GNU Emacs Manual

GNU Emacs Manual

Eleventh Edition, Updated for Emacs Version 19.29

Richard Stallman

Eleventh Edition
Updated for Emacs Version 19.29,
June 1995
ISBN 1-882114-52-3

Published by the Free Software Foundation
59 Temple Place, Suite 330
Boston, MA 02111-1307 USA

Cover art by Etienne Suvasa.

Short Contents

Table of Contents

Preface

This manual documents the use and simple customization of the Emacs editor. The reader is not expected to be a programmer; simple customizations do not require programming skill. But the user who is not interested in customizing can ignore the scattered customization hints.

This is primarily a reference manual, but can also be used as a primer. For complete beginners, it is a good idea to start with the on-line, learn-by-doing tutorial, before reading the manual. To run the tutorial, start Emacs and type C-h t. This way you can learn Emacs by using Emacs on a specially designed file which describes commands, tells you when to try them, and then explains the results you see.

On first reading, just skim chapters one and two, which describe the notational conventions of the manual and the general appearance of the Emacs display screen. Note which questions are answered in these chapters, so you can refer back later. After reading chapter four you should practice the commands there. The next few chapters describe fundamental techniques and concepts that are used constantly. You need to understand them thoroughly, experimenting with them if necessary.

Chapters 14 through 18 describe intermediate-level features that are useful for all kinds of editing. Chapter 19 and following chapters describe features that you may or may not want to use; read those chapters when you need them

Read the Trouble chapter if Emacs does not seem to be working properly. It explains how to cope with some common problems (see Section 31.2 [Lossage], page 374), as well as when and how to report Emacs bugs (see Section 31.3 [Bugs], page 377).

To find the documentation on a particular command, look in the index. Keys (character commands) and command names have separate indexes. There is also a glossary, with a cross reference for each term.

This manual is available as a printed book and also as an Info file. The Info file is for on-line perusal with the Info program, which will be the principle way of viewing documentation on-line in the GNU system. Both the Info file and the Info program itself are distributed along with GNU Emacs. The Info file and the printed book contain substantially the same text and are generated from the same source files, which are also distributed along with GNU Emacs.

GNU Emacs is a member of the Emacs editor family. There are many Emacs editors, all sharing common principles of organization. For information on the underlying philosophy of Emacs and the lessons learned from its development, write for a copy of AI memo 519a, "Emacs, the Extensible, Customizable Self-Documenting Display Editor", to Publications Department, Artificial Intelligence Lab, 545 Tech Square, Cambridge, MA 02139,

USA. At last report they charge $2.25 per copy. Another useful publication is LCS TM-165, "A Cookbook for an Emacs", by Craig Finseth, available from Publications Department, Laboratory for Computer Science, 545 Tech Square, Cambridge, MA 02139, USA. The price today is $3.

This edition of the manual is intended for use with GNU Emacs installed on GNU and Unix systems. GNU Emacs can also be used on VMS, MS-DOS (aka. MS-DOG) and Windows NT systems, but those systems have different file name syntax and do not support all GNU Emacs features. We don't try to describe VMS usage in this manual. See Appendix C [MS-DOS], page 409, for information about using Emacs on MS-DOS.

Distribution

GNU Emacs is *free software*; this means that everyone is free to use it and free to redistribute it on certain conditions. GNU Emacs is not in the public domain; it is copyrighted and there are restrictions on its distribution, but these restrictions are designed to permit everything that a good cooperating citizen would want to do. What is not allowed is to try to prevent others from further sharing any version of GNU Emacs that they might get from you. The precise conditions are found in the GNU General Public License that comes with Emacs and also appears following this section.

One way to get a copy of GNU Emacs is from someone else who has it. You need not ask for our permission to do so, or tell any one else; just copy it. If you have access to the Internet, you can get the latest distribution version of GNU Emacs by anonymous FTP; see the file 'etc/FTP' in the Emacs distribution for more information.

You may also receive GNU Emacs when you buy a computer. Computer manufacturers are free to distribute copies on the same terms that apply to everyone else. These terms require them to give you the full sources, including whatever changes they may have made, and to permit you to redistribute the GNU Emacs received from them under the usual terms of the General Public License. In other words, the program must be free for you when you get it, not just free for the manufacturer.

You can also order copies of GNU Emacs from the Free Software Foundation, on various magnetic media or on CD-ROM. This is a convenient and reliable way to get a copy; it is also a good way to help fund our work. (The Foundation has always received most of its funds in this way.) An order form is included at the end of manuals printed by the Foundation. It is also included in the file 'etc/ORDERS' in the Emacs distribution. For further information, write to

Free Software Foundation
59 Temple Place, Suite 330
Boston, MA 02111-1307 USA
USA

The income from distribution fees goes to support the foundation's purpose: the development of new free software, and improvements to our existing programs including GNU Emacs.

If you find GNU Emacs useful, please **send a donation** to the Free Software Foundation to support our work. Donations to the Free Software Foundation are tax deductible. If you use GNU Emacs at your workplace, suggest that the company make a donation. If company policy is unsympathetic to the idea of donating to charity, you might instead suggest ordering a CD-ROM from the Foundation occasionally, or subscribing to periodic updates.

Contributors to GNU Emacs include Per Abrahamsen, Jay K. Adams, Joe Arceneax, Boaz Ben-Zvi, Jim Blandy, Frank Bresz, Kevin Broadey, Vincent Broman, David M. Brown, Hans Chalupsky, Bob Chassell, James Clark, Mike Clarkson, Doug Cutting, Michael DeCorte, Gary Delp, Matthieu Devin, Scott Draves, Viktor Dukhovni, Rolf Ebert, Torbjörn Einarsson, Hans Henrik Eriksen, Michael Ernst, Ata Etemadi, Fred Fish, Karl Fogel, Noah Friedman, Keith Gabryelski, Kevin Gallagher, Howard Gayle, Stephen Gildea, David Gillespie, Boris Goldowsky, Michael Gschwind, Henry Guillaume, Doug Gwyn, Chris Hanson, K. Shane Hartman, Markus Heritsch, Karl Heuer, Manabu Higashida, Anders Holst, Lars Ingebrigtsen, Michael K. Johnson, Kyle Jones, Brewster Kahle, David Kaufman, Henry Kautz, Howard Kaye, Michael Kifer, Richard King, Larry K. Kolodney, Robert Krawitz, Sebastian Kremer, Geoff Kuenning, David Kågedal, Daniel LaLiberte, Aaron Larson, James R. Larus, Lars Lindberg, Neil M. Mager, Ken Manheimer, Bill Mann, Brian Marick, Simon Marshall, Bengt Martensson, Charlie Martin, Thomas May, Roland McGrath, David Megginson, Richard Mlynarik, Keith Moore, Thomas Neumann, Mike Newton, Jurgen Nickelsen, Jeff Norden, Jeff Peck, Damon Anton Permezel, Tom Perrine, Daniel Pfeiffer, Fred Pierresteguy, Christian Plaunt, Franceso A. Potorti, Michael D. Prange, Mukesh Prasad, Ashwin Ram, Eric S. Raymond, Paul Reilly, Edward M. Reingold, Rob Riepel, Roland B. Roberts, John Robinson, William Rosenblatt, Guillermo J. Rozas, Wolfgang Rupprecht, James B. Salem, Masahiko Sato, William Schelter, Gregor Schmid, Michael Schmidt, Ronald S. Schnell, Philippe Schnoebelen, Randal Schwartz, Mark Shapiro, Olin Shivers, Espen Skoglund, Rick Sladkey, Lynn Slater, Chris Smith, David Smith, William Sommerfeld, Ake Stenhoff, Jonathan Stigelman, Steve Strassman, Spencer Thomas, Jim Thompson, Masanobu Umeda, Geoffrey Voelker, Johan Vromans, Barry Warsaw, Morten Welinder, Joseph Brian Wells, Ed Wilkinson, Mike Williams, Steven A. Wood, Dale R. Worley, Felix S. T. Wu, Tom Wurgler, Jamie Zawinski, and Neal Ziring.

GNU GENERAL PUBLIC LICENSE

Version 2, June 1991

Copyright © 1989, 1991 Free Software Foundation, Inc.
675 Mass Ave, Cambridge, MA 02139, USA

Preamble

The licenses for most software are designed to take away your freedom to share and change it. By contrast, the GNU General Public License is intended to guarantee your freedom to share and change free software—to make sure the software is free for all its users. This General Public License applies to most of the Free Software Foundation's software and to any other program whose authors commit to using it. (Some other Free Software Foundation software is covered by the GNU Library General Public License instead.) You can apply it to your programs, too.

When we speak of free software, we are referring to freedom, not price. Our General Public Licenses are designed to make sure that you have the freedom to distribute copies of free software (and charge for this service if you wish), that you receive source code or can get it if you want it, that you can change the software or use pieces of it in new free programs; and that you know you can do these things.

To protect your rights, we need to make restrictions that forbid anyone to deny you these rights or to ask you to surrender the rights. These restrictions translate to certain responsibilities for you if you distribute copies of the software, or if you modify it.

For example, if you distribute copies of such a program, whether gratis or for a fee, you must give the recipients all the rights that you have. You must make sure that they, too, receive or can get the source code. And you must show them these terms so they know their rights.

We protect your rights with two steps: (1) copyright the software, and (2) offer you this license which gives you legal permission to copy, distribute and/or modify the software.

Also, for each author's protection and ours, we want to make certain that everyone understands that there is no warranty for this free software. If the software is modified by someone else and passed on, we want its recipients to know that what they have is not the original, so that any problems introduced by others will not reflect on the original authors' reputations.

Finally, any free program is threatened constantly by software patents. We wish to avoid the danger that redistributors of a free program will individually obtain patent licenses, in effect making the program proprietary. To prevent this, we have made it clear that any patent must be licensed for everyone's free use or not licensed at all.

The precise terms and conditions for copying, distribution and modification follow.

TERMS AND CONDITIONS FOR COPYING, DISTRIBUTION AND MODIFICATION

0. This License applies to any program or other work which contains a notice placed by the copyright holder saying it may be distributed under the terms of this General Public License. The "Program", below, refers to any such program or work, and a "work based on the Program" means either the Program or any derivative work under copyright law: that is to say, a work containing the Program or a portion of it, either verbatim or with modifications and/or translated into another language. (Hereinafter, translation is included without limitation in the term "modification".) Each licensee is addressed as "you".

   Activities other than copying, distribution and modification are not covered by this License; they are outside its scope. The act of running the Program is not restricted, and the output from the Program is covered only if its contents constitute a work based on the Program (independent of having been made by running the Program). Whether that is true depends on what the Program does.

1. You may copy and distribute verbatim copies of the Program's source code as you receive it, in any medium, provided that you conspicuously and appropriately publish on each copy an appropriate copyright notice and disclaimer of warranty; keep intact all the notices that refer to this License and to the absence of any warranty; and give any other recipients of the Program a copy of this License along with the Program.

   You may charge a fee for the physical act of transferring a copy, and you may at your option offer warranty protection in exchange for a fee.

2. You may modify your copy or copies of the Program or any portion of it, thus forming a work based on the Program, and copy and distribute such modifications or work under the terms of Section 1 above, provided that you also meet all of these conditions:

   a. You must cause the modified files to carry prominent notices stating that you changed the files and the date of any change.

   b. You must cause any work that you distribute or publish, that in whole or in part contains or is derived from the Program or any part thereof, to be licensed as a whole at no charge to all third parties under the terms of this License.

c. If the modified program normally reads commands interactively when run, you must cause it, when started running for such interactive use in the most ordinary way, to print or display an announcement including an appropriate copyright notice and a notice that there is no warranty (or else, saying that you provide a warranty) and that users may redistribute the program under these conditions, and telling the user how to view a copy of this License. (Exception: if the Program itself is interactive but does not normally print such an announcement, your work based on the Program is not required to print an announcement.)

These requirements apply to the modified work as a whole. If identifiable sections of that work are not derived from the Program, and can be reasonably considered independent and separate works in themselves, then this License, and its terms, do not apply to those sections when you distribute them as separate works. But when you distribute the same sections as part of a whole which is a work based on the Program, the distribution of the whole must be on the terms of this License, whose permissions for other licensees extend to the entire whole, and thus to each and every part regardless of who wrote it.

Thus, it is not the intent of this section to claim rights or contest your rights to work written entirely by you; rather, the intent is to exercise the right to control the distribution of derivative or collective works based on the Program.

In addition, mere aggregation of another work not based on the Program with the Program (or with a work based on the Program) on a volume of a storage or distribution medium does not bring the other work under the scope of this License.

3. You may copy and distribute the Program (or a work based on it, under Section 2) in object code or executable form under the terms of Sections 1 and 2 above provided that you also do one of the following:

a. Accompany it with the complete corresponding machine-readable source code, which must be distributed under the terms of Sections 1 and 2 above on a medium customarily used for software interchange; or,

b. Accompany it with a written offer, valid for at least three years, to give any third party, for a charge no more than your cost of physically performing source distribution, a complete machine-readable copy of the corresponding source code, to be distributed under the terms of Sections 1 and 2 above on a medium customarily used for software interchange; or,

c. Accompany it with the information you received as to the offer to distribute corresponding source code. (This alternative is allowed only for noncommercial distribution and only if you received the program in object code or executable form with such an offer, in accord with Subsection b above.)

The source code for a work means the preferred form of the work for making modifications to it. For an executable work, complete source code means all the source code for all modules it contains, plus any associated interface definition files, plus the scripts used to control compilation and installation of the executable. However, as a special exception, the source code distributed need not include anything that is normally distributed (in either source or binary form) with the major components (compiler, kernel, and so on) of the operating system on which the executable runs, unless that component itself accompanies the executable.

If distribution of executable or object code is made by offering access to copy from a designated place, then offering equivalent access to copy the source code from the same place counts as distribution of the source code, even though third parties are not compelled to copy the source along with the object code.

4. You may not copy, modify, sublicense, or distribute the Program except as expressly provided under this License. Any attempt otherwise to copy, modify, sublicense or distribute the Program is void, and will automatically terminate your rights under this License. However, parties who have received copies, or rights, from you under this License will not have their licenses terminated so long as such parties remain in full compliance.

5. You are not required to accept this License, since you have not signed it. However, nothing else grants you permission to modify or distribute the Program or its derivative works. These actions are prohibited by law if you do not accept this License. Therefore, by modifying or distributing the Program (or any work based on the Program), you indicate your acceptance of this License to do so, and all its terms and conditions for copying, distributing or modifying the Program or works based on it.

6. Each time you redistribute the Program (or any work based on the Program), the recipient automatically receives a license from the original licensor to copy, distribute or modify the Program subject to these terms and conditions. You may not impose any further restrictions on the recipients' exercise of the rights granted herein. You are not responsible for enforcing compliance by third parties to this License.

7. If, as a consequence of a court judgment or allegation of patent infringement or for any other reason (not limited to patent issues), conditions are imposed on you (whether by court order, agreement or otherwise)

that contradict the conditions of this License, they do not excuse you from the conditions of this License. If you cannot distribute so as to satisfy simultaneously your obligations under this License and any other pertinent obligations, then as a consequence you may not distribute the Program at all. For example, if a patent license would not permit royalty-free redistribution of the Program by all those who receive copies directly or indirectly through you, then the only way you could satisfy both it and this License would be to refrain entirely from distribution of the Program.

If any portion of this section is held invalid or unenforceable under any particular circumstance, the balance of the section is intended to apply and the section as a whole is intended to apply in other circumstances.

It is not the purpose of this section to induce you to infringe any patents or other property right claims or to contest validity of any such claims; this section has the sole purpose of protecting the integrity of the free software distribution system, which is implemented by public license practices. Many people have made generous contributions to the wide range of software distributed through that system in reliance on consistent application of that system; it is up to the author/donor to decide if he or she is willing to distribute software through any other system and a licensee cannot impose that choice.

This section is intended to make thoroughly clear what is believed to be a consequence of the rest of this License.

8. If the distribution and/or use of the Program is restricted in certain countries either by patents or by copyrighted interfaces, the original copyright holder who places the Program under this License may add an explicit geographical distribution limitation excluding those countries, so that distribution is permitted only in or among countries not thus excluded. In such case, this License incorporates the limitation as if written in the body of this License.

9. The Free Software Foundation may publish revised and/or new versions of the General Public License from time to time. Such new versions will be similar in spirit to the present version, but may differ in detail to address new problems or concerns.

Each version is given a distinguishing version number. If the Program specifies a version number of this License which applies to it and "any later version", you have the option of following the terms and conditions either of that version or of any later version published by the Free Software Foundation. If the Program does not specify a version number of this License, you may choose any version ever published by the Free Software Foundation.

10. If you wish to incorporate parts of the Program into other free programs whose distribution conditions are different, write to the author to ask

for permission. For software which is copyrighted by the Free Software Foundation, write to the Free Software Foundation; we sometimes make exceptions for this. Our decision will be guided by the two goals of preserving the free status of all derivatives of our free software and of promoting the sharing and reuse of software generally.

NO WARRANTY

11. BECAUSE THE PROGRAM IS LICENSED FREE OF CHARGE, THERE IS NO WARRANTY FOR THE PROGRAM, TO THE EXTENT PERMITTED BY APPLICABLE LAW. EXCEPT WHEN OTHERWISE STATED IN WRITING THE COPYRIGHT HOLDERS AND/OR OTHER PARTIES PROVIDE THE PROGRAM "AS IS" WITHOUT WARRANTY OF ANY KIND, EITHER EXPRESSED OR IMPLIED, INCLUDING, BUT NOT LIMITED TO, THE IMPLIED WARRANTIES OF MERCHANTABILITY AND FITNESS FOR A PARTICULAR PURPOSE. THE ENTIRE RISK AS TO THE QUALITY AND PERFORMANCE OF THE PROGRAM IS WITH YOU. SHOULD THE PROGRAM PROVE DEFECTIVE, YOU ASSUME THE COST OF ALL NECESSARY SERVICING, REPAIR OR CORRECTION.

12. IN NO EVENT UNLESS REQUIRED BY APPLICABLE LAW OR AGREED TO IN WRITING WILL ANY COPYRIGHT HOLDER, OR ANY OTHER PARTY WHO MAY MODIFY AND/OR REDISTRIBUTE THE PROGRAM AS PERMITTED ABOVE, BE LIABLE TO YOU FOR DAMAGES, INCLUDING ANY GENERAL, SPECIAL, INCIDENTAL OR CONSEQUENTIAL DAMAGES ARISING OUT OF THE USE OR INABILITY TO USE THE PROGRAM (INCLUDING BUT NOT LIMITED TO LOSS OF DATA OR DATA BEING RENDERED INACCURATE OR LOSSES SUSTAINED BY YOU OR THIRD PARTIES OR A FAILURE OF THE PROGRAM TO OPERATE WITH ANY OTHER PROGRAMS), EVEN IF SUCH HOLDER OR OTHER PARTY HAS BEEN ADVISED OF THE POSSIBILITY OF SUCH DAMAGES.

END OF TERMS AND CONDITIONS

How to Apply These Terms to Your New Programs

If you develop a new program, and you want it to be of the greatest possible use to the public, the best way to achieve this is to make it free software which everyone can redistribute and change under these terms.

To do so, attach the following notices to the program. It is safest to attach them to the start of each source file to most effectively convey the exclusion of warranty; and each file should have at least the "copyright" line and a pointer to where the full notice is found.

```
one line to give the program's name and an idea of what it does.
Copyright (C) 19yy   name of author

This program is free software; you can redistribute it and/or
modify it under the terms of the GNU General Public License
as published by the Free Software Foundation; either version 2
of the License, or (at your option) any later version.

This program is distributed in the hope that it will be useful,
but WITHOUT ANY WARRANTY; without even the implied warranty of
MERCHANTABILITY or FITNESS FOR A PARTICULAR PURPOSE.  See the
GNU General Public License for more details.

You should have received a copy of the GNU General Public License
along with this program; if not, write to the Free Software
Foundation, Inc., 675 Mass Ave, Cambridge, MA 02139, USA.
```

Also add information on how to contact you by electronic and paper mail.

If the program is interactive, make it output a short notice like this when it starts in an interactive mode:

```
Gnomovision version 69, Copyright (C) 19yy name of author
Gnomovision comes with ABSOLUTELY NO WARRANTY; for details
type 'show w'.  This is free software, and you are welcome
to redistribute it under certain conditions; type 'show c'
for details.
```

The hypothetical commands 'show w' and 'show c' should show the appropriate parts of the General Public License. Of course, the commands you use may be called something other than 'show w' and 'show c'; they could even be mouse-clicks or menu items—whatever suits your program.

You should also get your employer (if you work as a programmer) or your school, if any, to sign a "copyright disclaimer" for the program, if necessary. Here is a sample; alter the names:

```
Yoyodyne, Inc., hereby disclaims all copyright
interest in the program 'Gnomovision'
(which makes passes at compilers) written
by James Hacker.

signature of Ty Coon, 1 April 1989
Ty Coon, President of Vice
```

This General Public License does not permit incorporating your program into proprietary programs. If your program is a subroutine library, you may consider it more useful to permit linking proprietary applications with the library. If this is what you want to do, use the GNU Library General Public License instead of this License.

Introduction

You are reading about GNU Emacs, the GNU incarnation of the advanced, self-documenting, customizable, extensible real-time display editor Emacs. (The 'G' in 'GNU' is not silent.)

We say that Emacs is a *display* editor because normally the text being edited is visible on the screen and is updated automatically as you type your commands. See Chapter 1 [Screen], page 15.

We call it a *real-time* editor because the display is updated very frequently, usually after each character or pair of characters you type. This minimizes the amount of information you must keep in your head as you edit. See Chapter 4 [Basic Editing], page 27.

We call Emacs advanced because it provides facilities that go beyond simple insertion and deletion: controlling subprocesses; automatic indentation of programs; viewing two or more files at once; editing formatted text; and dealing in terms of characters, words, lines, sentences, paragraphs, and pages, as well as expressions and comments in several different programming languages.

Self-documenting means that at any time you can type a special character, `Control-h`, to find out what your options are. You can also use it to find out what any command does, or to find all the commands that pertain to a topic. See Chapter 7 [Help], page 47.

Customizable means that you can change the definitions of Emacs commands in little ways. For example, if you use a programming language in which comments start with '`<**`' and end with '`**>`', you can tell the Emacs comment manipulation commands to use those strings (see Section 21.7 [Comments], page 210). Another sort of customization is rearrangement of the command set. For example, if you prefer the four basic cursor motion commands (up, down, left and right) on keys in a diamond pattern on the keyboard, you can rebind the keys that way. See Chapter 30 [Customization], page 343.

Extensible means that you can go beyond simple customization and write entirely new commands, programs in the Lisp language to be run by Emacs's own Lisp interpreter. Emacs is an "on-line extensible" system, which means that it is divided into many functions that call each other, any of which can be redefined in the middle of an editing session. Almost any part of Emacs can be replaced without making a separate copy of all of Emacs. Most of the editing commands of Emacs are written in Lisp already; the few exceptions could have been written in Lisp but are written in C for efficiency. Although only a programmer can write an extension, anybody can use it afterward.

When run under the X Window System, Emacs provides its own menus and convenient bindings to mouse buttons. But Emacs can provide many of the benefits of a window system on a text-only terminal. For instance, you can look at or edit several files at once, move text between them, and edit files at the same time as you run shell commands.

1 The Organization of the Screen

On a text-only terminal, the Emacs display occupies the whole screen. On the X Window System, Emacs creates its own X windows to use. We use the term *frame* to mean an entire text-only screen or an entire X window used by Emacs. Emacs uses both kinds of frames in the same way to display your editing. Emacs normally starts out with just one frame, but you can create additional frames if you wish. See Chapter 17 [Frames], page 147.

When you start Emacs, the entire frame except for the last line is devoted to the text you are editing. This area is called *window*. The last line is a special *echo area* or *minibuffer window* where prompts appear and where you can enter responses. You can subdivide the large text window horizontally or vertically into multiple text windows, each of which can be used for a different file (see Chapter 16 [Windows], page 141). In this manual, the word "window" always refers to the subdivisions of a frame within Emacs.

The window that the cursor is in is the *selected window*, in which editing takes place. Most Emacs commands implicitly apply to the text in the selected window (though mouse commands generally operate on whatever window you click them in, whether selected or not). The other windows display text for reference only, unless/until you select them. If you use multiple frames under the X Window System, then giving the input focus to a particular frame selects a window in that frame.

Each window's last line is a *mode line* which describes what is going on in that window. It appears in inverse video if the terminal supports that, and contains text that starts like '`-----Emacs: something`'. Its purpose is to indicate what buffer is being displayed above it in the window; what major and minor modes are in use; and whether the buffer contains unsaved changes.

1.1 Point

Within Emacs, the terminal's cursor shows the location at which editing commands will take effect. This location is called *point*. Many Emacs commands move point through the text, so that you can edit at different places in it. You can also place point by clicking mouse button 1.

While the cursor appears to point *at* a character, you should think of point as *between* two characters; it points *before* the character that appears under the cursor. For example, if your text looks like '`frob`' with the cursor over the '`b`', then point is between the '`o`' and the '`b`'. If you insert the character '`!`' at that position, the result is '`fro!b`', with point between the '`!`' and the '`b`'. Thus, the cursor remains over the '`b`', as before.

Sometimes people speak of "the cursor" when they mean "point", or speak of commands that move point as "cursor motion" commands.

Terminals have only one cursor, and when output is in progress it must appear where the typing is being done. This does not mean that point is moving. It is only that Emacs has no way to show you the location of point except when the terminal is idle.

If you are editing several files in Emacs, each in its own buffer, each buffer has its own point location. A buffer that is not currently displayed remembers where point is in case you display it again later.

When there are multiple windows in a frame, each window has its own point location. The cursor shows the location of point in the selected window. This also is how you can tell which window is selected. If the same buffer appears in more than one window, each window has its own position for point in that buffer.

When there are multiple frames, each frame can display one cursor. The cursor in the selected frame is solid; the cursor in other frames is a hollow box, and appears in the window that would be selected if you give the input focus to that frame.

The term 'point' comes from the character '.', which was the command in TECO (the language in which the original Emacs was written) for accessing the value now called 'point'.

1.2 The Echo Area

The line at the bottom of the frame (below the mode line) is the *echo area*. It is used to display small amounts of text for several purposes.

Echoing means displaying the characters that you type. Outside Emacs, the operating system normally echoes all your input. Emacs handles echoing differently.

Single-character commands do not echo in Emacs, and multi-character commands echo only if you pause while typing them. As soon as you pause for more than a second in the middle of a command, Emacs echoes all the characters of the command so far. This is to *prompt* you for the rest of the command. Once echoing has started, the rest of the command echoes immediately as you type it. This behavior is designed to give confident users fast response, while giving hesitant users maximum feedback. You can change this behavior by setting a variable (see Section 11.6 [Display Vars], page 79).

If a command cannot be executed, it may print an *error message* in the echo area. Error messages are accompanied by a beep or by flashing the screen. Also, any input you have typed ahead is thrown away when an error happens.

Some commands print informative messages in the echo area. These messages look much like error messages, but they are not announced with a beep and do not throw away input. Sometimes the message tells you what the command has done, when this is not obvious from looking at the text being edited. Sometimes the sole purpose of a command is to print a message giving you specific information—for example, C-x = prints a message describing the character position of point in the text and its current column in the window. Commands that take a long time often display messages ending in '...' while they are working, and add 'done' at the end when they are finished.

Echo area informative messages appear also in a buffer named '*Messages*'. If you miss a message that appears briefly on the screen, you can switch to the '*Messages*' buffer to see it again. Garbage collection messages are omitted from '*Messages*', and successive progress messages are often collapsed into one.

The size of '*Messages*' is limited to a certain number of lines. The variable message-log-max specifies how many lines. Once the buffer has that many lines, each line added at the end deletes one line from the beginning. See Section 30.2 [Variables], page 345, for how to set variables such as message-log-max.

The echo area is also used to display the *minibuffer*, a window that is used for reading arguments to commands, such as the name of a file to be edited. When the minibuffer is in use, the echo area begins with a prompt string that usually ends with a colon; also, the cursor appears in that line because it is the selected window. You can always get out of the minibuffer by typing C-g. See Chapter 5 [Minibuffer], page 37.

1.3 The Mode Line

Each text window's last line is a *mode line* which describes what is going on in that window. When there is only one text window, the mode line appears right above the echo area. The mode line is in inverse video if the terminal supports that, it starts and ends with dashes, and it contains text like 'Emacs: *something*'.

A few special editing modes, such as Dired and Rmail, display something else in place of 'Emacs: *something*'. The rest of the mode line still has the usual meaning.

Normally, the mode line looks like this:

    --*ch*-Emacs: *buf*   (*major minor*)----*pos*------

This gives information about the buffer being displayed in the window: the buffer's name, what major and minor modes are in use, whether the buffer's text has been changed, and how far down the buffer you are currently looking.

ch contains two stars '**' if the text in the buffer has been edited (the buffer is "modified"), or '--' if the buffer has not been edited. For a read-only buffer, it is '%*' if the buffer is modified, and '%%' otherwise.

buf is the name of the window's *buffer*. In most cases this is the same as the name of a file you are editing. See Chapter 15 [Buffers], page 133.

The buffer displayed in the selected window (the window that the cursor is in) is also Emacs's selected buffer, the one that editing takes place in. When we speak of what some command does to "the buffer", we are talking about the currently selected buffer.

pos tells you whether there is additional text above the top of the window, or below the bottom. If your buffer is small and it is all visible in the window, *pos* is 'All'. Otherwise, it is 'Top' if you are looking at the beginning of the buffer, 'Bot' if you are looking at the end of the buffer, or '*nn*%', where *nn* is the percentage of the buffer above the top of the window.

major is the name of the *major mode* in effect in the buffer. At any time, each buffer is in one and only one of the possible major modes. The major modes available include Fundamental mode (the least specialized), Text mode, Lisp mode, C mode, Texinfo mode, and many others. See Chapter 18 [Major Modes], page 161, for details of how the modes differ and how to select one.

Some major modes display additional information after the major mode name. For example, Rmail buffers display the current message number and the total number of messages. Compilation buffers and Shell buffers display the status of the subprocess.

minor is a list of some of the *minor modes* that are turned on at the moment in the window's chosen buffer. For example, 'Fill' means that Auto Fill mode is on. 'Abbrev' means that Word Abbrev mode is on. 'Ovwrt' means that Overwrite mode is on. See Section 30.1 [Minor Modes], page 343, for more information. 'Narrow' means that the buffer being displayed has editing restricted to only a portion of its text. This is not really a minor mode, but is like one. See Section 29.7 [Narrowing], page 335. 'Def' means that a keyboard macro is being defined. See Section 30.3 [Keyboard Macros], page 352.

In addition, if Emacs is currently inside a recursive editing level, square brackets ('[...]') appear around the parentheses that surround the modes. If Emacs is in one recursive editing level within another, double square brackets appear, and so on. Since recursive editing levels affect Emacs globally, not just one buffer, the square brackets appear in every window's mode line or not in any of them. See Section 29.11 [Recursive Edit], page 339.

See Section 11.5 [Optional Mode Line], page 79, for features that add other handy information to the mode line, such as the current line number of point, the current time, and whether new mail for you has arrived.

2 Characters, Keys and Commands

This chapter explains the character sets used by Emacs for input commands and for the contents of files, and also explains the concepts of *keys* and *commands* which are fundamental for understanding how Emacs interprets your keyboard and mouse input.

2.1 Kinds of User Input

GNU Emacs uses an extension of the ASCII character set for keyboard input; it also accepts non-character input events including function keys and mouse button actions.

ASCII consists of 128 character codes. Some of these codes are assigned graphic symbols such as 'a' and '='; the rest are control characters, such as Control-a (usually written C-a for short). C-a gets its name from the fact that you type it by holding down the CTRL key while pressing a.

Some control characters have special names, and special keys you can type them with: for example, RET, TAB, LFD, DEL and ESC. The space character is usually referred to below as SPC, even though strictly speaking it is a graphic character whose graphic happens to be blank.

On ASCII terminals, there are only 32 possible control characters. These are the control variants of letters and '@[]\^_'. In addition, the shift key is meaningless with control characters: C-a and C-A are the same character, and Emacs cannot distinguish them.

But the Emacs character set has room for control variants of all characters, and for distinguishing between C-a and C-A. X Windows makes it possible to enter all these characters. For example, C-- (that's Control-Minus) and C-5 are meaningful Emacs commands under X.

Another Emacs character set extension is that characters have additional modifier bits. Only one modifier bit is commonly used; it is called Meta. Every character has a Meta variant; examples include Meta-a (normally written M-a, for short), M-A (not the same character as M-a, but those two characters normally have the same meaning in Emacs), M-RET, and M-C-a. For reasons of tradition, we usually write C-M-a rather than M-C-a; logically speaking, the order in which the modifier keys CTRL and META are mentioned does not matter.

Some terminals have a META key, and allow you to type Meta characters by holding this key down. Thus, Meta-a is typed by holding down META and pressing a. The META key works much like the SHIFT key. Such a key is not always labeled META, however, as this function is often a special option for a key with some other primary purpose.

If there is no META key, you can still type Meta characters using two-character sequences starting with ESC. Thus, to enter M-a, you could type ESC a. To enter C-M-a, you would type ESC C-a. ESC is allowed on terminals with META keys, too, in case you have formed a habit of using it.

X Windows provides several other modifier keys that can be applied to any input character. These are called SUPER, HYPER and ALT. We write 's-', 'H-' and 'A-' to say that a character uses these modifiers. Thus, s-H-C-x is short for Super-Hyper-Control-x. Not all X terminals actually provide keys for these modifier flags—in fact, many terminals have a key labeled ALT which is really a META key. The standard key bindings of Emacs do not include any characters with these modifiers. But you can assign them meanings of your own by customizing Emacs.

Keyboard input includes keyboard keys that are not characters at all: for example function keys and arrow keys. Mouse buttons are also outside the gamut of characters. You can modify these events with the modifier keys CONTROL, META, SUPER, HYPER and ALT like keyboard characters.

Input characters and non-character inputs are collectively called *input events*. See section "Input Events" in *The Emacs Lisp Manual*, for more information. If you are not doing Lisp programming, but simply want to redefine the meaning of some characters or non-character events, see Chapter 30 [Customization], page 343.

ASCII terminals cannot really send anything to the computer except ASCII characters. These terminals use a sequence of characters to represent each function key. But that is invisible to the Emacs user, because the keyboard input routines recognize these special sequences and convert them to function key events before any other part of Emacs gets to see them.

2.2 Keys

A *key sequence* (*key*, for short) is a sequence of input events that are meaningful as a unit—as "a single command." Some Emacs command sequences are just one character or one event; for example, just C-f is enough to move forward one character. But Emacs also has commands that take two or more events to invoke.

If a sequence of events is enough to invoke a command, it is a *complete key*. Examples of complete keys include C-a, X, RET, NEXT (a function key), DOWN (an arrow key), C-x C-f and C-x 4 C-f. If it isn't long enough to be complete, we call it a *prefix key*. The above examples show that C-x and C-x 4 are prefix keys. Every key sequence is either a complete key or a prefix key.

Most single characters constitute complete keys in the standard Emacs command bindings. A few of them are prefix keys. A prefix key combines with the following input event to make a longer key sequence, which may itself be complete or a prefix. For example, C-x is a prefix key, so C-x and the next input event combine to make a two-character key sequence. Most of these key sequences are complete keys, including C-x C-f and C-x b. A few, such as C-x 4 and C-x r, are themselves prefix keys that lead to three-character key sequences. There's no limit to the length of a key sequence, but in practice people rarely use sequences longer than four events.

By contrast, you can't add more events onto a complete key. For example, the two-character sequence C-f C-k is not a key, because the C-f is a complete key in itself. It's impossible to give C-f C-k an independent meaning as a command. C-f C-k is two key sequences, not one.

All told, the prefix keys in Emacs are C-c, C-h, C-x, C-x C-a, C-x n, C-x r, C-x v, C-x 4, C-x 5, C-x 6, and ESC. But this is not cast in concrete; it is just a matter of Emacs's standard key bindings. If you customize Emacs, you can make new prefix keys, or eliminate these. See Section 30.4 [Key Bindings], page 355.

If you do make or eliminate prefix keys, that changes the set of possible key sequences. For example, if you redefine C-f as a prefix, C-f C-k automatically becomes a key (complete, unless you define it too as a prefix). Conversely, if you remove the prefix definition of C-x 4, then C-x 4 f (or C-x 4 *anything*) is no longer a key.

Typing the help character (C-h or F1) after a prefix character displays a list of the commands starting with that prefix. There are a few prefix characters for which C-h does not work—for historical reasons, they have other meanings for C-h which are not easy to change. But F1 should work for all prefix characters.

2.3 Keys and Commands

This manual is full of passages that tell you what particular keys do. But Emacs does not assign meanings to keys directly. Instead, Emacs assigns meanings to named *commands*, and then gives keys their meanings by *binding* them to commands.

Every command has a name chosen by a programmer. The name is usually made of a few English words separated by dashes; for example, next-line or forward-word. A command also has a *function definition* which is a Lisp program; this is what makes the command do what it does. In Emacs Lisp, a command is actually a special kind of Lisp function; one which specifies how to read arguments for it and call it interactively. For more information on commands and functions, see section "What Is a Function" in *The Emacs Lisp Reference Manual*. (The definition we use in this manual is simplified slightly.)

The bindings between keys and commands are recorded in various tables called *keymaps*. See Section 30.4.1 [Keymaps], page 355.

When we say that "C-n moves down vertically one line" we are glossing over a distinction that is irrelevant in ordinary use but is vital in understanding how to customize Emacs. It is the command `next-line` that is programmed to move down vertically. C-n has this effect *because* it is bound to that command. If you rebind C-n to the command `forward-word` then C-n will move forward by words instead. Rebinding keys is a common method of customization.

In the rest of this manual, we usually ignore this subtlety to keep things simple. To give the information needed for customization, we state the name of the command which really does the work in parentheses after mentioning the key that runs it. For example, we will say that "The command C-n (`next-line`) moves point vertically down," meaning that `next-line` is a command that moves vertically down and C-n is a key that is standardly bound to it.

While we are on the subject of information for customization only, it's a good time to tell you about *variables*. Often the description of a command will say, "To change this, set the variable `mumble-foo`." A variable is a name used to remember a value. Most of the variables documented in this manual exist just to facilitate customization: some command or other part of Emacs examines the variable and behaves differently according to the value that you set. Until you are interested in customizing, you can ignore the information about variables. When you are ready to be interested, read the basic information on variables, and then the information on individual variables will make sense. See Section 30.2 [Variables], page 345.

2.4 Character Set for Text

Emacs buffers use an 8-bit character set, because bytes have 8 bits. ASCII graphic characters in Emacs buffers are displayed with their graphics. The newline character (which has the same character code as LFD) is displayed by starting a new line. The tab character is displayed by moving to the next tab stop column (normally every 8 columns). Other control characters are displayed as a caret ('^') followed by the non-control version of the character; thus, C-a is displayed as '^A'. Non-ASCII characters 128 and up are displayed with octal escape sequences; thus, character code 243 (octal) is displayed as '\243'.

You can customize the display of these character codes (or ASCII characters) by creating a *display table*. See section "Display Tables" in *The Emacs Lisp Reference Manual*. This is useful for editing files that use 8-bit European character sets. See Section 11.4 [European Display], page 77.

3 Entering and Exiting Emacs

The usual way to invoke Emacs is with the shell command 'emacs'. Emacs clears the screen and then displays an initial help message and copyright notice. Some operating systems discard all type-ahead when Emacs starts up; they give Emacs no way to prevent this. Therefore, it is advisable to wait until Emacs clears the screen before typing your first editing command.

If you run Emacs from a shell window under the X Window System, run it in the background with 'emacs&'. This way, Emacs does not tie up the shell window, so you can use that to run other shell commands while Emacs operates its own X windows. You can begin typing Emacs commands as soon as you direct your keyboard input to the Emacs frame.

When Emacs starts up, it makes a buffer named '*scratch*'. That's the buffer you start out in. The '*scratch*' buffer uses Lisp Interaction mode; you can use it to type Lisp expressions and evaluate them, or you can ignore that capability and simply doodle. (You can specify a different major mode for this buffer by setting the variable initial-major-mode in your init file. See Section 30.7 [Init File], page 366.)

It is possible to specify files to be visited, Lisp files to be loaded, and functions to be called, by giving Emacs arguments in the shell command line. See Appendix A [Command Arguments], page 389. But we don't recommend doing this. The feature exists mainly for compatibility with other editors.

Many other editors are designed to be started afresh each time you want to edit. You edit one file and then exit the editor. The next time you want to edit either another file or the same one, you must run the editor again. With these editors, it makes sense to use a command line argument to say which file to edit.

But starting a new Emacs each time you want to edit a different file does not make sense. For one thing, this would be annoyingly slow. For another, this would fail to take advantage of Emacs's ability to visit more than one file in a single editing session. And it would lose the other accumulated context, such as registers, undo history, and the mark ring.

The recommended way to use GNU Emacs is to start it only once, just after you log in, and do all your editing in the same Emacs session. Each time you want to edit a different file, you visit it with the existing Emacs, which eventually comes to have many files in it ready for editing. Usually you do not kill the Emacs until you are about to log out. See Chapter 14 [Files], page 103, for more information on visiting more than one file.

3.1 Exiting Emacs

There are two commands for exiting Emacs because there are two kinds of exiting: *suspending* Emacs and *killing* Emacs.

Suspending means stopping Emacs temporarily and returning control to its parent process (usually a shell), allowing you to resume editing later in the same Emacs job, with the same buffers, same kill ring, same undo history, and so on. This is the usual way to exit.

Killing Emacs means destroying the Emacs job. You can run Emacs again later, but you will get a fresh Emacs; there is no way to resume the same editing session after it has been killed.

C-z   Suspend Emacs (`suspend-emacs`) or iconify a frame (`iconify-or-deiconify-frame`).

C-x C-c   Kill Emacs (`save-buffers-kill-emacs`).

To suspend Emacs, type C-z (`suspend-emacs`). This takes you back to the shell from which you invoked Emacs. You can resume Emacs with the shell command '`%emacs`' in most common shells.

On systems that do not support suspending programs, C-z starts an inferior shell that communicates directly with the terminal. Emacs waits until you exit the subshell. (The way to do that is probably with C-d or '`exit`', but it depends on which shell you use.) The only way on these systems to get back to the shell from which Emacs was run (to log out, for example) is to kill Emacs.

Suspending also fails if you run Emacs under a shell that doesn't support suspending programs, even if the system itself does support it. In such a case, you can set the variable `cannot-suspend` to a non-`nil` value to force C-z to start an inferior shell. (One might also describe Emacs's parent shell as "inferior" for failing to support job control properly, but that is a matter of taste.)

When Emacs communicates directly with an X server and creates its own dedicated X windows, C-z has a different meaning. Suspending an applications that uses its own X windows is not meaningful or useful. Instead, C-z runs the command `iconify-or-deiconify-frame`, which temporarily closes up the selected Emacs frame (see Chapter 17 [Frames], page 147). The way to get back to a shell window is with the window manager.

To kill Emacs, type C-x C-c (`save-buffers-kill-emacs`). A two-character key is used for this to make it harder to type. This command first offers to save any modified file-visiting buffers. If you do not save them all, it asks for reconfirmation with `yes` before killing Emacs, since any changes not saved will be lost forever. Also, if any subprocesses are still running, C-x C-c asks for confirmation about them, since killing Emacs will kill the subprocesses immediately.

There is no way to restart an Emacs session once you have killed it. You can, however, arrange for Emacs to record certain session information, such as which files are visited, when you kill it, so that the next time you restart Emacs it will try to visit the same files and so on. See Section 29.10 [Saving Emacs Sessions], page 338.

The operating system usually listens for certain special characters whose meaning is to kill or suspend the program you are running. **This operating system feature is turned off while you are in Emacs.** The meanings of C-z and C-x C-c as keys in Emacs were inspired by the use of C-z and C-c on several operating systems as the characters for stopping or killing a program, but that is their only relationship with the operating system. You can customize these keys to run any commands of your choice (see Section 30.4.1 [Keymaps], page 355).

4 Basic Editing Commands

We now give the basics of how to enter text, make corrections, and save the text in a file. If this material is new to you, you might learn it more easily by running the Emacs learn-by-doing tutorial. To use the tutorial, run Emacs and type `Control-h t` (`help-with-tutorial`).

To clear the screen and redisplay, type `C-l` (`recenter`).

4.1 Inserting Text

To insert printing characters into the text you are editing, just type them. This inserts the characters you type into the buffer at the cursor (that is, at *point*; see Section 1.1 [Point], page 15). The cursor moves forward, and any text after the cursor moves forward too. If the text in the buffer is 'FOOBAR', with the cursor before the 'B', then if you type `XX`, you get 'FOOXXBAR', with the cursor still before the 'B'.

To *delete* text you have just inserted, use `DEL`. `DEL` deletes the character *before* the cursor (not the one that the cursor is on top of or under; that is the character *after* the cursor). The cursor and all characters after it move backwards. Therefore, if you type a printing character and then type `DEL`, they cancel out.

To end a line and start typing a new one, type `RET`. This inserts a newline character in the buffer. If point is in the middle of a line, `RET` splits the line. Typing `DEL` when the cursor is at the beginning of a line deletes the preceding newline, thus joining the line with the preceding line.

Emacs can split lines automatically when they become too long, if you turn on a special minor mode called *Auto Fill* mode. See Section 20.5 [Filling], page 174, for how to use Auto Fill mode.

If you prefer to have text characters replace (overwrite) existing text rather than shove it to the right, you can enable Overwrite mode, a minor mode. See Section 30.1 [Minor Modes], page 343.

Direct insertion works for printing characters and `SPC`, but other characters act as editing commands and do not insert themselves. If you need to insert a control character or a character whose code is above 200 octal, you must *quote* it by typing the character `Control-q` (`quoted-insert`) first. (This character's name is normally written `C-q` for short.) There are two ways to use `C-q`:

- `C-q` followed by any non-graphic character (even `C-g`) inserts that character.
- `C-q` followed by three octal digits inserts the character with the specified character code.

A numeric argument to C-q specifies how many copies of the quoted character should be inserted (see Section 4.10 [Arguments], page 35).

Customization information: DEL in most modes runs the command delete-backward-char; RET runs the command newline, and self-inserting printing characters run the command self-insert, which inserts whatever character was typed to invoke it. Some major modes rebind DEL to other commands.

4.2 Changing the Location of Point

To do more than insert characters, you have to know how to move point (see Section 1.1 [Point], page 15). The simplest way to do this is with arrow keys, or by clicking the left mouse button where you want to move to.

There are also control and meta characters for cursor motion. Some are equivalent to the arrow keys (these date back to the days before terminals had arrow keys, and are usable on terminals which don't have them). Others do more sophisticated things.

C-a   Move to the beginning of the line (beginning-of-line).

C-e   Move to the end of the line (end-of-line).

C-f   Move forward one character (forward-char).

C-b   Move backward one character (backward-char).

M-f   Move forward one word (forward-word).

M-b   Move backward one word (backward-word).

C-n   Move down one line, vertically (next-line). This command attempts to keep the horizontal position unchanged, so if you start in the middle of one line, you end in the middle of the next. When on the last line of text, C-n creates a new line and moves onto it.

C-p   Move up one line, vertically (previous-line).

M-r   Move point to left margin, vertically centered in the window (move-to-window-line). Text does not move on the screen.

           A numeric argument says which screen line to place point on. It counts screen lines down from the top of the window (zero for the top line). A negative argument counts lines from the bottom (−1 for the bottom line).

M-<   Move to the top of the buffer (beginning-of-buffer). With numeric argument n, move to n/10 of the way from the top. See Section 4.10 [Arguments], page 35, for more information on numeric arguments.

M->   Move to the end of the buffer (end-of-buffer).

M-x goto-char
               Read a number *n* and move point to character number *n*. Position 1 is the beginning of the buffer.

M-x goto-line
               Read a number *n* and move point to line number *n*. Line 1 is the beginning of the buffer.

C-x C-n   Use the current column of point as the *semipermanent goal column* for C-n and C-p (set-goal-column). Henceforth, those commands always move to this column in each line moved into, or as close as possible given the contents of the line. This goal column remains in effect until canceled.

C-u C-x C-n
               Cancel the goal column. Henceforth, C-n and C-p once again try to stick to a fixed horizontal position, as usual.

If you set the variable track-eol to a non-nil value, then C-n and C-p when at the end of the starting line move to the end of another line. Normally, track-eol is nil. See Section 30.2 [Variables], page 345, for how to set variables such as track-eol.

Normally, C-n on the last line of a buffer appends a newline to it. If the variable next-line-add-newlines is nil, then C-n gets an error instead (like C-p on the first line).

4.3 Erasing Text

DEL   Delete the character before point (delete-backward-char).

C-d   Delete the character after point (delete-char).

C-k   Kill to the end of the line (kill-line).

M-d   Kill forward to the end of the next word (kill-word).

M-DEL   Kill back to the beginning of the previous word (backward-kill-word).

You already know about the DEL key which deletes the character before point (that is, before the cursor). Another key, Control-d (C-d for short), deletes the character after point (that is, the character that the cursor is on). This shifts the rest of the text on the line to the left. If you type C-d at the end of a line, it joins together that line and the next line.

To erase a larger amount of text, use the C-k key, which kills a line at a time. If you type C-k at the beginning or middle of a line, it kills all the

text up to the end of the line. If you type C-k at the end of a line, it joins
that line and the next line.

See Section 9.1 [Killing], page 61, for more flexible ways of killing text.

4.4 Undoing Changes

You can undo all the recent changes in the buffer text, up to a certain
point. Each buffer records changes individually, and the undo command
always applies to the current buffer. Usually each editing command makes
a separate entry in the undo records, but some commands such as query-
replace make many entries, and very simple commands such as self-inserting
characters are often grouped to make undoing less tedious.

C-x u   Undo one batch of changes—usually, one command worth
             (undo).

C-_   The same.

The command C-x u or C-_ is how you undo. The first time you give
this command, it undoes the last change. Point moves back to where it was
before the command that made the change.

Consecutive repetitions of C-_ or C-x u undo earlier and earlier changes,
back to the limit of the undo information available. If all recorded changes
have already been undone, the undo command prints an error message and
does nothing.

Any command other than an undo command breaks the sequence of undo
commands. Starting from that moment, the previous undo commands become ordinary changes that you can undo. Thus, to redo changes you have
undone, type C-f or any other command that will harmlessly break the
sequence of undoing, then type more undo commands.

If you notice that a buffer has been modified accidentally, the easiest way
to recover is to type C-_ repeatedly until the stars disappear from the front
of the mode line. At this time, all the modifications you made have been
canceled. Whenever an undo command makes the stars disappear from the
mode line, it means that the buffer contents are the same as they were when
the file was last read in or saved.

If you do not remember whether you changed the buffer deliberately,
type C-_ once. When you see the last change you made undone, you will see
whether it was an intentional change. If it was an accident, leave it undone.
If it was deliberate, redo the change as described above.

Not all buffers record undo information. Buffers whose names start with
spaces don't; these buffers are used internally by Emacs and its extensions
to hold text that users don't normally look at or edit.

You cannot undo mere cursor motion; only changes in the buffer contents save undo information. However, some cursor motion commands set the mark, so if you use these commands from time to time, you can move back to the neighborhoods you have moved through by popping the mark ring (see Section 8.5 [Mark Ring], page 59).

When the undo information for a buffer becomes too large, Emacs discards the oldest undo information from time to time (during garbage collection). You can specify how much undo information to keep by setting two variables: `undo-limit` and `undo-strong-limit`. Their values are expressed in units of bytes of space.

The variable `undo-limit` sets a soft limit: Emacs keeps undo data for enough commands to reach this size, and perhaps exceed it, but does not keep data for any earlier commands beyond that. Its default value is 20000. The variable `undo-strong-limit` sets a stricter limit: the command which pushes the size past this amount is itself forgotten. Its default value is 30000.

Regardless of the values of those variables, the most recent change is never discarded, so there is no danger that garbage collection occurring right after an unintentional large change might prevent you from undoing it.

The reason the `undo` command has two keys, `C-x u` and `C-_`, set up to run it is that it is worthy of a single-character key, but on some keyboards it is not obvious how to type `C-_`. `C-x u` is an alternative you can type straightforwardly on any terminal.

4.5 Files

The commands described above are sufficient for creating and altering text in an Emacs buffer; the more advanced Emacs commands just make things easier. But to keep any text permanently you must put it in a *file*. Files are named units of text which are stored by the operating system for you to retrieve later by name. To look at or use the contents of a file in any way, including editing the file with Emacs, you must specify the file name.

Consider a file named '/usr/rms/foo.c'. In Emacs, to begin editing this file, type

```
C-x C-f /usr/rms/foo.c RET
```

Here the file name is given as an *argument* to the command `C-x C-f` (find-file). That command uses the *minibuffer* to read the argument, and you type RET to terminate the argument (see Chapter 5 [Minibuffer], page 37).

Emacs obeys the command by *visiting* the file: creating a buffer, copying the contents of the file into the buffer, and then displaying the buffer for you to edit. If you alter the text, you can *save* the new text in the file by typing `C-x C-s` (save-buffer). This makes the changes permanent by copying the altered buffer contents back into the file '/usr/rms/foo.c'. Until you save, the changes exist only inside Emacs, and the file 'foo.c' is unaltered.

To create a file, just visit the file with C-x C-f as if it already existed. This creates an empty buffer in which you can insert the text you want to put in the file. The file is actually created when you save this buffer with C-x C-s.

Of course, there is a lot more to learn about using files. See Chapter 14 [Files], page 103.

4.6 Help

If you forget what a key does, you can find out with the Help character, which is C-h (or F1, which is an alias for C-h). Type C-h k followed by the key you want to know about; for example, C-h k C-n tells you all about what C-n does. C-h is a prefix key; C-h k is just one of its subcommands (the command describe-key). The other subcommands of C-h provide different kinds of help. Type C-h twice to get a description of all the help facilities. See Chapter 7 [Help], page 47.

4.7 Blank Lines

Here are special commands and techniques for putting in and taking out blank lines.

C-o   Insert one or more blank lines after the cursor (open-line).

C-x C-o   Delete all but one of many consecutive blank lines (delete-blank-lines).

When you want to insert a new line of text before an existing line, you can do it by typing the new line of text, followed by RET. However, it may be easier to see what you are doing if you first make a blank line and then insert the desired text into it. This is easy to do using the key C-o (open-line), which inserts a newline after point but leaves point in front of the newline. After C-o, type the text for the new line. C-o F O O has the same effect as F O O RET, except for the final location of point.

You can make several blank lines by typing C-o several times, or by giving it a numeric argument to tell it how many blank lines to make. See Section 4.10 [Arguments], page 35, for how. If you have a fill prefix, then C-o command inserts the fill prefix on the new line, when you use it at the beginning of a line. See Section 20.5.3 [Fill Prefix], page 176.

The easy way to get rid of extra blank lines is with the command C-x C-o (delete-blank-lines). C-x C-o in a run of several blank lines deletes all but one of them. C-x C-o on a solitary blank line deletes that blank line.

When point is on a nonblank line, `C-x C-o` deletes any blank lines following that nonblank line.

4.8 Continuation Lines

If you add too many characters to one line without breaking it with `RET`, the line will grow to occupy two (or more) lines on the screen, with a '\' at the extreme right margin of all but the last of them. The '\' says that the following screen line is not really a distinct line in the text, but just the *continuation* of a line too long to fit the screen. Continuation is also called *line wrapping*.

Sometimes it is nice to have Emacs insert newlines automatically when a line gets too long. Continuation on the screen does not do that. Use Auto Fill mode (see Section 20.5 [Filling], page 174) if that's what you want.

As an alternative to continuation, Emacs can display long lines by *truncation*. This means that all the characters that do not fit in the width of the screen or window do not appear at all. They remain in the buffer, temporarily invisible. '$' is used in the last column instead of '\' to inform you that truncation is in effect.

Truncation instead of continuation happens whenever horizontal scrolling is in use, and optionally in all side-by-side windows (see Chapter 16 [Windows], page 141). You can enable truncation for a particular buffer by setting the variable `truncate-lines` to non-nil in that buffer. (See Section 30.2 [Variables], page 345.) Altering the value of `truncate-lines` makes it local to the current buffer; until that time, the default value is in effect. The default is initially `nil`. See Section 30.2.4 [Locals], page 348.

See Section 11.6 [Display Vars], page 79, for additional variables that affect how text is displayed.

4.9 Cursor Position Information

Here are commands to get information about the size and position of parts of the buffer, and to count lines.

`M-x what-page`
> Print page number of point, and line number within page.

`M-x what-line`
> Print line number of point in the buffer.

`M-x line-number-mode`
> Toggle automatic display of current line number.

M-=   Print number of lines in the current region (`count-lines-`
             `region`). See Chapter 8 [Mark], page 55, for information about
             the region.

C-x =   Print character code of character after point, character position
             of point, and column of point (`what-cursor-position`).

There are two commands for working with line numbers. `M-x what-line`
computes the current line number and displays it in the echo area. To go to
a given line by number, use `M-x goto-line`; it prompts you for the number.
These line numbers count from one at the beginning of the buffer.

`M-x line-number-mode` enables display of the current line number in the
mode line; once you turn this on, the number updates as you move point, so
it remains valid all the time. See Section 1.3 [Mode Line], page 17. If you
narrow the buffer, only the accessible portion counts for this feature.

By contrast, `M-x what-page` counts pages from the beginning of the file,
and counts lines within the page, printing both numbers. See Section 20.4
[Pages], page 173.

While on this subject, we might as well mention `M-=` (`count-lines-`
`region`), which prints the number of lines in the region (see Chapter 8
[Mark], page 55). See Section 20.4 [Pages], page 173, for the command
`C-x l` which counts the lines in the current page.

The command `C-x =` (`what-cursor-position`) can be used to find out
the column that the cursor is in, and other miscellaneous information about
point. It prints a line in the echo area that looks like this:

```
Char: x (0170)  point=65986 of 563027(12%)  x=44
```

(In fact, this is the output produced when point is before the '`x=44`' in the
example.)

The two values after '`Char:`' describe the character that follows point,
first by showing it and second by giving its octal character code.

'`point=`' is followed by the position of point expressed as a character
count. The front of the buffer counts as position 1, one character later as
2, and so on. The next, larger number is the total number of characters
in the buffer. Afterward in parentheses comes the position expressed as a
percentage of the total size.

'`x=`' is followed by the horizontal position of point, in columns from the
left edge of the window.

If the buffer has been narrowed, making some of the text at the beginning
and the end temporarily inaccessible, `C-x =` prints additional text describing
the currently accessible range. For example, it might display this:

```
Char: x (0170)  point=65986 of 563025(12%) <65102 - 68533>  x=44
```

where the two extra numbers give the smallest and largest character position that point is allowed to assume. The characters between those two positions are the accessible ones. See Section 29.7 [Narrowing], page 335.

If point is at the end of the buffer (or the end of the accessible part), C-x = omits any description of the character after point. The output looks like this:

```
point=563026 of 563025(100%)   x=0
```

4.10 Numeric Arguments

Any Emacs command can be given a *numeric argument* (also called a *prefix argument*). Some commands interpret the argument as a repetition count. For example, C-f with an argument of ten moves forward ten characters instead of one. With these commands, no argument is equivalent to an argument of one. Negative arguments tell most such commands to move or act in the opposite direction.

If your terminal keyboard has a META key, the easiest way to specify a numeric argument is to type digits and/or a minus sign while holding down the the META key. For example,

```
M-5 C-n
```

would move down five lines. The characters Meta-1, Meta-2, and so on, as well as Meta--, do this because they are keys bound to commands (digit-argument and negative-argument) that are defined to contribute to an argument for the next command. Digits and - modified with Control, or Control and Meta, also specify numeric arguments.

Another way of specifying an argument is to use the C-u (universal-argument) command followed by the digits of the argument. With C-u, you can type the argument digits without holding down modifier keys; C-u works on all terminals. To type a negative argument, type a minus sign after C-u. Just a minus sign without digits normally means −1.

C-u followed by a character which is neither a digit nor a minus sign has the special meaning of "multiply by four". It multiplies the argument for the next command by four. C-u twice multiplies it by sixteen. Thus, C-u C-u C-f moves forward sixteen characters. This is a good way to move forward "fast", since it moves about 1/5 of a line in the usual size screen. Other useful combinations are C-u C-n, C-u C-u C-n (move down a good fraction of a screen), C-u C-u C-o (make "a lot" of blank lines), and C-u C-k (kill four lines).

Some commands care only about whether there is an argument, and not about its value. For example, the command M-q (fill-paragraph) with no argument fills text; with an argument, it justifies the text as well. (See

Section 20.5 [Filling], page 174, for more information on M-q.) Plain C-u is a handy way of providing an argument for such commands.

Some commands use the value of the argument as a repeat count, but do something peculiar when there is no argument. For example, the command C-k (kill-line) with argument *n* kills *n* lines, including their terminating newlines. But C-k with no argument is special: it kills the text up to the next newline, or, if point is right at the end of the line, it kills the newline itself. Thus, two C-k commands with no arguments can kill a nonblank line, just like C-k with an argument of one. (See Section 9.1 [Killing], page 61, for more information on C-k.)

A few commands treat a plain C-u differently from an ordinary argument. A few others may treat an argument of just a minus sign differently from an argument of −1. These unusual cases are described when they come up; they are always for reasons of convenience of use of the individual command.

You can use a numeric argument to insert multiple copies of a character. This is straightforward unless the character is a digit; for example, C-u 6 4 a inserts 64 copies of the character 'a'. But this does not work for inserting digits; C-u 6 4 1 specifies an argument of 641, rather than inserting anything. To separate the digit to insert from the argument, type another C-u; for example, C-u 6 4 C-u 1 does insert 64 copies of the character '1'.

We use the term "prefix argument" as well as "numeric argument" to emphasize that you type the argument before the command, and to distinguish these arguments from minibuffer arguments that come after the command.

5 The Minibuffer

The *minibuffer* is the facility used by Emacs commands to read arguments more complicated than a single number. Minibuffer arguments can be file names, buffer names, Lisp function names, Emacs command names, Lisp expressions, and many other things, depending on the command reading the argument. You can use the usual Emacs editing commands in the minibuffer to edit the argument text.

When the minibuffer is in use, it appears in the echo area, and the terminal's cursor moves there. The beginning of the minibuffer line displays a *prompt* which says what kind of input you should supply and how it will be used. Often this prompt is derived from the name of the command that the argument is for. The prompt normally ends with a colon.

Sometimes a *default argument* appears in parentheses after the colon; it too is part of the prompt. The default will be used as the argument value if you enter an empty argument (e.g., just type RET). For example, commands that read buffer names always show a default, which is the name of the buffer that will be used if you type just RET.

The simplest way to enter a minibuffer argument is to type the text you want, terminated by RET which exits the minibuffer. You can cancel the command that wants the argument, and get out of the minibuffer, by typing C-g.

Since the minibuffer uses the screen space of the echo area, it can conflict with other ways Emacs customarily uses the echo area. Here is how Emacs handles such conflicts:

- If a command gets an error while you are in the minibuffer, this does not cancel the minibuffer. However, the echo area is needed for the error message and therefore the minibuffer itself is hidden for a while. It comes back after a few seconds, or as soon as you type anything.

- If in the minibuffer you use a command whose purpose is to print a message in the echo area, such as C-x =, the message is printed normally, and the minibuffer is hidden for a while. It comes back after a few seconds, or as soon as you type anything.

- Echoing of keystrokes does not take place while the minibuffer is in use.

5.1 Minibuffers for File Names

Sometimes the minibuffer starts out with text in it. For example, when you are supposed to give a file name, the minibuffer starts out containing the *default directory*, which ends with a slash. This is to inform you which directory the file will be found in if you do not specify a directory.

For example, the minibuffer might start out with these contents:

        Find File: /u2/emacs/src/

where 'Find File: ' is the prompt.   Typing buffer.c specifies the file
'/u2/emacs/src/buffer.c'.   To find files in nearby directories, use
..; thus, if you type ../lisp/simple.el, you will get the file named
'/u2/emacs/lisp/simple.el'. Alternatively, you can kill with M-DEL the
directory names you don't want (see Section 20.1 [Words], page 169).

    If you don't want any of the default, you can kill it with C-a C-k. But you
don't need to kill the default; you can simply ignore it. Insert an absolute file
name, one starting with a slash or a tilde, after the default directory. For
example, to specify the file '/etc/termcap', just insert that name, giving
these minibuffer contents:

        Find File: /u2/emacs/src//etc/termcap

Two slashes in a row are not normally meaningful in a file name, but they are
allowed in GNU Emacs. They mean, "ignore everything before the second
slash in the pair." Thus, '/u2/emacs/src/' is ignored in the example above,
and you get the file '/etc/termcap'.

    If you set insert-default-directory to nil, the default directory is
not inserted in the minibuffer. This way, the minibuffer starts out empty.
But the name you type, if relative, is still interpreted with respect to the
same default directory.

5.2 Editing in the Minibuffer

    The minibuffer is an Emacs buffer (albeit a peculiar one), and the usual
Emacs commands are available for editing the text of an argument you are
entering.

    Since RET in the minibuffer is defined to exit the minibuffer, you can't
use it to insert a newline in the minibuffer. To do that, type C-o or C-q LFD.
(Recall that a newline is really the LFD character.)

    The minibuffer has its own window which always has space on the screen
but acts as if it were not there when the minibuffer is not in use. When
the minibuffer is in use, its window is just like the others; you can switch to
another window with C-x o, edit text in other windows and perhaps even
visit more files, before returning to the minibuffer to submit the argument.
You can kill text in another window, return to the minibuffer window, and
then yank the text to use it in the argument. See Chapter 16 [Windows],
page 141.

    There are some restrictions on the use of the minibuffer window, how-
ever. You cannot switch buffers in it—the minibuffer and its window are
permanently attached. Also, you cannot split or kill the minibuffer window. But you can make it taller in the normal fashion with C-x ^. If you

enable Resize-Minibuffer mode, then the minibuffer window expands vertically as necessary to hold the text that you put in the minibuffer. Use `M-x resize-minibuffer-mode` to enable or disable this minor mode (see Section 30.1 [Minor Modes], page 343).

If while in the minibuffer you issue a command that displays help text of any sort in another window, you can use the `C-M-v` command while in the minibuffer to scroll the help text. This lasts until you exit the minibuffer. This feature is especially useful if a completing minibuffer gives you a list of possible completions. See Section 16.3 [Other Window], page 142.

Emacs normally disallows most commands that use the minibuffer while the minibuffer is selected. This rule is to prevent recursive minibuffers from confusing novice users. If you want to be able to use such commands in the minibuffer, set the variable `enable-recursive-minibuffers` to a non-`nil` value.

5.3 Completion

For certain kinds of arguments, you can use *completion* to enter the argument value. Completion means that you type part of the argument, then Emacs visibly fills in the rest, or as much as can be determined from the part you have typed.

When completion is available, certain keys—TAB, RET, and SPC—are rebound to complete the text present in the minibuffer into a longer string that it stands for, by matching it against a set of *completion alternatives* provided by the command reading the argument. ? is defined to display a list of possible completions of what you have inserted.

For example, when `M-x` uses the minibuffer to read the name of a command, it provides a list of all available Emacs command names to complete against. The completion keys match the text in the minibuffer against all the command names, find any additional name characters implied by the ones already present in the minibuffer, and add those characters to the ones you have given. This is what makes it possible to type `M-x ins SPC b RET` instead of `M-x insert-buffer RET` (for example).

Case is normally significant in completion, because it is significant in most of the names that you can complete (buffer names, file names and command names). Thus, 'fo' does not complete to 'Foo'. Completion does ignore case distinctions for certain arguments in which case does not matter.

5.3.1 Completion Example

A concrete example may help here. If you type `M-x au TAB`, the TAB looks for alternatives (in this case, command names) that start with 'au'. There are only two: `auto-fill-mode` and `auto-save-mode`. These are the same as far as `auto-`, so the 'au' in the minibuffer changes to 'auto-'.

If you type TAB again immediately, there are multiple possibilities for the very next character—it could be 's' or 'f'—so no more characters are added; instead, TAB displays a list of all possible completions in another window.

If you go on to type f TAB, this TAB sees 'auto-f'. The only command name starting this way is `auto-fill-mode`, so completion fills in the rest of that. You now have 'auto-fill-mode' in the minibuffer after typing just au TAB f TAB. Note that TAB has this effect because in the minibuffer it is bound to the command `minibuffer-complete` when completion is available.

5.3.2 Completion Commands

Here is a list of the completion commands defined in the minibuffer when completion is available.

TAB   Complete the text in the minibuffer as much as possible (`minibuffer-complete`).

SPC   Complete the minibuffer text, but don't go beyond one word (`minibuffer-complete-word`).

RET   Submit the text in the minibuffer as the argument, possibly completing first as described below (`minibuffer-complete-and-exit`).

?   Print a list of all possible completions of the text in the minibuffer (`minibuffer-list-completions`).

SPC completes much like TAB, but never goes beyond the next hyphen or space. If you have 'auto-f' in the minibuffer and type SPC, it finds that the completion is 'auto-fill-mode', but it stops completing after 'fill-'. This gives 'auto-fill-'. Another SPC at this point completes all the way to 'auto-fill-mode'. SPC in the minibuffer when completion is available runs the command `minibuffer-complete-word`.

Here are some commands you can use to choose a completion from a window that displays a list of completions:

Mouse-2   Clicking mouse button 2 on a completion in the list of possible completions chooses that completion (`mouse-choose-completion`). You normally use this command while point is in the minibuffer; but you must click in the list of completions, not in the minibuffer itself.

PRIOR
M-v   Typing PRIOR or PAGE-UP, or M-v, while in the minibuffer, selects the window showing the completion list buffer (`switch-to-completions`). This paves the way for using the commands

	below. (Selecting that window in the usual ways has the same effect, but this way is more convenient.)
RET	Typing RET *in the completion list buffer* chooses the completion that point is in or next to (choose-completion). To use this command, you must first switch windows to the window that shows the list of completions.
RIGHT	Typing the right-arrow key RIGHT *in the completion list buffer* moves point to the following completion (next-completion).
LEFT	Typing the left-arrow key LEFT *in the completion list buffer* moves point toward the beginning of the buffer, to the previous completion (previous-completion).

5.3.3 Strict Completion

There are three different ways that RET can work in completing minibuffers, depending on how the argument will be used.

- *Strict* completion is used when it is meaningless to give any argument except one of the known alternatives. For example, when C-x k reads the name of a buffer to kill, it is meaningless to give anything but the name of an existing buffer. In strict completion, RET refuses to exit if the text in the minibuffer does not complete to an exact match.

- *Cautious* completion is similar to strict completion, except that RET exits only if the text was an exact match already, not needing completion. If the text is not an exact match, RET does not exit, but it does complete the text. If it completes to an exact match, a second RET will exit.

  Cautious completion is used for reading file names for files that must already exist.

- *Permissive* completion is used when any string whatever is meaningful, and the list of completion alternatives is just a guide. For example, when C-x C-f reads the name of a file to visit, any file name is allowed, in case you want to create a file. In permissive completion, RET takes the text in the minibuffer exactly as given, without completing it.

The completion commands display a list of all possible completions in a window whenever there is more than one possibility for the very next character. Also, typing ? explicitly requests such a list. If the list of completions is long, you can scroll it with C-M-v (see Section 16.3 [Other Window], page 142).

5.3.4 Completion Options

When completion is done on file names, certain file names are usually ignored. The variable completion-ignored-extensions contains a list of strings; a file whose name ends in any of those strings is ignored as a possible completion. The standard value of this variable has several elements including ".o", ".elc", ".dvi" and "~". The effect is that, for example, 'foo' can complete to 'foo.c' even though 'foo.o' exists as well. However, if *all* the possible completions end in "ignored" strings, then they are not ignored. Ignored extensions do not apply to lists of completions—those always mention all possible completions.

Normally, a completion command that finds the next character is undetermined automatically displays a list of all possible completions. If the variable `completion-auto-help` is set to `nil`, this does not happen, and you must type ? to display the possible completions.

The `complete` library implements a more powerful kind of completion that can complete multiple words at a time. For example, it can complete the command name abbreviation p-b into `print-buffer`, because no other command starts with two words whose initials are 'p' and 'b'. To use this library, put (`load "complete"`) in your '~/.emacs' file (see Section 30.7 [Init File], page 366).

Icomplete mode presents a constantly-updated display that tells you what completions are available for the text you've entered so far. The command to enable or disable this minor mode is `M-x icomplete-mode`.

5.4 Minibuffer History

Every argument that you enter with the minibuffer is saved on a *minibuffer history list* so that you can use it again later in another argument. Special commands load the text of an earlier argument in the minibuffer. They discard the old minibuffer contents, so you can think of them as moving through the history of previous arguments.

M-p   Move to the next earlier argument string saved in the minibuffer history (`previous-history-element`).

M-n   Move to the next later argument string saved in the minibuffer history (`next-history-element`).

M-r *regexp* RET
           Move to an earlier saved argument in the minibuffer history that has a match for *regexp* (`previous-matching-history-element`).

M-s *regexp* RET
           Move to a later saved argument in the minibuffer history that has a match for *regexp* (`next-matching-history-element`).

The simplest way to reuse the saved arguments in the history list is to move through the history list one element at a time. While in the minibuffer, type M-p (previous-history-element) to "move to" the next earlier minibuffer input, and use M-n (next-history-element) to "move to" the next later input.

The previous input that you fetch from the history entirely replaces the contents of the minibuffer. To use it as the argument, exit the minibuffer as usual with RET. You can also edit the text before you reuse it; this does not change the history element that you "moved" to, but your new argument does go at the end of the history list in its own right.

There are also commands to search forward or backward through the history. As of this writing, they search for history elements that match a regular expression that you specify with the minibuffer. M-r (previous-matching-history-element) searches older elements in the history, while M-s (next-matching-history-element) searches newer elements. By special dispensation, these commands can use the minibuffer to read their arguments even though you are already in the minibuffer when you issue them.

All uses of the minibuffer record your input on a history list, but there are separate history lists for different kinds of arguments. For example, there is a list for file names, used by all the commands that read file names. There is a list for arguments of commands like query-replace. There are several very specific history lists, including one for command names read by M-X and one for compilation commands read by compile. Finally, there is one "miscellaneous" history list that most minibuffer arguments use.

5.5 Repeating Minibuffer Commands

Every command that uses the minibuffer at least once is recorded on a special history list, together with the values of its arguments, so that you can repeat the entire command. In particular, every use of M-x is recorded there, since M-x uses the minibuffer to read the command name.

C-x ESC ESC
> Re-execute a recent minibuffer command (repeat-complex-command).

M-x list-command-history
> Display the entire command history, showing all the commands C-x ESC ESC can repeat, most recent first.

C-x ESC ESC is used to re-execute a recent minibuffer-using command. With no argument, it repeats the last such command. A numeric argument specifies which command to repeat; one means the last one, and larger numbers specify earlier ones.

C-x ESC ESC works by turning the previous command into a Lisp expression and then entering a minibuffer initialized with the text for that expression. If you type just RET, the command is repeated as before. You can also change the command by editing the Lisp expression. Whatever expression you finally submit is what will be executed. The repeated command is added to the front of the command history unless it is identical to the most recently executed command already there.

Even if you don't understand Lisp syntax, it will probably be obvious which command is displayed for repetition. If you do not change the text, it will repeat exactly as before.

Once inside the minibuffer for C-x ESC ESC, you can use the minibuffer history commands (M-p, M-n, M-r, M-s; see Section 5.4 [Minibuffer History], page 42) to move through the history list of saved entire commands. After finding the desired previous command, you can edit its expression as usual and then resubmit it by typing RET as usual.

The list of previous minibuffer-using commands is stored as a Lisp list in the variable command-history. Each element is a Lisp expression which describes one command and its arguments. Lisp programs can reexecute a command by calling eval with the command-history element.

6 Running Commands by Name

The Emacs commands that are used often or that must be quick to type are bound to keys—short sequences of characters—for convenient use. Other Emacs commands that do not need to be brief are not bound to keys; to run them, you must refer to them by name.

A command name is, by convention, made up of one or more words, separated by hyphens; for example, `auto-fill-mode` or `manual-entry`. The use of English words makes the command name easier to remember than a key made up of obscure characters, even though it is more characters to type.

The way to run a command by name is to start with `M-x`, type the command name, and finish it with `RET`. `M-x` uses the minibuffer to read the command name. `RET` exits the minibuffer and runs the command. The string 'M-x' appears at the beginning of the minibuffer as a *prompt* to remind you to enter the name of a command to be run. See Chapter 5 [Minibuffer], page 37, for full information on the features of the minibuffer.

You can use completion to enter the command name. For example, the command `forward-char` can be invoked by name by typing

    M-x forward-char RET

or

    M-x forw TAB c RET

Note that `forward-char` is the same command that you invoke with the key `C-f`. You can run any Emacs command by name using `M-x`, whether or not any keys are bound to it.

If you type `C-g` while the command name is being read, you cancel the `M-x` command and get out of the minibuffer, ending up at top level.

To pass a numeric argument to the command you are invoking with `M-x`, specify the numeric argument before the `M-x`. `M-x` passes the argument along to the command it runs. The argument value appears in the prompt while the command name is being read.

Normally, when describing a command that is run by name, we omit the `RET` that is needed to terminate the name. Thus we might speak of `M-x auto-fill-mode` rather than `M-x auto-fill-mode RET`. We mention the `RET` only when there is a need to emphasize its presence, such as when we show the command together with following arguments.

`M-x` works by running the command `execute-extended-command`, which is responsible for reading the name of another command and invoking it.

7 Help

Emacs provides extensive help features accessible through a single character, C-h. C-h is a prefix key that is used only for documentation-printing commands. The characters that you can type after C-h are called *help options*. One help option is C-h; that is how you ask for help about using C-h. To cancel, type C-g. The function key F1 is equivalent to C-h.

C-h C-h displays a list of the possible help options, each with a brief description. Before you type a help option, you can use SPC or DEL to scroll through the list.

C-h or F1 means "help" in various other contexts as well. For example, in query-replace, it describes the options available. After a prefix key, it displays a list of the alternatives that can follow the prefix key. (A few prefix keys don't support this because they define other meanings for C-h.)

Here is a summary of the defined help commands.

C-h a *regexp* RET
:   Display list of commands whose names match *regexp* (command-apropos).

C-h b
:   Display a table of all key bindings in effect now, in this order: minor mode bindings, major mode bindings, and global bindings (describe-bindings).

C-h c *key*
:   Print the name of the command that *key* runs (describe-key-briefly). Here c stands for 'character'. For more extensive information on *key*, use C-h k.

C-h f *function* RET
:   Display documentation on the Lisp function named *function* (describe-function). Since commands are Lisp functions, a command name may be used.

C-h i
:   Run Info, the program for browsing documentation files (info). The complete Emacs manual is available on-line in Info.

C-h k *key*
:   Display name and documentation of the command that *key* runs (describe-key).

C-h l
:   Display a description of the last 100 characters you typed (view-lossage).

C-h m
:   Display documentation of the current major mode (describe-mode).

C-h n
:   Display documentation of Emacs changes, most recent first (view-emacs-news).

C-h p
:   Find packages by topic keyword (finder-by-keyword).

`C-h s`   Display current contents of the syntax table, plus an explana-
              tion of what they mean (`describe-syntax`). See Section 30.6
              [Syntax], page 366.

`C-h t`   Enter the Emacs interactive tutorial (`help-with-tutorial`).

`C-h v` *var* `RET`
              Display the documentation of the Lisp variable *var* (`describe-`
              `variable`).

`C-h w` *command* `RET`
              Print which keys run the command named *command* (`where-`
              `is`).

`C-h C-f` *function* `RET`
              Enter Info and go to the node documenting the Emacs function
              function (`info-goto-emacs-command-node`).

`C-h C-k` *key*
              Enter Info and go to the node where the key sequence *key* is
              documented (`info-goto-emacs-key-command-node`).

`C-h C-c`   Display the copying conditions for GNU Emacs.

`C-h C-d`   Display information about getting new versions of GNU Emacs.

`C-h C-p`   Display information about the GNU Project.

7.1 Documentation for a Key

The most basic `C-h` options are `C-h c` (`describe-key-briefly`) and
`C-h k` (`describe-key`). `C-h c` *key* prints in the echo area the name of
the command that *key* is bound to. For example, `C-h c C-f` prints
'`forward-char`'. Since command names are chosen to describe what the
commands do, this is a good way to get a very brief description of what *key*
does.

`C-h k` *key* is similar but gives more information: it displays the documentation string of the command as well as its name. This is too big for the
echo area, so a window is used for the display.

`C-h c` and `C-h k` work for any sort of key sequences, including function
keys and mouse events.

7.2 Help by Command or Variable Name

`C-h f` (`describe-function`) reads the name of a Lisp function using the
minibuffer, then displays that function's documentation string in a window.
Since commands are Lisp functions, you can use this to get the documentation of a command that you know by name. For example,

C-h f auto-fill-mode RET

displays the documentation of auto-fill-mode. This is the only way to get the documentation of a command that is not bound to any key (one which you would normally run using M-x).

C-h f is also useful for Lisp functions that you are planning to use in a Lisp program. For example, if you have just written the expression (make-vector len) and want to check that you are using make-vector properly, type C-h f make-vector RET. Because C-h f allows all function names, not just command names, you may find that some of your favorite abbreviations that work in M-x don't work in C-h f. An abbreviation may be unique among command names yet fail to be unique when other function names are allowed.

The function name for C-h f to describe has a default which is used if you type RET leaving the minibuffer empty. The default is the function called by the innermost Lisp expression in the buffer around point, *provided* that is a valid, defined Lisp function name. For example, if point is located following the text '(make-vector (car x)', the innermost list containing point is the one that starts with '(make-vector', so the default is to describe the function make-vector.

C-h f is often useful just to verify that you have the right spelling for the function name. If C-h f mentions a name from the buffer as the default, that name must be defined as a Lisp function. If that is all you want to know, just type C-g to cancel the C-h f command, then go on editing.

C-h w *command* RET tells you what keys are bound to *command*. It prints a list of the keys in the echo area. If it says the command is not on any key, you must use M-x to run it. C-h w runs the command where-is.

C-h v (describe-variable) is like C-h f but describes Lisp variables instead of Lisp functions. Its default is the Lisp symbol around or before point, but only if that is the name of a known Lisp variable. See Section 30.2 [Variables], page 345.

7.3 Apropos

A more sophisticated sort of question to ask is, "What are the commands for working with files?" To ask this question, type C-h a file RET, which displays a list of all command names that contain 'file', including copy-file, find-file, and so on. With each command name appears a brief description of how to use the command, and what keys you can currently invoke it with. For example, it would say that you can invoke find-file by typing C-x C-f. The a in C-h a stands for 'Apropos'; C-h a runs the command command-apropos.

Because C-h a looks only for functions whose names contain the string which you specify, you must use ingenuity in choosing the string. If you are looking for commands for killing backwards and C-h a kill-backwards RET doesn't reveal any, don't give up. Try just kill, or just backwards, or just back. Be persistent. Also note that you can use a regular expression as the argument, for more flexibility (see Section 12.5 [Regexps], page 88).

Here is a set of arguments to give to C-h a that covers many classes of Emacs commands, since there are strong conventions for naming the standard Emacs commands. By giving you a feel for the naming conventions, this set should also serve to aid you in developing a technique for picking apropos strings.

> char, line, word, sentence, paragraph, region, page, sexp, list, defun, rect, buffer, frame, window, face, file, dir, register, mode, beginning, end, forward, backward, next, previous, up, down, search, goto, kill, delete, mark, insert, yank, fill, indent, case, change, set, what, list, find, view, describe, default.

To list all Lisp symbols that contain a match for a regexp, not just the ones that are defined as commands, use the command M-x apropos instead of C-h a. This command does not check key bindings by default; specify a numeric argument if you want it to check them.

The super-apropos command is like apropos except that it searches documentation strings as well as symbol names for matches for the specified regular expression.

7.4 Keyword Search for Lisp Libraries

The C-h p command lets you search the standard Emacs Lisp libraries by topic keywords. Here is a partial list of keywords you can use:

'abbrev'   Abbreviation handling, typing shortcuts, macros.

'bib'   Support for the bibliography processor bib.

'c'   C and C++ language support.

'calendar'
            Calendar and time management support.

'comm'   Communications, networking, remote access to files.

'data'   Support for editing files of data.

'debugging'
            Support for debugging programs.

'docs'   Support for Emacs documentation.

`'emulations'`
> Emulations of other editors.

`'extensions'`
> Emacs Lisp language extensions.

`'faces'`   Support for using faces (fonts and colors; see Section 17.12 [Faces], page 156).

`'frames'`   Support for Emacs frames and window systems.

`'games'`   Games, jokes and amusements.

`'hardware'`
> Support for interfacing with exotic hardware.

`'help'`   Support for on-line help systems.

`'hypermedia'`
> Support for links within text, or other media types.

`'i18n'`   Internationalization and alternate character-set support.

`'internal'`
> Code for Emacs internals, build process, defaults.

`'languages'`
> Specialized modes for editing programming languages.

`'lisp'`   Support for using Lisp (including Emacs Lisp).

`'local'`   Libraries local to your site.

`'maint'`   Maintenance aids for the Emacs development group.

`'mail'`   Modes for electronic-mail handling.

`'matching'`
> Searching and matching.

`'news'`   Support for netnews reading and posting.

`'non-text'`
> Support for editing files that are not ordinary text.

`'oop'`   Support for object-oriented programming.

`'outlines'`
> Hierarchical outlining.

`'processes'`
> Process, subshell, compilation, and job control support.

`'terminals'`
> Support for terminal types.

'tex'   Support for the TEX formatter.

'tools'   Programming tools.

'unix'   Front-ends/assistants for, or emulators of, Unix features.

'vms'   Support code for VMS.

'wp'   Word processing.

7.5 Other Help Commands

C-h i (info) runs the Info program, which is used for browsing through structured documentation files. The entire Emacs manual is available within Info. Eventually all the documentation of the GNU system will be available. Type h after entering Info to run a tutorial on using Info.

There are two special help commands for accessing Emacs documentation through Info. C-h C-f *function* RET enters Info and goes straight to the documentation of the Emacs function *function*. C-h C-k *key* enters Info and goes straight to the documentation of the key *key*. These two keys run the commands Info-goto-emacs-command-node and Info-goto-emacs-key-command-node.

If something surprising happens, and you are not sure what commands you typed, use C-h l (view-lossage). C-h l prints the last 100 command characters you typed in. If you see commands that you don't know, you can use C-h c to find out what they do.

Emacs has numerous major modes, each of which redefines a few keys and makes a few other changes in how editing works. C-h m (describe-mode) prints documentation on the current major mode, which normally describes all the commands that are changed in this mode.

C-h b (describe-bindings) and C-h s (describe-syntax) present other information about the current Emacs mode. C-h b displays a list of all the key bindings now in effect; the local bindings defined by the current minor modes first, then the local bindings defined by the current major mode, and finally the global bindings (see Section 30.4 [Key Bindings], page 355). C-h s displays the contents of the syntax table, with explanations of each character's syntax (see Section 30.6 [Syntax], page 366).

You can get a similar list for a particular prefix key by typing C-h after the prefix key. (There are a few prefix keys for which this does not work—those that provide their own bindings for C-h. One of these is ESC, because ESC C-h is actually C-M-h, which marks a defun.)

The other C-h options display various files of useful information. C-h C-w displays the full details on the complete absence of warranty for GNU Emacs. C-h n (view-emacs-news) displays the file 'emacs/etc/NEWS', which contains documentation on Emacs changes arranged chronologically. C-h t (`help-with-tutorial`) displays the learn-by-doing Emacs tutorial. `C-h C-c` (`describe-copying`) displays the file 'emacs/etc/COPYING', which tells you the conditions you must obey in distributing copies of Emacs. `C-h C-d` (`describe-distribution`) displays the file 'emacs/etc/DISTRIB', which tells you how you can order a copy of the latest version of Emacs. `C-h C-p` (`describe-project`) displays general information about the GNU Project.

8 The Mark and the Region

Many Emacs commands operate on an arbitrary contiguous part of the current buffer. To specify the text for such a command to operate on, you set *the mark* at one end of it, and move point to the other end. The text between point and the mark is called *the region*. Emacs highlights the region whenever there is one, if you enable Transient Mark mode (see Section 8.2 [Transient Mark], page 56).

You can move point or the mark to adjust the boundaries of the region. It doesn't matter which one is set first chronologically, or which one comes earlier in the text. Once the mark has been set, it remains where you put it until you set it again at another place. Each Emacs buffer has its own mark, so that when you return to a buffer that had been selected previously, it has the same mark it had before.

Many commands that insert text, such as `C-y` (`yank`) and `M-x insert-buffer`, position point and the mark at opposite ends of the inserted text, so that the region contains the text just inserted.

Aside from delimiting the region, the mark is also useful for remembering a spot that you may want to go back to. To make this feature more useful, each buffer remembers 16 previous locations of the mark in the *mark ring*.

8.1 Setting the Mark

Here are some commands for setting the mark:

`C-SPC`   Set the mark where point is (`set-mark-command`).

`C-@`   The same.

`C-x C-x`   Interchange mark and point (`exchange-point-and-mark`).

`Drag-Mouse-1`
      Set point and the mark around the text you drag across.

`Mouse-3`   Set the mark where point is, then move point to where you click (`mouse-save-then-kill`).

For example, suppose you wish to convert part of the buffer to all upper-case, using the `C-x C-u` (`upcase-region`) command which operates on the text in the region. You can first go to the beginning of the text to be capitalized, type `C-SPC` to put the mark there, move to the end, and then type `C-x C-u`. Or, you can set the mark at the end of the text, move to the beginning, and then type `C-x C-u`.

The most common way to set the mark is with the `C-SPC` command (`set-mark-command`). This sets the mark where point is. Then you can move point away, leaving the mark behind.

There are two ways to set the mark with the mouse. You can drag mouse button one across a range of text; that puts point where you release the mouse button, and sets the mark at the other end of that range. Or you can click mouse button three, which sets the mark at point (like C-SPC) and them moves point (like Mouse-1). Both of these methods copy the region into the kill ring in addition to setting the mark; that gives behavior consistent with other window-driven applications, but if you don't want to modify the kill ring, you must use keyboard commands to set the mark. See Section 17.1 [Mouse Commands], page 147.

Ordinary terminals have only one cursor, so there is no way for Emacs to show you where the mark is located. You have to remember. The usual solution to this problem is to set the mark and then use it soon, before you forget where it is. Alternatively, you can see where the mark is with the command C-x C-x (exchange-point-and-mark) which puts the mark where point was and point where the mark was. The extent of the region is unchanged, but the cursor and point are now at the previous position of the mark. In Transient Mark mode, this command reactivates the mark.

C-x C-x is also useful when you are satisfied with the position of point but want to move the mark; do C-x C-x to put point at that end of the region, and then move it. A second use of C-x C-x, if necessary, puts the mark at the new position with point back at its original position.

There is no such character as C-SPC in ASCII; when you type SPC while holding down CTRL, what you get on most ordinary terminals is the character C-@. This key is actually bound to set-mark-command. But unless you are unlucky enough to have a terminal where typing C-SPC does not produce C-@, you might as well think of this character as C-SPC. Under X, C-SPC is actually a distinct character, but its binding is still set-mark-command.

8.2 Transient Mark Mode

Emacs can highlight the current region, using X Windows. But normally it does not. Why not?

Highlighting the region doesn't work well ordinarily in Emacs, because once you have set a mark, there is *always* a region (in that buffer). And highlighting the region all the time would be a nuisance.

You can turn on region highlighting by enabling Transient Mark mode. This is a more rigid mode of operation in which the region "lasts" only temporarily, so you must set up a region for each command that uses one. In Transient Mark mode, most of the time there is no region; therefore, highlighting the region when it exists is convenient.

To enable Transient Mark mode, type M-x transient-mark-mode. This command toggles the mode, so you can repeat the command to turn off the mode.

Here are the details of Transient Mark mode:

- To set the mark, type C-SPC (set-mark-command). This makes the mark active; as you move point, you will see the region highlighting change in extent.

- The mouse commands for specifying the mark also make it active. So do keyboard commands whose purpose is to specify a region, including M-@, C-M-@, M-h, C-M-h, C-x C-p, and C-x h.

- When the mark is active, you can execute commands that operate on the region, such as killing, indentation, or writing to a file.

- Any change to the buffer, such as inserting or deleting a character, de-activates the mark. This means any subsequent command that operates on a region will get an error and refuse to operate. You can make the region active again by typing C-x C-x.

- Commands like M-> and C-s that "leave the mark behind" in addition to some other primary purpose do not activate the new mark. You can activate the new region by executing C-x C-x (exchange-point-and-mark).

- C-s when the mark is active does not alter the mark.

- Quitting with C-g deactivates the mark.

Transient Mark mode is also sometimes known as "Zmacs mode" because the Zmacs editor on the MIT Lisp Machine handled the mark in a similar way.

When multiple windows show the same buffer, they can have different regions, because they can have different values of point (though they all share common one mark position). In Transient Mark mode, each window highlights its own region. The part that is highlighted in the selected window is the region that editing commands use. See Chapter 16 [Windows], page 141.

When Transient Mark mode is not enabled, every command that sets the mark also activates it, and nothing ever deactivates it.

8.3 Operating on the Region

Once you have a region and the mark is active, here are some of the ways you can operate on the region:

- Kill it with C-w (see Section 9.1 [Killing], page 61).

- Save it in a register with C-x r s (see Chapter 10 [Registers], page 71).

- Save it in a buffer or a file (see Section 9.3 [Accumulating Text], page 66).

- Convert case with C-x C-l or C-x C-u (see Section 20.6 [Case], page 178).

- Indent it with C-x TAB or C-M-\ (see Chapter 19 [Indentation], page 165).

- Fill it as text with M-x fill-region (see Section 20.5 [Filling], page 174).

- Print hardcopy with M-x print-region (see Section 29.4 [Hardcopy], page 331).

- Evaluate it as Lisp code with M-x eval-region (see Section 22.5 [Lisp Eval], page 247).

Most commands that operate on the text in the region have the word region in their names.

8.4 Commands to Mark Textual Objects

Here are the commands for placing point and the mark around a textual object such as a word, list, paragraph or page.

M-@   Set mark after end of next word (mark-word). This command and the following one do not move point.

C-M-@   Set mark after end of next Lisp expression (mark-sexp).

M-h   Put region around current paragraph (mark-paragraph).

C-M-h   Put region around current Lisp defun (mark-defun).

C-x h   Put region around entire buffer (mark-whole-buffer).

C-x C-p   Put region around current page (mark-page).

M-@ (mark-word) puts the mark at the end of the next word, while C-M-@ (mark-sexp) puts it at the end of the next Lisp expression. These commands handle arguments just like M-f and C-M-f.

Other commands set both point and mark, to delimit an object in the buffer. For example, M-h (mark-paragraph) moves point to the beginning of the paragraph that surrounds or follows point, and puts the mark at the end of that paragraph (see Section 20.3 [Paragraphs], page 172). It prepares the region so you can indent, case-convert, or kill a whole paragraph.

C-M-h (mark-defun) similarly puts point before and the mark after the current or following defun (see Section 21.4 [Defuns], page 202). C-x C-p (mark-page) puts point before the current page, and mark at the end (see Section 20.4 [Pages], page 173). The mark goes after the terminating page delimiter (to include it), while point goes after the preceding page delimiter (to exclude it). A numeric argument specifies a later page (if positive) or an earlier page (if negative) instead of the current page.

Finally, C-x h (mark-whole-buffer) sets up the entire buffer as the region, by putting point at the beginning and the mark at the end.

In Transient Mark mode, all of these commands activate the mark.

8.5 The Mark Ring

Aside from delimiting the region, the mark is also useful for remembering a spot that you may want to go back to. To make this feature more useful, each buffer remembers 16 previous locations of the mark, in the *mark ring*. Commands that set the mark also push the old mark onto this ring. To return to a marked location, use C-u C-SPC (or C-u C-@); this is the command **set-mark-command** given a numeric argument. It moves point to where the mark was, and restores the mark from the ring of former marks. Thus, repeated use of this command moves point to all of the old marks on the ring, one by one. The mark positions you move through in this way are not lost; they go to the end of the ring.

Each buffer has its own mark ring. All editing commands use the current buffer's mark ring. In particular, C-u C-SPC always stays in the same buffer.

Many commands that can move long distances, such as M-< (**beginning-of-buffer**), start by setting the mark and saving the old mark on the mark ring. This is to make it easier for you to move back later. Searches set the mark if they move point. You can tell when a command sets the mark because it displays '**Mark Set**' in the echo area.

If you want to move back to the same place over and over, the mark ring may not be convenient enough. If so, you can record the position in a register for later retrieval (see Section 10.1 [RegPos], page 71).

The variable **mark-ring-max** specifies the maximum number of entries to keep in the mark ring. If that many entries exist and another one is pushed, the last one in the list is discarded. Repeating C-u C-SPC circulates through the positions currently in the ring.

The variable **mark-ring** holds the mark ring itself, as a list of marker objects in the order most recent first. This variable is local in every buffer.

8.6 The Global Mark Ring

In addition to the ordinary mark ring that belongs to each buffer, Emacs has a single *global mark ring*. It records a sequence of buffers in which you have recently set the mark, so you can go back to those buffers.

Setting the mark always makes an entry on the current buffer's mark ring. If you have switched buffers since the previous mark setting, the new mark position makes an entry on the global mark ring also. The result is that the global mark ring records a sequence of buffers that you have been in, and, for each buffer, a place where you set the mark.

The command C-x C-SPC (**pop-global-mark**) jumps to the buffer and position of the latest entry in the global ring. It also rotates the ring, so that successive uses of C-x C-SPC take you to earlier and earlier buffers.

9 Killing and Moving Text

Killing means erasing text and copying it into the *kill ring*, from which it can be retrieved by *yanking* it. Some systems use the terms "cutting" and "pasting" for these operations.

The commonest way of moving or copying text within Emacs is to kill it and later yank elsewhere it in one or more places. This is very safe because Emacs remembers several recent kills, not just the last one. It is versatile, because the many commands for killing syntactic units can also be used for moving those units. But there are other ways of copying text for special purposes.

Emacs has only one kill ring for all buffers, so you can kill text in one buffer and yank it in another buffer.

9.1 Deletion and Killing

Most commands which erase text from the buffer save it in the kill ring so that you can move or copy it to other parts of the buffer. These commands are known as *kill* commands. The rest of the commands that erase text do not save it in the kill ring; they are known as *delete* commands. (This distinction is made only for erasure of text in the buffer.) If you do a kill or delete command by mistake, you can use the C-x u (undo) command to undo it (see Section 4.4 [Undo], page 30).

The delete commands include C-d (delete-char) and DEL (delete-backward-char), which delete only one character at a time, and those commands that delete only spaces or newlines. Commands that can destroy significant amounts of nontrivial data generally kill. The commands' names and individual descriptions use the words 'kill' and 'delete' to say which they do.

9.1.1 Deletion

C-d   Delete next character (delete-char).

DEL   Delete previous character (delete-backward-char).

M-\   Delete spaces and tabs around point (delete-horizontal-space).

M-SPC   Delete spaces and tabs around point, leaving one space (just-one-space).

C-x C-o   Delete blank lines around the current line (delete-blank-lines).

M-^   Join two lines by deleting the intervening newline, along with
               any indentation following it (`delete-indentation`).

The most basic delete commands are `C-d` (`delete-char`) and `DEL`
(`delete-backward-char`). `C-d` deletes the character after point, the one
the cursor is "on top of". This doesn't move point. `DEL` deletes the character before the cursor, and moves point back. You can delete newlines like any
other characters in the buffer; deleting a newline joins two lines. Actually,
`C-d` and `DEL` aren't always delete commands; when given arguments, they
kill instead, since they can erase more than one character this way.

The other delete commands are those which delete only whitespace characters: spaces, tabs and newlines. `M-\` (`delete-horizontal-space`) deletes
all the spaces and tab characters before and after point. `M-SPC` (`just-one-
space`) does likewise but leaves a single space after point, regardless of the
number of spaces that existed previously (even zero).

`C-x C-o` (`delete-blank-lines`) deletes all blank lines after the current
line. If the current line is blank, it deletes all blank lines preceding the
current line as well (leaving one blank line, the current line).

`M-^` (`delete-indentation`) joins the current line and the previous line,
by deleting a newline and all surrounding spaces, usually leaving a single
space. See Chapter 19 [Indentation], page 165.

9.1.2 Killing by Lines

C-k   Kill rest of line or one or more lines (`kill-line`).

The simplest kill command is `C-k`. If given at the beginning of a line, it
kills all the text on the line, leaving it blank. When used on a blank line,
it kills the whole line including its newline. To kill an entire non-blank line,
go to the beginning and type `C-k` twice.

More generally, `C-k` kills from point up to the end of the line, unless it
is at the end of a line. In that case it kills the newline following point, thus
merging the next line into the current one. Spaces and tabs that you can't
see at the end of the line are ignored when deciding which case applies, so if
point appears to be at the end of the line, you can be sure `C-k` will kill the
newline.

When `C-k` is given a positive argument, it kills that many lines and the
newlines that follow them (however, text on the current line before point is
spared). With a negative argument $-n$, it kills n lines preceding the current
line (together with the text on the current line before point). Thus, `C-u - 2
C-k` at the front of a line kills the two previous lines.

`C-k` with an argument of zero kills the text before point on the current
line.

If the variable `kill-whole-line` is non-nil, `C-k` at the very beginning of a line kills the entire line including the following newline. This variable is normally `nil`.

9.1.3 Other Kill Commands

`C-w`   Kill region (from point to the mark) (`kill-region`).

`M-d`   Kill word (`kill-word`). See Section 20.1 [Words], page 169.

`M-DEL`   Kill word backwards (`backward-kill-word`).

`C-x DEL`   Kill back to beginning of sentence (`backward-kill-sentence`). See Section 20.2 [Sentences], page 171.

`M-k`   Kill to end of sentence (`kill-sentence`).

`C-M-k`   Kill sexp (`kill-sexp`). See Section 21.2 [Lists], page 200.

`M-z` *char*   Kill through the next occurrence of *char* (`zap-to-char`).

A kill command which is very general is `C-w` (`kill-region`), which kills everything between point and the mark. With this command, you can kill any contiguous sequence of characters, if you first set the region around them.

A convenient way of killing is combined with searching: `M-z` (`zap-to-char`) reads a character and kills from point up to (and including) the next occurrence of that character in the buffer. A numeric argument acts as a repeat count. A negative argument means to search backward and kill text before point.

Other syntactic units can be killed: words, with `M-DEL` and `M-d` (see Section 20.1 [Words], page 169); sexps, with `C-M-k` (see Section 21.2 [Lists], page 200); and sentences, with `C-x DEL` and `M-k` (see Section 20.2 [Sentences], page 171).

You can use kill commands in read-only buffers. They don't actually change the buffer, and they beep to warn you of that, but they do copy the text you tried to kill into the kill ring, so you can yank it into other buffers. Most of the kill commands move point across the text they copy in this way, so that successive kill commands build up a single kill ring entry as usual.

9.2 Yanking

Yanking means reinserting text previously killed. This is what some systems call "pasting". The usual way to move or copy text is to kill it and then yank it elsewhere one or more times.

`C-y`   Yank last killed text (`yank`).

M-y   Replace text just yanked with an earlier batch of killed text
             (yank-pop).

M-w   Save region as last killed text without actually killing it (kill-
             ring-save).

C-M-w   Append next kill to last batch of killed text (append-next-
             kill).

9.2.1 The Kill Ring

All killed text is recorded in the *kill ring*, a list of blocks of text that have
been killed. There is only one kill ring, shared by all buffers, so you can kill
text in one buffer and yank it in another buffer. This is the usual way to
move text from one file to another. (See Section 9.3 [Accumulating Text],
page 66, for some other ways.)

The command C-y (yank) reinserts the text of the most recent kill. It
leaves the cursor at the end of the text. It sets the mark at the beginning
of the text. See Chapter 8 [Mark], page 55.

C-u C-y leaves the cursor in front of the text, and sets the mark after
it. This happens only if the argument is specified with just a C-u, precisely.
Any other sort of argument, including C-u and digits, specifies an earlier kill
to yank (see Section 9.2.3 [Earlier Kills], page 65).

To copy a block of text, you can use M-w (kill-ring-save), which copies
the region into the kill ring without removing it from the buffer. This is
approximately equivalent to C-w followed by C-x u, except that M-w does
not alter the undo history and does not temporarily change the screen.

9.2.2 Appending Kills

Normally, each kill command pushes a new entry onto the kill ring. However, two or more kill commands in a row combine their text into a single
entry, so that a single C-y yanks all the text as a unit, just as it was before
it was killed.

Thus, if you want to yank text as a unit, you need not kill all of it with
one command; you can keep killing line after line, or word after word, until
you have killed it all, and you can still get it all back at once.

Commands that kill forward from point add onto the end of the previous killed text. Commands that kill backward from point add text onto
the beginning. This way, any sequence of mixed forward and backward kill
commands puts all the killed text into one entry without rearrangement. Numeric arguments do not break the sequence of appending kills. For example,
suppose the buffer contains this text:

```
    This is a line *of sample text.
```

with point shown by ⋆. If you type M-d M-DEL M-d M-DEL, killing alternately forward and backward, you end up with 'a line of sample' as one entry in the kill ring, and 'This is text.' in the buffer. (Note the double space, which you can clean up with M-SPC or M-q.)

Another way to kill the same text is to move back two words with M-b M-b, then kill all four words forward with C-u M-d. This produces exactly the same results in the buffer and in the kill ring. M-f M-f C-u M-DEL kills the same text, all going backward; once again, the result is the same. The text in the kill ring entry always has the same order that it had in the buffer before you killed it.

If a kill command is separated from the last kill command by other commands (not just numeric arguments), it starts a new entry on the kill ring. But you can force it to append by first typing the command C-M-w (append-next-kill) right before it. The C-M-w tells the following command, if it is a kill command, to append the text it kills to the last killed text, instead of starting a new entry. With C-M-w, you can kill several separated pieces of text and accumulate them to be yanked back in one place.

A kill command following M-w does not append to the text that M-w copied into the kill ring.

9.2.3 Yanking Earlier Kills

To recover killed text that is no longer the most recent kill, use the M-y command (yank-pop). It takes the text previously yanked and replaces it with the text from an earlier kill. So, to recover the text of the next-to-the-last kill, first use C-y to yank the last kill, and then use M-y to replace it with the previous kill. M-y is allowed only after a C-y or another M-y.

You can understand M-y in terms of a "last yank" pointer which points at an entry in the kill ring. Each time you kill, the "last yank" pointer moves to the newly made entry at the front of the ring. C-y yanks the entry which the "last yank" pointer points to. M-y moves the "last yank" pointer to a different entry, and the text in the buffer changes to match. Enough M-y commands can move the pointer to any entry in the ring, so you can get any entry into the buffer. Eventually the pointer reaches the end of the ring; the next M-y moves it to the first entry again.

M-y moves the "last yank" pointer around the ring, but it does not change the order of the entries in the ring, which always runs from the most recent kill at the front to the oldest one still remembered.

M-y can take a numeric argument, which tells it how many entries to advance the "last yank" pointer by. A negative argument moves the pointer toward the front of the ring; from the front of the ring, it moves "around" to the last entry and continues forward from there.

Once the text you are looking for is brought into the buffer, you can stop doing M-y commands and it will stay there. It's just a copy of the kill ring entry, so editing it in the buffer does not change what's in the ring. As long as no new killing is done, the "last yank" pointer remains at the same place in the kill ring, so repeating C-y will yank another copy of the same previous kill.

If you know how many M-y commands it would take to find the text you want, you can yank that text in one step using C-y with a numeric argument. C-y with an argument restores the text the specified number of entries back in the kill ring. Thus, C-u 2 C-y gets the next to the last block of killed text. It is equivalent to C-y M-y. C-y with a numeric argument starts counting from the "last yank" pointer, and sets the "last yank" pointer to the entry that it yanks.

The length of the kill ring is controlled by the variable kill-ring-max; no more than that many blocks of killed text are saved.

The actual contents of the kill ring are stored in a variable named kill-ring; you can view the entire contents of the kill ring with the command C-h v kill-ring.

9.3 Accumulating Text

Usually we copy or move text by killing it and yanking it, but there are other methods convenient for copying one block of text in many places, or for copying many scattered blocks of text into one place. To copy one block to many places, store it in a register (see Chapter 10 [Registers], page 71). Here we describe the commands to accumulate scattered pieces of text into a buffer or into a file.

M-x append-to-buffer
> Append region to contents of specified buffer.

M-x prepend-to-buffer
> Prepend region to contents of specified buffer.

M-x copy-to-buffer
> Copy region into specified buffer, deleting that buffer's old contents.

M-x insert-buffer
> Insert contents of specified buffer into current buffer at point.

M-x append-to-file
> Append region to contents of specified file, at the end.

To accumulate text into a buffer, use M-x append-to-buffer. This reads a buffer name, them inserts a copy of the region into the buffer specified. If you specify a nonexistent buffer, `append-to-buffer` creates the buffer. The text is inserted wherever point is in that buffer. If you have been using the buffer for editing, the copied text goes into the middle of the text of the buffer, wherever point happens to be in it.

Point in that buffer is left at the end of the copied text, so successive uses of `append-to-buffer` accumulate the text in the specified buffer in the same order as they were copied. Strictly speaking, `append-to-buffer` does not always append to the text already in the buffer—only if point in that buffer is at the end. However, if `append-to-buffer` is the only command you use to alter a buffer, then point is always at the end.

`M-x prepend-to-buffer` is just like `append-to-buffer` except that point in the other buffer is left before the copied text, so successive prependings add text in reverse order. `M-x copy-to-buffer` is similar except that any existing text in the other buffer is deleted, so the buffer is left containing just the text newly copied into it.

To retrieve the accumulated text from another buffer, use `M-x insert-buffer`; this too takes *buffername* as an argument. It inserts a copy of the text in buffer *buffername* into the selected buffer. You can alternatively select the other buffer for editing, then optionally move text from it by killing. See Chapter 15 [Buffers], page 133, for background information on buffers.

Instead of accumulating text within Emacs, in a buffer, you can append text directly into a file with `M-x append-to-file`, which takes *filename* as an argument. It adds the text of the region to the end of the specified file. The file is changed immediately on disk.

You should use `append-to-file` only with files that are *not* being visited in Emacs. Using it on a file that you are editing in Emacs would change the file behind Emacs's back, which can lead to losing some of your editing.

9.4 Rectangles

The rectangle commands operate on rectangular areas of the text: all the characters between a certain pair of columns, in a certain range of lines. Commands are provided to kill rectangles, yank killed rectangles, clear them out, fill them with blanks or text, or delete them. Rectangle commands are useful with text in multicolumn formats, and for changing text into or out of such formats.

When you must specify a rectangle for a command to work on, you do it by putting the mark at one corner and point at the opposite corner. The rectangle thus specified is called the *region-rectangle* because you control it in about the same way the region is controlled. But remember that a given combination of point and mark values can be interpreted either as a region or as a rectangle, depending on the command that uses them.

If point and the mark are in the same column, the rectangle they delimit is empty. If they are in the same line, the rectangle is one line high.
This asymmetry between lines and columns comes about because point (and
likewise the mark) is between two columns, but within a line.

C-x r k   Kill the text of the region-rectangle, saving its contents as the
             "last killed rectangle" (`kill-rectangle`).

C-x r d   Delete the text of the region-rectangle (`delete-rectangle`).

C-x r y   Yank the last killed rectangle with its upper left corner at point
             (`yank-rectangle`).

C-x r o   Insert blank space to fill the space of the region-rectangle (`open-
             rectangle`). This pushes the previous contents of the region-
             rectangle rightward.

M-x clear-rectangle
             Clear the region-rectangle by replacing its contents with spaces.

M-x string-rectangle RET *string* RET
             Insert *string* on each line of the region-rectangle.

The rectangle operations fall into two classes: commands deleting and
inserting rectangles, and commands for blank rectangles.

There are two ways to get rid of the text in a rectangle: you can discard
the text (delete it) or save it as the "last killed" rectangle. The commands
for these two ways are C-x r d (`delete-rectangle`) and C-x r k (`kill-
rectangle`). In either case, the portion of each line that falls inside the
rectangle's boundaries is deleted, causing following text (if any) on the line
to move left into the gap.

Note that "killing" a rectangle is not killing in the usual sense; the rectangle is not stored in the kill ring, but in a special place that can only record
the most recent rectangle killed. This is because yanking a rectangle is so
different from yanking linear text that different yank commands have to be
used and yank-popping is hard to make sense of.

To yank the last killed rectangle, type C-x r y (`yank-rectangle`). Yanking a rectangle is the opposite of killing one. Point specifies where to put
the rectangle's upper left corner. The rectangle's first line is inserted there,
the rectangle's second line is inserted at a position one line vertically down,
and so on. The number of lines affected is determined by the height of the
saved rectangle.

You can convert single-column lists into double-column lists using rectangle killing and yanking; kill the second half of the list as a rectangle and
then yank it beside the first line of the list. See Section 29.8 [Two-Column],
page 336, for another way to edit multi-column text.

You can also copy rectangles into and out of registers with C-x r r r and
C-x r i r. See Section 10.3 [Rectangle Registers], page 72.

There are two commands for making with blank rectangles: `M-x clear-rectangle` to blank out existing text, and `C-x r o` (`open-rectangle`) to insert a blank rectangle. Clearing a rectangle is equivalent to deleting it and then inserting a blank rectangle of the same size.

The command `M-x string-rectangle` is similar to `C-x r o`, but it inserts a specified string instead of blanks. You specify the string with the minibuffer. Since the length of the string specifies how many columns to insert, the width of the region-rectangle does not matter for this command. What does matter is the position of the left edge (which specifies the column position for the insertion in each line) and the range of lines that the rectangle occupies. The previous contents of the text beyond the insertion column are pushed rightward.

10 Registers

Emacs *registers* are places you can save text or positions for later use. Once you save text or a rectangle in a register, you can copy it into the buffer once or many times; you can move point to a position saved in a register once or many times.

Each register has a name which is a single character. A register can store a piece of text, a rectangle, a position, a window configuration, or a file name, but only one thing at any given time. Whatever you store in a register remains there until you store something else in that register. To see what a register *r* contains, use `M-x view-register`.

`M-x view-register RET` *r*
> Display a description of what register *r* contains.

10.1 Saving Positions in Registers

Saving a position records a place in a buffer so that you can move back there later. Moving to a saved position switches to that buffer and moves point to that place in it.

`C-x r SPC` *r*
> Save position of point in register *r* (`point-to-register`).

`C-x r j` *r*   Jump to the position saved in register *r* (`jump-to-register`).

To save the current position of point in a register, choose a name *r* and type `C-x r SPC` *r*. The register *r* retains the position thus saved until you store something else in that register.

The command `C-x r j` *r* moves point to the position recorded in register *r*. The register is not affected; it continues to record the same position. You can jump to the saved position any number of times.

10.2 Saving Text in Registers

When you want to insert a copy of the same piece of text several times, it may be inconvenient to yank it from the kill ring, since each subsequent kill moves that entry further down the ring. An alternative is to store the text in a register and later retrieve it.

`C-x r s` *r*   Copy region into register *r* (`copy-to-register`).

`C-x r i` *r*   Insert text from register *r* (`insert-register`).

`C-x r s` *r* stores a copy of the text of the region into the register named *r*. Given a numeric argument, `C-x r s` *r* deletes the text from the buffer as well.

C-x r i r inserts in the buffer the text from register r. Normally it leaves point before the text and places the mark after, but with a numeric argument (C-u) it puts point after the text and the mark before.

10.3 Saving Rectangles in Registers

A register can contain a rectangle instead of linear text. The rectangle is represented as a list of strings. See Section 9.4 [Rectangles], page 67, for basic information on how to specify a rectangle in the buffer.

C-x r r r   Copy the region-rectangle into register r (copy-region-to-rectangle). With numeric argument, delete it as well.

C-x r i r   Insert the rectangle stored in register r (if it contains a rectangle) (insert-register).

The C-x r i r command inserts a text string if the register contains one, and inserts a rectangle if the register contains one.

See also the command sort-columns, which you can think of as sorting a rectangle. See Section 29.6 [Sorting], page 333.

10.4 Saving Window Configurations in Registers

You can save the window configuration of the selected frame in a register, or even the configuration of all windows in all frames, and restore the configuration later.

C-x r w r   Save the state of the selected frame's windows in register r (window-configuration-to-register).

C-x r f r   Save the state of all frames, including all their windows, in register r (frame-configuration-to-register).

Use C-x r j r to restore a window or frame configuration. This is the same command used to restore a cursor position. When you restore a frame configuration, any existing frames not included in the configuration become invisible. If you wish to delete these frames instead, use C-u C-x r j r.

10.5 Keeping File Names in Registers

If you visit certain file names frequently, you can visit them more conveniently if you put their names in registers. Here's the Lisp code used to put a file name in a register:

```
(set-register ?r '(file . name))
```

For example,

```
(set-register ?z '(file . "/gd/gnu/emacs/19.0/src/ChangeLog"))
```

puts the file name shown in register 'z'.

To visit the file whose name is in register r, type C-x r j r. (This is the same command used to jump to a position or restore a frame configuration.)

10.6 Bookmarks

Bookmarks are somewhat like registers in that they record positions you can jump to. Unlike registers, they have long names, and they persist automatically from one Emacs session to the next. The prototypical use of bookmarks is to record "where you were reading" in various files.

C-x r m RET
>   Set the bookmark for the visited file, at point.

C-x r m *bookmark* RET
>   Set the bookmark named *bookmark* at point (bookmark-set).

C-x r b *bookmark* RET
>   Jump to the bookmark named *bookmark* (bookmark-jump).

C-x r l   List all bookmarks (list-bookmarks).

M-x bookmark-save
>   Save all the current bookmark values in the default bookmark file.

The prototypical use for bookmarks is to record one current position in each of several files. So the command C-x r m, which sets a bookmark, uses the visited file name as the default for the bookmark name. If you name each bookmark after the file it points to, then you can conveniently revisit any of those files with C-x r b, and move to the position of the bookmark at the same time.

To display a list of all your bookmarks in a separate buffer, type C-x r l (list-bookmarks). If you switch to that buffer, you can use it to edit your bookmark definitions or annotate the bookmarks. Type C-h m in that buffer for more information about its special editing commands.

When you kill Emacs, Emacs offers to save your bookmark values in your default bookmark file, '~/.emacs.bmk', if you have changed any bookmark values. You can also save the bookmarks at any time with the M-x bookmark-save command. The bookmark commands load your default bookmark file automatically. This saving and loading is how bookmarks persist from one Emacs session to the next.

If you set the variable `bookmark-save-flag` to 1, then each command that sets a bookmark will also save your bookmarks; this way, you don't lose any bookmark values even if Emacs crashes. (The value, if a number, says how many bookmark modifications should go by between saving.)

Bookmark position values are saved with surrounding context, so that `bookmark-jump` can find the proper position even if the file is modified slightly. The variable `bookmark-search-size` says how many characters of context to record, on each side of the bookmark's position.

Here are some additional commands for working with bookmarks:

`M-x bookmark-load RET` *filename* `RET`

> Load a file named *filename* that contains a list of bookmark values. You can use this command, as well as `bookmark-write`, to work with other files of bookmark values in addition to your default bookmark file.

`M-x bookmark-write RET` *filename* `RET`

> Save all the current bookmark values in the file *filename*.

`M-x bookmark-delete RET` *bookmark* `RET`

> Delete the bookmark named *bookmark*.

`M-x bookmark-locate RET` *bookmark* `RET`

> Insert in the buffer the name of the file that bookmark *bookmark* points to.

`M-x bookmark-insert RET` *bookmark* `RET`

> Insert in the buffer the *contents* of the file that bookmark *bookmark* points to.

11 Controlling the Display

Since only part of a large buffer fits in the window, Emacs tries to show the part that is likely to be interesting. The display control commands allow you to specify which part of the text you want to see.

C-l   Clear screen and redisplay, scrolling the selected window to center point vertically within it (recenter).

C-v   Scroll forward (a windowful or a specified number of lines) (scroll-up).

NEXT   Likewise, scroll forward.

M-v   Scroll backward (scroll-down).

PRIOR   Likewise, scroll backward.

arg C-l   Scroll so point is on screen line arg (recenter).

C-x <   Scroll text in current window to the left (scroll-left).

C-x >   Scroll to the right (scroll-right).

C-x $ Make deeply indented lines invisible (set-selective-display).

The names of all scroll commands are based on the direction that the text moves in the window. Thus, the command to scrolling forward is called scroll-up, since the text moves up.

11.1 Scrolling

If a buffer contains text that is too large to fit entirely within a window that is displaying the buffer, Emacs shows a contiguous portion of the text. The portion shown always contains point.

Scrolling means moving text up or down in the window so that different parts of the text are visible. Scrolling forward means that text moves up, and new text appears at the bottom. Scrolling backward moves text down and new text appears at the top.

Scrolling happens automatically if you move point past the bottom or top of the window. You can also explicitly request scrolling with the commands in this section.

The most basic scrolling command is C-l (recenter) with no argument. It clears the entire screen and redisplays all windows. In addition, it scrolls the selected window so that point is halfway down from the top of the window.

The scrolling commands C-v and M-v let you move all the text in the window up or down a few lines. C-v (scroll-up) with an argument shows you that many more lines at the bottom of the window, moving the text and point up together as C-l might. C-v with a negative argument shows you more lines at the top of the window. M-v (scroll-down) is like C-v, but moves in the opposite direction. The function keys NEXT and PRIOR are equivalent to C-v and M-v.

To read the buffer a windowful at a time, use C-v with no argument. It takes the last two lines at the bottom of the window and puts them at the top, followed by nearly a whole windowful of lines not previously visible. If point was in the text scrolled off the top, it moves to the new top of the window. M-v with no argument moves backward with overlap similarly. The number of lines of overlap across a C-v or M-v is controlled by the variable next-screen-context-lines; by default, it is two.

Another way to do scrolling is with C-l with a numeric argument. C-l does not clear the screen when given an argument; it only scrolls the selected window. With a positive argument n, it repositions text to put point n lines down from the top. An argument of zero puts point on the very top line. Point does not move with respect to the text; rather, the text and point move rigidly on the screen. C-l with a negative argument puts point that many lines from the bottom of the window. For example, C-u - 1 C-l puts point on the bottom line, and C-u - 5 C-l puts it five lines from the bottom. Just C-u as argument, as in C-u C-l, scrolls point to the center of the screen.

The C-M-l command (reposition-window) scrolls the current window heuristically in a way designed to get useful information onto the screen. For example, in a Lisp file, this command tries to get the entire current defun onto the screen if possible.

Scrolling happens automatically if point has moved out of the visible portion of the text when it is time to display. Usually the scrolling is done so as to put point vertically centered within the window. However, if the variable scroll-step has a nonzero value, an attempt is made to scroll the buffer by that many lines; if that is enough to bring point back into visibility, that is what is done.

11.2 Horizontal Scrolling

The text in a window can also be scrolled horizontally. This means that each line of text is shifted sideways in the window, and one or more characters at the beginning of each line are not displayed at all. When a window has been scrolled horizontally in this way, text lines are truncated rather than continued (see Section 4.8 [Continuation Lines], page 33), with a '$' appearing in the first column when there is text truncated to the left, and in the last column when there is text truncated to the right.

The command C-x < (scroll-left) scrolls the selected window to the left by n columns with argument n. This moves part of the beginning of each line off the left edge of the window. With no argument, it scrolls by almost the full width of the window (two columns less, to be precise).

C-x > (scroll-right) scrolls similarly to the right. The window cannot be scrolled any farther to the right once it is displayed normally (with each line starting at the window's left margin); attempting to do so has no effect. This means that you don't have to calculate the argument precisely for C-x >; any sufficiently large argument will restore normally display.

11.3 Selective Display

Emacs has the ability to hide lines indented more than a certain number of columns (you specify how many columns). You can use this to get an overview of a part of a program.

To hide lines, type C-x $ (set-selective-display) with a numeric argument n. Then lines with at least n columns of indentation disappear from the screen. The only indication of their presence is that three dots ('...') appear at the end of each visible line that is followed by one or more invisible ones.

The commands C-n and C-p move across the invisible lines as if they were not there.

The invisible lines are still present in the buffer, and most editing commands see them as usual, so you may find point in the middle of invisible text. When this happens, the cursor appears at the end of the previous line, after the three dots. If point is at the end of the visible line, before the newline that ends it, the cursor appears before the three dots.

To make all lines visible again, type C-x $ with no argument.

If you set the variable selective-display-ellipses to nil, the three dots do not appear at the end of a line that precedes invisible lines. Then there is no visible indication of the invisible lines. This variable becomes local automatically when set.

11.4 European Character Set Display

Some European languages use accented letters and other special symbols. The ISO 8859 Latin-1 character set defines character codes for many European languages in the range 160 to 255.

Emacs can display those characters according to Latin-1, provided the terminal or font in use supports them. The M-x standard-display-european command toggles European character display mode. With a numeric argument, M-x standard-display-european enables European character display if and only if the argument is positive. Load the library iso-syntax

to specify the correct syntactic properties and case conversion table for the
Latin-1 character set.

Some operating systems let you specify the language you are using by
setting a locale. Emacs handles one common special case of this: if your locale name for character types contains the string '8859-1' or '88591', Emacs
automatically enables European character display mode and its syntax.

There are three different ways you can enter Latin-1 characters:

- If your keyboard can generate character codes 128 and up, representing ISO Latin-1 characters, execute the following expression to enable
  Emacs to understand them:

  ```
  (set-input-mode (car (current-input-mode))
                  (nth 1 (current-input-mode))
                  0)
  ```

- You can load the library `iso-transl` to turn the key C-x 8 into a "compose character" prefix for entry of the extra ISO Latin-1 printing characters. C-x 8 is good for insertion (in the minibuffer as well as other
  buffers), for searching, and in any other context where a key sequence
  is allowed. The ALT modifier key, if you have one, serves the same purpose as C-x 8; use ALT together with an accent character to modify the
  following letter.

- You can use ISO Accents mode. This minor mode is convenient if
  you enter non-ASCII ISO Latin-1 characters often. When this minor
  mode is enabled, the characters "'", "'", '"', '^', '/' and '~' modify the
  following letter by adding the corresponding diacritical mark to it, if
  possible. To enable or disable ISO Accents mode, use the command
  M-x iso-accents-mode. This command affects only the current buffer.

  To enter one of those six special characters while in ISO Accents mode,
  type the character, followed by a space. Some of those characters have
  a corresponding "dead key" accent character in the ISO Latin-1 character set; to enter that character, type the corresponding ASCII character
  twice. For example, '' enters the Latin-1 character acute-accent (character code 0264).

  ISO Accents mode input is available whenever a key sequence is expected: for ordinary insertion, for searching, for the minibuffer, and for
  certain command arguments.

  In addition to the accented letters, you can use these special sequences
  in ISO Accents mode to enter certain other ISO Latin-1 characters:

  /A   'A' with ring.

  ~C   'C' with cedilla.

  ~D   'D' with stroke.

  /E   'AE' ligature.

/a	'a' with ring.
~c	'c' with cedilla.
~d	'd' with stroke.
/e	'ae' ligature.
"s	German sharp 's'.
~<	Left guillemet.
~>	Right guillemet.
~!	Inverted exclamation mark.
~?	Inverted question mark.

11.5 Optional Mode Line Features

To add the current line number of point to the mode line, enable Line Number mode with the command M-x line-number-mode. The line number appears before the buffer percentage *pos*, with the letter 'L' to indicate what it is. See Section 30.1 [Minor Modes], page 343, for more information about minor modes and about how to use this command.

If the buffer is very large (larger than the value of line-number-display-limit), then the line number doesn't appear. Emacs doesn't compute the line number when the buffer is large, because that would be too slow. If you have narrowed the buffer (see Section 29.7 [Narrowing], page 335), the displayed line number is relative to the accessible portion of the buffer.

Emacs can optionally display the time and system load in all mode lines. To enable this feature, type M-x display-time. The information added to the mode line usually appears after the buffer name, before the mode names and their parentheses. It looks like this:

> *hh*:*mm*pm *l.ll*

Here *hh* and *mm* are the hour and minute, followed always by 'am' or 'pm'. *l.ll* is the average number of running processes in the whole system recently. (Some fields may be missing if your operating system cannot support them.)

The word 'Mail' appears after the load level if there is mail for you that you have not read yet.

11.6 Variables Controlling Display

This section contains information for customization only. Beginning users should skip it.

The variable `mode-line-inverse-video` controls whether the mode line is displayed in inverse video (assuming the terminal supports it); `nil` means don't do so. See Section 1.3 [Mode Line], page 17. If you specify the foreground color for the `modeline` face, and `mode-line-inverse-video` is non-`nil`, then the default background color for that face is the usual foreground color. See Section 17.12 [Faces], page 156.

If the variable `inverse-video` is non-`nil`, Emacs attempts to invert all the lines of the display from what they normally are.

If the variable `visible-bell` is non-`nil`, Emacs attempts to make the whole screen blink when it would normally make an audible bell sound. This variable has no effect if your terminal does not have a way to make the screen blink.

When you reenter Emacs after suspending, Emacs normally clears the screen and redraws the entire display. On some terminals with more than one page of memory, it is possible to arrange the termcap entry so that the 'ti' and 'te' strings (output to the terminal when Emacs is entered and exited, respectively) switch between pages of memory so as to use one page for Emacs and another page for other output. Then you might want to set the variable `no-redraw-on-reenter` non-`nil`; this tells Emacs to assume, when resumed, that the screen page it is using still contains what Emacs last wrote there.

The variable `echo-keystrokes` controls the echoing of multi-character keys; its value is the number of seconds of pause required to cause echoing to start, or zero meaning don't echo at all. See Section 1.2 [Echo Area], page 16.

If the variable `ctl-arrow` is `nil`, control characters in the buffer are displayed with octal escape sequences, all except newline and tab. Altering the value of `ctl-arrow` makes it local to the current buffer; until that time, the default value is in effect. The default is initially `t`. See section "Display Tables" in *The Emacs Lisp Reference Manual*.

Normally, a tab character in the buffer is displayed as whitespace which extends to the next display tab stop position, and display tab stops come at intervals equal to eight spaces. The number of spaces per tab is controlled by the variable `tab-width`, which is made local by changing it, just like `ctl-arrow`. Note that how the tab character in the buffer is displayed has nothing to do with the definition of TAB as a command. The variable `tab-width` must have an integer value between 1 and 1000, inclusive.

If the variable `truncate-lines` is non-`nil`, then each line of text gets just one screen line for display; if the text line is too long, display shows only the part that fits. If `truncate-lines` is `nil`, then long text lines display as more than one screen line, enough to show the whole text of the line. See Section 4.8 [Continuation Lines], page 33. Altering the value of `truncate-`

`lines` makes it local to the current buffer; until that time, the default value is in effect. The default is initially `nil`.

If the variable `truncate-partial-width-windows` is non-`nil`, it forces truncation rather than continuation in any window less than the full width of the screen or frame, regardless of the value of `truncate-lines`. For information about side-by-side windows, see Section 16.2 [Split Window], page 142. See also section "Display" in *The Emacs Lisp Reference Manual*.

The variable `baud-rate` holds the thc output speed of the terminal, as far as Emacs knows. Setting this variable does not change the speed of actual data transmission, but the value is used for calculations such as padding. It also affects decisions about whether to scroll part of the screen or redraw it instead—even when using a window system. (We designed it this way, despite the fact that a window system has no true "output speed", to give you a way to tune these decisions.)

12 Searching and Replacement

Like other editors, Emacs has commands for searching for occurrences of a string. The principal search command is unusual in that it is *incremental*; it begins to search before you have finished typing the search string. There are also nonincremental search commands more like those of other editors.

Besides the usual `replace-string` command that finds all occurrences of one string and replaces them with another, Emacs has a fancy replacement command called `query-replace` which asks interactively which occurrences to replace.

12.1 Incremental Search

An incremental search begins searching as soon as you type the first character of the search string. As you type in the search string, Emacs shows you where the string (as you have typed it so far) would be found. When you have typed enough characters to identify the place you want, you can stop. Depending on what you plan to do next, you may or may not need to terminate the search explicitly with RET.

C-s   Incremental search forward (`isearch-forward`).

C-r   Incremental search backward (`isearch-backward`).

C-s starts an incremental search. C-s reads characters from the keyboard and positions the cursor at the first occurrence of the characters that you have typed. If you type C-s and then F, the cursor moves right after the first 'F'. Type an O, and see the cursor move to after the first 'FO'. After another O, the cursor is after the first 'FOO' after the place where you started the search. Meanwhile, the search string 'FOO' has been echoed in the echo area.

If you make a mistake in typing the search string, you can cancel characters with DEL. Each DEL cancels the last character of search string. This does not happen until Emacs is ready to read another input character; first it must either find, or fail to find, the character you want to erase. If you do not want to wait for this to happen, use C-g as described below.

When you are satisfied with the place you have reached, you can type RET, which stops searching, leaving the cursor where the search brought it. Also, any command not specially meaningful in searches stops the searching and is then executed. Thus, typing C-a would exit the search and then move to the beginning of the line. RET is necessary only if the next command you want to type is a printing character, DEL, RET, or another control character that is special within searches (C-q, C-w, C-r, C-s, C-y, M-y, M-r, or M-s).

Sometimes you search for 'FOO' and find it, but not the one you expected to find. There was a second 'FOO' that you forgot about, before the one you were looking for. In this event, type another C-s to move to the next occurrence of the search string. This can be done any number of times. If you overshoot, you can cancel some C-s characters with DEL.

After you exit a search, you can search for the same string again by typing just C-s C-s: the first C-s is the key that invokes incremental search, and the second C-s means "search again".

To reuse earlier search strings, use the *search ring*. The commands M-p and M-n move through the ring to pick a search string to reuse. These commands leave the selected search ring element in the minibuffer, where you can edit it. Type C-s or C-r to terminate editing the string and search for it.

If your string is not found at all, the echo area says 'Failing I-Search'. The cursor is after the place where Emacs found as much of your string as it could. Thus, if you search for 'FOOT', and there is no 'FOOT', you might see the cursor after the 'FOO' in 'FOOL'. At this point there are several things you can do. If your string was mistyped, you can rub some of it out and correct it. If you like the place you have found, you can type RET or some other Emacs command to "accept what the search offered". Or you can type C-g, which removes from the search string the characters that could not be found (the 'T' in 'FOOT'), leaving those that were found (the 'FOO' in 'FOOT'). A second C-g at that point cancels the search entirely, returning point to where it was when the search started.

An upper-case letter in the search string makes the search case-sensitive. If you delete the upper-case character from the search string, it ceases to have this effect. See Section 12.6 [Search Case], page 92.

If a search is failing and you ask to repeat it by typing another C-s, it starts again from the beginning of the buffer. Repeating a failing reverse search with C-r starts again from the end. This is called *wrapping around*. 'Wrapped' appears in the search prompt once this has happened.

The C-g "quit" character does special things during searches; just what it does depends on the status of the search. If the search has found what you specified and is waiting for input, C-g cancels the entire search. The cursor moves back to where you started the search. If C-g is typed when there are characters in the search string that have not been found—because Emacs is still searching for them, or because it has failed to find them—then the search string characters which have not been found are discarded from the search string. With them gone, the search is now successful and waiting for more input, so a second C-g will cancel the entire search.

To search for a newline, type LFD (also known as C-j). To search for another control character such as control-S or carriage return, you must quote it by typing C-q first. This function of C-q is analogous to its meaning as an Emacs command: it causes the following character to be treated the way a graphic character would normally be treated in the same context. You can also specify a character by its octal code: enter C-q followed by three octal digits.

You can change to searching backwards with C-r. If a search fails because the place you started was too late in the file, you should do this. Repeated C-r keeps looking for more occurrences backwards. A C-s starts going forwards again. C-r in a search can be canceled with DEL.

If you know initially that you want to search backwards, you can use C-r instead of C-s to start the search, because C-r as a key runs a command (isearch-backward) to search backward.

The characters C-y and C-w can be used in incremental search to grab text from the buffer into the search string. This makes it convenient to search for another occurrence of text at point. C-w copies the word after point as part of the search string, advancing point over that word. Another C-s to repeat the search will then search for a string including that word. C-y is similar to C-w but copies all the rest of the current line into the search string. Both C-y and C-w convert the text they copy to lower case if the search is current not case-sensitive; this is so the search remains case-insensitive.

The character M-y copies text from the kill ring into the search string. It uses the same text that C-y as a command would yank. See Section 9.2 [Yanking], page 63.

When you exit the incremental search, it sets the mark to where point *was*, before the search. That is convenient for moving back there. In Transient Mark mode, incremental search sets the mark without activating it, and does so only if the mark is not already active.

To customize the special characters that incremental search understands, alter their bindings in the keymap isearch-mode-map. For a list of bindings, look at the documentation of isearch-mode with C-h f isearch-mode RET.

12.1.1 Slow Terminal Incremental Search

Incremental search on a slow terminal uses a modified style of display that is designed to take less time. Instead of redisplaying the buffer at each place the search gets to, it creates a new single-line window and uses that to display the line that the search has found. The single-line window comes into play as soon as point gets outside of the text that is already on the screen.

When you terminate the search, the single-line window is removed. Then Emacs redisplays the window in which the search was done, to show its new position of point.

The slow terminal style of display is used when the terminal baud rate is less than or equal to the value of the variable search-slow-speed, initially 1200.

The number of lines to use in slow terminal search display is controlled by the variable `search-slow-window-lines`. 1 is its normal value.

12.2 Nonincremental Search

Emacs also has conventional nonincremental search commands, which require you to type the entire search string before searching begins.

C-s RET *string* RET
>Search for *string*.

C-r RET *string* RET
>Search backward for *string*.

To do a nonincremental search, first type `C-s RET`. This enters the mini-buffer to read the search string; terminate the string with `RET`, and then the search takes place. If the string is not found, the search command gets an error.

The way `C-s RET` works is that the `C-s` invokes incremental search, which is specially programmed to invoke nonincremental search if the argument you give it is empty. (Such an empty argument would otherwise be useless.) `C-r RET` also works this way.

However, nonincremental searches performed using `C-s RET` do not call `search-forward` right away. The first thing done is to see if the next character is `C-w`, which requests a word search.

Forward and backward nonincremental searches are implemented by the commands `search-forward` and `search-backward`. These commands may be bound to keys in the usual manner. The feature that you can get to them via the incremental search commands exists for historical reasons, and to avoid the need to find suitable key sequences for them.

12.3 Word Search

Word search searches for a sequence of words without regard to how the words are separated. More precisely, you type a string of many words, using single spaces to separate them, and the string can be found even if there are multiple spaces, newlines or other punctuation between the words.

Word search is useful for editing a printed document made with a text formatter. If you edit while looking at the printed, formatted version, you can't tell where the line breaks are in the source file. With word search, you can search without having to know them.

C-s RET C-w *words* RET
>Search for *words*, ignoring details of punctuation.

C-r RET C-w *words* RET

    Search backward for *words*, ignoring details of punctuation.

Word search is a special case of nonincremental search and is invoked with C-s RET C-w. This is followed by the search string, which must always be terminated with RET. Being nonincremental, this search does not start until the argument is terminated. It works by constructing a regular expression and searching for that; see Section 12.4 [Regexp Search], page 87.

Use C-r RET C-w to do backward word search.

Forward and backward word searches are implemented by the commands word-search-forward and word-search-backward. These commands may be bound to keys in the usual manner. The feature that you can get to them via the incremental search commands exists for historical reasons, and to avoid the need to find suitable key sequences for them.

12.4 Regular Expression Search

A *regular expression* (*regexp*, for short) is a pattern that denotes a class of alternative strings to match, possibly infinitely many. In GNU Emacs, you can search for the next match for a regexp either incrementally or not.

Incremental search for a regexp is done by typing C-M-s (isearch-forward-regexp). This command reads a search string incrementally just like C-s, but it treats the search string as a regexp rather than looking for an exact match against the text in the buffer. Each time you add text to the search string, you make the regexp longer, and the new regexp is searched for. To search backward in the buffer, use C-M-r (isearch-backward-regexp).

All of the control characters that do special things within an ordinary incremental search have the same function in incremental regexp search. Typing C-s or C-r immediately after starting the search retrieves the last incremental search regexp used; that is to say, incremental regexp and non-regexp searches have independent defaults. They also have separate search rings that you can access with M-p and M-n.

If you type SPC in incremental regexp search, it matches any sequence of whitespace characters, including newlines. If you want to match just a space, type C-q SPC.

Note that adding characters to the regexp in an incremental regexp search can make the cursor move back and start again. For example, if you have searched for 'foo' and you add '\|bar', the cursor backs up in case the first 'bar' precedes the first 'foo'.

Nonincremental search for a regexp is done by the functions re-search-forward and re-search-backward. You can invoke these with M-x, or bind them to keys, or invoke them by way of incremental regexp search with C-M-s RET and C-M-r RET.

12.5 Syntax of Regular Expressions

Regular expressions have a syntax in which a few characters are special
constructs and the rest are *ordinary*. An ordinary character is a simple
regular expression which matches that same character and nothing else. The
special characters are '$', '^', '.', '*', '+', '?', '[', ']' and '\'. Any other
character appearing in a regular expression is ordinary, unless a '\' precedes
it.

For example, 'f' is not a special character, so it is ordinary, and therefore
'f' is a regular expression that matches the string 'f' and no other string.
(It does *not* match the string 'ff'.) Likewise, 'o' is a regular expression that
matches only 'o'. (When case distinctions are being ignored, these regexps
also match 'F' and 'O', but we consider this a generalization of "the same
string", rather than an exception.)

Any two regular expressions a and b can be concatenated. The result is a
regular expression which matches a string if a matches some amount of the
beginning of that string and b matches the rest of the string.

As a simple example, we can concatenate the regular expressions 'f' and
'o' to get the regular expression 'fo', which matches only the string 'fo'.
Still trivial. To do something nontrivial, you need to use one of the special
characters. Here is a list of them.

. (Period)   is a special character that matches any single character except a
              newline. Using concatenation, we can make regular expressions
              like 'a.b' which matches any three-character string which begins
              with 'a' and ends with 'b'.

*   is not a construct by itself; it is a postfix operator, which means
              to match the preceding regular expression repetitively as many
              times as possible. Thus, 'o*' matches any number of 'o's (in-
              cluding no 'o's).

              '*' always applies to the *smallest* possible preceding expression.
              Thus, 'fo*' has a repeating 'o', not a repeating 'fo'. It matches
              'f', 'fo', 'foo', and so on.

              The matcher processes a '*' construct by matching, immediately,
              as many repetitions as can be found. Then it continues with the
              rest of the pattern. If that fails, backtracking occurs, discarding
              some of the matches of the '*'-modified construct in case that
              makes it possible to match the rest of the pattern. For example,
              matching 'ca*ar' against the string 'caaar', the 'a*' first tries to
              match all three 'a's; but the rest of the pattern is 'ar' and there
              is only 'r' left to match, so this try fails. The next alternative
              is for 'a*' to match only two 'a's. With this choice, the rest of
              the regexp matches successfully.

+   is a postfix character, similar to '*' except that it must match
           the preceding expression at least once. So, for example, 'ca+r'
           matches the strings 'car' and 'caaaar' but not the string 'cr',
           whereas 'ca*r' matches all three strings.

?   is a postfix character, similar to '*' except that it can match
           the preceding expression either once or not at all. For example,
           'ca?r' matches 'car' or 'cr'; nothing else.

[...]   is a *character set*, which begins with '[' and is terminated by ']'.
           In the simplest case, the characters between the two brackets are
           what this set can match.

           Thus, '[ad]' matches either one 'a' or one 'd', and '[ad]*'
           matches any string composed of just 'a's and 'd's (including
           the empty string), from which it follows that 'c[ad]*r' matches
           'cr', 'car', 'cdr', 'caddaar', etc.

           You can also include character ranges a character set, by writing
           two characters with a '-' between them. Thus, '[a-z]' matches
           any lower-case letter. Ranges may be intermixed freely with
           individual characters, as in '[a-z$%.]', which matches any lower
           case letter or '$', '%' or period.

           Note that the usual regexp special characters are not special
           inside a character set. A completely different set of special char-
           acters exists inside character sets: ']', '-' and '^'.

           To include a ']' in a character set, you must make it the first
           character. For example, '[]a]' matches ']' or 'a'. To include a
           '-', write '-' as the first or last character of the set, or put it
           after a range. Thus, '[]-]' matches both ']' and '-'.

           To include '^', make it other than the first character in the set.

[^ ...]   '[^' begins a *complemented character set*, which matches any
           character except the ones specified. Thus, '[^a-z0-9A-Z]'
           matches all characters *except* letters and digits.

           '^' is not special in a character set unless it is the first character.
           The character following the '^' is treated as if it were first ('-'
           and ']' are not special there).

           A complemented character set can match a newline, unless new-
           line is mentioned as one of the characters not to match. This is
           in contrast to the handling of regexps in programs such as grep.

^   is a special character that matches the empty string, but only
           at the beginning of a line in the text being matched. Otherwise
           it fails to match anything. Thus, '^foo' matches a 'foo' which
           occurs at the beginning of a line.

**$**   is similar to '^' but matches only at the end of a line. Thus, 'xx*$' matches a string of one 'x' or more at the end of a line.

****   has two functions: it quotes the special characters (including '\\'), and it introduces additional special constructs.

    Because '\\' quotes special characters, '\\$' is a regular expression which matches only '$', and '\\[' is a regular expression which matches only '[', etc.

Note: for historical compatibility, special characters are treated as ordinary ones if they are in contexts where their special meanings make no sense. For example, '*foo' treats '*' as ordinary since there is no preceding expression on which the '*' can act. It is poor practice to depend on this behavior; better to quote the special character anyway, regardless of where is appears.

For the most part, '\\' followed by any character matches only that character. However, there are several exceptions: two-character sequences starting with '\\' which have special meanings. The second character in the sequence is always an ordinary character on their own. Here is a table of '\\' constructs.

\\| specifies an alternative. Two regular expressions *a* and *b* with '\\|' in between form an expression that matches anything that either *a* or *b* matches.

    Thus, 'foo\\|bar' matches either 'foo' or 'bar' but no other string.

    '\\|' applies to the largest possible surrounding expressions. Only a surrounding '\\(... \\)' grouping can limit the scope of '\\|'.

    Full backtracking capability exists to handle multiple uses of '\\|'.

\\(... \\) is a grouping construct that serves three purposes:

    1. To enclose a set of '\\|' alternatives for other operations. Thus, '\\(foo\\|bar\\)x' matches either 'foox' or 'barx'.

    2. To enclose a complicated expression for the postfix operators '*', '+' and '?' to operate on. Thus, 'ba\\(na\\)*' matches 'bananana', etc., with any (zero or more) number of 'na' strings.

    3. To mark a matched substring for future reference.

    This last application is not a consequence of the idea of a parenthetical grouping; it is a separate feature which is assigned as a second meaning to the same '\\(... \\)' construct. In practice there is no conflict between the two meanings. Here is an explanation of this feature:

\d   after the end of a '\(... \)' construct, the matcher remembers
                      the beginning and end of the text matched by that construct.
                      Then, later on in the regular expression, you can use '\' followed
                      by the digit *d* to mean "match the same text matched the *d*th
                      time by the '\(... \)' construct."

                      The strings matching the first nine '\(... \)' constructs ap-
                      pearing in a regular expression are assigned numbers 1 through
                      9 in order that the open-parentheses appear in the regular ex-
                      pression. '\1' through '\9' refer to the text previously matched
                      by the corresponding '\(... \)' construct.

                      For example, '\(.*\)\1' matches any newline-free string that
                      is composed of two identical halves. The '\(.*\)' matches the
                      first half, which may be anything, but the '\1' that follows must
                      match the same exact text.

                      If a particular '\(... \)' construct matches more than once
                      (which can easily happen if it is followed by '*'), only the last
                      match is recorded.

\`   matches the empty string, provided it is at the beginning of the
                      buffer.

\'   matches the empty string, provided it is at the end of the buffer.

\b   matches the empty string, provided it is at the beginning or end
                      of a word. Thus, '\bfoo\b' matches any occurrence of 'foo' as
                      a separate word. '\bballs?\b' matches 'ball' or 'balls' as a
                      separate word.

                      '\b' matches at the beginning or end of the buffer regardless of
                      what text appears next to it.

\B   matches the empty string, provided it is *not* at the beginning or
                      end of a word.

\<   matches the empty string, provided it is at the beginning of
                      a word. '\<' matches at the beginning of the buffer only if a
                      word-constituent character follows.

\>   matches the empty string, provided it is at the end of a word.
                      '\>' matches at the end of the buffer only if the contents end
                      with a word-constituent character.

\w   matches any word-constituent character. The syntax table de-
                      termines which characters these are. See Section 30.6 [Syntax],
                      page 366.

\W   matches any character that is not a word-constituent.

\s*c*   matches any character whose syntax is *c*. Here *c* is a character
                      which represents a syntax code: thus, 'w' for word constituent,

'(' for open-parenthesis, etc. Represent a character of whitespace (which can be a newline) by either '-' or a space character.

\Sc   matches any character whose syntax is not c.

The constructs that pertain to words and syntax are controlled by the setting of the syntax table (see Section 30.6 [Syntax], page 366).

Here is a complicated regexp, used by Emacs to recognize the end of a sentence together with any whitespace that follows. It is given in Lisp syntax to enable you to distinguish the spaces from the tab characters. In Lisp syntax, the string constant begins and ends with a double-quote. '\"' stands for a double-quote as part of the regexp, '\\' for a backslash as part of the regexp, '\t' for a tab and '\n' for a newline.

```
"[.?!][]\"')]*\\($\\|\t\\|  \\)[ \t\n]*"
```

This contains four parts in succession: a character set matching period, '?', or '!'; a character set matching close-brackets, quotes, or parentheses, repeated any number of times; an alternative in backslash-parentheses that matches end-of-line, a tab, or two spaces; and a character set matching whitespace characters, repeated any number of times.

To enter the same regexp interactively, you would type TAB to enter a tab, and C-q C-j to enter a newline. You would also type single slashes as themselves, instead of doubling them for Lisp syntax.

12.6 Searching and Case

Incremental searches in Emacs normally ignore the case of the text they are searching through, if you specify the text in lower case. Thus, if you specify searching for 'foo', then 'Foo' and 'foo' are also considered a match. Regexps, and in particular character sets, are included: '[ab]' would match 'a' or 'A' or 'b' or 'B'.

An upper-case letter in the incremental search string makes the search case-sensitive. Thus, searching for 'Foo' does not find 'foo' or 'FOO'. This applies to regular expression search as well as to string search. The effect ceases if you delete the upper-case letter from the search string.

If you set the variable case-fold-search to nil, then all letters must match exactly, including case. This is a per-buffer variable; altering the variable affects only the current buffer, but there is a default value which you can change as well. See Section 30.2.4 [Locals], page 348. This variable applies to nonincremental searches also, including those performed by the replace commands (see Section 12.7 [Replace], page 93).

12.7 Replacement Commands

Global search-and-replace operations are not needed as often in Emacs as they are in other editors[1], but they are available. In addition to the simple `M-x replace-string` command which is like that found in most editors, there is a `M-x query-replace` command which asks you, for each occurrence of the pattern, whether to replace it.

The replace commands all replace one string (or regexp) with one replacement string. It is possible to perform several replacements in parallel using the command `expand-region-abbrevs`. See Section 23.3 [Expanding Abbrevs], page 252.

12.7.1 Unconditional Replacement

`M-x replace-string` RET *string* RET *newstring* RET
> Replace every occurrence of *string* with *newstring*.

`M-x replace-regexp` RET *regexp* RET *newstring* RET
> Replace every match for *regexp* with *newstring*.

To replace every instance of 'foo' after point with 'bar', use the command `M-x replace-string` with the two arguments 'foo' and 'bar'. Replacement happens only in the text after point, so if you want to cover the whole buffer you must go to the beginning first. All occurrences up to the end of the buffer are replaced; to limit replacement to part of the buffer, narrow to that part of the buffer before doing the replacement (see Section 29.7 [Narrowing], page 335).

When `replace-string` exits, it leaves point at the last occurrence replaced. It sets the mark to the prior position of point (where the `replace-string` command was issued); use `C-u C-SPC` to move back there.

A numeric argument restricts replacement to matches that are surrounded by word boundaries. The argument's value doesn't matter.

12.7.2 Regexp Replacement

The `M-x replace-string` command replaces exact matches for a single string. The similar command `M-x replace-regexp` replaces any match for a specified pattern.

In `replace-regexp`, the *newstring* need not be constant: it can refer to all or part of what is matched by the *regexp*. '\&' in *newstring* stands for the entire match being replaced. '\d' in *newstring*, where *d* is a digit, stands

---

[1] In some editors, search-and-replace operations are the only convenient way to make a single change in the text.

for whatever matched the *d*th parenthesized grouping in *regexp*. To include a '\' in the text to replace with, you must enter '\\'. For example,

    `M-x replace-regexp RET c[ad]+r RET \&-safe RET`

replaces (for example) 'cadr' with 'cadr-safe' and 'cddr' with 'cddr-safe'.

    `M-x replace-regexp RET \(c[ad]+r\)-safe RET \1 RET`

performs the inverse transformation.

12.7.3 Replace Commands and Case

If the arguments to a replace command are in lower case, it preserves case when it makes a replacement. Thus, the command

    `M-x replace-string RET foo RET bar RET`

replaces a lower case 'foo' with a lower case 'bar', an all-caps 'FOO' with 'BAR', and a capitalized 'Foo' with 'Bar'. (These three alternatives–lower case, all caps, and capitalized, are the only ones that `replace-string` can distinguish.)

If upper case letters are used in the second argument, they remain upper case every time that argument is inserted. If upper case letters are used in the first argument, the second argument is always substituted exactly as given, with no case conversion. Likewise, if the variable `case-replace` is set to `nil`, replacement is done without case conversion. If `case-fold-search` is set to `nil`, case is significant in matching occurrences of 'foo' to replace; this also inhibits case conversion of the replacement string.

12.7.4 Query Replace

`M-%` *string* `RET` *newstring* `RET`
`M-x query-replace RET` *string* `RET` *newstring* `RET`
        Replace some occurrences of *string* with *newstring*.

`M-x query-replace-regexp RET` *regexp* `RET` *newstring* `RET`
        Replace some matches for *regexp* with *newstring*.

If you want to change only some of the occurrences of 'foo' to 'bar', not all of them, then you cannot use an ordinary `replace-string`. Instead, use `M-%` (`query-replace`). This command finds occurrences of 'foo' one by one, displays each occurrence and asks you whether to replace it. A numeric argument to `query-replace` tells it to consider only occurrences that are bounded by word-delimiter characters. This preserves case, just like `replace-string`, provided `case-replace` is non-`nil`, as it normally is.

Aside from querying, `query-replace` works just like `replace-string`, and `query-replace-regexp` works just like `replace-regexp`. The shortest way to type this command name is `M-x que SPC SPC SPC RET`.

The things you can type when you are shown an occurrence of *string* or a match for *regexp* are:

SPC   to replace the occurrence with *newstring*.

DEL   to skip to the next occurrence without replacing this one.

, (Comma)
           to replace this occurrence and display the result. You are then asked for another input character to say what to do next. Since the replacement has already been made, DEL and SPC are equivalent in this situation; both move to the next occurrence.

           You could type C-r at this point (see below) to alter the replaced text. You could also type C-x u to undo the replacement; this exits the query-replace, so if you want to do further replacement you must use C-x ESC ESC RET to restart (see Section 5.5 [Repetition], page 43).

RET   to exit without doing any more replacements.

. (Period) to replace this occurrence and then exit without searching for more occurrences.

!   to replace all remaining occurrences without asking again.

^   to go back to the position of the previous occurrence (or what used to be an occurrence), in case you changed it by mistake. This works by popping the mark ring. Only one ^ in a row is meaningful, because only one previous replacement position is kept during query-replace.

C-r   to enter a recursive editing level, in case the occurrence needs to be edited rather than just replaced with *newstring*. When you are done, exit the recursive editing level with C-M-c to proceed to the next occurrence. See Section 29.11 [Recursive Edit], page 339.

C-w   to delete the occurrence, and then enter a recursive editing level as in C-r. Use the recursive edit to insert text to replace the deleted occurrence of *string*. When done, exit the recursive editing level with C-M-c to proceed to the next occurrence.

C-l   to redisplay the screen. Then you must type another character to specify what to do with this occurrence.

C-h   to display a message summarizing these options. Then you must type another character to specify what to do with this occurrence.

Some other characters are aliases for the ones listed above: y, n and q are equivalent to SPC, DEL and RET.

Aside from this, any other character exits the `query-replace`, and is then reread as part of a key sequence. Thus, if you type C-k, it exits the `query-replace` and then kills to end of line.

To restart a `query-replace` once it is exited, use C-x ESC ESC, which repeats the `query-replace` because it used the minibuffer to read its arguments. See Section 5.5 [Repetition], page 43.

See also Section 27.9 [Transforming File Names], page 294, for Dired commands to rename, copy, or link files by replacing regexp matches in file names.

12.8 Other Search-and-Loop Commands

Here are some other commands that find matches for a regular expression. They all operate from point to the end of the buffer.

M-x occur RET *regexp* RET

> Display a list showing each line in the buffer that contains a match for *regexp*. A numeric argument specifies the number of context lines to print before and after each matching line; the default is none. To limit the search to part of the buffer, narrow to that part (see Section 29.7 [Narrowing], page 335).
>
> The buffer '*Occur*' containing the output serves as a menu for finding the occurrences in their original context. Click Mouse-2 on an occurrence listed in '*Occur*', or position point there and type RET; this switches to the buffer that was searched and moves point to the original of the chosen occurrence.

M-x list-matching-lines

> Synonym for M-x occur.

M-x count-matches RET *regexp* RET

> Print the number of matches for *regexp* after point.

M-x flush-lines RET *regexp* RET

> Delete each line that follows point and contains a match for *regexp*.

M-x keep-lines RET *regexp* RET

> Delete each line that follows point and *does not* contain a match for *regexp*.

13 Commands for Fixing Typos

In this chapter we describe the commands that are especially useful for the times when you catch a mistake in your text just after you have made it, or change your mind while composing text on the fly.

The most fundamental command for correcting erroneous editing is the undo command, C-x u or C-_. This command undoes a single command (usually), a part of a command (in the case of query-replace), or several consecutive self-inserting characters. Consecutive repetitions of C-_ or C-x u undo earlier and earlier changes, back to the limit of the undo information available. See Section 4.4 [Undo], page 30, for for more information.

13.1 Killing Your Mistakes

DEL   Delete last character (delete-backward-char).

M-DEL   Kill last word (backward-kill-word).

C-x DEL   Kill to beginning of sentence (backward-kill-sentence).

The DEL character (delete-backward-char) is the most important correction command. It deletes the character before point. When DEL follows a self-inserting character command, you can think of it as canceling that command. However, avoid the mistake of thinking of DEL as a general way to cancel a command!

When your mistake is longer than a couple of characters, it might be more convenient to use M-DEL or C-x DEL. M-DEL kills back to the start of the last word, and C-x DEL kills back to the start of the last sentence. C-x DEL is particularly useful when you change your mind about the phrasing of the text you are writing. M-DEL and C-x DEL save the killed text for C-y and M-y to retrieve. See Section 9.2 [Yanking], page 63.

M-DEL is often useful even when you have typed only a few characters wrong, if you know you are confused in your typing and aren't sure exactly what you typed. At such a time, you cannot correct with DEL except by looking at the screen to see what you did. Often it requires less thought to kill the whole word and start again.

13.2 Transposing Text

C-t   Transpose two characters (transpose-chars).

M-t   Transpose two words (transpose-words).

C-M-t   Transpose two balanced expressions (transpose-sexps).

C-x C-t   Transpose two lines (`transpose-lines`).

The common error of transposing two characters can be fixed, when they
are adjacent, with the C-t command (`transpose-chars`). Normally, C-t
transposes the two characters on either side of point. When given at the
end of a line, rather than transposing the last character of the line with the
newline, which would be useless, C-t transposes the last two characters on
the line. So, if you catch your transposition error right away, you can fix
it with just a C-t. If you don't catch it so fast, you must move the cursor
back to between the two transposed characters. If you transposed a space
with the last character of the word before it, the word motion commands
are a good way of getting there. Otherwise, a reverse search (C-r) is often
the best way. See Chapter 12 [Search], page 83.

M-t (`transpose-words`) transposes the word before point with the word
after point. It moves point forward over a word, dragging the word preceding
or containing point forward as well. The punctuation characters between
the words do not move. For example, 'FOO, BAR' transposes into 'BAR, FOO'
rather than 'BAR FOO,'.

C-M-t (`transpose-sexps`) is a similar command for transposing two
expressions (see Section 21.2 [Lists], page 200), and C-x C-t (`transpose-lines`) exchanges lines. They work like M-t except in determining the division of the text into syntactic units.

A numeric argument to a transpose command serves as a repeat count: it
tells the transpose command to move the character (word, sexp, line) before
or containing point across several other characters (words, sexps, lines). For
example, C-u 3 C-t moves the character before point forward across three
other characters. It would change 'f*oobar' into 'oobf*ar'. This is equivalent to repeating C-t three times. C-u - 4 M-t moves the word before point
backward across four words. C-u - C-M-t would cancel the effect of plain
C-M-t.

A numeric argument of zero is assigned a special meaning (because otherwise a command with a repeat count of zero would do nothing): to transpose
the character (word, sexp, line) ending after point with the one ending after
the mark.

13.3 Case Conversion

M-- M-l   Convert last word to lower case. Note `Meta--` is Meta-minus.

M-- M-u   Convert last word to all upper case.

M-- M-c   Convert last word to lower case with capital initial.

A very common error is to type words in the wrong case. Because of this,
the word case-conversion commands M-l, M-u and M-c have a special feature

when used with a negative argument: they do not move the cursor. As soon as you see you have mistyped the last word, you can simply case-convert it and go on typing. See Section 20.6 [Case], page 178.

13.4 Checking and Correcting Spelling

This section describes the commands to check the spelling of a single word or of a portion of a buffer. These commands work with the spelling checker program Ispell, which is not part of Emacs.

M-$ Check and correct spelling of word at point (`ispell-word`).

M-TAB   Complete the word before point based on the spelling dictionary
           (`ispell-complete-word`).

M-x ispell-buffer
           Check and correct spelling of each word in the buffer.

M-x ispell-region
           Check and correct spelling of each word in the region.

M-x ispell-message
           Check and correct spelling of each word in a draft mail message,
           excluding cited material.

M-x ispell-change-dictionary RET *dict* RET
           Restart the ispell process, using *dict* as the dictionary.

M-x ispell-kill-ispell
           Kill the Ispell subprocess.

To check the spelling of the word around or next to point, and optionally correct it as well, use the command M-$ (`ispell-word`). If the word is not correct, the command offers you various alternatives for what to do about it.

To check the entire current buffer, use M-x ispell-buffer. Use M-x ispell-region to check just the current region. To check spelling in an email message you are writing, use M-x ispell-message; that checks the whole buffer, but does not check material that is indented or appears to be cited from other messages.

Each time these commands encounter an incorrect word, they ask you what to do. It displays a list of alternatives, usually including several "near-misses"—words that are close to the word being checked. Then you must type a character. Here are the valid responses:

SPC   Skip this word—continue to consider it incorrect, but don't
           change it here.

r *new* RET Replace the word (just this time) with *new*.

R *new* RET   Replace the word with *new*, and do a `query-replace` so you can replace it elsewhere in the buffer if you wish.

digit   Replace the word (just this time) with one of the displayed near-misses. Each near-miss is listed with a digit; type that digit to select it.

a   Accept the incorrect word—treat it as correct, but only in this editing session.

A   Accept the incorrect word—treat it as correct, but only in this editing session and for this buffer.

i   Insert this word in your private dictionary file so that Ispell will consider it correct it from now on, even in future sessions.

u   Insert a lower-case version of this word in your private dictionary file.

m   Like i, but you can also specify dictionary completion information.

l *word* RET

               Look in the dictionary for words that match *word*. These words become the new list of "near-misses"; you can select one of them to replace with by typing a digit. You can use '*' in *word* as a wildcard.

C-g   Quit interactive spell checking. You can restart it again afterward with C-u M-$.

X   Same as C-g.

x   Quit interactive spell checking and move point back to where it was when you started spell checking.

q   Quit interactive spell checking and kill the Ispell subprocess.

C-l   Refresh the screen.

C-z   This key has its normal command meaning (suspend Emacs or iconify this frame).

The command `ispell-complete-word`, which is bound to the key M-TAB in Text mode and related modes, shows a list of completions based on spelling correction. Insert the beginning of a word, and then type M-TAB; the command displays a completion list window. To choose one of the completions listed, click Mouse-2 on it, or move the cursor there in the completions window and type RET. See Section 20.7 [Text Mode], page 179.

Once started, the Ispell subprocess continues to run (waiting for something to do), so that subsequent spell checking commands complete more quickly. If you want to get rid of the Ispell process, use M-x `ispell-kill-ispell`. This is not usually necessary, since the process uses no time except when you do spelling correction.

Ispell uses two dictionaries: the standard dictionary and your private dictionary. The variable `ispell-dictionary` specifies the file name of the standard dictionary to use. A value of `nil` says to use the default dictionary. The command `M-x ispell-change-dictionary` sets this variable and then restarts the Ispell subprocess, so that it will use a different dictionary.

14 File Handling

The operating system stores data permanently in named *files*. So most of the text you edit with Emacs comes from a file and is ultimately stored in a file.

To edit a file, you must tell Emacs to read the file and prepare a buffer containing a copy of the file's text. This is called *visiting* the file. Editing commands apply directly to text in the buffer; that is, to the copy inside Emacs. Your changes appear in the file itself only when you *save* the buffer back into the file.

In addition to visiting and saving files, Emacs can delete, copy, rename, and append to files, keep multiple versions of them, and operate on file directories.

14.1 File Names

Most Emacs commands that operate on a file require you to specify the file name. (Saving and reverting are exceptions; the buffer knows which file name to use for them.) You enter the file name using the minibuffer (see Chapter 5 [Minibuffer], page 37). *Completion* is available, to make it easier to specify long file names. See Section 5.3 [Completion], page 39.

For most operations, there is a *default file name* which is used if you type just RET to enter an empty argument. Normally the default file name is the name of the file visited in the current buffer; this makes it easy to operate on that file with any of the Emacs file commands.

Each buffer has a default directory, normally the same as the directory of the file visited in that buffer. When you enter a file name without a directory, the default directory is used. If you specify a directory in a relative fashion, with a name that does not start with a slash, it is interpreted with respect to the default directory. The default directory is kept in the variable `default-directory`, which has a separate value in every buffer.

For example, if the default file name is '/u/rms/gnu/gnu.tasks' then the default directory is '/u/rms/gnu/'. If you type just 'foo', which does not specify a directory, it is short for '/u/rms/gnu/foo'. '../.login' would stand for '/u/rms/.login'. 'new/foo' would stand for the file name '/u/rms/gnu/new/foo'.

The command M-x pwd prints the current buffer's default directory, and the command M-x cd sets it (to a value read using the minibuffer). A buffer's default directory changes only when the cd command is used. A file-visiting buffer's default directory is initialized to the directory of the file that is visited there. If you create a buffer with C-x b, its default directory is copied from that of the buffer that was current at the time.

The default directory actually appears in the minibuffer when the mini-buffer becomes active to read a file name. This serves two purposes: it *shows* you what the default is, so that you can type a relative file name and know with certainty what it will mean, and it allows you to *edit* the default to specify a different directory. This insertion of the default directory is inhibited if the variable `insert-default-directory` is set to `nil`.

Note that it is legitimate to type an absolute file name after you enter the minibuffer, ignoring the presence of the default directory name as part of the text. The final minibuffer contents may look invalid, but that is not so. For example, if the minibuffer starts out with '`/usr/tmp/`' and you add '`/x1/rms/foo`', you get '`/usr/tmp//x1/rms/foo`'; but Emacs ignores every-thing through the first slash in the double slash; the result is '`/x1/rms/foo`'. See Section 5.1 [Minibuffer File], page 37.

You can refer to files on other machines using a special file name syntax:

> /*host*:*filename*
> /*user*@*host*:*filename*

When you do this, Emacs uses the FTP program to read and write files on the specified host. It logs in through FTP using your user name or the name *user*. It may ask you for a password from time to time; this is used for logging in on *host*.

You can turn off the FTP file name feature by setting the variable `file-name-handler-alist` to `nil`.

'`$`' in a file name is used to substitute environment variables. For example, if you have used the shell command '`export FOO=rms/hacks`' to set up an environment variable named `FOO`, then you can use '`/u/$FOO/test.c`' or '`/u/${FOO}/test.c`' as an abbreviation for '`/u/rms/hacks/test.c`'. The environment variable name consists of all the alphanumeric characters after the '`$`'; alternatively, it may be enclosed in braces after the '`$`'. Note that shell commands to set environment variables affect Emacs only if done before Emacs is started.

To access a file with '`$`' in its name, type '`$$`'. This pair is converted to a single '`$`' at the same time as variable substitution is performed for single '`$`'. The Lisp function that performs the substitution is called `substitute-in-file-name`. The substitution is performed only on file names read as such using the minibuffer.

14.2 Visiting Files

C-x C-f Visit a file (`find-file`).

C-x C-r Visit a file for viewing, without allowing changes to it (`find-file-read-only`).

C-x C-v   Visit a different file instead of the one visited last (find-alternate-file).

C-x 4 C-f Visit a file, in another window (find-file-other-window). Don't change the selected window.

C-x 5 C-f Visit a file, in a new frame (find-file-other-frame). Don't change the selected frame.

Visiting a file means copying its contents into an Emacs buffer so you can edit them. Emacs makes a new buffer for each file that you visit. We say that this buffer is visiting the file that it was created to hold. Emacs constructs the buffer name from the file name by throwing away the directory, keeping just the name proper. For example, a file named '/usr/rms/emacs.tex' would get a buffer named 'emacs.tex'. If there is already a buffer with that name, a unique name is constructed by appending '<2>', '<3>', or so on, using the lowest number that makes a name that is not already in use.

Each window's mode line shows the name of the buffer that is being displayed in that window, so you can always tell what buffer you are editing.

The changes you make with editing commands are made in the Emacs buffer. They do not take effect in the file that you visited, or any place permanent, until you *save* the buffer. Saving the buffer means that Emacs writes the current contents of the buffer into its visited file. See Section 14.3 [Saving], page 107.

If a buffer contains changes that have not been saved, we say the buffer is *modified*. This is important because it implies that some changes will be lost if the buffer is not saved. The mode line displays two stars near the left margin to indicate that the buffer is modified.

To visit a file, use the command C-x C-f (find-file). Follow the command with the name of the file you wish to visit, terminated by a RET.

The file name is read using the minibuffer (see Chapter 5 [Minibuffer], page 37), with defaulting and completion in the standard manner (see Section 14.1 [File Names], page 103). While in the minibuffer, you can abort C-x C-f by typing C-g.

Your confirmation that C-x C-f has completed successfully is the appearance of new text on the screen and a new buffer name in the mode line. If the specified file does not exist and could not be created, or cannot be read, then you get an error, with an error message displayed in the echo area.

If you visit a file that is already in Emacs, C-x C-f does not make another copy. It selects the existing buffer containing that file. However, before doing so, it checks that the file itself has not changed since you visited or saved it last. If the file has changed, a warning message is printed. See Section 14.3.2 [Simultaneous Editing], page 111.

What if you want to create a new file? Just visit it. Emacs prints '(New File)' in the echo area, but in other respects behaves as if you had visited an existing empty file. If you make any changes and save them, the file is created.

If the file you specify is actually a directory, C-x C-f invokes Dired, the Emacs directory browser so that you can "edit" the contents of the directory (see Chapter 27 [Dired], page 287). Dired is a convenient way to delete, look at, or operate on the files in the directory. However, if the variable find-file-run-dired is nil, then it is an error to try to visit a directory.

If you visit a file that the operating system won't let you modify, Emacs makes the buffer read-only, so that you won't go ahead and make changes that you'll have trouble saving afterward. You can make the buffer writable with C-x C-q (vc-toggle-read-only). See Section 15.3 [Misc Buffer], page 135.

Occasionally you might want to visit a file as read-only in order to protect yourself from entering changes accidentally; do so by visiting the file with the command C-x C-r (find-file-read-only).

If you visit a nonexistent file unintentionally (because you typed the wrong file name), use the C-x C-v command (find-alternate-file) to visit the file you really wanted. C-x C-v is similar to C-x C-f, but it kills the current buffer (after first offering to save it if it is modified). When it reads the file name to visit, it inserts the entire default file name in the buffer, with point just after the directory part; this is convenient if you made a slight error in typing the name.

C-x 4 f (find-file-other-window) is like C-x C-f except that the buffer containing the specified file is selected in another window. The window that was selected before C-x 4 f continues to show the same buffer it was already showing. If this command is used when only one window is being displayed, that window is split in two, with one window showing the same buffer as before, and the other one showing the newly requested file. See Chapter 16 [Windows], page 141.

C-x 5 f (find-file-other-frame) is similar, but opens a new frame, or makes visible any existing frame showing the file you seek. This feature is available only when you are using a window system. See Chapter 17 [Frames], page 147.

Two special hook variables allow extensions to modify the operation of visiting files. Visiting a file that does not exist runs the functions in the list find-file-not-found-hooks; this variable holds a list of functions, and the functions are called one by one until one of them returns non-nil. Any visiting of a file, whether extant or not, expects find-file-hooks to contain a list of functions and calls them all, one by one. In both cases the functions receive no arguments. Of these two variables, find-file-not-found-hooks takes effect first. These variables are *not* normal hooks, and their names end in '-hooks' rather than '-hook' to indicate that fact. See Section 30.2.3 [Hooks], page 347.

There are several ways to specify automatically the major mode for editing the file (see Section 18.1 [Choosing Modes], page 161), and to specify local variables defined for that file (see Section 30.2.5 [File Variables], page 350).

14.3 Saving Files

Saving a buffer in Emacs means writing its contents back into the file that was visited in the buffer.

C-x C-s   Save the current buffer in its visited file (save-buffer).

C-x s   Save any or all buffers in their visited files (save-some-buffers).

M-~   Forget that the current buffer has been changed (not-modified).

C-x C-w   Save the current buffer in a specified file (write-file).

M-x set-visited-file-name
           Change file the name under which the current buffer will be saved.

When you wish to save the file and make your changes permanent, type C-x C-s (save-buffer). After saving is finished, C-x C-s displays a message like this:

    Wrote /u/rms/gnu/gnu.tasks

If the selected buffer is not modified (no changes have been made in it since the buffer was created or last saved), saving is not really done, because it would have no effect. Instead, C-x C-s displays a message like this in the echo area:

    (No changes need to be written)

The command C-x s (save-some-buffers) offers to save any or all modified buffers. It asks you what to do with each buffer. The possible responses are analogous to those of query-replace:

y   Save this buffer and ask about the rest of the buffers.

n   Don't save this buffer, but ask about the rest of the buffers.

!   Save this buffer and all the rest with no more questions.

RET   Terminate save-some-buffers without any more saving.

.   Save this buffer, then exit save-some-buffers without even asking about other buffers.

C-r   View the buffer that you are currently being asked about. When
             you exit View mode, you get back to `save-some-buffers`, which
             asks the question again.

C-h   Display a help message about these options.

C-x C-c, the key sequence to exit Emacs, invokes `save-some-buffers`
and therefore asks the same questions.

If you have changed a buffer but you do not want to save the changes, you
should take some action to prevent it. Otherwise, each time you use C-x s or
C-x C-c, you are liable to save this buffer by mistake. One thing you can do
is type M-~ (`not-modified`), which clears out the indication that the buffer
is modified. If you do this, none of the save commands will believe that the
buffer needs to be saved. ('~' is often used as a mathematical symbol for
'not'; thus M-~ is 'not', metafied.) You could also use `set-visited-file-
name` (see below) to mark the buffer as visiting a different file name, one
which is not in use for anything important. Alternatively, you can cancel all
the changes made since the file was visited or saved, by reading the text from
the file again. This is called *reverting*. See Section 14.4 [Reverting], page 112.
You could also undo all the changes by repeating the undo command C-x u
until you have undone all the changes; but reverting is easier.

M-x `set-visited-file-name` alters the name of the file that the current
buffer is visiting. It reads the new file name using the minibuffer. Then it
specifies the visited file name and changes the buffer name correspondingly
(as long as the new name is not in use). `set-visited-file-name` does not
save the buffer in the newly visited file; it just alters the records inside Emacs
in case you do save later. It also marks the buffer as "modified" so that C-x
C-s in that buffer *will* save.

If you wish to mark the buffer as visiting a different file and save it right
away, use C-x C-w (`write-file`). It is precisely equivalent to `set-visited-
file-name` followed by C-x C-s. C-x C-s used on a buffer that is not visiting
with a file has the same effect as C-x C-w; that is, it reads a file name, marks
the buffer as visiting that file, and saves it there. The default file name in a
buffer that is not visiting a file is made by combining the buffer name with
the buffer's default directory.

If Emacs is about to save a file and sees that the date of the latest version on disk does not match what Emacs last read or wrote, Emacs notifies
you of this fact, because it probably indicates a problem caused by simultaneous editing and requires your immediate attention. See Section 14.3.2
[Simultaneous Editing], page 111.

If the variable `require-final-newline` is non-`nil`, Emacs puts a newline
at the end of any file that doesn't already end in one, every time a file is
saved or written.

14.3.1 Backup Files

On most operating systems, rewriting a file automatically destroys all record of what the file used to contain. Thus, saving a file from Emacs throws away the old contents of the file—or it would, except that Emacs carefully copies the old contents to another file, called the *backup* file, before actually saving. (This assumes that the variable `make-backup-files` is non-`nil`. Backup files are not written if this variable is `nil`.)

At your option, Emacs can keep either a single backup file or a series of numbered backup files for each file that you edit.

Emacs makes a backup for a file only the first time the file is saved from one buffer. No matter how many times you save a file, its backup file continues to contain the contents from before the file was visited. Normally this means that the backup file contains the contents from before the current editing session; however, if you kill the buffer and then visit the file again, a new backup file will be made by the next save.

14.3.1.1 Single or Numbered Backups

If you choose to have a single backup file (this is the default), the backup file's name is constructed by appending '~' to the file name being edited; thus, the backup file for 'eval.c' would be 'eval.c~'.

If you choose to have a series of numbered backup files, backup file names are made by appending '.~', the number, and another '~' to the original file name. Thus, the backup files of 'eval.c' would be called 'eval.c.~1~', 'eval.c.~2~', and so on, through names like 'eval.c.~259~' and beyond.

If protection stops you from writing backup files under the usual names, the backup file is written as '%backup%~' in your home directory. Only one such file can exist, so only the most recently made such backup is available.

The choice of single backup or numbered backups is controlled by the variable `version-control`. Its possible values are

t   Make numbered backups.

nil   Make numbered backups for files that have numbered backups already. Otherwise, make single backups.

never   Do not in any case make numbered backups; always make single backups.

You can set `version-control` locally in an individual buffer to control the making of backups for that buffer's file. For example, Rmail mode locally sets `version-control` to `never` to make sure that there is only one backup for an Rmail file. See Section 30.2.4 [Locals], page 348.

If you set the environment variable VERSION_CONTROL, to tell various GNU utilities what to do with backup files, Emacs also obeys the environment variable by setting the Lisp variable version-control accordingly at startup. If the environment variable's value is 't' or 'numbered', then version-control becomes t; if the value is 'nil' or 'existing', then version-control becomes nil; if it is 'never' or 'simple', then version-control becomes never.

For files under version control (see Section 14.7 [Version Control], page 116), the variable vc-make-backup-files determines whether to make backup files. By default, it is nil, since backup files are redundant when you store all the previous versions in a version control system. See Section 14.7.3 [Editing with VC], page 117.

14.3.1.2 Automatic Deletion of Backups

To prevent unlimited consumption of disk space, Emacs can delete numbered backup versions automatically. Generally Emacs keeps the first few backups and the latest few backups, deleting any in between. This happens every time a new backup is made.

The two variables kept-old-versions and kept-new-versions control this deletion. Their values are, respectively the number of oldest (lowest-numbered) backups to keep and the number of newest (highest-numbered) ones to keep, each time a new backup is made. Recall that these values are used just after a new backup version is made; that newly made backup is included in the count in kept-new-versions. By default, both variables are 2.

If delete-old-versions is non-nil, the excess middle versions are deleted without a murmur. If it is nil, the default, then you are asked whether the excess middle versions should really be deleted.

Dired's . (Period) command can also be used to delete old versions. See Section 27.3 [Dired Deletion], page 287.

14.3.1.3 Copying vs. Renaming

Backup files can be made by copying the old file or by renaming it. This makes a difference when the old file has multiple names. If the old file is renamed into the backup file, then the alternate names become names for the backup file. If the old file is copied instead, then the alternate names remain names for the file that you are editing, and the contents accessed by those names will be the new contents.

The method of making a backup file may also affect the file's owner and group. If copying is used, these do not change. If renaming is used, you become the file's owner, and the file's group becomes the default (different operating systems have different defaults for the group).

Having the owner change is usually a good idea, because then the owner always shows who last edited the file. Also, the owners of the backups show who produced those versions. Occasionally there is a file whose owner should not change; it is a good idea for such files to contain local variable lists to set `backup-by-copying-when-mismatch` locally (see Section 30.2.5 [File Variables], page 350).

The choice of renaming or copying is controlled by three variables. Renaming is the default choice. If the variable `backup-by-copying` is non-nil, copying is used. Otherwise, if the variable `backup-by-copying-when-linked` is non-nil, then copying is used for files that have multiple names, but renaming may still used when the file being edited has only one name. If the variable `backup-by-copying-when-mismatch` is non-nil, then copying is used if renaming would cause the file's owner or group to change.

14.3.2 Protection against Simultaneous Editing

Simultaneous editing occurs when two users visit the same file, both make changes, and then both save them. If nobody were informed that this was happening, whichever user saved first would later find that his changes were lost. On some systems, Emacs notices immediately when the second user starts to change the file, and issues an immediate warning.

For the sake of systems where that is not possible, and in case someone else proceeds to change the file despite the warning, Emacs also checks when the file is saved, and issues a second warning if you are about to overwrite a file containing another user's changes. You can prevent loss of the other user's work by taking the proper corrective action at that time.

When you make the first modification in an Emacs buffer that is visiting a file, Emacs records that the file is *locked* by you. (It does this by writing another file in a directory reserved for this purpose.) The lock is removed when you save the changes. The idea is that the file is locked whenever an Emacs buffer visiting it has unsaved changes.

If you begin to modify the buffer while the visited file is locked by someone else, this constitutes a *collision*. When Emacs detects a collision, it asks you what to do, by calling the Lisp function `ask-user-about-lock`. You can redefine this function for the sake of customization. The standard definition of this function asks you a question and accepts three possible answers:

s   Steal the lock. Whoever was already changing the file loses the lock, and you gain the lock.

p   Proceed. Go ahead and edit the file despite its being locked by someone else.

q   Quit. This causes an error (`file-locked`) and the modification
                     you were trying to make in the buffer does not actually take
                     place.

Note that locking works on the basis of a file name; if a file has multiple names, Emacs does not realize that the two names are the same file
and cannot prevent two users from editing it simultaneously under different
names. However, basing locking on names means that Emacs can interlock
the editing of new files that will not really exist until they are saved.

Some systems are not configured to allow Emacs to make locks. On these
systems, Emacs cannot detect trouble in advance, but it still can detect the
collision when you try to save a file and overwrite someone else's changes.

Every time Emacs saves a buffer, it first checks the last-modification date
of the existing file on disk to verify that it has not changed since the file was
last visited or saved. If the date does not match, it implies that changes
were made in the file in some other way, and these changes are about to be
lost if Emacs actually does save. To prevent this, Emacs prints a warning
message and asks for confirmation before saving. Occasionally you will know
why the file was changed and know that it does not matter; then you can
answer yes and proceed. Otherwise, you should cancel the save with C-g
and investigate the situation.

The first thing you should do when notified that simultaneous editing has
already taken place is to list the directory with C-u C-x C-d (see Section 14.8
[Directories], page 130). This shows the file's current author. You should
attempt to contact him to warn him not to continue editing. Often the next
step is to save the contents of your Emacs buffer under a different name, and
use `diff` to compare the two files.

Simultaneous editing checks are also made when you visit with C-x C-f
a file that is already visited and when you start to modify a file. This is not
strictly necessary, but it can cause you to find out about the collision earlier,
when perhaps correction takes less work.

14.4 Reverting a Buffer

If you have made extensive changes to a file and then change your mind
about them, you can get rid of them by reading in the previous version of
the file. To do this, use M-x `revert-buffer`, which operates on the current
buffer. Since reverting a buffer unintentionally could lose a lot of work, you
must confirm this command with yes.

`revert-buffer` keeps point at the same distance (measured in characters)
from the beginning of the file. If the file was edited only slightly, you will be
at approximately the same piece of text after reverting as before. If you have

made drastic changes, the same value of point in the old file may address a totally different piece of text.

Reverting marks the buffer as "not modified" until another change is made.

Some kinds of buffers whose contents reflect data bases other than files, such as Dired buffers, can also be reverted. For them, reverting means recalculating their contents from the appropriate data base. Buffers created randomly with C-x b cannot be reverted; revert-buffer reports an error when asked to do so.

14.5 Auto-Saving: Protection Against Disasters

Emacs saves all the visited files from time to time (based on counting your keystrokes) without being asked. This is called *auto-saving*. It prevents you from losing more than a limited amount of work if the system crashes.

When Emacs determines that it is time for auto-saving, each buffer is considered, and is auto-saved if auto-saving is turned on for it and it has been changed since the last time it was auto-saved. The message 'Auto-saving...' is displayed in the echo area during auto-saving, if any files are actually auto-saved. Errors occurring during auto-saving are caught so that they do not interfere with the execution of commands you have been typing.

14.5.1 Auto-Save Files

Auto-saving does not normally save in the files that you visited, because it can be very undesirable to save a program that is in an inconsistent state when you have made half of a planned change. Instead, auto-saving is done in a different file called the *auto-save file*, and the visited file is changed only when you request saving explicitly (such as with C-x C-s).

Normally, the auto-save file name is made by appending '#' to the front and rear of the visited file name. Thus, a buffer visiting file 'foo.c' is auto-saved in a file '#foo.c#'. Most buffers that are not visiting files are auto-saved only if you request it explicitly; when they are auto-saved, the auto-save file name is made by appending '#%' to the front and '#' to the rear of buffer name. For example, the '*mail*' buffer in which you compose messages to be sent is auto-saved in a file named '#%*mail*#'. Auto-save file names are made this way unless you reprogram parts of Emacs to do something different (the functions make-auto-save-file-name and auto-save-file-name-p). The file name to be used for auto-saving in a buffer is calculated when auto-saving is turned on in that buffer.

When you delete a substantial part of the text in a large buffer, auto save turns off temporarily in that buffer. This is so that if you delete text accidentally, it is likely to remain present in the auto save file. To reenable auto-saving after this happens, simply save the file explicitly with `C-x C-s`. Using `C-u 1 M-x auto-save-mode` also cancels this particular state.

If you want auto-saving to be done in the visited file, set the variable `auto-save-visited-file-name` to be non-`nil`. In this mode, there is really no difference between auto-saving and explicit saving.

A buffer's auto-save file is deleted when you save the buffer in its visited file. To inhibit this, set the variable `delete-auto-save-files` to `nil`. Changing the visited file name with `C-x C-w` or `set-visited-file-name` renames any auto-save file to go with the new visited name.

When you delete a large amount of a buffer's text, auto-saving turns off in that buffer. This is because if you deleted the text unintentionally, you might find the auto-save file more useful if it contains the deleted text. To restart auto-saving in that buffer, save the buffer with `C-x C-s`, or use `M-x auto-save`.

14.5.2 Controlling Auto-Saving

Each time you visit a file, auto-saving is turned on for that file's buffer if the variable `auto-save-default` is non-`nil` (but not in batch mode; see Chapter 3 [Entering Emacs], page 23). The default for this variable is `t`, so auto-saving is the usual practice for file-visiting buffers. Auto-saving can be turned on or off for any existing buffer with the command `M-x auto-save-mode`. Like other minor mode commands, `M-x auto-save-mode` turns auto-saving on with a positive argument, off with a zero or negative argument; with no argument, it toggles.

Emacs does auto-saving periodically based on counting how many characters you have typed since the last time auto-saving was done. The variable `auto-save-interval` specifies how many characters there are between auto-saves. By default, it is 300.

Auto-saving also takes place when you stop typing for a while. The variable `auto-save-timeout` says how many seconds Emacs should wait before it does an auto save (and perhaps also a garbage collection). (The actual time period is longer if the current buffer is long; this is a heuristic which aims to keep out of your way when you are editing long buffers in which auto-save takes an appreciable amount of time.) Auto-saving during idle periods accomplishes two things: first, it makes sure all your work is saved if you go away from the terminal for a while; second, it may avoid some auto-saving while you are actually typing.

Emacs also does auto-saving whenever it gets a fatal error. This includes killing the Emacs job with a shell command such as '`kill %emacs`', or disconnecting a phone line or network connection.

You can request an auto-save explicitly with the command `M-x do-auto-save`.

14.5.3 Recovering Data from Auto-Saves

You can use the contents of an auto-save file to recover from a loss of data with the command `M-x recover-file RET` *file* `RET`. This visits *file* and then (after your confirmation) restores the contents from from its auto-save file '#*file*#'. You can then save with `C-x C-s` to put the recovered text into *file* itself. For example, to recover file 'foo.c' from its auto-save file '#foo.c#', do:

```
M-x recover-file RET foo.c RET
yes RET
C-x C-s
```

Before asking for confirmation, `M-x recover-file` displays a directory listing describing the specified file and the auto-save file, so you can compare their sizes and dates. If the auto-save file is older, `M-x recover-file` does not offer to read it.

If Emacs or the computer crashes, you can recover all the files you were editing from their auto save files with the command `M-x recover-session`. This first shows you a list of recorded interrupted sessions. Move point to the one you choose, and type `C-c C-c`.

Then `recover-session` asks about each of the files that were being edited during that session, asking whether to recover that file. If you answer `y`, it calls `recover-file`, which works in its normal fashion. It shows the dates of the original file and its auto-save file, and asks once again whether to recover that file.

When `recover-session` is done, the files you've chosen to recover are present in Emacs buffers. You should then save them. Only this—saving them—updates the files themselves.

14.6 File Name Aliases

Symbolic links and hard links both make it possible for several file names to refer to the same file. Hard links are alternate names that refer directly to the file; all the names are equally valid, and no one of them is preferred. By contrast, a symbolic link is a kind of defined alias: when 'foo' is a symbolic link to 'bar', you can use either name to refer to the file, but 'bar' is the real name, while 'foo' is just an alias. More complex cases occur when symbolic links point to directories.

If you visit two names for the same file, normally Emacs makes two different buffers, but it warns you about the situation.

If you wish to avoid visiting the same file in two buffers under different names, set the variable `find-file-existing-other-name` to a non-`nil` value. Then `find-file` uses the existing buffer visiting the file, no matter which of the file's names you specify.

If the variable `find-file-visit-truename` is non-`nil`, then the file name recorded for a buffer is the file's *truename* (made by replacing all symbolic links with their target names), rather than the name you specify. Setting `find-file-visit-truename` also implies the effect of `find-file-existing-other-name`.

14.7 Version Control

Version control systems are packages that can record multiple versions of a source file, usually storing the unchanged parts of the file just once. Version control systems also record history information such as the creation time of each version, who created it, and a description of what was changed in that version.

The Emacs version control commands work with three version control systems—RCS, CVS and SCCS. The GNU project recommends the version control system known as RCS, which is free software and available from the Free Software Foundation.

14.7.1 Supported Version Control Systems

VC currently works with three different version control systems or "back ends": RCS, CVS, and SCCS.

RCS is a free version control system that is available from the Free Software Foundation. It is perhaps the most mature of the supported back ends, and the VC commands are conceptually closest to RCS. Almost everything you can do with RCS can be done through VC.

CVS is built on top of RCS, and extends the features of RCS, allowing for more sophisticated release management, and concurrent multi-user development. However, its concepts are rather different from those of RCS and VC; consequently, some VC commands work differently when used with CVS. Note that before using CVS you must set up a repository, which is a subject too complex to treat here. See Section 14.7.3.6 [CVS and VC], page 120.

SCCS is a proprietary but widely used version control system. In terms of capabilities, it is the weakest of the the three that VC supports. VC compensates for certain features missing in SCCS (snapshots, for example) by implementing them itself, but some other VC features, such as multiple branches, are not available with SCCS. You should use SCCS only if for some reason you cannot use RCS.

14.7.2 Concepts of Version Control

When a file is under version control, we also say that it is *registered* in the version control system. Each registered file has a corresponding *master file* which represents the file's present state plus its change history, so that you can reconstruct from it either the current version or any specified earlier version. Usually the master file also records a *log entry* for each version describing what was changed in that version.

The file that is maintained under version control is sometimes called the *work file* corresponding to its master file.

To examine a file, you *check it out*. This extracts a version of the source file (typically, the most recent) from the master file. If you want to edit the file, you must check it out *locked*. Only one user can do this at a time for any given source file. (This kind of locking is completely unrelated to the locking that Emacs uses to detect simultaneous editing of a file.)

When you are done with your editing, you must *check in* the new version. This records the new version in the master file, and unlocks the source file so that other people can lock it and thus modify it.

Checkin and checkout are the basic operations of version control. You can do both of them with a single Emacs command: `C-x C-q` (`vc-toggle-read-only`).

A *snapshot* is a coherent collection of versions of the various files that make up a program. See Section 14.7.10 [Snapshots], page 126.

The model of checkin and checkout does not quite fit CVS. CVS has no such thing as locking; multiple users can simultaneously edit their copies of a file, and then check in their own variants of the file, but these variants must be reconciled later. See Section 14.7.3.6 [CVS and VC], page 120.

14.7.3 Editing with Version Control

These are the commands for editing a file maintained with version control:

`C-x C-q`
`C-x v v`   Check the visited file in or out.

`C-x v u`   Revert the buffer and the file to the last checked in version.

`C-x v c`   Remove the last-entered change from the master for the visited file. This undoes your last check-in.

`C-x v i`   Register the visited file for version control.

(`C-x v` is the prefix key for version control commands; all of these commands except for `C-x C-q` start with `C-x v`.)

14.7.3.1 Check-Out

When you want to modify a file maintained with version control, type C-x C-q (vc-toggle-read-only). This *checks out* the file, and tells RCS or SCCS to lock the file. This means making the file writable for you (but not for anyone else).

If you specify a prefix argument (C-u C-x C-q) for checkout, Emacs asks you for a version number, and checks out that version *unlocked*. This lets you move to old versions, or existing branches of the file (see Section 14.7.7 [Branches], page 123). You can then start editing the selected version by typing C-x C-q again. (If you edit an old version of a file this way, checking it in again creates a new branch.)

14.7.3.2 Check-In

When you are finished editing the file, type C-x C-q again. When used on a file that is checked out, this command checks the file in. But check-in does not start immediately; first, you must enter the *log entry*—a description of the changes in the new version. C-x C-q pops up a buffer for you to enter this in. When you are finished typing in the log entry, type C-c C-c to terminate it; this is when actual check-in takes place. See Section 14.7.4 [Log Entries], page 120.

With RCS and SCCS, a checked-out file is also *locked*, which means it is writable for you, but not for anyone else. As long as you own the lock on the file, nobody else can modify it, and nobody can check in any changes to that particular version. Checking in your changes unlocks the file, so that other users can lock it and modify it.

CVS, on the contrary, doesn't have a concept of locking. The working files are always modifiable, allowing concurrent development, with possible conflicts being resolved at check-in time. See Section 14.7.3.6 [CVS and VC], page 120.

To specify the version number for the new version, type C-u C-x C-q to check in a file. Then Emacs asks you for the new version number in the minibuffer. This can be used to create a new *branch* of the file (see Section 14.7.7 [Branches], page 123), or to increment the file's major version number.

It is not impossible to lock a file that someone else has locked. If you try to check out a file that is locked, C-x C-q asks you whether you want to "steal the lock." If you say yes, the file becomes locked by you, but a message is sent to the person who had formerly locked the file, to inform him of what has happened. The mode line indicates that a file is locked by someone else by displaying the login name of that person, before the version number.

14.7.3.3 Registering a File for Version Control

C-x v i   Register the visited file for version control.

You can put any file under version control by simply visiting it, and then typing C-x v i (vc-register). After C-x v i, the file is unlocked and read-only. Type C-x C-q if you wish to start editing it.

When you register the file, Emacs must choose which version control system to use for it. You can specify your choice explicitly by setting vc-default-back-end to RCS, CVS or SCCS. Otherwise, if there is a subdirectory named 'RCS', 'SCCS', or 'CVS', Emacs uses the corresponding version control system. In the absence of any specification, the default choice is RCS if RCS is installed, otherwise SCCS.

After registering a file with CVS, you must subsequently commit the initial version by typing C-x C-q. See Section 14.7.3.6 [CVS and VC], page 120.

The initial version number for a newly registered file is 1.1, by default. To specify a different number, give C-x v i a numeric argument; then it reads the initial version number using the minibuffer.

If vc-initial-comment is non-nil, C-x v i reads an initial comment (much like a log entry) to describe the purpose of this source file.

14.7.3.4 Undoing Version Control Actions

C-x v u   Revert the buffer and the file to the last checked in version.

C-x v c   Remove the last-entered change from the master for the visited file. This undoes your last checkin.

If you want to discard your current set of changes and revert to the last version checked in, use C-x v u (vc-revert-buffer). This cancels your last check-out, leaving the file unlocked. If you want to make a different set of changes, you must first check the file out again. C-x v u requires confirmation, unless it sees that you haven't made any changes since the last checked-in version.

C-x v u is also the command to use to unlock a file if you lock it and then decide not to change it.

You can cancel a change after checking it in, with C-x v c (vc-cancel-version). This command discards all record of the most recent checked in version. C-x v c also offers to revert your work file and buffer to the previous version (the one that precedes the version that is deleted). If you say no, then the buffer and work file do not change.

Be careful when invoking C-x v c, as it is easy to throw away a lot of work with it. To help you be careful, this command always requires confirmation with yes.

14.7.3.5 The VC Mode Line

When you visit a file that is under version control, the mode line indicates the current status of the file: the name of the version control back end system, the locking state, and the version.

The locking state is displayed as a single character, which can be either '-' or ':'. '-' means the file is not locked or not modified by you. Once you lock the file, the state indicator changes to ':'. If the file is locked by someone else, that user's name appears after the version number.

For example, 'RCS-1.3' means you are looking at RCS version 1.3, which is not locked. 'RCS:1.3' means that you have locked the file, and possibly already changed it. 'RCS:jim:1.3' means that the file is locked by jim.

14.7.3.6 Using VC with CVS

In CVS, files are never locked. Two users can check out the same file at the same time; each user has a separate copy and can edit it. Work files are always writable; once you have one, you need not type a VC command to start editing the file. You can edit it at any time.

CVS terminology speaks of *committing* a change rather than checking it in. But in practical terms they work the same way: Emacs asks you to type in a log entry, and you finish it with C-c C-c. When using RCS and SCCS, you normally use C-x C-q twice for each change; once before the change, for checkout, and once after, for checkin. With CVS, it's different: you normally use C-x C-q just once for each change, to commit the change when it is done. The work file remains writable, so you can begin editing again with no special commands.

When you commit a change in a file, and someone else has committed another change in the meanwhile, that creates a *conflict*. Then C-x C-q asks you to resolve the conflict and try again.

VC does not provide a way to check out a working copy of an existing file in the repository. You have to use the CVS shell commands to do that. Once you have a work file, you can start using VC for that file.

14.7.4 Log Entries

When you're editing an initial comment or log entry for inclusion in a master file, finish your entry by typing C-c C-c.

C-c C-c   Finish the comment edit normally (vc-finish-logentry). This finishes check-in.

To abort check-in, just **don't** type C-c C-c in that buffer. You can switch buffers and do other editing. As long as you don't try to check in another file, the entry you were editing remains in its buffer, and you can go back to that buffer at any time to complete the check-in.

If you change several source files for the same reason, it is often convenient to specify the same log entry for many of the files. To do this, use the history of previous log entries. The commands M-n, M-p, M-s and M-r for doing this work just like the minibuffer history commands (except that these versions are used outside the minibuffer).

Each time you check in a file, the log entry buffer is put into VC Log mode, which involves running two hooks: text-mode-hook and vc-log-mode-hook. See Section 30.2.3 [Hooks], page 347.

14.7.5 Change Logs and VC

If you use RCS for a program and also maintain a change log file for it (see Section 21.11 [Change Log], page 214), you can generate change log entries automatically from the version control log entries:

C-x v a   Visit the current directory's change log file and create new entries for versions checked in since the most recent entry in the change log file (vc-update-change-log).

This command works with RCS only; it does not work with CVS or SCCS.

For example, suppose the first line of 'ChangeLog' is dated 10 April 1992, and that the only check-in since then was by Nathaniel Bowditch to 'rcs2log' on 8 May 1992 with log text 'Ignore log messages that start with '#'.'. Then C-x v a visits 'ChangeLog' and inserts text like this:

```
Fri May  8 21:45:00 1992  Nathaniel Bowditch  <nat@apn.org>

        * rcs2log: Ignore log messages that start with '#'.
```

You can then edit the new change log entry further as you wish.

Normally, the log entry for file 'foo' is displayed as '* foo: *text of log entry*'. The ':' after 'foo' is omitted if the text of the log entry starts with '(*functionname*): '. For example, if the log entry for 'vc.el' is '(vc-do-command): Check call-process status.', then the text in 'ChangeLog' looks like this:

```
Wed May  6 10:53:00 1992  Nathaniel Bowditch  <nat@apn.org>

        * vc.el (vc-do-command): Check call-process status.
```

When C-x v a adds several change log entries at once, it groups related log entries together if they all are checked in by the same author at nearly the same time. If the log entries for several such files all have the same text, it coalesces them into a single entry. For example, suppose the most recent checkins have the following log entries:

- For 'vc.texinfo': 'Fix expansion typos.'
- For 'vc.el': 'Don't call expand-file-name.'
- For 'vc-hooks.el': 'Don't call expand-file-name.'

They appear like this in 'ChangeLog':

```
Wed Apr  1 08:57:59 1992  Nathaniel Bowditch  <nat@apn.org>

    * vc.texinfo: Fix expansion typos.

    * vc.el, vc-hooks.el: Don't call expand-file-name.
```

Normally, C-x v a separates log entries by a blank line, but you can mark several related log entries to be clumped together (without an intervening blank line) by starting the text of each related log entry with a label of the form '{*clumpname*} '. The label itself is not copied to 'ChangeLog'. For example, suppose the log entries are:

- For 'vc.texinfo': '{expand} Fix expansion typos.'
- For 'vc.el': '{expand} Don't call expand-file-name.'
- For 'vc-hooks.el': '{expand} Don't call expand-file-name.'

Then the text in 'ChangeLog' looks like this:

```
Wed Apr  1 08:57:59 1992  Nathaniel Bowditch  <nat@apn.org>

    * vc.texinfo: Fix expansion typos.
    * vc.el, vc-hooks.el: Don't call expand-file-name.
```

A log entry whose text begins with '#' is not copied to 'ChangeLog'. For example, if you merely fix some misspellings in comments, you can log the change with an entry beginning with '#' to avoid putting such trivia into 'ChangeLog'.

14.7.6 Examining And Comparing Old Versions

C-u C-x C-q *version* RET
> Select version *version* as the current work file version.

C-x v ~ *version* RET
> Examine version *version* of the visited file, in a buffer of its own.

C-x v =
> Compare the current buffer contents with the latest checked-in version of the file.

C-u C-x v = *file* RET *oldvers* RET *newvers* RET
> Compare the specified two versions of *file*.

There are two ways to work with an old version of a file. You can make the old version your current work file, for example if you want to reproduce a former stage of development, or if you want to create a branch from the old version (see Section 14.7.7 [Branches], page 123). To do this, visit the file and type C-u C-x C-q *version* RET. (This works only with RCS.)

If you want only to examine an old version, without changing your work file, visit the file and then type C-x v ~ *version* RET (vc-version-other-window). This puts the text of version *version* in a file named '*file-name.~version~*', and visits it in its own buffer in a separate window.

To compare two versions of a file, use the command C-x v = (vc-diff). Plain C-x v = compares the current buffer contents (saving them in the file if necessary) with the last checked-in version of the file. C-u C-x v =, with a numeric argument, reads a file name and two version numbers, then compares those versions of the specified file.

If you supply a directory name instead of the name of a work file, this command compares the two specified versions of all registered files in that directory and its subdirectories. You can also specify a snapshot name (see Section 14.7.10 [Snapshots], page 126) instead of one or both version numbers.

You can specify a checked-in version by its number; an empty input specifies the current contents of the work file (which may be different from all the checked-in versions).

This command works by running the diff utility, getting the options from the variable diff-switches. It displays the output in a special buffer in another window. Unlike the M-x diff command, C-x v = does not try to locate the changes in the old and new versions. This is because normally one or both versions do not exist as files when you compare them; they exist only in the records of the master file. See Section 14.9 [Comparing Files], page 130, for more information about M-x diff.

14.7.7 Multiple Branches of a File

One use of version control is to maintain multiple "current" versions of a file. For example, you might have different versions of a program in which you are gradually adding various unfinished new features. Each such independent line of development is called a *branch*. VC allows you to create branches, and switch between existing branches. Note, however, that branches are supported only with RCS.

A file's main line of development is usually called the *trunk*. The versions on the trunk are normally numbered 1.1, 1.2, 1.3, etc. At any such version, you may start an independent branch. A branch starting at version 1.2 would have version number 1.2.1.1. Consecutive versions on this branch would have numbers 1.2.1.2, 1.2.1.3, 1.2.1.4, and so on. If there is a second branch also starting at version 1.2; it would consist of versions 1.2.2.1, 1.2.2.2, 1.2.2.3, and so on.

If you omit the final component of a version number, that is called a *branch number*. It refers to the highest existing version on that branch. The branches in the example above have branch numbers 1.2.1 and 1.2.2.

A version which is the last in its branch is called a *head* version.

14.7.7.1 Switching between Branches

To switch between branches, type C-u C-x C-q and specify the version number you want to select. This version is then checked out *unlocked* (write-protected), so you can examine it before really checking it out. Switching branches in this way is allowed only when the file is not locked.

You may omit the minor version number, thus giving only the branch number; this takes you to the highest version on the indicated branch. If you only type RET, Emacs goes to the highest version on the trunk.

After you have switched to any branch (including the main branch), you stay on it for subsequent VC commands, until you explicitly select some other branch.

14.7.7.2 Creating New Branches

To create a new branch from a head version (one that is the latest in the branch that contains it), first select that version if necessary, lock it with C-x C-q, and make whatever changes you want. Then, when you check in the changes, use C-u C-x C-q. This lets you specify the version number for the new version. You should specify a suitable branch number for a branch starting at the current version. For example, if the current version is 2.5, the branch number should be 2.5.1, 2.5.2, and so on, depending on the number of existing branches at that point.

To create a new branch at an older version (one that is no longer the head of a branch), first select that version, lock it with C-x C-q, and make your changes. Then type C-x C-q again to check in a new version. This automatically creates a new branch starting from the selected version. You need not specially request a new branch, because that's the only way to add a new version at a point that is not the head of a branch.

After the branch is created, you "stay" on it. That means that subsequent checkouts and checkins create new versions on that branch. To leave the branch, you must explicitly select a different version with C-u C-x C-q for checkout.

14.7.7.3 Multi-User Branching

It is sometimes useful for multiple developers to work simultaneously on different branches of a file. This is possible if you create multiple source directories. Each source directory should have a link named 'RCS' which points to a common directory of RCS master files. Then each source directory can have its own choice of versions checked out, but all share the same common RCS records.

This technique works reliably and automatically, provided that the source files contain RCS version headers (see Section 14.7.11 [Version Headers], page 127). The headers enable Emacs to be sure, at all times, which version number is present in the work file.

If the files do not have version headers, you must instead tell Emacs explicitly in each session which branch you are working on. To do this, first find the file, then type C-u C-x C-q and specify the correct branch number. This ensures that Emacs knows which branch it is using during this particular editing session.

14.7.8 VC Status Commands

To view the detailed version control status and history of a file, type C-x v l (vc-print-log). It displays the history of changes to the current file, including the text of the log entries. The output appears in a separate window.

When you are working on a large program, it's often useful to find all the files that are currently locked, or all the files maintained in version control at all. You can use C-x v d (vc-directory) to show all the locked files in or beneath the current directory. This includes all files that are locked by any user. C-u C-x v d lists all files in or beneath the current directory that are maintained with version control.

The list of files is displayed as a buffer that uses an augmented Dired mode. The names of the users locking various files are shown (in parentheses) in place of the owner and group. All the normal Dired commands work in this buffer. Most interactive VC commands work also, and apply to the file name on the current line.

The C-x v v command (vc-next-action), when used in the augmented Dired buffer, operates on all the marked files (or the file on the current line). If it operates on more than one file, it handles each file according to its current state; thus, it may check out one file and check in another (because it is already checked out). If it has to check in any files, it reads a single log entry, then uses that text for all the files being checked in. This can be convenient for registering or checking in several files at once, as part of the same change.

14.7.9 Renaming VC Work Files and Master Files

When you rename a registered file, you must also rename its master file correspondingly to get proper results. Use `vc-rename-file` to rename the source file as you specify, and rename its master file accordingly. It also updates any snapshots (see Section 14.7.10 [Snapshots], page 126) that mention the file, so that they use the new name; despite this, the snapshot thus modified may not completely work (see Section 14.7.10.2 [Snapshot Caveats], page 127).

You cannot use `vc-rename-file` on a file that is locked by someone else.

14.7.10 Snapshots

A *snapshot* is a named set of file versions (one for each registered file) that you can treat as a unit. One important kind of snapshot is a *release*, a (theoretically) stable version of the system that is ready for distribution to users.

14.7.10.1 Making and Using Snapshots

There are two basic commands for snapshots; one makes a snapshot with a given name, the other retrieves a named snapshot.

C-x v s *name* RET
> Define the last saved versions of every registered file in or under the current directory as a snapshot named *name* (`vc-create-snapshot`).

C-x v r *name* RET
> Check out all registered files at or below the current directory level using whatever versions correspond to the snapshot *name* (`vc-retrieve-snapshot`).
>
> This command reports an error if any files are locked at or below the current directory, without changing anything; this is to avoid overwriting work in progress.

A snapshot uses a very small amount of resources—just enough to record the list of file names and which version belongs to the snapshot. Thus, you need not hesitate to create snapshots whenever they are useful.

You can give a snapshot name as an argument to C-x v = or C-x v ~ (see Section 14.7.6 [Old Versions], page 122). Thus, you can use it to compare a snapshot against the current files, or two snapshots against each other, or a snapshot against a named version.

14.7.10.2 Snapshot Caveats

VC's snapshot facilities are modeled on RCS's named-configuration support. They use RCS's native facilities for this, so under VC snapshots made using RCS are visible even when you bypass VC.

For SCCS, VC implements snapshots itself. The files it uses contain name/file/version-number triples. These snapshots are visible only through VC.

A snapshot is a set of checked-in versions. So make sure that all the files are checked in and not locked when you make a snapshot.

File renaming and deletion can create some difficulties with snapshots. This is not a VC-specific problem, but a general design issue in version control systems that no one has solved very well yet.

If you rename a registered file, you need to rename its master along with it (the command `vc-rename-file` does this automatically). If you are using SCCS, you must also update the records of the snapshot, to mention the file by its new name (`vc-rename-file` does this, too). An old snapshot that refers to a master file that no longer exists under the recorded name is invalid; VC can no longer retrieve it. It would be beyond the scope of this manual to explain enough about RCS and SCCS to explain how to update the snapshots by hand.

Using `vc-rename-file` makes the snapshot remain valid for retrieval, but it does not solve all problems. For example, some of the files in the program probably refer to others by name. At the very least, the makefile probably mentions the file that you renamed. If you retrieve an old snapshot, the renamed file is retrieved under its new name, which is not the name that the makefile expects. So the program won't really work as retrieved.

14.7.11 Inserting Version Control Headers

Sometimes it is convenient to put version identification strings directly into working files. Certain special strings called *version headers* are replaced in each successive version by the number of that version.

If you are using RCS, and version headers are present in your working files, Emacs can use them to determine the current version and the locking state of the files. This is more reliable than referring to the master files, which is done when there are no version headers. Note that in a multi-branch environment, version headers are necessary to make VC behave correctly (see Section 14.7.7.3 [Multi-User Branching], page 124).

Searching for version headers is controlled by the variable `vc-consult-headers`. If it is non-`nil`, Emacs searches for headers to determine the version number you are editing. Setting it to `nil` disables this feature.

You can use the `C-x v h` command (`vc-insert-headers`) to insert a suitable header string.

C-x v h   Insert headers in a file for use with your version-control system.

The default header string is '`$Id$`' for RCS and '`%W%`' for SCCS. You can specify other headers to insert by setting the variable `vc-header-alist`. Its value is a list of elements of the form (*program* . *string*) where *program* is RCS or SCCS and *string* is the string to use.

Instead of a single string, you can specify a list of strings; then each string in the list is inserted as a separate header on a line of its own.

It is often necessary to use "superfluous" backslashes when writing the strings that you put in this variable. This is to prevent the string in the constant from being interpreted as a header itself if the Emacs Lisp file containing it is maintained with version control.

Each header is inserted surrounded by tabs, inside comment delimiters, on a new line at the start of the buffer. Normally the ordinary comment start and comment end strings of the current mode are used, but for certain modes, there are special comment delimiters for this purpose; the variable `vc-comment-alist` specifies them. Each element of this list has the form (*mode starter ender*).

The variable `vc-static-header-alist` specifies further strings to add based on the name of the buffer. Its value should be a list of elements of the form (*regexp* . *format*). Whenever *regexp* matches the buffer name, *format* is inserted as part of the header. A header line is inserted for each element that matches the buffer name, and for each string specified by `vc-header-alist`. The header line is made by processing the string from `vc-header-alist` with the format taken from the element. The default value for `vc-static-header-alist` is as follows:

```
(("\\.c$" .
  "\n#ifndef lint\nstatic char vcid[] = \"\%s\";\n\
#endif /* lint */\n"))
```

It specifies insertion of text of this form:

```
#ifndef lint
static char vcid[] = "string";
#endif /* lint */
```

Note that the text above starts with a blank line.

If you use more than one version header in a file, put them close together in the file. The mechanism in `revert-buffer` that preserves markers may not handle markers positioned between two version headers.

14.7.12 Customizing VC

Emacs normally does not save backup files for source files that are maintained with version control. If you want to make backup files even for files that use version control, set the variable `vc-make-backup-files` to a non-`nil` value.

Normally the work file exists all the time, whether it is locked or not. If you set `vc-keep-workfiles` to `nil`, then checking in a new version with `C-x C-q` deletes the work file; but any attempt to visit the file with Emacs creates it again. (With CVS, work files are always kept.)

If `vc-suppress-confirm` is non-`nil`, then `C-x C-q` and `C-x v i` can save the current buffer without asking, and `C-x v u` also operates without asking for confirmation. (This variable does not affect `C-x v c`; that operation is so drastic that it should always ask for confirmation.)

VC mode does much of its work by running the shell commands for RCS, CVS and SCCS. If `vc-command-messages` is non-`nil`, VC displays messages to indicate which shell commands it runs, and additional messages when the commands finish.

When deducing the locked/unlocked state of a file, VC first looks for an RCS version header string in the file (see Section 14.7.11 [Version Headers], page 127). If there is no header string (or if the backend system is SCCS), VC normally looks at the file permissions of the work file; this is fast. But there might be situations when the file permissions cannot be trusted. In this case the master file has to be consulted, which is rather expensive. Also the master file can only tell you *if* there's any lock on the file, but not whether your work file really contains that locked version.

You can tell VC not to use version headers to determine lock status by setting `vc-consult-headers` to `nil`. VC then always uses the file permissions (if it can trust them), or else checks the master file.

You can specify the criterion for whether to trust the file permissions by setting the variable `vc-mistrust-permissions`. Its value may be `t` (always mistrust the file permissions and check the master file), `nil` (always trust the file permissions), or a function of one argument which makes the decision. The argument is the directory name of the 'RCS', 'CVS' or 'SCCS' subdirectory. A non-`nil` value from the function says to mistrust the file permissions. If you find that the file permissions of work files are changed erroneously, set `vc-mistrust-permissions` to `t`. Then VC always checks the master file to determine the file's status.

You can specify additional directories to search for version control programs by setting the variable `vc-path`. These directories are searched before the usual search path. But the proper files are usually found automatically.

14.8 File Directories

The file system groups files into *directories*. A *directory listing* is a list of all the files in a directory. Emacs provides commands to create and delete directories, and to make directory listings in brief format (file names only) and verbose format (sizes, dates, and authors included). There is also a directory browser called Dired; see Chapter 27 [Dired], page 287.

C-x C-d *dir-or-pattern* RET
> Display a brief directory listing (`list-directory`).

C-u C-x C-d *dir-or-pattern* RET
> Display a verbose directory listing.

M-x make-directory RET *dirname* RET
> Create a new directory named *dirname*.

M-x delete-directory RET *dirname* RET
> Delete the directory named *dirname*. It must be empty, or you get an error.

The command to display a directory listing is C-x C-d (`list-directory`). It reads using the minibuffer a file name which is either a directory to be listed or a wildcard-containing pattern for the files to be listed. For example,

    C-x C-d /u2/emacs/etc RET

lists all the files in directory '`/u2/emacs/etc`'. Here is an example of specifying a file name pattern:

    C-x C-d /u2/emacs/src/*.c RET

Normally, C-x C-d prints a brief directory listing containing just file names. A numeric argument (regardless of value) tells it to make a verbose listing including sizes, dates, and authors (like '`ls -l`').

The text of a directory listing is obtained by running `ls` in an inferior process. Two Emacs variables control the switches passed to `ls`: `list-directory-brief-switches` is a string giving the switches to use in brief listings ("`-CF`" by default), and `list-directory-verbose-switches` is a string giving the switches to use in a verbose listing ("`-l`" by default).

14.9 Comparing Files

The command M-x diff compares two files, displaying the differences in an Emacs buffer named '`*Diff*`'. It works by running the `diff` program, using options taken from the variable `diff-switches`, whose value should be a string.

The buffer '`*Diff*`' has Compilation mode as its major mode, so you can use C-x ' to visit successive changed locations in the two source files. You can also move to a particular hunk of changes and type RET or C-c C-c, or click Mouse-2 on it, to move to the corresponding source location. You can also use the other special commands of Compilation mode: SPC and DEL for scrolling, and M-p and M-n for cursor motion. See Section 22.1 [Compilation], page 239.

The command M-x diff-backup compares a specified file with its most recent backup. If you specify the name of a backup file, diff-backup compares it with the source file that it is a backup of.

The command M-x compare-windows compares the text in the current window with that in the next window. Comparison starts at point in each window, and each starting position is pushed on the mark ring in its respective buffer. Then point moves forward in each window, a character at a time, until a mismatch between the two windows is reached. Then the command is finished. For more information about windows in Emacs, Chapter 16 [Windows], page 141.

With a numeric argument, compare-windows ignores changes in whitespace. If the variable compare-ignore-case is non-nil, it ignores differences in case as well.

See also Section 21.13 [Emerge], page 223, for convenient facilities for merging two similar files.

14.10 Miscellaneous File Operations

Emacs has commands for performing many other operations on files. All operate on one file; they do not accept wild card file names.

M-x view-file allows you to scan or read a file by sequential screenfuls. It reads a file name argument using the minibuffer. After reading the file into an Emacs buffer, view-file displays the beginning. You can then type SPC to scroll forward one windowful, or DEL to scroll backward. Various other commands are provided for moving around in the file, but none for changing it; type C-h while viewing for a list of them. They are mostly the same as normal Emacs cursor motion commands. To exit from viewing, type C-c. The commands for viewing are defined by a special major mode called View mode.

A related command, M-x view-buffer, views a buffer already present in Emacs. See Section 15.3 [Misc Buffer], page 135.

M-x insert-file inserts a copy of the contents of the specified file into the current buffer at point, leaving point unchanged before the contents and the mark after them.

M-x write-region is the inverse of M-x insert-file; it copies the contents of the region into the specified file. M-x append-to-file adds the text of the region to the end of the specified file. See Section 9.3 [Accumulating Text], page 66.

M-x delete-file deletes the specified file, like the rm command in the shell. If you are deleting many files in one directory, it may be more convenient to use Dired (see Chapter 27 [Dired], page 287).

M-x rename-file reads two file names *old* and *new* using the minibuffer, then renames file *old* as *new*. If a file named *new* already exists, you must confirm with yes or renaming is not done; this is because renaming causes the old meaning of the name *new* to be lost. If *old* and *new* are on different file systems, the file *old* is copied and deleted.

The similar command M-x add-name-to-file is used to add an additional name to an existing file without removing its old name. The new name must belong on the same file system that the file is on.

M-x copy-file reads the file *old* and writes a new file named *new* with the same contents. Confirmation is required if a file named *new* already exists, because copying has the consequence of overwriting the old contents of the file *new*.

M-x make-symbolic-link reads two file names *old* and *linkname*, then creates a symbolic link named *linkname* and pointing at *old*. The effect is that future attempts to open file *linkname* will refer to whatever file is named *old* at the time the opening is done, or will get an error if the name *old* is not in use at that time. This command does not expand the argument *filename*, so that it allows you to specify a relative name as the target of the link.

Confirmation is required when creating the link if *linkname* is in use. Note that not all systems support symbolic links.

15 Using Multiple Buffers

The text you are editing in Emacs resides in an object called a *buffer*. Each time you visit a file, a buffer is created to hold the file's text. Each time you invoke Dired, a buffer is created to hold the directory listing. If you send a message with C-x m, a buffer named '*mail*' is used to hold the text of the message. When you ask for a command's documentation, that appears in a buffer called '*Help*'.

At any time, one and only one buffer is *selected*. It is also called the *current buffer*. Often we say that a command operates on "the buffer" as if there were only one; but really this means that the command operates on the selected buffer (most commands do).

When Emacs has multiple windows, each window has a chosen buffer which is displayed there, but at any time only one of the windows is selected and its chosen buffer is the selected buffer. Each window's mode line displays the name of the buffer that the window is displaying (see Chapter 16 [Windows], page 141).

Each buffer has a name, which can be of any length, and you can select any buffer by giving its name. Most buffers are made by visiting files, and their names are derived from the files' names. But you can also create an empty buffer with any name you want. A newly started Emacs has a buffer named '*scratch*' which can be used for evaluating Lisp expressions in Emacs. The distinction between upper and lower case matters in buffer names.

Each buffer records individually what file it is visiting, whether it is modified, and what major mode and minor modes are in effect in it (see Chapter 18 [Major Modes], page 161). Any Emacs variable can be made *local to* a particular buffer, meaning its value in that buffer can be different from the value in other buffers. See Section 30.2.4 [Locals], page 348.

15.1 Creating and Selecting Buffers

C-x b *buffer* RET
> Select or create a buffer named *buffer* (switch-to-buffer).

C-x 4 b *buffer* RET
> Similar, but select *buffer* in another window (switch-to-buffer-other-window).

C-x 5 b *buffer* RET
> Similar, but select *buffer* in a separate frame (switch-to-buffer-other-frame).

To select the buffer named *bufname*, type C-x b *bufname* RET. This runs the command switch-to-buffer with argument *bufname*. You can use completion on an abbreviation for the buffer name you want (see Section 5.3 [Completion], page 39). An empty argument to C-x b specifies the most recently selected buffer that is not displayed in any window.

Most buffers are created by visiting files, or by Emacs commands that want to display some text, but you can also create a buffer explicitly by typing C-x b *bufname* RET. This makes a new, empty buffer which is not visiting any file, and selects it for editing. Such buffers are used for making notes to yourself. If you try to save one, you are asked for the file name to use. The new buffer's major mode is determined by the value of default-major-mode (see Chapter 18 [Major Modes], page 161).

Note that C-x C-f, and any other command for visiting a file, can also be used to switch to an existing file-visiting buffer. See Section 14.2 [Visiting], page 104.

15.2 Listing Existing Buffers

C-x C-b   List the existing buffers (list-buffers).

To display a list of all the buffers that exist, type C-x C-b. Each line in the list shows one buffer's name, major mode and visited file. The buffers are listed in the order, most recently visited first.

'*' at the beginning of a line indicates the buffer is "modified". If several buffers are modified, it may be time to save some with C-x s (see Section 14.3 [Saving], page 107). '%' indicates a read-only buffer. '.' marks the selected buffer. Here is an example of a buffer list:

```
MR Buffer          Size  Mode            File
-- ------          ----  ----            ----
.* emacs.tex       383402 Texinfo        /u2/emacs/man/emacs.tex
   *Help*          1287   Fundamental
   files.el        23076 Emacs-Lisp      /u2/emacs/lisp/files.el
 % RMAIL           64042 RMAIL           /u/rms/RMAIL
*% man             747    Dired           /u2/emacs/man/
   net.emacs       343885 Fundamental    /u/rms/net.emacs
   fileio.c        27691 C               /u2/emacs/src/fileio.c
   NEWS            67340 Text            /u2/emacs/etc/NEWS
   *scratch*       0  Lisp Interaction
```

Note that the buffer '*Help*' was made by a help request; it is not visiting any file. The buffer man was made by Dired on the directory '/u2/emacs/man/'.

15.3 Miscellaneous Buffer Operations

C-x C-q   Toggle read-only status of buffer (vc-toggle-read-only).

M-x rename-buffer RET *name* RET
> Change the name of the current buffer.

M-x rename-uniquely
> Rename the current buffer by adding '<*number*>' to the end.

M-x view-buffer RET *buffer* RET
> Scroll through buffer *buffer*.

A buffer can be *read-only*, which means that commands to change its contents are not allowed. The mode line indicates read-only buffers with '%%' or '%*' near the left margin. Read-only buffers are usually made by subsystems such as Dired and Rmail that have special commands to operate on the text; also by visiting a file whose access control says you cannot write it.

If you wish to make changes in a read-only buffer, use the command C-x C-q (vc-toggle-read-only). It makes a read-only buffer writable, and makes a writable buffer read-only. In most cases, this works by setting the variable buffer-read-only, which has a local value in each buffer and makes the buffer read-only if its value is non-nil. If the file is maintained with version control, C-x C-q works through the version control system to change the read-only status of the file as well as the buffer. See Section 14.7 [Version Control], page 116.

M-x rename-buffer changes the name of the current buffer. Specify the new name as a minibuffer argument. There is no default. If you specify a name that is in use for some other buffer, an error happens and no renaming is done.

M-x rename-uniquely renames the current buffer to a similar name with a numeric suffix added to make it both different and unique. This command does not need an argument. It is useful for creating multiple shell buffers: if you rename the '*Shell*' buffer, then do M-x shell again, it makes a new shell buffer named '*Shell*'; meanwhile, the old shell buffer continues to exist under its new name. This method is also good for mail buffers, compilation buffers, and most Emacs features that create special buffers with particular names.

M-x view-buffer is much like M-x view-file (see Section 14.10 [Misc File Ops], page 131) except that it examines an already existing Emacs buffer. View mode provides commands for scrolling through the buffer conveniently but not for changing it. When you exit View mode, the value of point that resulted from your perusal remains in effect.

The commands `M-x append-to-buffer` and `M-x insert-buffer` can be used to copy text from one buffer to another. See Section 9.3 [Accumulating Text], page 66.

15.4 Killing Buffers

If you continue an Emacs session for a while, you may accumulate a large number of buffers. You may then find it convenient to *kill* the buffers you no longer need. On most operating systems, killing a buffer releases its space back to the operating system so that other programs can use it. Here are some commands for killing buffers:

`C-x k` *bufname* `RET`
>   Kill buffer *bufname* (`kill-buffer`).

`M-x kill-some-buffers`
>   Offer to kill each buffer, one by one.

`C-x k` (`kill-buffer`) kills one buffer, whose name you specify in the minibuffer. The default, used if you type just `RET` in the minibuffer, is to kill the current buffer. If you kill the current buffer, another buffer is selected; one that has been selected recently but does not appear in any window now. If you ask to kill a file-visiting buffer that is modified (has unsaved editing), then you must confirm with `yes` before the buffer is killed.

The command `M-x kill-some-buffers` asks about each buffer, one by one. An answer of `y` means to kill the buffer. Killing the current buffer or a buffer containing unsaved changes selects a new buffer or asks for confirmation just like `kill-buffer`.

The buffer menu feature (see Section 15.5 [Several Buffers], page 136) is also convenient for killing various buffers.

If you want to do something special every time a buffer is killed, you can add hook functions to the hook `kill-buffer-hook` (see Section 30.2.3 [Hooks], page 347).

15.5 Operating on Several Buffers

The *buffer-menu* facility is like a "Dired for buffers"; it allows you to request operations on various Emacs buffers by editing an Emacs buffer containing a list of them. You can save buffers, kill them (here called *deleting* them, for consistency with Dired), or display them.

`M-x buffer-menu`
>   Begin editing a buffer listing all Emacs buffers.

The command `buffer-menu` writes a list of all Emacs buffers into the buffer '*Buffer List*', and selects that buffer in Buffer Menu mode. The buffer is read-only, and can be changed only through the special commands described in this section. The usual Emacs cursor motion commands can be used in the '*Buffer List*' buffer. The following commands apply to the buffer described on the current line.

d   Request to delete (kill) the buffer, then move down. The request shows as a 'D' on the line, before the buffer name. Requested deletions take place when you type the x command.

C-d   Like d but move up afterwards instead of down.

s   Request to save the buffer. The request shows as an 'S' on the line. Requested saves take place when you type the x command. You may request both saving and deletion for the same buffer.

x   Perform previously requested deletions and saves.

u   Remove any request made for the current line, and move down.

DEL   Move to previous line and remove any request made for that line.

The d, C-d, s and u commands to add or remove flags also move down (or up) one line. They accept a numeric argument as a repeat count.

These commands operate immediately on the buffer listed on the current line:

~   Mark the buffer "unmodified". The command ~ does this immediately when you type it.

%   Toggle the buffer's read-only flag. The command % does this immediately when you type it.

t   Visit the buffer as a tags table. See Section 21.12.3 [Select Tags Table], page 219.

There are also commands to select another buffer or buffers:

q   Quit the buffer menu—immediately display the most recent formerly visible buffer in its place.

RET
f   Immediately select this line's buffer in place of the '*Buffer List*' buffer.

o   Immediately select this line's buffer in another window as if by C-x 4 b, leaving '*Buffer List*' visible.

C-o   Immediately display this line's buffer in another window, but don't select the window.

1   Immediately select this line's buffer in a full-screen window.

2   Immediately set up two windows, with this line's buffer in
             one, and the previously selected buffer (aside from the buffer
             '*Buffer List*') in the other.

m   Mark this line's buffer to be displayed in another window if you
             exit with the v command. The request shows as a '>' at the
             beginning of the line. (A single buffer may not have both a
             delete request and a display request.)

v   Immediately select this line's buffer, and also display in other
             windows any buffers previously marked with the m command. If
             you have not marked any buffers, this command is equivalent to
             1.

All that `buffer-menu` does directly is create and switch to a suitable
buffer, and turn on Buffer Menu mode. Everything else described above is
implemented by the special commands provided in Buffer Menu mode. One
consequence of this is that you can switch from the '*Buffer List*' buffer
to another Emacs buffer, and edit there. You can reselect the '*Buffer
List*' buffer later, to perform the operations already requested, or you can
kill it, or pay no further attention to it.

The only difference between `buffer-menu` and `list-buffers` is that
`buffer-menu` switches to the '*Buffer List*' buffer in the selected window;
`list-buffers` displays it in another window. If you run `list-buffers` (that
is, type C-x C-b) and select the buffer list manually, you can use all of the
commands described here.

The buffer '*Buffer List*' is not updated automatically when buffers
are created and killed; its contents are just text. If you have created, deleted
or renamed buffers, the way to update '*Buffer List*' to show what you
have done is to type g (`revert-buffer`) or repeat the `buffer-menu` command.

15.6 Indirect Buffers

An *indirect buffer* shares the text of some other buffer, which is called
the *base buffer* of the indirect buffer. In some ways it is the analogue, for
buffers, of a symbolic link between files.

M-x make-indirect-buffer *base-buffer* RET *indirect-name* RET
             Create an indirect buffer named *indirect-name* whose base buffer
             is *base-buffer*.

The text of the indirect buffer is always identical to the text of its base
buffer; changes made by editing either one are visible immediately in the

other. But in all other respects, the indirect buffer and its base buffer are completely separate. They have different names, different values of point, different narrowing, different markers, different major modes, and different local variables.

An indirect buffer cannot visit a file, but its base buffer can. If you try to save the indirect buffer, that actually works by saving the base buffer. Killing the base buffer effectively kills the indirect buffer, but killing an indirect buffer has no effect on its base buffer.

One way to use indirect buffers is to display multiple views of an outline. See Section 20.8.4 [Outline Views], page 183.

16 Multiple Windows

Emacs can split a frame into two or many windows. Multiple windows can display parts of different buffers, or different parts of one buffer. Multiple frames always imply multiple windows, because each frame has its own set of windows. Each window belongs to one and only one frame.

16.1 Concepts of Emacs Windows

Each Emacs window displays one Emacs buffer at any time. A single buffer may appear in more than one window; if it does, any changes in its text are displayed in all the windows where it appears. But the windows showing the same buffer can show different parts of it, because each window has its own value of point.

At any time, one of the windows is the *selected window*; the buffer this window is displaying is the current buffer. The terminal's cursor shows the location of point in this window. Each other window has a location of point as well, but since the terminal has only one cursor there is no way to show where those locations are. When multiple frames are visible in X Windows, each frame has a cursor which appears in the frame's selected window. The cursor in the selected frame is solid; the cursor in other frames is a hollow box.

Commands to move point affect the value of point for the selected Emacs window only. They do not change the value of point in any other Emacs window, even one showing the same buffer. The same is true for commands such as C-x b to change the selected buffer in the selected window; they do not affect other windows at all. However, there are other commands such as C-x 4 b that select a different window and switch buffers in it. Also, all commands that display information in a window, including (for example) C-h f (describe-function) and C-x C-b (list-buffers), work by switching buffers in a nonselected window without affecting the selected window.

When multiple windows show the same buffer, they can have different regions, because they can have different values of point. This means that in Transient Mark mode, each window highlights a different part of the buffer. The part that is highlighted in the selected window is the region that editing commands use.

Each window has its own mode line, which displays the buffer name, modification status and major and minor modes of the buffer that is displayed in the window. See Section 1.3 [Mode Line], page 17, for full details on the mode line.

16.2 Splitting Windows

C-x 2   Split the selected window into two windows, one above the other
            (`split-window-vertically`).

C-x 3   Split the selected window into two windows positioned side by
            side (`split-window-horizontally`).

C-Mouse-2

            In the mode line or scroll bar of a window, split that window.

The command C-x 2 (`split-window-vertically`) breaks the selected
window into two windows, one above the other. Both windows start out
displaying the same buffer, with the same value of point. By default the two
windows each get half the height of the window that was split; a numeric
argument specifies how many lines to give to the top window.

C-x 3 (`split-window-horizontally`) breaks the selected window into
two side-by-side windows. A numeric argument specifies how many columns
to give the one on the left. A line of vertical bars separates the two windows.
Windows that are not the full width of the screen have mode lines, but they
are truncated; also, they do not always appear in inverse video, because
the Emacs display routines have not been taught how to display a region of
inverse video that is only part of a line on the screen.

You can split a window horizontally or vertically by clicking C-Mouse-2
in the mode line or the scroll bar. The line of splitting goes through the place
where you click: if you click on the mode line, the new scroll bar goes above
the spot; if you click in the scroll bar, the mode line of the split window is
side by side with your click.

When a window is less than the full width, text lines too long to fit
are frequent. Continuing all those lines might be confusing. The variable
`truncate-partial-width-windows` can be set non-nil to force truncation
in all windows less than the full width of the screen, independent of the
buffer being displayed and its value for `truncate-lines`. See Section 4.8
[Continuation Lines], page 33.

Horizontal scrolling is often used in side-by-side windows. See Chapter 11
[Display], page 75.

If `split-window-keep-point` is non-nil, C-x 2 tries to avoid shifting any
text on the screen by putting point in whichever window happens to contain
the screen line the cursor is already on. The default is that `split-window-keep-point` is non-nil on slow terminals.

16.3 Using Other Windows

C-x o   Select another window (`other-window`). That is o, not zero.

C-M-v   Scroll the next window (`scroll-other-window`).

M-x compare-windows
             Find next place where the text in the selected window does not
             match the text in the next window.

Mouse-1   Mouse-1, in a window's mode line, selects that window but does
             not move point in it (`mouse-select-region`).

To select a different window, click with Mouse-1 on its mode line. With
the keyboard, you can switch windows by typing C-x o (`other-window`).
That is an o, for 'other', not a zero. When there are more than two windows,
this command moves through all the windows in a cyclic order, generally top
to bottom and left to right. After the rightmost and bottommost window,
it goes back to the one at the upper left corner. A numeric argument means
to move several steps in the cyclic order of windows. A negative argument
moves around the cycle in the opposite order. When the minibuffer is active,
the minibuffer is the last window in the cycle; you can switch from the
minibuffer window to one of the other windows, and later switch back and
finish supplying the minibuffer argument that is requested. See Section 5.2
[Minibuffer Edit], page 38.

The usual scrolling commands (see Chapter 11 [Display], page 75) apply to the selected window only, but there is one command to scroll the
next window. C-M-v (`scroll-other-window`) scrolls the window that C-x
o would select. It takes arguments, positive and negative, like C-v. (In
the minibuffer, C-M-v scrolls the window that contains the minibuffer help
display, if any, rather than the next window in the standard cyclic order.)

The command M-x compare-windows lets you compare two files or buffers
visible in two windows, by moving through them to the next mismatch. See
Section 14.9 [Comparing Files], page 130, for details.

16.4 Displaying in Another Window

C-x 4 is a prefix key for commands that select another window (splitting
the window if there is only one) and select a buffer in that window. Different
C-x 4 commands have different ways of finding the buffer to select.

C-x 4 b *bufname* RET
             Select buffer *bufname* in another window. This runs `switch-
             to-buffer-other-window`.

C-x 4 C-o *bufname* RET
             Display buffer *bufname* in another window, but don't select that
             buffer or that window. This runs `display-buffer`.

`C-x 4 f` *filename* `RET`
>   Visit file *filename* and select its buffer in another window. This
>   runs `find-file-other-window`. See Section 14.2 [Visiting],
>   page 104.

`C-x 4 d` *directory* `RET`
>   Select a Dired buffer for directory *directory* in another win-
>   dow. This runs `dired-other-window`. See Chapter 27 [Dired],
>   page 287.

`C-x 4 m`   Start composing a mail message in another window. This runs
>   `mail-other-window`; its same-window analogue is `C-x m` (see
>   Chapter 25 [Sending Mail], page 261).

`C-x 4 .`   Find a tag in the current tags table, in another window. This
>   runs `find-tag-other-window`, the multiple-window variant of
>   `M-.` (see Section 21.12 [Tags], page 216).

`C-x 4 r` *filename* `RET`
>   Visit file *filename* read-only, and select its buffer in another win-
>   dow. This runs `find-file-read-only-other-window`. See Sec-
>   tion 14.2 [Visiting], page 104.

16.5 Forcing Display in the Same Window

Certain Emacs commands switch to a specific buffer with special contents. For example, `M-x shell` switches to a buffer named '`*Shell*`'. By
convention, all these commands are written to pop up the buffer in a separate window. But you can specify that certain of these buffers should appear
in the selected window.

If you add a buffer name to the list `same-window-buffer-names`, the
effect is that such commands display that particular buffer by switching to
it in the selected window. For example, if you add the element `"*grep*"`
to the list, the `grep` command will display its output buffer in the selected
window.

The default value of `same-window-buffer-names` is not `nil`. It specifies
the buffers '`*info*`', '`*mail*`' and '`*shell*`'. This is why `M-x shell` normally switches to the '`*shell*`' buffer in the selected window. If you delete
this element from the value of `same-window-buffer-names`, the behavior of
`M-x shell` will change—it will pop up the buffer in another window instead.

You can specify these buffers more generally with the variable `same-
window-regexps`. Set it to a list of regular expressions; then any buffer whose
name matches one of those regular expressions is displayed by switching to
it in the selected window. (Once again, this applies only to buffers that
normally get displayed for you in a separate window.) The default value of
this variable specifies Telnet and rlogin buffers.

An analogous feature lets you specify buffers which should be displayed in their own individual frames. See Section 17.8 [Special Buffer Frames], page 152.

16.6 Deleting and Rearranging Windows

C-x 0   Delete the selected window (`delete-window`). That is a zero.

C-x 1   Delete all windows in the selected frame except the selected window (`delete-other-windows`).

C-x ^   Make selected window taller (`enlarge-window`).

C-x }   Make selected window wider (`enlarge-window-horizontally`).

Drag-Mouse-1
             Dragging a window's mode line up or down with Mouse-1 changes window heights.

Mouse-2   Mouse-2 in a window's mode line deletes all other windows in the frame (`mouse-delete-other-windows`).

Mouse-3   Mouse-3 in a window's mode line deletes that window (`mouse-delete-window`).

To delete a window, type C-x 0 (`delete-window`). (That is a zero.) The space occupied by the deleted window is given to an adjacent window (but not the minibuffer window, even if that is active at the time). Once a window is deleted, its attributes are forgotten; only restoring a window configuration can bring it back. Deleting the window has no effect on the buffer it used to display; the buffer continues to exist, and you can select it in any window with C-x b.

C-x 1 (`delete-other-windows`) is more powerful than C-x 0; it deletes all the windows except the selected one (and the minibuffer); the selected window expands to use the whole frame except for the echo area.

You can also delete a window by clicking on its mode line with Mouse-2, and expand a window to fill its frame by clicking on its mode line with Mouse-3.

The easiest way to adjust window heights is with a mouse. If you press Mouse-1 on a mode line, you can drag that mode line up or down, changing the heights of the windows above and below it.

To readjust the division of space among vertically adjacent windows, use C-x ^ (`enlarge-window`). It makes the currently selected window get one line bigger, or as many lines as is specified with a numeric argument. With a negative argument, it makes the selected window smaller. C-x } (`enlarge-window-horizontally`) makes the selected window wider by the specified number of columns. The extra screen space given to a window comes from one of its neighbors, if that is possible. If this makes any window too small, it is deleted and its space is given to an adjacent window. The minimum size is specified by the variables `window-min-height` and `window-min-width`.

See Section 5.2 [Minibuffer Edit], page 38, for information about the Resize-Minibuffer mode, which automatically changes the size of the mini-buffer window to fit the text in the minibuffer.

17 Frames and X Windows

When using the X Window System, you can create multiple windows at the X level in a single Emacs session. Each X window that belongs to Emacs displays a *frame* which can contain one or several Emacs windows. A frame initially contains a single general-purpose Emacs window which you can subdivide vertically or horizontally into smaller windows. A frame normally contains its own echo area and minibuffer, but you can make frames that don't have these—they use the echo area and minibuffer of another frame.

Editing you do in one frame also affects the other frames. For instance, if you put text in the kill ring in one frame, you can yank it in another frame. If you exit Emacs through C-x C-c in one frame, it terminates all the frames. To delete just one frame, use C-x 5 0.

To avoid confusion, we reserve the word "window" for the subdivisions that Emacs implements, and never use it to refer to a frame.

17.1 Mouse Commands for Editing

The mouse commands for selecting and copying a region are mostly compatible with the xterm program. You can use the same mouse commands for copying between Emacs and other X client programs.

Mouse-1   Move point to where you click (mouse-set-point). This is normally the left button.

Drag-Mouse-1

     Set the region to the text you select by dragging, and copy it to the kill ring (mouse-set-region). You can specify both ends of the region with this single command.

     If you move the mouse off the top or bottom of the window while dragging, the window scrolls at a steady rate until you move the mouse back into the window. This way, you can select regions that don't fit entirely on the screen.

Mouse-2   Yank the last killed text, where you click (mouse-yank-at-click). This is normally the middle button.

Mouse-3   This command, mouse-save-then-kill, has several functions depending on where you click and the status of the region.

     The most basic case is when you click Mouse-1 in one place and then Mouse-3 in another. This selects the text between those two positions as the region. It also copies the new region to the kill ring, so that you can copy it to someplace else.

     If you click Mouse-1, scroll with the scroll bar, and then click Mouse-3, it remembers where point was before scrolling (where you put it with Mouse-1), and uses that position as the other end of the region. This is so that you can select a region that doesn't fit entirely on the screen.

More generally, if you do not have a highlighted region, Mouse-3 selects the text between point and the click position as the region. It does this by setting the mark where point was, and moving point to where you click.

If you have a highlighted region, or if the region was set just before by dragging button 1, Mouse-3 adjusts the nearer end of the region by moving it to where you click. The adjusted region's text also replaces the old region's text in the kill ring.

If you originally specified the region using a double or triple Mouse-1, so that the region is defined to consist of entire words or lines, then adjusting the region with Mouse-3 also proceeds by entire words or lines.

If you use Mouse-3 a second time consecutively, at the same place, that kills the region already selected.

Double-Mouse-1
:   This key sets the region around the word which you click on.

Double-Drag-Mouse-1
:   This key selects a region made up of the words that you drag across.

Triple-Mouse-1
:   This key sets the region around the line which you click on.

Triple-Drag-Mouse-1
:   This key selects a region made up of the lines that you drag across.

The simplest way to kill text with the mouse is to press Mouse-1 at one end, then press Mouse-3 twice at the other end. See Section 9.1 [Killing], page 61. To copy the text into the kill ring without deleting it from the buffer, press Mouse-3 just once—or just drag across the text with Mouse-1. Then you can copy it elsewhere by yanking it.

To yank the killed or copied text somewhere else, move the mouse there and press Mouse-2. See Section 9.2 [Yanking], page 63. However, if mouse-yank-at-point is non-nil, Mouse-2 yanks at point. Then it does not matter precisely where you click; all that matters is which window you click on. The default value is nil. This variable also effects yanking the secondary selection.

To copy text to another X window, kill it or save it in the kill ring. Under X, this also sets the *primary selection*. Then use the "paste" or "yank" command of the program operating the other window to insert the text from the selection.

To copy text from another X window, use the "cut" or "copy" command of the program operating the other window, to select the text you want. Then yank it in Emacs with `C-y` or `Mouse-2`.

When Emacs puts text into the kill ring, or rotates text to the front of the kill ring, it sets the *primary selection* in the X server. This is how other X clients can access the text. Emacs also stores the text in the cut buffer, but only if the text is short enough (`x-cut-buffer-max` specifies the maximum number of characters); putting long strings in the cut buffer can be slow.

The commands to yank the first entry in the kill ring actually check first for a primary selection in another program; after that, they check for text in the cut buffer. If neither of those sources provides text to yank, the kill ring contents are used.

17.2 Secondary Selection

The *secondary selection* is another way of selecting text using X. It does not use point or the mark, so you can use it to kill text without setting point or the mark.

`M-Drag-Mouse-1`

> Set the secondary selection, with one end at the place where you press down the button, and the other end at the place where you release it (`mouse-set-secondary`). The highlighting appears and changes as you drag.
>
> If you move the mouse off the top or bottom of the window while dragging, the window scrolls at a steady rate until you move the mouse back into the window. This way, you can mark regions that don't fit entirely on the screen.

`M-Mouse-1`

> Set one endpoint for the *secondary selection* (`mouse-start-secondary`).

`M-Mouse-3`

> Make a secondary selection, using the place specified with `M-Mouse-1` as the other end (`mouse-secondary-save-then-kill`). A second click at the same place kills the secondary selection just made.

`M-Mouse-2`

> Insert the secondary selection where you click (`mouse-kill-secondary`). This places point at the end of the yanked text.

Double or triple clicking of M-Mouse-1 operates on words and lines, much like Mouse-1.

If mouse-yank-at-point is non-nil, M-Mouse-2 yanks at point. Then it does not matter precisely where you click; all that matters is which window you click on. See Section 17.1 [Mouse Commands], page 147.

17.3 Following References with the Mouse

Some Emacs buffers display lists of various sorts. These include lists of files, of buffers, of possible completions, of matches for a pattern, and so on.

Since yanking text into these buffers is not very useful, most of them define Mouse-2 specially, as a command to use or view the item you click on.

For example, if you click Mouse-2 on a file name in a Dired buffer, you visit the that file. If you click Mouse-2 on an error message in the '*Compilation*' buffer, you go to the source code for that error message. If you click Mouse-2 on a completion in the '*Completions*' buffer, you choose that completion.

You can usually tell when Mouse-2 has this special sort of meaning because the sensitive text highlights when you move the mouse over it.

17.4 Mouse Clicks for Menus

Mouse clicks modified with the CONTROL bring up menus.

C-Mouse-1

> This menu is for specifying the frame's lefault font.

C-Mouse-2

> This menu is for specifying faces and)ther text properties for editing formatted text. See Section 20.11 [Formatted Text], page 190.

C-Mouse-3

> This menu is mode-specific. For mcst modes, this menu has the same items as all the mode-specific menu bar menus put together. Some modes may specify a different menu for this button.[1]

---

[1] Some systems use Mouse-3 for a mode-specific menu. We took a survey of users, and found they preferred to keep Mouse-3 for selecting and killing regions. Hence the decision to use C-Mouse-3 for this menu.

17.5 Mode Line Mouse Commands

You can use mouse clicks on window mode lines to select and manipulate windows.

Mouse-1   Mouse-1 on a mode line selects the window above. By dragging Mouse-1 on the mode line, you can move it, thus changing the height of the windows above and below.

Mouse-2   Mouse-2 on a mode line expands that window to fill its frame.

Mouse-3   Mouse-3 on a mode line deletes the window above.

C-Mouse-2

C-Mouse-2 on a mode line splits the window above horizontally, above the place in the mode line where you click.

C-Mouse-2 on a scroll bar splits the corresponding window vertically. See Section 16.2 [Split Window], page 142.

17.6 Creating Frames

The prefix key C-x 5 is analogous to C-x 4, with parallel subcommands. The difference is that C-x 5 commands create a new frame rather than just a new window in the selected frame (See Section 16.4 [Pop Up Window], page 143). If an existing visible or iconified frame already displays the requested material, these commands use the existing frame, after raising or deiconifying as necessary.

The various C-x 5 commands differ in how they find or create the buffer to select:

C-x 5 2   Create a new frame (make-frame).

C-x 5 b *bufname* RET

Select buffer *bufname* in another window. This runs switch-to-buffer-other-frame.

C-x 5 f *filename* RET

Visit file *filename* and select its buffer in another frame. This runs find-file-other-frame. See Section 14.2 [Visiting], page 104.

C-x 5 d *directory* RET

Select a Dired buffer for directory *directory* in another frame. This runs dired-other-frame. See Chapter 27 [Dired], page 287.

C-x 5 m   Start composing a mail message in another frame. This runs mail-other-frame. It is the other-frame variant of C-x m. See Chapter 25 [Sending Mail], page 261.

C-x 5 .   Find a tag in the current tag table in another frame. This runs
               `find-tag-other-frame`, the multiple-frame variant of M-.. See
               Section 21.12 [Tags], page 216.

C-x 5 r *filename* RET
               Visit file *filename* read-only, and select its buffer in another
               frame. This runs `find-file-read-only-other-frame`. See
               Section 14.2 [Visiting], page 104.

You can control the appearance of new frames you create by setting
the frame parameters in `default-frame-alist`. You can use the variable `initial-frame-alist` to specify parameters that affect only the initial
frame. See section "Initial Parameters" in *The Emacs Lisp Manual*, for more
information.

17.7 Multiple Displays

A single Emacs can talk to more than one X Windows display. Initially, Emacs uses just one display—the one specified with the `DISPLAY` environment variable or with the '`--display`' option (see Section A.2 [Initial
Options], page 390). To connect to another display, use the command `make-`
`frame-on-display`:

M-x make-frame-on-display RET *display* RET
               Create a new frame on display *display*.

A single X server can handle more than one screen. When you open
frames on two screens belonging to one server, Emacs knows they share a
single keyboard, and it treats all the commands arriving from these screens
as a single stream of input.

When you open frames on different X servers, Emacs makes a separate
input stream for each server. This way, two users can type simultaneously
on the two displays, and Emacs will not garble their input. Each server also
has its own selected frame. The commands you enter with a particular X
server apply to that server's selected frame.

Despite these features, people using the same Emacs job from different
displays can still interfere with each other if they are not careful. For example, if any one types C-x C-c, that exits the Emacs job for all of them!

17.8 Special Buffer Frames

You can make certain chosen buffers, for which Emacs normally creates a
second window when you have just one window, appear in special frames of
their own. To do this, set the variable `special-display-buffer-names` to a
list of buffer names; any buffer whose name is in that list automatically gets

a special frame, when an Emacs command wants to display it "in another window."

For example, if you set the variable this way,

```
(setq special-display-buffer-names
      '("*Completions*" "*grep*" "*tex-shell*"))
```

then completion lists, `grep` output and the TEX mode shell buffer get individual frames of their own. These frames, and the windows in them, are never automatically split or reused for any other buffers. They continue to show the buffers they were created for, unless you alter them by hand. Killing the special buffer deletes its frame automatically.

More generally, you can set `special-display-regexps` to a list of regular expressions; then a buffer gets its own frame if its name matches any of those regular expressions. (Once again, this applies only to buffers that normally get displayed for you in a separate window.)

The variable `special-display-frame-alist` specifies the frame parameters for these frames. It has a default value, so you don't need to set it.

For those who know Lisp, an element of `special-display-buffer-names` or `special-display-regexps` can also be a list. Then the first element is the buffer name or regular expression; the rest of the list specifies how to create the frame. It can be an association list specifying frame parameter values; these values take precedence over parameter values specified in `special-display-frame-alist`. Alternatively, it can have this form:

    (*function args...*)

where *function* is a symbol. Then the frame is constructed by calling *function*; its first argument is the buffer, and its remaining arguments are *args*.

17.9 Setting Frame Parameters

This section describes commands for altering the display style and window management behavior of the selected frame.

`M-x set-foreground-color` RET *color* RET
> Specify color *color* for the foreground of the selected frame.

`M-x set-background-color` RET *color* RET
> Specify color *color* for the background of the selected frame. This changes the foreground color of the `modeline` face also, so that it remains in inverse video compared with the default.

`M-x set-cursor-color` RET *color* RET
> Specify color *color* for the cursor of the selected frame.

`M-x set-mouse-color RET` *color* `RET`

> Specify color *color* for the mouse cursor when it is over the selected frame.

`M-x set-border-color RET` *color* `RET`

> Specify color *color* for the border of the selected frame.

`M-x list-colors-display`

> Display the defined color names and show what the colors look like. This command is somewhat slow.

`M-x auto-raise-mode`

> Toggle whether or not the selected frame should auto-raise. Auto-raise means that every time you move the mouse onto the frame, it raises the frame.

> Note that this auto-raise feature is implemented by Emacs itself. Some window managers also implement auto-raise. If you enable auto-raise for Emacs frames in your X window manager, it should work, but it is beyond Emacs's control and therefore `auto-raise-mode` has no effect on it.

`M-x auto-lower-mode`

> Toggle whether or not the selected frame should auto-lower. Auto-lower means that every time you move the mouse off of the frame, the frame moves to the bottom of the stack of X windows.

> The command `auto-lower-mode` has no effect on auto-lower implemented by the X window manager. To control that, you must use the appropriate window manager features.

`M-x set-default-font RET` *font* `RET`

> Specify font *font* as the default for the selected frame. See Section A.7 [Font X], page 396, for ways to list the available fonts on your system.

> You can also set a frame's default font through a pop-up menu. Press `C-Mouse-1` to activate this menu.

In Emacs versions that use an X toolkit, the color-setting and font-setting functions don't affect menus and the menu bar, since they are displayed by their own widget classes. To change the appearance of the menus and menu bar, you must use X resources (see Section A.12 [Resources X], page 401). See Section A.8 [Colors X], page 398, regarding colors. See Section A.7 [Font X], page 396, regarding choice of font.

For information on frame parameters and customization, see section "Frame Parameters" in *The Emacs Lisp Manual*.

17.10 Scroll Bars

When using X, Emacs normally makes a *scroll bar* at the right of each Emacs window. The scroll bar runs the height of the window, and shows a moving rectangular inner box which represents the portion of the buffer currently displayed. The entire height of the scroll bar represents the entire length of the buffer.

You can use `Mouse-2` (normally, the middle button) in the scroll bar to move or drag the inner box up and down. If you move it to the top of the scroll bar, you see the top of the buffer. If you move it to the bottom of the scroll bar, you see the bottom of the buffer.

The left and right buttons in the scroll bar scroll by controlled increments. `Mouse-1` (normally, the left button) moves the line at the level where you click up to the top of the window. `Mouse-3` (normally, the right button) moves the line at the top of the window down to the level where you click. By clicking repeatedly in the same place, you can scroll by the same distance over and over.

Aside from scrolling, you can also click `C-Mouse-2` in the scroll bar to split a window vertically. The split occurs on the line where you click.

You can enable or disable Scroll Bar mode with the command `M-x scroll-bar-mode`. With no argument, it toggles the use of scroll bars. With an argument, it turns use of scroll bars on if and only if the argument is positive. This command applies to all frames, including frames yet to be created. You can use the X resource 'verticalScrollBars' to control the initial setting of Scroll Bar mode. See Section A.12 [Resources X], page 401.

To enable or disable scroll bars for just the selected frame, use the `M-x toggle-scroll-bar` command.

17.11 Menu Bars

By default, each Emacs frame has a menu bar at the top which you can use to perform certain common operations. There's no need to describe them in detail here, as you can more easily see for yourself; also, we may change them and add to them in subsequent Emacs versions.

Each of the operations in the menu bar is bound to an ordinary Emacs command which you can invoke equally well with `M-x` or with its own key bindings. The menu lists one equivalent key binding (if the command has any) at the right margin. To see the command's name and documentation, type `C-h k` and then select the menu bar item you are interested in.

You can turn display of menu bars on or off with `M-x menu-bar-mode`. With no argument, this command toggles Menu Bar mode, a minor mode. With an argument, the command turns Menu Bar mode on if the argument

is positive, off if the argument is not positive. You can use the X resource
'menuBarLines' to control the initial setting of Menu Bar mode. See Section A.12 [Resources X], page 401.

17.12 Using Multiple Typefaces

When using Emacs with X, you can set up multiple styles of displaying
characters. The aspects of style that you can control are the type font, the
foreground color, the background color, and whether to underline. Emacs
19.29 does not support faces on MS-DOS, but future versions may support
them partially (see Appendix C [MS-DOS], page 409).

The way you control display style is by defining named *faces*. Each face
can specify a type font, a foreground color, a background color, and an
underline flag; but it does not have to specify all of them.

The style of display used for a given character in the text is determined by
combining several faces. Any aspect of the display style that isn't specified
by overlays or text properties comes from the frame itself.

Enriched mode, the mode for editing formatted text, includes several
commands and menus for specifying faces. See Section 20.11.4 [Format
Faces], page 192, for how to specify the font for text in the buffer. See
Section 20.11.5 [Format Colors], page 193, for how to specify the foreground
and background color.

To see what faces are currently defined, and what they look like, type
M-x list-faces-display. It's possible for a given face to look different in
different frames; this command shows the appearance in the frame in which
you type it. Here's a list of the standardly defined faces:

default   This face is used for ordinary text that doesn't specify any other
             face.

modeline   This face is used for mode lines. By default, it's set up as
             the inverse of the default face. See Section 11.6 [Display Vars],
             page 79.

highlight
             This face is used for highlighting portions of text, in various
             modes.

region   This face is used for displaying a selected region (when Transient
             Mark mode is enabled—see below).

secondary-selection
             This face is used for displaying a secondary selection (see Sec-
             tion 17.2 [Secondary Selection], page 149).

bold   This face uses a bold variant of the default font, if it has one.

italic   This face uses an italic variant of the default font, if it has one.

bold-italic

> This face uses a bold italic variant of the default font, if it has one.

underline

> This face underlines text.

When Transient Mark mode is enabled, the text of the region is highlighted when the mark is active. This uses the face named `region`; you can control the style of highlighting by changing the style of this face (see Section 17.13 [Modifying Faces], page 157). See Section 8.2 [Transient Mark], page 56, for more information about Transient Mark mode and activation and deactivation of the mark.

One easy way to use faces is to turn on Font-Lock mode. This minor mode, which is always local to a particular buffer, arranges to choose faces according to the syntax of the text you are editing. It can recognize comments and strings in most languages; in several languages, it can also recognize and properly highlight various other important constructs—for example, names of functions being defined.

Font-Lock mode is a minor mode. The command `M-x font-lock-mode` turns the mode on or off. The function `turn-on-font-lock` unconditionally enables Font-Lock mode. This is useful in mode-hook functions. For example, to enable Font-Lock mode whenever you edit a C file, you can do this:

```
(add-hook 'c-mode-hook 'turn-on-font-lock)
```

To get the full benefit of Font-Lock mode, you need to choose a default font which has bold, italic, and bold-italic variants; or else you need to have a color or grayscale screen. The variable `font-lock-display-type` specifies whether Font-Lock mode should use font styles, colors, or shades of gray to distinguish the various kinds of text. Emacs chooses the default value according to the characteristics of your display.

17.13 Modifying Faces

Here are the commands for changing the font of a face:

`M-x set-face-font` RET *face* RET *font* RET

> Change face *face* to use font *font*. See Section A.7 [Font X], page 396, for more information about font naming under X.

`M-x make-face-bold` RET *face* RET

> Convert face *face* to use a bold version of its current font.

`M-x make-face-italic` RET *face* RET

> Convert face *face* to use a italic version of its current font.

`M-x make-face-bold-italic RET` *face* `RET`
> Convert face *face* to use a bold-italic version of its current font.

`M-x make-face-unbold RET` *face* `RET`
> Convert face *face* to use a non-bold version of its current font.

`M-x make-face-unitalic RET` *face* `RET`
> Convert face *face* to use a non-italic version of its current font.

Here are the commands for setting the colors and underline flag of a face:

`M-x set-face-foreground RET` *face* `RET` *color* `RET`
> Use color *color* for the foreground of characters in face *face*.

`M-x set-face-background RET` *face* `RET` *color* `RET`
> Use color *color* for the background of characters in face *face*.
>
> On a black-and-white display, the colors you can use for the background are 'black', 'white', 'gray', 'gray1' and 'gray3'. Emacs supports the gray colors by using background stipple patterns instead of a color.

`M-x set-face-stipple RET` *face* `RET` *pattern* `RET`
> Use stipple pattern *pattern* for the background of characters in face *face*.

`M-x list-colors-display`
> Display the defined color names and show what the colors look like.

`M-x set-face-underline-p RET` *face* `RET` *flag* `RET`
> Specify whether to underline characters in face *face*.

`M-x invert-face RET` *face* `RET`
> Swap the foreground and background colors of face *face*.

`M-x modify-face RET` *face* `RET` *attributes...*
> Change various attributes of face *face*. This command prompts for all the attribute of the face, one attribute at a time. For the color and stipple attributes, the attribute's current value is the default—type just `RET` if you don't want to change that attribute. Type 'none' if you want to clear out the attribute.

You can also use X resources to specify attributes of particular faces. See Section A.12 [Resources X], page 401.

17.14 Miscellaneous X Window Features

The following commands let you create, delete and operate on frames:

C-z   To iconify the selected Emacs frame, type C-z (iconify-or-
             deiconify-frame). The normal meaning of C-z, to suspend
             Emacs, is not useful under a window system, so it has a different
             binding in that case.

             If you type this command on an Emacs frame's icon, it deiconi-
             fies the frame.

C-x 5 0   To delete the selected frame, type C-x 5 0 (delete-frame).
             This is not allowed if there is only one frame.

M-x transient-mark-mode
             Under X Windows, when Transient Mark mode is enabled,
             Emacs highlights the region when the mark is active. This
             feature is the main motive for using Transient Mark mode.
             To toggle the state of this mode, use the command M-x
             transient-mark-mode. See Chapter 8 [Mark], page 55.

18 Major Modes

Emacs provides many alternative *major modes*, each of which customizes Emacs for editing text of a particular sort. The major modes are mutually exclusive, and each buffer has one major mode at any time. The mode line normally shows the name of the current major mode, in parentheses (see Section 1.3 [Mode Line], page 17).

The least specialized major mode is called *Fundamental mode*. This mode has no mode-specific redefinitions or variable settings, so that each Emacs command behaves in its most general manner, and each option is in its default state. For editing text of a specific type that Emacs knows about, such as Lisp code or English text, you should switch to the appropriate major mode, such as Lisp mode or Text mode.

Selecting a major mode changes the meanings of a few keys to become more specifically adapted to the language being edited. The ones which are changed frequently are TAB, DEL, and LFD. The prefix key C-c normally contains mode-specific commands. In addition, the commands which handle comments use the mode to determine how comments are to be delimited. Many major modes redefine the syntactical properties of characters appearing in the buffer. See Section 30.6 [Syntax], page 366.

The major modes fall into three major groups. Lisp mode (which has several variants), C mode, Fortran mode and others are for specific programming languages. Text mode, Nroff mode, TEX mode and Outline mode are for editing English text. The remaining major modes are not intended for use on users' files; they are used in buffers created for specific purposes by Emacs, such as Dired mode for buffers made by Dired (see Chapter 27 [Dired], page 287), and Mail mode for buffers made by C-x m (see Chapter 25 [Sending Mail], page 261), and Shell mode for buffers used for communicating with an inferior shell process (see Section 29.2.2 [Interactive Shell], page 323).

Most programming language major modes specify that only blank lines separate paragraphs. This is to make the paragraph commands useful. (See Section 20.3 [Paragraphs], page 172.) They also cause Auto Fill mode to use the definition of TAB to indent the new lines it creates. This is because most lines in a program are usually indented. (See Chapter 19 [Indentation], page 165.)

18.1 How Major Modes are Chosen

You can select a major mode explicitly for the current buffer, but most of the time Emacs determines which mode to use based on the file name or on special text in the file.

Explicit selection of a new major mode is done with a M-x command. From the name of a major mode, add -mode to get the name of a command to select that mode. Thus, you can enter Lisp mode by executing M-x lisp-mode.

When you visit a file, Emacs usually chooses the right major mode based on the file's name. For example, files whose names end in '.c' are edited in C mode. The correspondence between file names and major mode is controlled by the variable auto-mode-alist. Its value is a list in which each element has the form

    (regexp . mode-function)

For example, one element normally found in the list has the form ("\\.c\\'" . c-mode), and it is responsible for selecting C mode for files whose names end in '.c'. (Note that '\\' is needed in Lisp syntax to include a '\' in the string, which is needed to suppress the special meaning of '.' in regexps.) The only practical way to change this variable is with Lisp code.

You can specify which major mode should be used for editing a certain file by a special sort of text in the first nonblank line of the file. The mode name should appear in this line both preceded and followed by '-*-'. Other text may appear on the line as well. For example,

    ;-*-Lisp-*-

tells Emacs to use Lisp mode. Such an explicit specification overrides any defaulting based on the file name. Note how the semicolon is used to make Lisp treat this line as a comment.

Another format of mode specification is

    -*-Mode: modename;-*-

which allows you to specify local variables as well, like this:

    -*- mode: modename; var: value; ... -*-

See Section 30.2.5 [File Variables], page 350, for more information about this.

When a file's contents begin with '#!', it can serve as an executable shell command, which works by running an interpreter named on the file's first line. The rest of the file is used as input to the interpreter.

When you visit such a file in Emacs, if the file's name does not specify a major mode, Emacs uses the interpreter name on the first line to choose a mode. If the first line is the name of a recognized interpreter program, such as 'perl' or 'tcl', Emacs uses a mode appropriate for programs for that interpreter. The variable interpreter-mode-alist specifies the correspondence between interpreter program names and major modes.

When you visit a file that does not specify a major mode to use, or when you create a new buffer with C-x b, the variable default-major-mode specifies which major mode to use. Normally its value is the symbol fundamental-mode, which specifies Fundamental mode. If default-major-mode is nil, the major mode is taken from the previously selected buffer.

If you change the major mode of a buffer, you can go back to the major mode Emacs would choose automatically: use the command M-x normal-mode to do this. This is the same function that find-file calls to choose the major mode. It also processes the file's local variables list if any.

19 Indentation

This chapter describes the Emacs commands that add, remove, or adjust indentation.

TAB   Indent current line "appropriately" in a mode-dependent fashion.

LFD   Perform RET followed by TAB (`newline-and-indent`).

M-^   Merge two lines (`delete-indentation`). This would cancel out the effect of LFD.

C-M-o   Split line at point; text on the line after point becomes a new line indented to the same column that it now starts in (`split-line`).

M-m   Move (forward or back) to the first nonblank character on the current line (`back-to-indentation`).

C-M-\   Indent several lines to same column (`indent-region`).

C-x TAB   Shift block of lines rigidly right or left (`indent-rigidly`).

M-i   Indent from point to the next prespecified tab stop column (`tab-to-tab-stop`).

M-x indent-relative
                Indent from point to under an indentation point in the previous line.

Most programming languages have some indentation convention. For Lisp code, lines are indented according to their nesting in parentheses. The same general idea is used for C code, though many details are different.

Whatever the language, to indent a line, use the TAB command. Each major mode defines this command to perform the sort of indentation appropriate for the particular language. In Lisp mode, TAB aligns the line according to its depth in parentheses. No matter where in the line you are when you type TAB, it aligns the line as a whole. In C mode, TAB implements a subtle and sophisticated indentation style that knows about many aspects of C syntax.

In Text mode, TAB runs the command `tab-to-tab-stop`, which indents to the next tab stop column. You can set the tab stops with M-x `edit-tab-stops`.

19.1 Indentation Commands and Techniques

To move over the indentation on a line, do M-m (`back-to-indentation`). This command, given anywhere on a line, positions point at the first nonblank character on the line.

To insert an indented line before the current line, do `C-a C-o TAB`. To make an indented line after the current line, use `C-e LFD`.

If you just want to insert a tab character in the buffer, you can type `C-q TAB`.

`C-M-o` (`split-line`) moves the text from point to the end of the line vertically down, so that the current line becomes two lines. `C-M-o` first moves point forward over any spaces and tabs. Then it inserts after point a newline and enough indentation to reach the same column point is on. Point remains before the inserted newline; in this regard, `C-M-o` resembles `C-o`.

To join two lines cleanly, use the `M-^` (`delete-indentation`) command. It deletes the indentation at the front of the current line, and the line boundary as well, replacing them with a single space. As a special case (useful for Lisp code) the single space is omitted if the characters to be joined are consecutive open parentheses or closing parentheses, or if the junction follows another newline. To delete just the indentation of a line, go to the beginning of the line and use `M-\` (`delete-horizontal-space`), which deletes all spaces and tabs around the cursor.

If you have a fill prefix, `M-^` deletes the fill prefix if it appears after the newline that is deleted. See Section 20.5.3 [Fill Prefix], page 176.

There are also commands for changing the indentation of several lines at once. `C-M-\` (`indent-region`) applies to all the lines that begin in the region; it indents each line in the "usual" way, as if you had typed `TAB` at the beginning of the line. A numeric argument specifies the column to indent to, and each line is shifted left or right so that its first nonblank character appears in that column. `C-x TAB` (`indent-rigidly`) moves all of the lines in the region right by its argument (left, for negative arguments). The whole group of lines moves rigidly sideways, which is how the command gets its name.

`M-x indent-relative` indents at point based on the previous line (actually, the last nonempty line). It inserts whitespace at point, moving point, until it is underneath an indentation point in the previous line. An indentation point is the end of a sequence of whitespace or the end of the line. If point is farther right than any indentation point in the previous line, the whitespace before point is deleted and the first indentation point then applicable is used. If no indentation point is applicable even then, `indent-relative` runs `tab-to-tab-stop` (see next section).

`indent-relative` is the definition of `TAB` in Indented Text mode. See Chapter 20 [Text], page 169.

See Section 20.11.6 [Format Indentation], page 194, for another way of specifying the indentation for part of your text.

19.2 Tab Stops

For typing in tables, you can use Text mode's definition of TAB, tab-to-tab-stop. This command inserts indentation before point, enough to reach the next tab stop column. If you are not in Text mode, this command can be found on the key M-i.

You can specify the tab stops used by M-i. They are stored in a variable called tab-stop-list, as a list of column-numbers in increasing order.

The convenient way to set the tab stops is with M-x edit-tab-stops, which creates and selects a buffer containing a description of the tab stop settings. You can edit this buffer to specify different tab stops, and then type C-c C-c to make those new tab stops take effect. In the tab stop buffer, C-c C-c runs the function edit-tab-stops-note-changes rather than its usual definition save-buffer. edit-tab-stops records which buffer was current when you invoked it, and stores the tab stops back in that buffer; normally all buffers share the same tab stops and changing them in one buffer affects all, but if you happen to make tab-stop-list local in one buffer then edit-tab-stops in that buffer will edit the local settings.

Here is what the text representing the tab stops looks like for ordinary tab stops every eight columns.

```
        :       :       :       :       :       :
0       1       2       3       4
012345678901234567890123456789012345678901234678
To install changes, type C-c C-c
```

The first line contains a colon at each tab stop. The remaining lines are present just to help you see where the colons are and know what to do.

Note that the tab stops that control tab-to-tab-stop have nothing to do with displaying tab characters in the buffer. See Section 11.6 [Display Vars], page 79, for more information on that.

19.3 Tabs vs. Spaces

Emacs normally uses both tabs and spaces to indent lines. If you prefer, all indentation can be made from spaces only. To request this, set indent-tabs-mode to nil. This is a per-buffer variable; altering the variable affects only the current buffer, but there is a default value which you can change as well. See Section 30.2.4 [Locals], page 348.

There are also commands to convert tabs to spaces or vice versa, always preserving the columns of all nonblank text. M-x tabify scans the region for sequences of spaces, and converts sequences of at least three spaces to tabs if that can be done without changing indentation. M-x untabify changes all tabs in the region to appropriate numbers of spaces.

20 Commands for Human Languages

The term *text* has two widespread meanings in our area of the computer field. One is data that is a sequence of characters. Any file that you edit with Emacs is text, in this sense of the word. The other meaning is more restrictive: a sequence of characters in a human language for humans to read (possibly after processing by a text formatter), as opposed to a program or commands for a program.

Human languages have syntactic/stylistic conventions that can be supported or used to advantage by editor commands: conventions involving words, sentences, paragraphs, and capital letters. This chapter describes Emacs commands for all of these things. There are also commands for *filling*, which means rearranging the lines of a paragraph to be approximately equal in length. The commands for moving over and killing words, sentences and paragraphs, while intended primarily for editing text, are also often useful for editing programs.

Emacs has several major modes for editing human language text. If the file contains text pure and simple, use Text mode, which customizes Emacs in small ways for the syntactic conventions of text. Outline mode provides special commands for operating on text with an outline structure. See Section 20.8 [Outline Mode], page 179.

For text which contains embedded commands for text formatters, Emacs has other major modes, each for a particular text formatter. Thus, for input to TeX, you would use TeX mode (see Section 20.9 [TeX Mode], page 184). For input to nroff, use Nroff mode.

Instead of using a text formatter, you can edit formatted text in WYSIWYG style ("what you see is what you get"), with Enriched mode. Then the formatting appears on the screen in Emacs while you edit. See Section 20.11 [Formatted Text], page 190.

20.1 Words

Emacs has commands for moving over or operating on words. By convention, the keys for them are all Meta characters.

M-f   Move forward over a word (`forward-word`).

M-b   Move backward over a word (`backward-word`).

M-d   Kill up to the end of a word (`kill-word`).

M-DEL   Kill back to the beginning of a word (`backward-kill-word`).

M-@   Mark the end of the next word (`mark-word`).

`M-t`   Transpose two words or drag a word across other words
             (`transpose-words`).

Notice how these keys form a series that parallels the character-based
`C-f`, `C-b`, `C-d`, `C-t` and DEL. `M-@` is cognate to `C-@`, which is an alias for
`C-SPC`.

The commands `M-f` (`forward-word`) and `M-b` (`backward-word`) move forward and backward over words. These Meta characters are thus analogous to the corresponding control characters, `C-f` and `C-b`, which move over single characters in the text. The analogy extends to numeric arguments, which serve as repeat counts. `M-f` with a negative argument moves backward, and `M-b` with a negative argument moves forward. Forward motion stops right after the last letter of the word, while backward motion stops right before the first letter.

`M-d` (`kill-word`) kills the word after point. To be precise, it kills everything from point to the place `M-f` would move to. Thus, if point is in the middle of a word, `M-d` kills just the part after point. If some punctuation comes between point and the next word, it is killed along with the word. (If you wish to kill only the next word but not the punctuation before it, simply do `M-f` to get the end, and kill the word backwards with `M-DEL`.) `M-d` takes arguments just like `M-f`.

`M-DEL` (`backward-kill-word`) kills the word before point. It kills everything from point back to where `M-b` would move to. If point is after the space in 'FOO, BAR', then 'FOO, ' is killed. (If you wish to kill just 'FOO', do `M-b` `M-d` instead of `M-DEL`.)

`M-t` (`transpose-words`) exchanges the word before or containing point with the following word. The delimiter characters between the words do not move. For example, 'FOO, BAR' transposes into 'BAR, FOO' rather than 'BAR FOO,'. See Section 13.2 [Transpose], page 97, for more on transposition and on arguments to transposition commands.

To operate on the next n words with an operation which applies between point and mark, you can either set the mark at point and then move over the words, or you can use the command `M-@` (`mark-word`) which does not move point, but sets the mark where `M-f` would move to. `M-@` accepts a numeric argument that says how many words to scan for the place to put the mark. In Transient Mark mode, this command activates the mark.

The word commands' understanding of syntax is completely controlled by the syntax table. Any character can, for example, be declared to be a word delimiter. See Section 30.6 [Syntax], page 366.

20.2 Sentences

The Emacs commands for manipulating sentences and paragraphs are mostly on Meta keys, so as to be like the word-handling commands.

M-a   Move back to the beginning of the sentence (backward-sentence).

M-e   Move forward to the end of the sentence (forward-sentence).

M-k   Kill forward to the end of the sentence (kill-sentence).

C-x DEL Kill back to the beginning of the sentence (backward-kill-sentence).

The commands M-a and M-e (backward-sentence and forward-sentence) move to the beginning and end of the current sentence, respectively. They were chosen to resemble C-a and C-e, which move to the beginning and end of a line. Unlike them, M-a and M-e if repeated or given numeric arguments move over successive sentences.

Moving backward over a sentence places point just before the first character of the sentence; moving forward places point right after the punctuation that ends the sentence. Neither one moves over the whitespace at the sentence boundary.

Just as C-a and C-e have a kill command, C-k, to go with them, so M-a and M-e have a corresponding kill command M-k (kill-sentence) which kills from point to the end of the sentence. With minus one as an argument it kills back to the beginning of the sentence. Larger arguments serve as a repeat count. There is also a command, C-x DEL (backward-kill-sentence), for killing back to the beginning of a sentence. This command is useful when you change your mind in the middle of composing text.

The sentence commands assume that you follow the American typist's convention of putting two spaces at the end of a sentence; they consider a sentence to end wherever there is a '.', '?' or '!' followed by the end of a line or two spaces, with any number of ')', ']', '’', or '"' characters allowed in between. A sentence also begins or ends wherever a paragraph begins or ends.

The variable sentence-end controls recognition of the end of a sentence. It is a regexp that matches the last few characters of a sentence, together with the whitespace following the sentence. Its normal value is

```
"[.?!][]\"’’)]*\\($\\|\t\\|  \\)[ \t\n]*"
```

This example is explained in the section on regexps. See Section 12.5 [Regexps], page 88.

If you want to use just one space between sentences, you should set sentence-end to this value:

```
"[.?!][]\"')]*\\($\\|\t\\| \\)[ \t\n]*"
```

You should also set the variable `sentence-end-double-space` to `nil` so that the fill commands expect and leave just one space at the end of a sentence. Note that this makes it impossible to distinguish between periods that end sentences and those that indicate abbreviations.

20.3 Paragraphs

The Emacs commands for manipulating paragraphs are also Meta keys.

M-{   Move back to previous paragraph beginning (`backward-paragraph`).

M-}   Move forward to next paragraph end (`forward-paragraph`).

M-h   Put point and mark around this or next paragraph (`mark-paragraph`).

M-{ moves to the beginning of the current or previous paragraph, while M-} moves to the end of the current or next paragraph. Blank lines and text formatter command lines separate paragraphs and are not considered part of any paragraph. Also, an indented line starts a new paragraph.

In major modes for programs (as opposed to Text mode), paragraphs begin and end only at blank lines. This makes the paragraph commands continue to be useful even though there are no paragraphs per se.

When there is a fill prefix, then paragraphs are delimited by all lines which don't start with the fill prefix. See Section 20.5 [Filling], page 174.

When you wish to operate on a paragraph, you can use the command M-h (`mark-paragraph`) to set the region around it. Thus, for example, M-h C-w kills the paragraph around or after point. The M-h command puts point at the beginning and mark at the end of the paragraph point was in. In Transient Mark mode, it activates the mark. If point is between paragraphs (in a run of blank lines, or at a boundary), the paragraph following point is surrounded by point and mark. If there are blank lines preceding the first line of the paragraph, one of these blank lines is included in the region.

The precise definition of a paragraph boundary is controlled by the variables `paragraph-separate` and `paragraph-start`. The value of `paragraph-start` is a regexp that should match any line that either starts or separates paragraphs. The value of `paragraph-separate` is another regexp that should match only lines that separate paragraphs without being part of any paragraph. Lines that start a new paragraph and are contained in it must match only `paragraph-start`, not `paragraph-separate`. For example, normally `paragraph-start` is `"^[ \t\n\f]"` and `paragraph-separate` is `"^[ \t\f]*$"`.

Normally it is desirable for page boundaries to separate paragraphs. The default values of these variables recognize the usual separator for pages.

20.4 Pages

Files are often thought of as divided into *pages* by the *formfeed* character (ASCII control-L, octal code 014). When you print hardcopy for a file, this character forces a page break; thus, each page of the file goes on a separate page on paper. Most Emacs commands treat the page-separator character just like any other character: you can insert it with C-q C-l, and delete it with DEL. Thus, you are free to paginate your file or not. However, since pages are often meaningful divisions of the file, Emacs provides commands to move over them and operate on them.

C-x [Move point to previous page boundary (backward-page).

C-x]   Move point to next page boundary (forward-page).

C-x C-p   Put point and mark around this page (or another page) (mark-page).

C-x l   Count the lines in this page (count-lines-page).

The C-x [(backward-page) command moves point to immediately after the previous page delimiter. If point is already right after a page delimiter, it skips that one and stops at the previous one. A numeric argument serves as a repeat count. The C-x] (forward-page) command moves forward past the next page delimiter.

The C-x C-p command (mark-page) puts point at the beginning of the current page and the mark at the end. The page delimiter at the end is included (the mark follows it). The page delimiter at the front is excluded (point follows it). C-x C-p C-w is a handy way to kill a page to move it elsewhere. If you move to another page delimiter with C-x [and C-x], then yank the killed page, all the pages will be properly delimited once again. The reason C-x C-p includes only the following page delimiter in the region is to ensure that.

A numeric argument to C-x C-p is used to specify which page to go to, relative to the current one. Zero means the current page. One means the next page, and −1 means the previous one.

The C-x l command (count-lines-page) is good for deciding where to break a page in two. It prints in the echo area the total number of lines in the current page, and then divides it up into those preceding the current line and those following, as in

    Page has 96 (72+25) lines

Notice that the sum is off by one; this is correct if point is not at the beginning of a line.

The variable `page-delimiter` controls where pages begin. Its value is a regexp that matches the beginning of a line that separates pages. The normal value of this variable is `"^\f"`, which matches a formfeed character at the beginning of a line.

20.5 Filling Text

Filling text means breaking it up into lines that fit a specified width. Emacs does filling in two ways. In Auto Fill mode, inserting text with self-inserting characters also automatically fills it. There are also explicit fill commands that you can use when editing text leaves it unfilled. When you edit formatted text, you can specify a style of filling for each portion of the text (see Section 20.11 [Formatted Text], page 190).

20.5.1 Auto Fill Mode

Auto Fill mode is a minor mode in which lines are broken automatically when they become too wide. Breaking happens only when you type a `SPC` or `RET`.

`M-x auto-fill-mode`
          Enable or disable Auto Fill mode.

`SPC`
`RET`   In Auto Fill mode, break lines when appropriate.

`M-x auto-fill-mode` turns Auto Fill mode on if it was off, or off if it was on. With a positive numeric argument it always turns Auto Fill mode on, and with a negative argument always turns it off. You can see when Auto Fill mode is in effect by the presence of the word 'Fill' in the mode line, inside the parentheses. Auto Fill mode is a minor mode which is enabled or disabled for each buffer individually. See Section 30.1 [Minor Modes], page 343.

In Auto Fill mode, lines are broken automatically at spaces when they get longer than the desired width. Line breaking and rearrangement takes place only when you type `SPC` or `RET`. If you wish to insert a space or newline without permitting line-breaking, type `C-q SPC` or `C-q LFD` (recall that a newline is really a linefeed). Also, `C-o` inserts a newline without line breaking.

Auto Fill mode works well with Lisp mode, because when it makes a new line in Lisp mode it indents that line with `TAB`. If a line ending in a comment gets too long, the text of the comment is split into two comment lines. Optionally new comment delimiters are inserted at the end of the first line and the beginning of the second so that each line is a separate comment; the variable `comment-multi-line` controls the choice (see Section 21.7 [Comments], page 210).

Auto Fill mode does not refill entire paragraphs; it can break lines but cannot merge lines. So editing in the middle of a paragraph can result in a paragraph that is not correctly filled. The easiest way to make the paragraph properly filled again is usually with the explicit fill commands.

Many users like Auto Fill mode and want to use it in all text files. The section on init files says how to arrange this permanently for yourself. See Section 30.7 [Init File], page 366.

20.5.2 Explicit Fill Commands

M-q   Fill current paragraph (`fill-paragraph`).

C-x f   Set the fill column (`set-fill-column`).

M-x fill-region
             Fill each paragraph in the region (`fill-region`).

M-x fill-region-as-paragraph.
             Fill the region, considering it as one paragraph.

M-s   Center a line.

To refill a paragraph, use the command M-q (`fill-paragraph`). This operates on the paragraph that point is inside, or the one after point if point is between paragraphs. Refilling works by removing all the line-breaks, then inserting new ones where necessary.

To refill many paragraphs, use M-x `fill-region`, which divides the region into paragraphs and fills each of them.

M-q and `fill-region` use the same criteria as M-h for finding paragraph boundaries (see Section 20.3 [Paragraphs], page 172). For more control, you can use M-x `fill-region-as-paragraph`, which refills everything between point and mark. This command deletes any blank lines within the region, so separate blocks of text end up combined into one block.

A numeric argument to M-q causes it to *justify* the text as well as filling it. This means that extra spaces are inserted to make the right margin line up exactly at the fill column. To remove the extra spaces, use M-q with no argument. (Likewise for `fill-region`.) Another way to control justification, and choose other styles of filling, is with the `justification` text property; see Section 20.11.7 [Format Justification], page 195.

When `adaptive-fill-mode` is non-nil (which is normally the case), if you use `fill-region-as-paragraph` on an indented paragraph and you don't have a fill prefix, it uses the indentation of the second line of the paragraph as the fill prefix. The effect of adaptive filling is not noticeable in Text mode, because an indented line counts as a paragraph starter and thus each line of an indented paragraph is considered a paragraph of its own. But you do notice the effect in Indented Text mode and some other major modes.

The command `M-s` (`center-line`) centers the current line within the current fill column. With an argument *n*, it centers *n* lines individually and moves past them.

The maximum line width for filling is in the variable `fill-column`. Altering the value of `fill-column` makes it local to the current buffer; until that time, the default value is in effect. The default is initially 70. See Section 30.2.4 [Locals], page 348. The easiest way to set `fill-column` is to use the command `C-x f` (`set-fill-column`). With no argument, it sets `fill-column` to the current horizontal position of point. With a numeric argument, it uses that as the new fill column.

Emacs commands normally consider a period followed by two spaces or by a newline as the end of a sentence; a period followed by just one space indicates an abbreviation and not the end of a sentence. To preserve the distinction between these two ways of using a period, the fill commands do not break a line after a period followed by just one space.

If the variable `sentence-end-double-space` is `nil`, the fill commands expect and leave just one space at the end of a sentence. Ordinarily this variable is `t`, so the fill commands insist on two spaces for the end of a sentence, as explained above. See Section 20.2 [Sentences], page 171.

20.5.3 The Fill Prefix

To fill a paragraph in which each line starts with a special marker (which might be a few spaces, giving an indented paragraph), use the *fill prefix* feature. The fill prefix is a string which Emacs expects every line to start with, and which is not included in filling.

`C-x .`   Set the fill prefix (`set-fill-prefix`).

`M-q`   Fill a paragraph using current fill prefix (`fill-paragraph`).

`M-x fill-individual-paragraphs`
              Fill the region, considering each change of indentation as starting
              a new paragraph.

`M-x fill-nonuniform-paragraphs`
              Fill the region, considering only paragraph-separator lines as
              starting a new paragraph.

To specify a fill prefix, move to a line that starts with the desired prefix, put point at the end of the prefix, and give the command `C-x .` (`set-fill-`

prefix). That's a period after the C-x. To turn off the fill prefix, specify an empty prefix: type C-x . with point at the beginning of a line.

When a fill prefix is in effect, the fill commands remove the fill prefix from each line before filling and insert it on each line after filling. Auto Fill mode also inserts the fill prefix automatically when it makes a new line. The C-o command inserts the fill prefix on new lines it creates, when you use it at the beginning of a line (see Section 4.7 [Blank Lines], page 32). Conversely, the command M-^ deletes the prefix (if it occurs) after the newline that it deletes (see Chapter 19 [Indentation], page 165).

For example, if fill-column is 40 and you set the fill prefix to '; ; ', then M-q in the following text

```
;; This is an
;; example of a paragraph
;; inside a Lisp-style comment.
```

produces this:

```
;; This is an example of a paragraph
;; inside a Lisp-style comment.
```

Lines that do not start with the fill prefix are considered to start paragraphs, both in M-q and the paragraph commands; this is gives good results for paragraphs with hanging indentation (every line indented except the first one). Lines which are blank or indented once the prefix is removed also separate or start paragraphs; this is what you want if you are writing multi-paragraph comments with a comment delimiter on each line.

You can use M-x fill-individual-paragraphs to set the fill prefix for each paragraph automatically. This command divides the region into paragraphs, treating every change in the amount of indentation as the start of a new paragraph, and fills each of these paragraphs. Thus, all the lines in one "paragraph" have the same amount of indentation. That indentation serves as the fill prefix for that paragraph.

M-x fill-nonuniform-paragraphs is a similar command that divides the region into paragraphs in a different way. It considers only paragraph-separating lines (as defined by paragraph-separate) as starting a new paragraph. Since this means that the lines of one paragraph may have different amounts of indentation, the fill prefix used is the smallest amount of indentation of any of the lines of the paragraph. This gives good results with styles that indent a paragraph's first line more or less that the rest of the paragraph.

The fill prefix is stored in the variable fill-prefix. Its value is a string, or nil when there is no fill prefix. This is a per-buffer variable; altering the variable affects only the current buffer, but there is a default value which you can change as well. See Section 30.2.4 [Locals], page 348.

The `indentation` text property provides another way to control the amount of indentation paragraphs receive. See Section 20.11.6 [Format Indentation], page 194.

20.6 Case Conversion Commands

Emacs has commands for converting either a single word or any arbitrary range of text to upper case or to lower case.

M-l   Convert following word to lower case (`downcase-word`).

M-u   Convert following word to upper case (`upcase-word`).

M-c   Capitalize the following word (`capitalize-word`).

C-x C-l   Convert region to lower case (`downcase-region`).

C-x C-u   Convert region to upper case (`upcase-region`).

The word conversion commands are the most useful. M-l (`downcase-word`) converts the word after point to lower case, moving past it. Thus, repeating M-l converts successive words. M-u (`upcase-word`) converts to all capitals instead, while M-c (`capitalize-word`) puts the first letter of the word into upper case and the rest into lower case. All these commands convert several words at once if given an argument. They are especially convenient for converting a large amount of text from all upper case to mixed case, because you can move through the text using M-l, M-u or M-c on each word as appropriate, occasionally using M-f instead to skip a word.

When given a negative argument, the word case conversion commands apply to the appropriate number of words before point, but do not move point. This is convenient when you have just typed a word in the wrong case: you can give the case conversion command and continue typing.

If a word case conversion command is given in the middle of a word, it applies only to the part of the word which follows point. This is just like what M-d (`kill-word`) does. With a negative argument, case conversion applies only to the part of the word before point.

The other case conversion commands are C-x C-u (`upcase-region`) and C-x C-l (`downcase-region`), which convert everything between point and mark to the specified case. Point and mark do not move.

The region case conversion commands `upcase-region` and `downcase-region` are normally disabled. This means that they ask for confirmation if you try to use them. When you confirm, you may enable the command, which means it will not ask for confirmation again. See Section 30.4.10 [Disabling], page 365.

20.7 Text Mode

When you edit files of text in a human language, it's more convenient to use Text mode rather than Fundamental mode. Invoke M-x text-mode to enter Text mode. In Text mode, TAB runs the function tab-to-tab-stop, which allows you to use arbitrary tab stops set with M-x edit-tab-stops (see Section 19.2 [Tab Stops], page 167). Features concerned with comments in programs are turned off in Text mode except when explicitly invoked. The syntax table is changed so that periods are not considered part of a word, while apostrophes, backspaces and underlines are part of words.

A similar variant mode is Indented Text mode, intended for editing text in which most lines are indented. This mode defines TAB to run indent-relative (see Chapter 19 [Indentation], page 165), and makes Auto Fill indent the lines it creates. The result is that normally a line made by Auto Filling, or by LFD, is indented just like the previous line. In Indented Text mode, only blank lines separate paragraphs—indented lines continue the current paragraph. Use M-x indented-text-mode to select this mode.

Text mode, and all the modes based on it, define M-TAB as the command ispell-complete-word, which performs completion of the partial word in the buffer before point, using the spelling dictionary as the space of possible words. See Section 13.4 [Spelling], page 99.

Entering Text mode or Indented Text mode runs the hook text-mode-hook. Other major modes related to Text mode also run this hook, followed by hooks of their own; this includes Nroff mode, TEX mode, Outline mode and Mail mode. Hook functions on text-mode-hook can look at the value of major-mode to see which of these modes is actually being entered. See Section 30.2.3 [Hooks], page 347.

20.8 Outline Mode

Outline mode is a major mode much like Text mode but intended for editing outlines. It allows you to make parts of the text temporarily invisible so that you can see the outline structure. Type M-x outline-mode to switch to Outline mode as the major mode of the current buffer.

When Outline mode makes a line invisible, the line does not appear on the screen. The screen appears exactly as if the invisible line were deleted, except that an ellipsis (three periods in a row) appears at the end of the previous visible line (only one ellipsis no matter how many invisible lines follow).

All editing commands treat the text of the invisible line as part of the previous visible line. For example, C-n moves onto the next visible line. Killing an entire visible line, including its terminating newline, really kills all the following invisible lines along with it; yanking it all back yanks the invisible lines and they remain invisible.

Outline minor mode provides the same commands as the major mode, Outline mode, but you can use it in conjunction with other major modes. Type `M-x outline-minor-mode` to enable the Outline minor mode in the current buffer. You can also specify this in the text of a file, with a file local variable of the form 'mode: outline-minor' (see Section 30.2.5 [File Variables], page 350).

The major mode, Outline mode, provides special key bindings on the `C-c` prefix. Outline minor mode provides similar bindings with `C-c @` as the prefix; this is to reduce the conflicts with the major mode's special commands. (The variable `outline-minor-mode-prefix` controls the prefix used.)

Entering Outline mode runs the hook `text-mode-hook` followed by the hook `outline-mode-hook` (see Section 30.2.3 [Hooks], page 347).

20.8.1 Format of Outlines

Outline mode assumes that the lines in the buffer are of two types: *heading lines* and *body lines*. A heading line represents a topic in the outline. Heading lines start with one or more stars; the number of stars determines the depth of the heading in the outline structure. Thus, a heading line with one star is a major topic; all the heading lines with two stars between it and the next one-star heading are its subtopics; and so on. Any line that is not a heading line is a body line. Body lines belong with the preceding heading line. Here is an example:

```
* Food

This is the body,
which says something about the topic of food.

** Delicious Food

This is the body of the second-level header.

** Distasteful Food

This could have
a body too, with
several lines.

*** Dormitory Food
```

```
* Shelter
```

`Another first-level topic with its header line.`

A heading line together with all following body lines is called collectively an *entry*. A heading line together with all following deeper heading lines and their body lines is called a *subtree*.

You can customize the criterion for distinguishing heading lines by setting the variable `outline-regexp`. Any line whose beginning has a match for this regexp is considered a heading line. Matches that start within a line (not at the left margin) do not count. The length of the matching text determines the level of the heading; longer matches make a more deeply nested level. Thus, for example, if a text formatter has commands '`@chapter`', '`@section`' and '`@subsection`' to divide the document into chapters and sections, you could make those lines count as heading lines by setting `outline-regexp` to '`"@chap\\|@\\(sub\\)*section"`'. Note the trick: the two words '`chapter`' and '`section`' are equally long, but by defining the regexp to match only '`chap`' we ensure that the length of the text matched on a chapter heading is shorter, so that Outline mode will know that sections are contained in chapters. This works as long as no other command starts with '`@chap`'.

It is possible to change the rule for calculating the level of a heading line by setting the variable `outline-level`. The value of `outline-level` should be a function that takes no arguments and returns the level of the current heading. Some major modes such as C, Nroff, and Emacs Lisp mode set this variable in order to work with Outline minor mode.

Outline mode makes a line invisible by changing the newline before it into an ASCII control-M (code 015). Most editing commands that work on lines treat an invisible line as part of the previous line because, strictly speaking, it *is* part of that line, since there is no longer a newline in between. When you save the file in Outline mode, control-M characters are saved as newlines, so the invisible lines become ordinary lines in the file. But saving does not change the visibility status of a line inside Emacs.

20.8.2 Outline Motion Commands

Outline mode provides special motion commands that move backward and forward to heading lines.

C-c C-n   Move point to the next visible heading line (`outline-next-visible-heading`).

C-c C-p   Move point to the previous visible heading line (`outline-previous-visible-heading`).

C-c C-f   Move point to the next visible heading line at the same level as the one point is on (`outline-forward-same-level`).

C-c C-b   Move point to the previous visible heading line at the same level
           (`outline-backward-same-level`).

C-c C-u   Move point up to a lower-level (more inclusive) visible heading
           line (`outline-up-heading`).

C-c C-n (`next-visible-heading`) moves down to the next heading line.
C-c C-p (`previous-visible-heading`) moves similarly backward. Both accept numeric arguments as repeat counts. The names emphasize that invisible headings are skipped, but this is not really a special feature. All editing
commands that look for lines ignore the invisible lines automatically.

More powerful motion commands understand the level structure of headings. C-c C-f (`outline-forward-same-level`) and C-c C-b (`outline-
backward-same-level`) move from one heading line to another visible head-
ing at the same depth in the outline. C-c C-u (`outline-up-heading`) moves
backward to another heading that is less deeply nested.

20.8.3 Outline Visibility Commands

The other special commands of outline mode are used to make lines visible
or invisible. Their names all start with **hide** or **show**. Most of them fall into
pairs of opposites. They are not undoable; instead, you can undo right past
them. Making lines visible or invisible is simply not recorded by the undo
mechanism.

C-c C-t   Make all body lines in the buffer invisible (**hide-body**).

C-c C-a   Make all lines in the buffer visible (**show-all**).

C-c C-d   Make everything under this heading invisible, not including this
           heading itself
           (**hide-subtree**).

C-c C-s   Make everything under this heading visible, including body, sub-
           headings, and their bodies (**show-subtree**).

C-c C-l   Make the body of this heading line, and of all its subheadings,
           invisible (**hide-leaves**).

C-c C-k   Make all subheadings of this heading line, at all levels, visible
           (**show-branches**).

C-c C-i   Make immediate subheadings (one level down) of this heading
           line visible (**show-children**).

C-c C-c   Make this heading line's body invisible (**hide-entry**).

C-c C-e   Make this heading line's body visible (**show-entry**).

C-c C-q   Hide everything except the top _n_ levels of heading lines (**hide-
           sublevels**).

C-c C-o   Hide everything except for the heading or body that point is in, plus the headings leading up from there to the top level of the outline (`hide-other`).

Two commands that are exact opposites are C-c C-c (`hide-entry`) and C-c C-e (`show-entry`). They are used with point on a heading line, and apply only to the body lines of that heading. Subheadings and their bodies are not affected.

Two more powerful opposites are C-c C-d (`hide-subtree`) and C-c C-s (`show-subtree`). Both expect to be used when point is on a heading line, and both apply to all the lines of that heading's *subtree*: its body, all its subheadings, both direct and indirect, and all of their bodies. In other words, the subtree contains everything following this heading line, up to and not including the next heading of the same or higher rank.

Intermediate between a visible subtree and an invisible one is having all the subheadings visible but none of the body. There are two commands for doing this, depending on whether you want to hide the bodies or make the subheadings visible. They are C-c C-l (`hide-leaves`) and C-c C-k (`show-branches`).

A little weaker than `show-branches` is C-c C-i (`show-children`). It makes just the direct subheadings visible—those one level down. Deeper subheadings remain invisible, if they were invisible.

Two commands have a blanket effect on the whole file. C-c C-t (`hide-body`) makes all body lines invisible, so that you see just the outline structure. C-c C-a (`show-all`) makes all lines visible. These commands can be thought of as a pair of opposites even though C-c C-a applies to more than just body lines.

The command C-c C-q (`hide-sublevels`) hides all but the top level headings. With a numeric argument n, it hides everything except the top n levels of heading lines.

The command C-c C-o (`hide-other`) hides everything except the heading or body text that point is in, plus its parents (the headers leading up from there to top level in the outline).

You can turn off the use of ellipses at the ends of visible lines by setting `selective-display-ellipses` to `nil`. Then there is no visible indication of the presence of invisible lines.

20.8.4 Viewing One Outline in Multiple Views

You can display two views of a single outline at the same time, in different windows, by means of an alternative implementation of Outline mode called `noutline`.

To do this, first load the library `noutline` with `M-x load-library RET` `noutline RET`. This loads the alternative implementation of Outline mode. It provides the same command names and key bindings as regular Outline mode, but it implements them differently.

Then, to display a second view of an outline buffer, you must create an indirect buffer using `M-x make-indirect-buffer`. The first argument of this command is the existing outline buffer name, and its second argument is the name to use for the new indirect buffer. See Section 15.6 [Indirect Buffers], page 138.

Once the indirect buffer exists, you can display it in a window in the normal fashion, with `C-x 4 b` or other Emacs commands. The Outline mode commands to show and hide parts of the text operate on each buffer independently; as a result, each buffer can have its own view. If you want more than two views on the same outline, create additional indirect buffers.

In a future Emacs version, the alternative `noutline` implementation will probably become the principal implementation.

20.9 TeX Mode

TeX is a powerful text formatter written by Donald Knuth; it is also free, like GNU Emacs. LaTeX is a simplified input format for TeX, implemented by TeX macros; it comes with TeX. SliTeX is a special form of LaTeX.

Emacs has a special TeX mode for editing TeX input files. It provides facilities for checking the balance of delimiters and for invoking TeX on all or part of the file.

TeX mode has three variants, Plain TeX mode, LaTeX mode, and SliTeX mode (these three distinct major modes differ only slightly). They are designed for editing the three different formats. The command `M-x tex-mode` looks at the contents of the buffer to determine whether the contents appear to be either LaTeX input or SliTeX input; if so, it selects the appropriate mode. If the file contents do not appear to be LaTeX or SliTeX, it selects Plain TeX mode. If the contents are insufficient to determine this, the variable `tex-default-mode` controls which mode is used.

When `M-x tex-mode` does not guess right, you can use the commands `M-x plain-tex-mode`, `M-x latex-mode`, and `M-x slitex-mode` to select explicitly the particular variants of TeX mode.

20.9.1 TeX Editing Commands

Here are the special commands provided in TeX mode for editing the text of the file.

"   Insert, according to context, either ' '' ' or '"' or ' '' ' (tex-
             insert-quote).

LFD   Insert a paragraph break (two newlines) and check the pre-
             vious paragraph for unbalanced braces or dollar signs (tex-
             terminate-paragraph).

M-x validate-tex-region
             Check each paragraph in the region for unbalanced braces or
             dollar signs.

C-c {   Insert '{}' and position point between them (tex-insert-
             braces).

C-c }   Move forward past the next unmatched close brace (up-list).

In TEX, the character '"' is not normally used; we use ' '' ' to start a
quotation and ' '' ' to end one. To make editing easier under this formatting
convention, TEX mode overrides the normal meaning of the key " with a
command that inserts a pair of single-quotes or backquotes (tex-insert-
quote). To be precise, this command inserts ' '' ' after whitespace or an
open brace, '"' after a backslash, and ' '' ' after any other character.

If you need the character '"' itself in unusual contexts, use C-q to insert it.
Also, " with a numeric argument always inserts that number of '"' characters.

In TEX mode, '$' has a special syntax code which attempts to understand
the way TEX math mode delimiters match. When you insert a '$' that is
meant to exit math mode, the position of the matching '$' that entered math
mode is displayed for a second. This is the same feature that displays the
open brace that matches a close brace that is inserted. However, there is no
way to tell whether a '$' enters math mode or leaves it; so when you insert
a '$' that enters math mode, the previous '$' position is shown as if it were
a match, even though they are actually unrelated.

TEX uses braces as delimiters that must match. Some users prefer to keep
braces balanced at all times, rather than inserting them singly. Use C-c {
(tex-insert-braces) to insert a pair of braces. It leaves point between the
two braces so you can insert the text that belongs inside. Afterward, use the
command C-c } (up-list) to move forward past the close brace.

There are two commands for checking the matching of braces. LFD (tex-
terminate-paragraph) checks the paragraph before point, and inserts two
newlines to start a new paragraph. It prints a message in the echo area if any
mismatch is found. M-x validate-tex-region checks a region, paragraph
by paragraph. When it finds a paragraph that contains a mismatch, it
displays point at the beginning of the paragraph for a few seconds and sets
the mark at that spot. Scanning continues until the whole buffer has been
checked or until you type another key. Afterward, you can use the mark
ring to find the last several paragraphs that had mismatches (see Section 8.5
[Mark Ring], page 59).

Note that Emacs commands count square brackets and parentheses in TEX mode, not just braces. This is not strictly correct for the purpose of checking TEX syntax. However, parentheses and square brackets are likely to be used in text as matching delimiters and it is useful for the various motion commands and automatic match display to work with them.

20.9.2 LaTEX Editing Commands

LaTEX mode, and its variant, SliTEX mode, provide a few extra features not applicable to plain TEX.

C-c C-o   Insert '\begin' and '\end' for LaTEX block and position point on a line between them. (tex-latex-block).

C-c C-e   Close the last unended block for LaTEX (tex-close-latex-block).

In LaTEX input, '\begin' and '\end' commands are used to group blocks of text. To insert a '\begin' and a matching '\end' (on a new line following the '\begin'), use C-c C-o (tex-latex-block). A blank line is inserted between the two, and point is left there. You can use completion when you enter the block type; to specify additional block type names beyond the standard list, set the variable latex-block-names. For example, here's how to add 'theorem', 'corollary', and 'proof':

    (setq latex-block-names '("theorem" "corollary" "proof"))

In LaTEX input, '\begin' and '\end' commands must balance. You can use C-c C-e (tex-close-latex-block) to insert automatically a matching '\end' to match the last unmatched '\begin'. It indents the '\end' to match the corresponding '\begin'. It inserts a newline after '\end' if point is at the beginning of a line.

20.9.3 TEX Printing Commands

You can invoke TEX as an inferior of Emacs on either the entire contents of the buffer or just a region at a time. Running TEX in this way on just one chapter is a good way to see what your changes look like without taking the time to format the entire file.

C-c C-r   Invoke TEX on the current region, together with the buffer's header (tex-region).

C-c C-b   Invoke TEX on the entire current buffer (tex-buffer).

C-c TAB   Invoke BibTEX on the current file (tex-bibtex-file).

C-c C-f   Invoke TEX on the current file (tex-file).

C-c C-l   Recenter the window showing output from the inferior TeX so that the last line can be seen (`tex-recenter-output-buffer`).

C-c C-k   Kill the TeX subprocess (`tex-kill-job`).

C-c C-p   Print the output from the last C-c C-r, C-c C-b, or C-c C-f command (`tex-print`).

C-c C-v   Preview the output from the last C-c C-r, C-c C-b, or C-c C-f command (`tex-view`).

C-c C-q   Show the printer queue (`tex-show-print-queue`).

You can pass the current buffer through an inferior TeX by means of C-c C-b (`tex-buffer`). The formatted output appears in a temporary file; to print it, type C-c C-p (`tex-print`). Afterward, you can use C-c C-q (`tex-show-print-queue`) to view the progress of your output towards being printed. If your terminal has the ability to display TeX output files, you can preview the output on the terminal with C-c C-v (`tex-view`).

You can specify the directory to use for running TeX by setting the variable `tex-directory`. "." is the default value. If your environment variable `TEXINPUTS` contains relative directory names, or if your files contains '\input' commands with relative file names, then `tex-directory` *must* be "." or you will get the wrong results. Otherwise, it is safe to specify some other directory, such as "/tmp".

If you want to specify which shell commands are used in the inferior TeX, you can do so by setting the values of the variables `tex-run-command`, `latex-run-command`, `slitex-run-command`, `tex-dvi-print-command`, `tex-dvi-view-command`, and `tex-show-queue-command`. You *must* set the value of `tex-dvi-view-command` for your particular terminal; this variable has no default value. The other variables have default values that may (or may not) be appropriate for your system.

Normally, the file name given to these commands comes at the end of the command string; for example, '`latex filename`'. In some cases, however, the file name needs to be embedded in the command; an example is when you need to provide the file name as an argument to one command whose output is piped to another. You can specify where to put the file name with '*' in the command string. For example,

```
(setq tex-dvi-print-command "dvips -f * | lpr")
```

The terminal output from TeX, including any error messages, appears in a buffer called '`*tex-shell*`'. If TeX gets an error, you can switch to this buffer and feed it input (this works as in Shell mode; see Section 29.2.2 [Interactive Shell], page 323). Without switching to this buffer you can scroll it so that its last line is visible by typing C-c C-l.

Type C-c C-k (`tex-kill-job`) to kill the TEX process if you see that its output is no longer useful. Using C-c C-b or C-c C-r also kills any TEX process still running.

You can also pass an arbitrary region through an inferior TEX by typing C-c C-r (`tex-region`). This is tricky, however, because most files of TEX input contain commands at the beginning to set parameters and define macros, without which no later part of the file will format correctly. To solve this problem, C-c C-r allows you to designate a part of the file as containing essential commands; it is included before the specified region as part of the input to TEX. The designated part of the file is called the *header*.

To indicate the bounds of the header in Plain TEX mode, you insert two special strings in the file. Insert '`%**start of header`' before the header, and '`%**end of header`' after it. Each string must appear entirely on one line, but there may be other text on the line before or after. The lines containing the two strings are included in the header. If '`%**start of header`' does not appear within the first 100 lines of the buffer, C-c C-r assumes that there is no header.

In LaTEX mode, the header begins with '`\documentstyle`' and ends with '`\begin{document}`'. These are commands that LaTEX requires you to use in any case, so nothing special needs to be done to identify the header.

The commands (`tex-buffer`) and (`tex-region`) do all of their work in a temporary directory, and do not have available any of the auxiliary files needed by TEX for cross-references; these commands are generally not suitable for running the final copy in which all of the cross-references need to be correct. When you want the auxiliary files, use C-c C-f (`tex-file`) which runs TEX on the current buffer's file, in that file's directory. Before TEX runs, you will be asked about saving any modified buffers. Generally, you need to use (`tex-file`) twice to get cross-references correct.

For LaTEX files, you can use BibTEX to process the auxiliary file for the current buffer's file. BibTEX looks up bibliographic citations in a data base and prepares the cited references for the bibliography section. The command C-c TAB (`tex-bibtex-file`) runs the shell command (`tex-bibtex-command`) to produce a '`.bbl`' file for the current buffer's file. Generally, you need to do C-c C-f (`tex-file`) once to generate the '`.aux`' file, then do C-c TAB (`tex-bibtex-file`), and then repeat C-c C-f (`tex-file`) twice more to get the cross-references correct.

Entering any kind of TEX mode runs the hooks `text-mode-hook` and `tex-mode-hook`. Then it runs either `plain-tex-mode-hook` or `latex-mode-hook`, whichever is appropriate. For SliTEX files, it calls `slitex-mode-hook`. Starting the TEX shell runs the hook `tex-shell-hook`. See Section 30.2.3 [Hooks], page 347.

20.9.4 Unix TeX Distribution

TeX for Unix systems can be obtained from the University of Washington for a distribution fee.

To order a full distribution, specify whether you prefer 1/4 inch QIC-24 or 4mm DAT tape (9-track reel-to-reel is no longer available) and send $210.00 for a (tar or cpio) cartridge, payable to the University of Washington to:

Pierre MacKay
Department of Classics
Denny Hall, Mail Stop DH-10
University of Washington
Seattle, Washington 98195

Purchase orders are acceptable, but there is an extra charge of $10.00, to pay for processing charges.

For overseas orders please add $20.00 to the base cost for shipment via air parcel post, or $30.00 for shipment via courier.

The normal distribution is a tar tape, blocked 20, 1600 bpi, on an industry standard 2400 foot half-inch reel. The physical format for the 1/4 inch streamer cartridges is QIC-24. System V tapes can be written in cpio format, blocked 5120 bytes, with ASCII headers.

20.10 Nroff Mode

Nroff mode is a mode like Text mode but modified to handle nroff commands present in the text. Invoke `M-x nroff-mode` to enter this mode. It differs from Text mode in only a few ways. All nroff command lines are considered paragraph separators, so that filling will never garble the nroff commands. Pages are separated by '`.bp`' commands. Comments start with backslash-doublequote. Also, three special commands are provided that are not in Text mode:

M-n   Move to the beginning of the next line that isn't an nroff command (`forward-text-line`). An argument is a repeat count.

M-p   Like `M-n` but move up (`backward-text-line`).

M-?   Prints in the echo area the number of text lines (lines that are not nroff commands) in the region (`count-text-lines`).

The other feature of Nroff mode is that you can turn on Electric Nroff mode. This is a minor mode that you can turn on or off with `M-x electric-nroff-mode` (see Section 30.1 [Minor Modes], page 343). When the mode is on, each time you use RET to end a line that contains an nroff command that opens a kind of grouping, the matching nroff command to close that grouping is automatically inserted on the following line. For example, if you are at the beginning of a line and type `. ( b RET`, this inserts the matching command '`.)b`' on a new line following point.

If you use Outline minor mode with Nroff mode (see Section 20.8 [Outline Mode], page 179), heading lines are lines of the form '`.H`' followed by a number (the header level).

Entering Nroff mode runs the hook `text-mode-hook`, followed by the hook `nroff-mode-hook` (see Section 30.2.3 [Hooks], page 347).

20.11 Editing Formatted Text

Enriched mode is a minor mode for editing files that contain formatted text in WYSIWYG fashion, as in a word processor. Currently, formatted text in Enriched mode can specify fonts, colors, underlining, margins, and types of filling and justification. In the future, we plan to implement other formatting features as well.

Enriched mode is a minor mode (see Section 30.1 [Minor Modes], page 343). Typically it is used in conjunction with Text mode (see Section 20.7 [Text Mode], page 179). However, you can also use it with other major modes such as Outline mode and Indented Text mode.

Potentially, Emacs can store formatted text files in various file formats. Currently, only one format is implemented: *text/enriched* format, which is defined by the MIME protocol. See section "Format Conversion" in *the Emacs Lisp Reference Manual*, for details of how Emacs recognizes and converts file formats.

The Emacs distribution contains a formatted text file that can serve as an example. Its name is '`etc/enriched.doc`'. It contains samples illustrating all the features described in this section. It also contains a list of ideas for future enhancements.

20.11.1 Requesting to Edit Formatted Text

Whenever you visit a file that Emacs saved in the text/enriched format, Emacs automatically converts the formatting information in the file into Emacs's own internal format (text properties), and turns on Enriched mode.

To create a new file of formatted text, first visit the nonexistent file, then type `M-x enriched-mode` before you start inserting text. This command turns on Enriched mode. Do this before you begin inserting text, to ensure that the text you insert is handled properly.

More generally, the command `enriched-mode` turns Enriched mode on if it was off, and off if it was on. With a prefix argument, this command turns Enriched mode on if the argument is positive, and turns the mode off otherwise.

When you save a buffer while Enriched mode is enabled in it, Emacs automatically converts the text to text/enriched format while writing it into the file. When you visit the file again, Emacs will automatically recognize the format, reconvert the text, and turn on Enriched mode again.

Normally, after reading a file in text/enriched format, Emacs refills each paragraph to fit the width of the window. You can turn off this refilling, to save time, by setting the variable `enriched-fill-after-visiting` to `nil` or to `ask`.

In any case, if the window width is the same as the width with which the file was saved, Emacs trusts that the file is already properly filled.

You can add annotations for saving additional text properties, which Emacs normally does not save, by adding to `enriched-translations`. Note that the text/enriched standard requires any non-standard annotations to have names starting with 'x-', as in 'x-read-only'. This ensures that they will not conflict with standard annotations that may be added later.

20.11.2 Hard and Soft Newlines

In formatted text, Emacs distinguishes between two different kinds of newlines, *hard* newlines and *soft* newlines.

Hard newlines are used to separate paragraphs, or items in a list, or anywhere that there should always be a line break regardless of the margins. The RET command (`newline`) and C-o (`open-line`) insert hard newlines.

Soft newlines are used to make text fit between the margins. All the fill commands, including Auto Fill, insert soft newlines—and they delete only soft newlines.

Although hard and soft newlines look the same, it is important to bear the difference in mind. Do not use RET to break lines in the middle of filled paragraphs, or else you will get hard newlines that are barriers to further filling. Instead, let Auto Fill mode break lines, so that if the text or the margins change, Emacs can refill the lines properly. See Section 20.5.1 [Auto Fill], page 174.

On the other hand, in tables and lists, where the lines should always remain as you type them, you can use RET to end lines. For these lines, you may also want to set the justification style to `unfilled`. See Section 20.11.7 [Format Justification], page 195.

20.11.3 Editing Format Information

There are two ways to alter the formatting information for a formatted text file: with keyboard commands, and with the mouse.

The easiest way to add properties to your document is by using the Text Properties menu. You can get to this menu in two ways: from the Edit menu in the menu bar, or with `C-mouse-2` (hold the `CTRL` key and press the middle mouse button).

Most of the items in the Text Properties menu lead to other submenus. These are described in the sections that follow. Some items run commands directly:

Remove Properties
> Delete from the region all the text properties that the Text Properties menu works with (`facemenu-remove-props`).

Remove All
> Delete *all* text properties from the region (`facemenu-remove-all`).

List Properties
> List all the text properties of the character following point (`list-text-properties-at`).

Display Faces
> Display a list of all the defined faces.

Display Colors
> Display a list of all the defined colors.

20.11.4 Faces in Formatted Text

The Faces submenu lists various Emacs faces including `bold`, `italic`, and `underline`. Selecting one of these adds the chosen face to the region. See Section 17.12 [Faces], page 156. You can also specify a face with these keyboard commands:

`M-g d`   Set the region, or the next inserted character, to the `default` face (`facemenu-set-default`).

`M-g b`   Set the region, or the next inserted character, to the `bold` face (`facemenu-set-bold`).

`M-g i`   Set the region, or the next inserted character, to the `italic` face (`facemenu-set-italic`).

`M-g l`   Set the region, or the next inserted character, to the `bold-italic` face (`facemenu-set-bold-italic`).

M-g u   Set the region, or the next inserted character, to the `underline` face (`facemenu-set-underline`).

M-g o *face* RET
             Set the region, or the next inserted character, to the face *face* (`facemenu-set-face`).

If you use these commands with a prefix argument—or, in Transient Mark mode, if the region is not active—then these commands specify a face to use for your next self-inserting input. See Section 8.2 [Transient Mark], page 56. This applies to both the keyboard commands and the menu commands.

Enriched mode defines two additional faces: `excerpt` and `fixed`. These correspond to codes used in the text/enriched file format.

The `excerpt` face is intended for quotations. This face is the same as `italic` unless you customize it (see Section 17.13 [Modifying Faces], page 157).

The `fixed` face is meant to say, "Use a fixed-width font for this part of the text." Emacs currently supports only fixed-width fonts; therefore, the `fixed` annotation is not necessary now. However, we plan to support variable width fonts in future Emacs versions, and other systems that display text/enriched format may not use a fixed-width font as the default. So if you specifically want a certain part of the text to use a fixed-width font, you should specify the `fixed` face for that part.

The `fixed` face is normally defined to use a different font from the default. However, systems have different fonts installed, you may need to customize this.

If your terminal cannot display different faces, you will not be able to see them, but you can still edit documents containing faces. You can even add faces and colors to documents. They will be visible when the file is viewed on a terminal that can display them.

20.11.5 Colors in Formatted Text

You can specify foreground and background colors for portions of the text. There is a menu for specifying the foreground color and a menu for specifying the background color. Each color menu lists all the colors that you have used in Enriched mode in the current Emacs session.

If you specify a color with a prefix argument—or, in Transient Mark mode, if the region is not active—then it applies to your next self-inserting input. See Section 8.2 [Transient Mark], page 56. Otherwise, the command applies to the region.

Each color menu contains one additional item: 'Other'. You can use this item to specify a color that is not listed in the menu; it reads the color name with the minibuffer. To display list of available colors and their

names, use the 'Display Colors' menu item in the Text Properties menu
(see Section 20.11.3 [Editing Format Info], page 192).

Any color that you specify in this way, or that is mentioned in a formatted
text file that you read in, is added to both color menus for the duration of
the Emacs session.

There are no key bindings for specifying colors, but you can do so
with the extended commands M-x facemenu-set-foreground and M-x
facemenu-set-background. Both of these commands read the name of
the color with the minibuffer.

20.11.6 Indentation in Formatted Text

When editing formatted text, you can specify different amounts of indentation for the right or left margin of an entire paragraph or a part of a
paragraph. The margins you specify automatically affect the Emacs fill commands (see Section 20.5 [Filling], page 174) and line-breaking commands.

The Indentation submenu provides a convenient interface for specifying
these properties. The submenu contains four items:

Indent More
> Indent the region by 4 columns (increase-left-margin). In
> Enriched mode, this command is also available on C-x TAB; if
> you supply a numeric argument, that says how many columns
> to add to the margin (a negative argument reduces the number
> of columns).

Indent Less
> Remove 4 columns of indentation from the region.

Indent Right More
> Make the text narrower by indenting 4 columns at the right
> margin.

Indent Right Less
> Remove 4 columns of indentation from the right margin.

You can use these commands repeatedly to increase or decrease the indentation.

The most common way to use these commands is to change the indentation of an entire paragraph. However, that is not the only use. You can
change the margins at any point; the new values take effect at the end of the
line (for right margins) or the beginning of the next line (for left margins).

This makes it possible to format paragraphs with *hanging indents*, which
means that the first line is indented less than subsequent lines. To set up a
hanging indent, increase the indentation of the region starting after the first
word of the paragraph and running until the end of the paragraph.

Indenting the first line of a paragraph is easier. Set the margin for the whole paragraph where you want it to be for the body of the paragraph, then indent the first line by inserting extra spaces or tabs.

Sometimes, as a result of editing, the filling of a paragraph becomes messed up—parts of the paragraph may extend past the left or right margins. When this happens, use M-q (fill-paragraph) to refill the paragraph.

The variable standard-indent specifies how many columns these commands should add to or subtract from the indentation. The default value is 4.

Enriched mode automatically sets the variable fill-column based on the window width: it leaves a certain number of columns for the right margin. The variable enriched-default-right-margin says how many columns. The default value is 10.

20.11.7 Justification in Formatted Text

When editing formatted text, you can specify various styles of justification for a paragraph. The style you specify automatically affects the Emacs fill commands.

The Justification submenu provides a convenient interface for specifying the style. The submenu contains five items:

Flush Left
> This is the most common style of justification (at least for English). Lines are aligned at the left margin but left uneven at the right.

Flush Right
> This aligns each line with the right margin. Spaces and tabs are added on the left, if necessary, to make lines line up on the right.

Full
> This justifies the text, aligning both edges of each line. Justified text looks very nice in a printed book, where the spaces can all be adjusted equally, but it does not look as nice with a fixed-width font on the screen. Perhaps a future version of Emacs will be able to adjust the width of spaces in a line to achieve elegant justification.

Center
> This centers every line between the current margins.

None
> This turns off filling entirely. Each line will remain as you wrote it; the fill and auto-fill functions will have no effect on text which has this setting. You can, however, still indent the left margin. In unfilled regions, all newlines are treated as hard newlines (see Section 20.11.2 [Hard and Soft Newlines], page 191) .

In Enriched mode, you can also specify justification from the keyboard using the M-j prefix character:

M-j l   Make the region left-filled (set-justification-left).

M-j r   Make the region right-filled (set-justification-right).

M-j f   Make the region fully-justified (set-justification-full).

M-j c
M-S   Make the region centered (set-justification-center).

M-j u   Make the region unfilled (set-justification-none).

Justification styles apply to entire paragraphs. All the justification-changing commands operate on the paragraph containing point, or, if the region is active, on all paragraphs which overlap the region.

The default justification style is specified by the variable default-justification. Its value should be one of the symbols left, right, full, center, or none.

20.11.8 Setting Other Text Properties

The Other Properties menu lets you add or remove three other useful text properties: read-only, invisible and intangible. The intangible property disallows moving point within the text, the invisible text property hides text from display, and the read-only property disallows alteration of the text.

Each of these special properties has a menu item to add it to the region. The last menu item, 'Remove Special', removes all of these special properties from the text in the region.

Currently, the invisible and intangible properties are *not* saved in the text/enriched format. The read-only property is saved, but it is not a standard part of the text/enriched format, so other editors may not respect it.

20.11.9 Forcing Enriched Mode

Normally, Emacs knows when you are editing formatted text because it recognizes the special annotations used in the file that you visited. However, there are situations in which you must take special actions to convert file contents or turn on Enriched mode:

* When you visit a file that was created with some other editor, Emacs may not recognize the file as being in the text/enriched format. In this case, when you visit the file you will see the formatting commands rather than the formatted text. Type M-x format-decode-buffer to translate it.

- When you *insert* a file into a buffer, rather than visiting it. Emacs does the necessary conversions on the text which you insert, but it does not enable Enriched mode. If you wish to do that, type `M-x enriched-mode`.

The command `format-decode-buffer` translates text in various formats into Emacs's internal format. It asks you to specify the format to translate from; however, normally you can type just `RET`, which tells Emacs to guess the format.

21 Editing Programs

Emacs has many commands designed to understand the syntax of programming languages such as Lisp and C. These commands can

- Move over or kill balanced expressions or *sexps* (see Section 21.2 [Lists], page 200).
- Move over or mark top-level expressions—*defuns*, in Lisp; functions, in C (see Section 21.4 [Defuns], page 202).
- Show how parentheses balance (see Section 21.6 [Matching], page 209).
- Insert, kill or align comments (see Section 21.7 [Comments], page 210).
- Follow the usual indentation conventions of the language (see Section 21.5 [Program Indent], page 203).

The commands for words, sentences and paragraphs are very useful in editing code even though their canonical application is for editing human language text. Most symbols contain words (see Section 20.1 [Words], page 169); sentences can be found in strings and comments (see Section 20.2 [Sentences], page 171). Paragraphs per se don't exist in code, but the paragraph commands are useful anyway, because programming language major modes define paragraphs to begin and end at blank lines (see Section 20.3 [Paragraphs], page 172). Judicious use of blank lines to make the program clearer will also provide useful chunks of text for the paragraph commands to work on.

The selective display feature is useful for looking at the overall structure of a function (see Section 11.3 [Selective Display], page 77). This feature causes only the lines that are indented less than a specified amount to appear on the screen.

21.1 Major Modes for Programming Languages

Emacs also has major modes for the programming languages Lisp, Scheme (a variant of Lisp), Awk, C, C++, Fortran, Icon, Pascal, Perl and Tcl. There is also a major mode for makefiles, called Makefile mode.

Ideally, a major mode should be implemented for each programming language that you might want to edit with Emacs; but often the mode for one language can serve for other syntactically similar languages. The language modes that exist are those that someone decided to take the trouble to write.

There are several forms of Lisp mode, which differ in the way they interface to Lisp execution. See Section 22.3 [Executing Lisp], page 245.

Each of the programming language modes defines the TAB key to run an indentation function that knows the indentation conventions of that language and updates the current line's indentation accordingly. For example, in C mode `TAB` is bound to `c-indent-line`. `LFD` is normally defined to do `RET` followed by `TAB`; thus, it too indents in a mode-specific fashion.

In most programming languages, indentation is likely to vary from line to line. So the major modes for those languages rebind `DEL` to treat a tab as if it were the equivalent number of spaces (using the command `backward-delete-char-untabify`). This makes it possible to rub out indentation one column at a time without worrying whether it is made up of spaces or tabs. Use `C-b C-d` to delete a tab character before point, in these modes.

Programming language modes define paragraphs to be separated only by blank lines, so that the paragraph commands remain useful. Auto Fill mode, if enabled in a programming language major mode, indents the new lines which it creates.

Turning on a major mode runs a normal hook called the *mode hook*, which is the value of a Lisp variable. Each major mode has a mode hook, and the hook's name is always made from the mode command's name by adding '-hook'. For example, turning on C mode runs the hook `c-mode-hook`, while turning on Lisp mode runs the hook `lisp-mode-hook`. See Section 30.2.3 [Hooks], page 347.

21.2 Lists and Sexps

By convention, Emacs keys for dealing with balanced expressions are usually Control-Meta characters. They tend to be analogous in function to their Control and Meta equivalents. These commands are usually thought of as pertaining to expressions in programming languages, but can be useful with any language in which some sort of parentheses exist (including human languages).

These commands fall into two classes. Some deal only with *lists* (parenthetical groupings). They see nothing except parentheses, brackets, braces (whichever ones must balance in the language you are working with), and escape characters that might be used to quote those.

The other commands deal with expressions or *sexps*. The word 'sexp' is derived from *s-expression*, the ancient term for an expression in Lisp. But in Emacs, the notion of 'sexp' is not limited to Lisp. It refers to an expression in whatever language your program is written in. Each programming language has its own major mode, which customizes the syntax tables so that expressions in that language count as sexps.

Sexps typically include symbols, numbers, and string constants, as well as anything contained in parentheses, brackets or braces.

In languages that use prefix and infix operators, such as C, it is not possible for all expressions to be sexps. For example, C mode does not recognize 'foo + bar' as a sexp, even though it *is* a C expression; it recognizes 'foo' as one sexp and 'bar' as another, with the '+' as punctuation between them. This is a fundamental ambiguity: both 'foo + bar' and 'foo' are legitimate choices for the sexp to move over if point is at the 'f'. Note that '(foo + bar)' is a single sexp in C mode.

Some languages have obscure forms of expression syntax that nobody has bothered to make Emacs understand properly.

21.3 List And Sexp Commands

C-M-f   Move forward over a sexp (forward-sexp).

C-M-b   Move backward over a sexp (backward-sexp).

C-M-k   Kill sexp forward (kill-sexp).

C-M-DEL   Kill sexp backward (backward-kill-sexp).

C-M-u   Move up and backward in list structure (backward-up-list).

C-M-d   Move down and forward in list structure (down-list).

C-M-n   Move forward over a list (forward-list).

C-M-p   Move backward over a list (backward-list).

C-M-t   Transpose expressions (transpose-sexps).

C-M-@   Put mark after following expression (mark-sexp).

To move forward over a sexp, use C-M-f (forward-sexp). If the first significant character after point is an opening delimiter ('(' in Lisp; '(', '[' or '{' in C), C-M-f moves past the matching closing delimiter. If the character begins a symbol, string, or number, C-M-f moves over that.

The command C-M-b (backward-sexp) moves backward over a sexp. The detailed rules are like those above for C-M-f, but with directions reversed. If there are any prefix characters (single-quote, backquote and comma, in Lisp) preceding the sexp, C-M-b moves back over them as well. The sexp commands move across comments as if they were whitespace in most modes.

C-M-f or C-M-b with an argument repeats that operation the specified number of times; with a negative argument, it moves in the opposite direction.

Killing a sexp at a time can be done with C-M-k (kill-sexp) or C-M-DEL (backward-kill-sexp). C-M-k kills the characters that C-M-f would move over, and C-M-DEL kills the characters that C-M-b would move over.

The *list commands* move over lists like the sexp commands but skip blithely over any number of other kinds of sexps (symbols, strings, etc). They are C-M-n (forward-list) and C-M-p (backward-list). The main reason they are useful is that they usually ignore comments (since the comments usually do not contain any lists).

C-M-n and C-M-p stay at the same level in parentheses, when that's possible. To move *up* one (or *n*) levels, use C-M-u (backward-up-list). C-M-u moves backward up past one unmatched opening delimiter. A positive argument serves as a repeat count; a negative argument reverses direction of motion and also requests repetition, so it moves forward and up one or more levels.

To move *down* in list structure, use C-M-d (down-list). In Lisp mode, where '(' is the only opening delimiter, this is nearly the same as searching for a '('. An argument specifies the number of levels of parentheses to go down.

A somewhat random-sounding command which is nevertheless handy is C-M-t (transpose-sexps), which drags the previous sexp across the next one. An argument serves as a repeat count, and a negative argument drags backwards (thus canceling out the effect of C-M-t with a positive argument). An argument of zero, rather than doing nothing, transposes the sexps ending after point and the mark.

To set the region around the next sexp in the buffer, use C-M-@ (mark-sexp), which sets mark at the same place that C-M-f would move to. C-M-@ takes arguments like C-M-f. In particular, a negative argument is useful for putting the mark at the beginning of the previous sexp.

The list and sexp commands' understanding of syntax is completely controlled by the syntax table. Any character can, for example, be declared to be an opening delimiter and act like an open parenthesis. See Section 30.6 [Syntax], page 366.

21.4 Defuns

In Emacs, a parenthetical grouping at the top level in the buffer is called a *defun*. The name derives from the fact that most top-level lists in a Lisp file are instances of the special form defun, but any top-level parenthetical grouping counts as a defun in Emacs parlance regardless of what its contents are, and regardless of the programming language in use. For example, in C, the body of a function definition is a defun.

C-M-a   Move to beginning of current or preceding defun (beginning-of-defun).

C-M-e   Move to end of current or following defun (end-of-defun).

C-M-h   Put region around whole current or following defun (mark-defun).

The commands to move to the beginning and end of the current defun are C-M-a (beginning-of-defun) and C-M-e (end-of-defun).

If you wish to operate on the current defun, use C-M-h (mark-defun) which puts point at the beginning and mark at the end of the current or next defun. For example, this is the easiest way to get ready to move the defun to a different place in the text. In C mode, C-M-h runs the function mark-c-function, which is almost the same as mark-defun; the difference is that it backs up over the argument declarations, function name and returned data type so that the entire C function is inside the region. See Section 8.4 [Marking Objects], page 58.

Emacs assumes that any open-parenthesis found in the leftmost column is the start of a defun. Therefore, **never put an open-parenthesis at the left margin in a Lisp file unless it is the start of a top level list. Never put an open-brace or other opening delimiter at the beginning of a line of C code unless it starts the body of a function.** The most likely problem case is when you want an opening delimiter at the start of a line inside a string. To avoid trouble, put an escape character ('\', in C and Emacs Lisp, '/' in some other Lisp dialects) before the opening delimiter. It will not affect the contents of the string.

In the remotest past, the original Emacs found defuns by moving upward a level of parentheses until there were no more levels to go up. This always required scanning all the way back to the beginning of the buffer, even for a small function. To speed up the operation, Emacs was changed to assume that any '(' (or other character assigned the syntactic class of opening-delimiter) at the left margin is the start of a defun. This heuristic is nearly always right and avoids the costly scan; however, it mandates the convention described above.

21.5 Indentation for Programs

The best way to keep a program properly indented is to use Emacs to re-indent it as you change it. Emacs has commands to indent properly either a single line, a specified number of lines, or all of the lines inside a single parenthetical grouping.

Emacs also provides a Lisp pretty-printer in the library pp. This program prints a Lisp object with indentation chosen to look nice.

21.5.1 Basic Program Indentation Commands

TAB   Adjust indentation of current line.

LFD   Equivalent to RET followed by TAB (newline-and-indent).

The basic indentation command is TAB, which gives the current line the correct indentation as determined from the previous lines. The function that TAB runs depends on the major mode; it is lisp-indent-line in Lisp mode, c-indent-line in C mode, etc. These functions understand different syntaxes for different languages, but they all do about the same thing. TAB in any programming language major mode inserts or deletes whitespace at the beginning of the current line, independent of where point is in the line. If point is inside the whitespace at the beginning of the line, TAB leaves it at the end of that whitespace; otherwise, TAB leaves point fixed with respect to the characters around it.

Use C-q TAB to insert a tab at point.

When entering lines of new code, use LFD (newline-and-indent), which is equivalent to a RET followed by a TAB. LFD creates a blank line, and then gives it the appropriate indentation.

TAB indents the second and following lines of the body of a parenthetical grouping each under the preceding one; therefore, if you alter one line's indentation to be nonstandard, the lines below will tend to follow it. This behavior is convenient in cases where you have overridden the standard result of TAB because you find it unaesthetic for a particular line.

Remember that an open-parenthesis, open-brace or other opening delimiter at the left margin is assumed by Emacs (including the indentation routines) to be the start of a function. Therefore, you must never have an opening delimiter in column zero that is not the beginning of a function, not even inside a string. This restriction is vital for making the indentation commands fast; you must simply accept it. See Section 21.4 [Defuns], page 202, for more information on this.

21.5.2 Indenting Several Lines

When you wish to re-indent several lines of code which have been altered or moved to a different level in the list structure, you have several commands available.

C-M-q   Re-indent all the lines within one list (indent-sexp).

C-u TAB   Shift an entire list rigidly sideways so that its first line is properly indented.

C-M-\   Re-indent all lines in the region (indent-region).

You can re-indent the contents of a single list by positioning point before the beginning of it and typing C-M-q (indent-sexp in Lisp mode, indent-c-exp in C mode; also bound to other suitable commands in other modes). The indentation of the line the sexp starts on is not changed; therefore, only the relative indentation within the list, and not its position, is changed. To correct the position as well, type a TAB before the C-M-q.

If the relative indentation within a list is correct but the indentation of its first line is not, go to that line and type C-u TAB. TAB with a numeric argument reindents the current line as usual, then reindents by the same amount all the lines in the grouping starting on the current line. In other words, it reindents the whole grouping rigidly as a unit. It is clever, though, and does not alter lines that start inside strings, or C preprocessor lines when in C mode.

Another way to specify the range to be re-indented is with the region. The command C-M-\ (indent-region) applies TAB to every line whose first character is between point and mark.

21.5.3 Customizing Lisp Indentation

The indentation pattern for a Lisp expression can depend on the function called by the expression. For each Lisp function, you can choose among several predefined patterns of indentation, or define an arbitrary one with a Lisp program.

The standard pattern of indentation is as follows: the second line of the expression is indented under the first argument, if that is on the same line as the beginning of the expression; otherwise, the second line is indented underneath the function name. Each following line is indented under the previous line whose nesting depth is the same.

If the variable lisp-indent-offset is non-nil, it overrides the usual indentation pattern for the second line of an expression, so that such lines are always indented lisp-indent-offset more columns than the containing list.

The standard pattern is overridden for certain functions. Functions whose names start with def always indent the second line by lisp-body-indent extra columns beyond the open-parenthesis starting the expression.

The standard pattern can be overridden in various ways for individual functions, according to the lisp-indent-function property of the function name. There are four possibilities for this property:

nil   This is the same as no property; the standard indentation pattern is used.

defun   The pattern used for function names that start with def is used for this function also.

a number, *number*

The first *number* arguments of the function are *distinguished* arguments; the rest are considered the *body* of the expression. A line in the expression is indented according to whether the first argument on it is distinguished or not. If the argument is part of the body, the line is indented lisp-body-indent more columns than the open-parenthesis starting the containing expression. If the argument is distinguished and is either the first or second argument, it is indented *twice* that many extra columns. If the argument is distinguished and not the first or second argument, the standard pattern is followed for that line.

a symbol, *symbol*

> *symbol* should be a function name; that function is called to calculate the indentation of a line within this expression. The function receives two arguments:
>
> *state*   The value returned by `parse-partial-sexp` (a Lisp primitive for indentation and nesting computation) when it parses up to the beginning of this line.
>
> *pos*   The position at which the line being indented begins.
>
> It should return either a number, which is the number of columns of indentation for that line, or a list whose car is such a number. The difference between returning a number and returning a list is that a number says that all following lines at the same nesting level should be indented just like this one; a list says that following lines might call for different indentations. This makes a difference when the indentation is being computed by `C-M-q`; if the value is a number, `C-M-q` need not recalculate indentation for the following lines until the end of the list.

21.5.4 Customizing C Indentation

Two variables control which commands perform C indentation and when.

If `c-auto-newline` is non-`nil`, newlines are inserted both before and after braces that you insert, and after colons and semicolons. Correct C indentation is done on all the lines that are made this way.

If `c-tab-always-indent` is nil, the TAB command in C mode does indentation only if point is at the left margin or within the line's indentation. If there is non-whitespace to the left of point, then TAB just inserts a tab character in the buffer. Normally, this variable is `t`, and TAB always reindents the current line. The default behavior means that to insert a real tab character you must quote it by typing `C-q` TAB.

C does not have anything analogous to particular function names for which special forms of indentation are desirable. However, it has a different need for customization facilities: many different styles of C indentation are in common use.

There are six variables you can set to control the style that Emacs C mode uses.

`c-indent-level`
>   Indentation of C statements within surrounding block. The surrounding block's indentation is the indentation of the line on which the open-brace appears.

`c-continued-statement-offset`
>   Extra indentation given to a substatement, such as the thenclause of an if or body of a while.

`c-brace-offset`
>   Extra indentation for line if it starts with an open brace.

`c-brace-imaginary-offset`
>   An open brace following other text is treated as if it were this far to the right of the start of its line.

`c-argdecl-indent`
>   Indentation level of declarations of C function arguments.

`c-label-offset`
>   Extra indentation for line that is a label, or case or default.

The variable `c-indent-level` controls the indentation for C statements with respect to the surrounding block. In the example

```
{
    foo ();
```

the difference in indentation between the lines is `c-indent-level`. Its standard value is 2.

If the open-brace beginning the compound statement is not at the beginning of its line, the `c-indent-level` is added to the indentation of the line, not the column of the open-brace. For example,

```
if (losing) {
    do_this ();
```

One popular indentation style is that which results from setting `c-indent-level` to 8 and putting open-braces at the end of a line in this way. I prefer to put the open-brace on a separate line.

In fact, the value of the variable `c-brace-imaginary-offset` is also added to the indentation of such a statement. Normally this variable is zero. Think of this variable as the imaginary position of the open brace, relative to the first nonblank character on the line. By setting this variable to 4 and `c-indent-level` to 0, you can get this style:

```
if (x == y) {
    do_it ();
    }
```

When `c-indent-level` is zero, the statements inside most braces will line up right under the open brace. But there is an exception made for braces in column zero, such as surrounding a function's body. The statements just inside it do not go at column zero. Instead, `c-brace-offset` and `c-continued-statement-offset` (see below) are added to produce a typical offset between brace levels, and the statements are indented that far.

`c-continued-statement-offset` controls the extra indentation for a line that starts within a statement (but not within parentheses or brackets). These lines are usually statements that are within other statements, such as the then-clauses of `if` statements and the bodies of `while` statements. This parameter is the difference in indentation between the two lines in

```
if (x == y)
    do_it ();
```

Its standard value is 2. Some popular indentation styles correspond to a value of zero for `c-continued-statement-offset`.

`c-brace-offset` is the extra indentation given to a line that starts with an open-brace. Its standard value is zero; compare

```
if (x == y)
  {
```

with

```
if (x == y)
    do_it ();
```

if `c-brace-offset` were set to 4, the first example would become

```
if (x == y)
      {
```

`c-argdecl-indent` controls the indentation of declarations of the arguments of a C function. It is absolute: argument declarations receive exactly `c-argdecl-indent` spaces. The standard value is 5, resulting in code like this:

```
char *
index (string, c)
     char *string;
     int c;
```

`c-label-offset` is the extra indentation given to a line that contains a label, a case statement, or a `default:` statement. Its standard value is −2, resulting in code like this

```
switch (c)
  {
  case 'x':
```

If `c-label-offset` were zero, the same code would be indented as

```
switch (c)
  {
    case 'x':
```

This example assumes that the other variables above also have their standard values.

I strongly recommend that you try out the indentation style produced by the standard settings of these variables, together with putting open braces on separate lines. You can see how it looks in all the C source files of GNU Emacs.

21.6 Automatic Display Of Matching Parentheses

The Emacs parenthesis-matching feature is designed to show automatically how parentheses match in the text. Whenever you type a self-inserting character that is a closing delimiter, the cursor moves momentarily to the location of the matching opening delimiter, provided that is on the screen. If it is not on the screen, some text near it is displayed in the echo area. Either way, you can tell what grouping is being closed off.

In Lisp, automatic matching applies only to parentheses. In C, it applies to braces and brackets too. Emacs knows which characters to regard as matching delimiters based on the syntax table, which is set by the major mode. See Section 30.6 [Syntax], page 366.

If the opening delimiter and closing delimiter are mismatched—such as in '[x)'—a warning message is displayed in the echo area. The correct matches are specified in the syntax table.

Three variables control parenthesis match display. `blink-matching-paren` turns the feature on or off; `nil` turns it off, but the default is `t` to turn match display on. `blink-matching-delay` says how many seconds to wait; the default is 1, but on some systems it is useful to specify a fraction of a second. `blink-matching-paren-distance` specifies how many characters back to search to find the matching opening delimiter. If the match is not found in that far, scanning stops, and nothing is displayed. This is to prevent scanning for the matching delimiter from wasting lots of time when there is no match. The default is 12,000.

When using X Windows, you can request a more powerful kind of automatic parenthesis matching by loading the **paren** library. To load it, type `M-x load-library` RET `paren` RET. This library turns off the usual kind of matching parenthesis display and substitutes another: whenever point is after a close parenthesis, the close parenthesis and its matching open parenthesis are both highlighted; otherwise, if point is before an open parenthesis, the matching close parenthesis is highlighted. (There is no need to highlight the open parenthesis after point because the cursor appears on top of that character.)

21.7 Manipulating Comments

Because comments are such an important part of programming, Emacs provides special commands for editing and inserting comments.

21.7.1 Comment Commands

The comment commands insert, kill and align comments.

M-;   Insert or align comment (`indent-for-comment`).

C-x ;   Set comment column (`set-comment-column`).

C-u - C-x ;
           Kill comment on current line (`kill-comment`).

M-LFD   Like `RET` followed by inserting and aligning a comment (`indent-new-comment-line`).

M-x comment-region
           Add or remove comment delimiters on all the lines in the region.

The command that creates a comment is M-; (`indent-for-comment`). If there is no comment already on the line, a new comment is created, aligned at a specific column called the *comment column*. The comment is created by inserting the string Emacs thinks comments should start with (the value of `comment-start`; see below). Point is left after that string. If the text of the line extends past the comment column, then the indentation is done to a suitable boundary (usually, at least one space is inserted). If the major mode has specified a string to terminate comments, that is inserted after point, to keep the syntax valid.

M-; can also be used to align an existing comment. If a line already contains the string that starts comments, then M-; just moves point after it and re-indents it to the conventional place. Exception: comments starting in column 0 are not moved.

Some major modes have special rules for indenting certain kinds of comments in certain contexts. For example, in Lisp code, comments which start with two semicolons are indented as if they were lines of code, instead of at the comment column. Comments which start with three semicolons are supposed to start at the left margin. Emacs understands these conventions by indenting a double-semicolon comment using `TAB`, and by not changing the indentation of a triple-semicolon comment at all.

```
;; This function is just an example
;;; Here either two or three semicolons are appropriate.
(defun foo (x)
;;; And now, the first part of the function:
  ;; The following line adds one.
  (1+ x))             ; This line adds one.
```

In C code, a comment preceded on its line by nothing but whitespace is indented like a line of code.

Even when an existing comment is properly aligned, M-; is still useful for moving directly to the start of the comment.

C-u - C-x ; (kill-comment) kills the comment on the current line, if there is one. The indentation before the start of the comment is killed as well. If there does not appear to be a comment in the line, nothing is done. To reinsert the comment on another line, move to the end of that line, do C-y, and then do M-; to realign it. Note that C-u - C-x ; is not a distinct key; it is C-x ; (set-comment-column) with a negative argument. That command is programmed so that when it receives a negative argument it calls kill-comment. However, kill-comment is a valid command which you could bind directly to a key if you wanted to.

21.7.2 Multiple Lines of Comments

If you are typing a comment and wish to continue it on another line, you can use the command M-LFD (indent-new-comment-line). This terminates the comment you are typing, creates a new blank line afterward, and begins a new comment indented under the old one. When Auto Fill mode is on, going past the fill column while typing a comment causes the comment to be continued in just this fashion. If point is not at the end of the line when M-LFD is typed, the text on the rest of the line becomes part of the new comment line.

To turn existing lines into comment lines, use the M-x comment-region command. It adds comment delimiters to the lines that start in the region, thus commenting them out. With a negative argument, it does the opposite—it deletes comment delimiters from the lines in the region.

With a positive argument, comment-region duplicates the last character of the comment start sequence it adds; the argument specifies how many copies of the character to insert. Thus, in Lisp mode, C-u 2 M-x comment-region adds ';;' to each line. Duplicating the comment delimiter is a way of calling attention to the comment. It can also affect how the comment is indented. In Lisp, for proper indentation, you should use an argument of two, if between defuns, and three, if within a defun.

21.7.3 Options Controlling Comments

The comment column is stored in the variable `comment-column`. You can set it to a number explicitly. Alternatively, the command `C-x ;` (set-comment-column) sets the comment column to the column point is at. `C-u C-x ;` sets the comment column to match the last comment before point in the buffer, and then does a `M-;` to align the current line's comment under the previous one. Note that `C-u - C-x ;` runs the function `kill-comment` as described above.

The variable `comment-column` is per-buffer: setting the variable in the normal fashion affects only the current buffer, but there is a default value which you can change with `setq-default`. See Section 30.2.4 [Locals], page 348. Many major modes initialize this variable for the current buffer.

The comment commands recognize comments based on the regular expression that is the value of the variable `comment-start-skip`. Make sure this regexp does not match the null string. It may match more than the comment starting delimiter in the strictest sense of the word; for example, in C mode the value of the variable is `"/\\*+ *"`, which matches extra stars and spaces after the '/*' itself. (Note that '\\' is needed in Lisp syntax to include a '\' in the string, which is needed to deny the first star its special meaning in regexp syntax. See Section 12.5 [Regexps], page 88.)

When a comment command makes a new comment, it inserts the value of `comment-start` to begin it. The value of `comment-end` is inserted after point, so that it will follow the text that you will insert into the comment. In C mode, `comment-start` has the value `"/* "` and `comment-end` has the value `" */"`.

The variable `comment-multi-line` controls how M-LFD (indent-new-comment-line) behaves when used inside a comment. If `comment-multi-line` is `nil`, as it normally is, then the comment on the starting line is terminated and a new comment is started on the new following line. If `comment-multi-line` is not `nil`, then the new following line is set up as part of the same comment that was found on the starting line. This is done by not inserting a terminator on the old line, and not inserting a starter on the new line. In languages where multi-line comments work, the choice of value for this variable is a matter of taste.

The variable `comment-indent-function` should contain a function that will be called to compute the indentation for a newly inserted comment or for aligning an existing comment. It is set differently by various major modes. The function is called with no arguments, but with point at the beginning of the comment, or at the end of a line if a new comment is to be inserted. It should return the column in which the comment ought to start. For example, in Lisp mode, the indent hook function bases its decision on how many semicolons begin an existing comment, and on the code in the preceding lines.

21.8 Editing Without Unbalanced Parentheses

M-(Put parentheses around next sexp(s) (`insert-parentheses`).

M-)   Move past next close parenthesis and re-indent (`move-over-close-and-reindent`).

The commands M-((`insert-parentheses`) and M-) (`move-over-close-and-reindent`) are designed to facilitate a style of editing which keeps parentheses balanced at all times. M-(inserts a pair of parentheses, either together as in '()', or, if given an argument, around the next several sexps. It leaves point after the open parenthesis. The command M-) moves past the close parenthesis, deleting any indentation preceding it (in this example there is none), and indenting with LFD after it.

For example, instead of typing (F O O), you can type M-(F O O, which has the same effect except for leaving the cursor before the close parenthesis.

M-(may insert a space before the open parenthesis, depending on the syntax class of the preceding character. Set `parens-dont-require-spaces` to a non-`nil` value if you wish to inhibit this.

21.9 Completion for Symbol Names

Usually completion happens in the minibuffer. But one kind of completion is available in all buffers: completion for symbol names.

The character M-TAB runs a command to complete the partial symbol before point against the set of meaningful symbol names. Any additional characters determined by the partial name are inserted at point.

If the partial name in the buffer has more than one possible completion and they have no additional characters in common, a list of all possible completions is displayed in another window.

There are two ways of determining the set of legitimate symbol names to complete against. In most major modes, this uses a tags table (see Section 21.12 [Tags], page 216); the legitimate symbol names are the tag names listed in the tags table file. The command which implements this is `complete-tag`.

In Emacs-Lisp mode, the name space for completion normally consists of nontrivial symbols present in Emacs—those that have function definitions, values or properties. However, if there is an open-parenthesis immediately before the beginning of the partial symbol, only symbols with function definitions are considered as completions. The command which implements this is `lisp-complete-symbol`.

In Text mode and related modes, `M-TAB` completes words based on the spell-checker's dictionary. See Section 13.4 [Spelling], page 99.

21.10 Documentation Commands

As you edit Lisp code to be run in Emacs, the commands `C-h f` (`describe-function`) and `C-h v` (`describe-variable`) can be used to print documentation of functions and variables that you want to call. These commands use the minibuffer to read the name of a function or variable to document, and display the documentation in a window.

For extra convenience, these commands provide default arguments based on the code in the neighborhood of point. `C-h f` sets the default to the function called in the innermost list containing point. `C-h v` uses the symbol name around or adjacent to point as its default.

Documentation on operating system commands, library functions and system calls can be obtained with the `M-x manual-entry` command. This reads a topic as an argument, and displays the "man page" on that topic. `manual-entry` starts a background process that formats the manual page, by running the `man` program. The result goes in a buffer named '*man *topic**'. These buffers use a special major mode, Man mode, that facilitates scrolling and examining other manual pages. For details, type `C-h m` while in a man page buffer.

For a long man page, setting the faces properly can take substantial time. By default, Emacs uses faces in man pages if you are using X Windows. You can turn off use of faces in man pages by setting the variable `Man-fontify-manpage-flag` to `nil`.

If you insert the text of a man page into an Emacs buffer in some other fashion, you can use the command `M-x Man-fontify-manpage` to perform the same conversions that `M-x manual-entry` does.

Eventually the GNU project hopes to replace most man pages with better-organized manuals that you can browse with Info. See Section 7.5 [Misc Help], page 52. Since this process is only partially completed, it is still useful to read manual pages.

21.11 Change Logs

The Emacs command `C-x 4 a` adds a new entry to the change log file for the file you are editing (`add-change-log-entry-other-window`).

A change log file contains a chronological record of when and why you have changed a program, consisting of a sequence of entries describing individual changes. Normally it is kept in a file called 'ChangeLog' in the same directory as the file you are editing, or one of its parent directories. A single 'ChangeLog' file can record changes for all the files in its directory and all its subdirectories.

A change log entry starts with a header line that contains your name, your email address (taken from the variable user-mail-address), and the current date and time. Aside from these header lines, every line in the change log starts with a space or a tab. The bulk of the entry consists of *items*, each of which starts with a line starting with whitespace and a star. Here are two entries, each with two items:

```
Wed May  5 14:11:45 1993  Richard Stallman   <rms@gnu.ai.mit.edu>

        * man.el: Rename symbols 'man-*' to 'Man-*'.
        (manual-entry): Make prompt string clearer.

        * simple.el (blink-matching-paren-distance):
        Change default to 12,000.

Tue May  4 12:42:19 1993  Richard Stallman   <rms@gnu.ai.mit.edu>

        * vc.el (minor-mode-map-alist): Don't use it if it's void.
        (vc-cancel-version): Doc fix.
```

One entry can describe several changes; each change should have its own item. Normally there should be a blank line between items. When items are related (parts of the same change, in different places), group them by leaving no blank line between them. The second entry above contains two items grouped in this way.

C-x 4 a visits the change log file and creates a new entry unless the most recent entry is for today's date and your name. It also creates a new item for the current file. For many languages, it can even guess the name of the function or other object that was changed.

The change log file is visited in Change Log mode. In this major mode, each bunch of grouped items counts as one paragraph, and each entry is considered a page. This facilitates editing the entries. LFD and auto-fill indent each new line like the previous line; this is convenient for entering the contents of an entry.

Version control systems are another way keep track of changes in your program and keep a change log. See Section 14.7.4 [Log Entries], page 120.

21.12 Tags Tables

A *tags table* is a description of how a multi-file program is broken up into files. It lists the names of the component files and the names and positions of the functions (or other named subunits) in each file. Grouping the related files makes it possible to search or replace through all the files with one command. Recording the function names and positions makes possible the M-. command which finds the definition of a function by looking up which of the files it is in.

Tags tables are stored in files called *tags table files*. The conventional name for a tags table file is 'TAGS'.

Each entry in the tags table records the name of one tag, the name of the file that the tag is defined in (implicitly), and the position in that file of the tag's definition.

Just what names from the described files are recorded in the tags table depends on the programming language of the described file. They normally include all functions and subroutines, and may also include global variables, data types, and anything else convenient. Each name recorded is called a *tag*.

21.12.1 Source File Tag Syntax

- In Lisp code, any function defined with defun, any variable defined with defvar or defconst, and in general the first argument of any expression that starts with '(def' in column zero, is a tag.

- In Scheme code, tags include anything defined with def or with a construct whose name starts with 'def'. They also include variables set with set! at top level in the file.

- In C code, any C function or typedef is a tag, and so are definitions of struct, union and enum. Any #define is also a tag, unless '--no-defines' is specified when the tags table is constructed, which sometimes makes the tags file much smaller. In C++ code, member functions are also recognized.

- In Yacc or Bison input files, each rule defines as a tag the nonterminal it constructs. The portions of the file that contain C code are parsed as C code.

- In Fortran code, functions and subroutines are tags.

- In Pascal code, the tags are the functions and procedures defined in the file.

- In Prolog code, a tag name appears at the left margin.

- In assembler code, labels appearing at the beginning of a line, followed by a colon, are tags.

- In LaTeX text, the argument of any of the commands \chapter, \section, \subsection, \subsubsection, \eqno, \label, \ref, \cite, \bibitem and \typeout is a tag.
- You can also generate tags based on regexp matching (see Section 21.12.2 [Create Tags Table], page 217) for any text file.

21.12.2 Creating Tags Tables

The etags program is used to create a tags table file. It knows the syntax of several languages, as described in the previous section. Here is how to run etags:

    etags inputfiles...

The etags program reads the specified files, and writes a tags table named 'TAGS' in the current working directory. etags recognizes the language used in an input file based on its file name and contents. You can specify the language with the '--language=name' option, described below.

If the tags table data become outdated due to changes in the files described in the table, the way to update the tags table is the same way it was made in the first place. It is not necessary to do this often.

If the tags table fails to record a tag, or records it for the wrong file, then Emacs cannot possibly find its definition. However, if the position recorded in the tags table becomes a little bit wrong (due to some editing in the file that the tag definition is in), the only consequence is a slight delay in finding the tag. Even if the stored position is very wrong, Emacs will still find the tag, but it must search the entire file for it.

So you should update a tags table when you define new tags that you want to have listed, or when you move tag definitions from one file to another, or when changes become substantial. Normally there is no need to update the tags table after each edit, or even every day.

One tags table can effectively include another. Specify the included tags file name with the '--include=file' option when creating the file that is to include it. The latter file then acts as if it contained all the files specified in the included file, as well as the files it directly contains.

When you want to make a tags table from a great number of files, you may have problems listing them on the command line, because some systems have a limit on its length. The simplest way to circumvent this limit is to tell etags to read the file names from its standard input, by typing a dash in place of the file names, like this:

    find . -name "*.[chCH]" -print | etags -

Use the option '--language=name' to specify the language explicitly. You can intermix these options with file names; each one applies to the

file names that follow it. Specify '--language=auto' to tell etags to resume guessing the language from the file names and file contents. Specify
'--language=none' to turn off language-specific processing entirely; then
etags recognizes tags by regexp matching alone. 'etags --help' prints the
list of the languages etags knows, and the file name rules for guessing the
language.

The '--regex' option provides a general way of recognizing tags based on
regexp matching. You can freely intermix it with file names. Each '--regex'
option adds to the preceding ones, and applies only to the following files.
The syntax is:

    --regex=/*tagregexp*[/*nameregexp*]/

where *tagregexp* is used to match the lines to tag. It is always anchored, that
is, it behaves as if preceded by '^'. If you want to account for indentation,
just match any initial number of blanks by beginning your regular expression
with '[\t]*'. In the regular expressions, '\' quotes the next character, and
'\t' stands for the tab character. Note that etags does not handle the other
C escape sequences for special characters.

You should not match more characters with *tagregexp* than that needed
to recognize what you want to tag. If the match is such that more characters
than needed are unavoidably matched by *tagregexp*, you may find useful to
add a *nameregexp*, in order to narrow the tag scope. You can find some
examples below.

The '-R' option deletes all the regexps defined with '--regex' options.
It applies to the file names following it, as you can see from the following
example:

    etags --regex=/*reg1*/ voo.doo --regex=/*reg2*/ \
        bar.ber -R --lang=lisp los.er

Here etags chooses the parsing language for 'voo.doo' and 'bar.ber' according to their contents. etags also uses *reg1* to recognize additional tags in
'voo.doo', and both *reg1* and *reg2* to recognize additional tags in 'bar.ber'.
etags uses the Lisp tags rules, and no regexp matching, to recognize tags in
'los.er'.

Here are some more examples. The regexps are quoted to protect them
from shell interpretation.

Tag the DEFVAR macros in the emacs source files:

    --regex='/[\t]*DEFVAR_[A-Z_ \t(]+"\([^"]+\)"/'

Tag VHDL files (this example is a single long line, broken here for formatting
reasons):

    --language=none
    --regex='/[\t]*\(ARCHITECTURE\|CONFIGURATION\) +[^]* +OF/'
    --regex='/[\t]*\(ATTRIBUTE\|ENTITY\|FUNCTION\|PACKAGE\

```
\( BODY\)?\|PROCEDURE\|PROCESS\|TYPE\)[ \t]+\([^ \t(]+\)/\3/'
```

Tag Cobol files (every label starting in column seven):

```
--language=none --regex='/.......[a-zA-Z0-9-]+\./'
```

Tag Postscript files (every label starting in column one):

```
--language=none --regex='#/[^ \t{]+#/'
```

Tag TCL files (this last example shows the usage of a *nameregexp*):

```
--lang=none --regex='/proc[ \t]+\([^ \t]+\)/\1/'
```

For a list of the other available **etags** options, execute **etags --help**.

21.12.3 Selecting a Tags Table

Emacs has at any time one *selected* tags table, and all the commands for working with tags tables use the selected one. To select a tags table, type M-x visit-tags-table, which reads the tags table file name as an argument. The name 'TAGS' in the default directory is used as the default file name.

All this command does is store the file name in the variable **tags-file-name**. Emacs does not actually read in the tags table contents until you try to use them. Setting this variable yourself is just as good as using **visit-tags-table**. The variable's initial value is **nil**; that value tells all the commands for working with tags tables that they must ask for a tags table file name to use.

Using **visit-tags-table** when a tags table is already loaded gives you a choice: you can add the new tags table to the current list of tags tables, or start a new list. The tags commands use all the tags tables in the current list. If you start a new list, the new tags table is used *instead* of others. If you add the new table to the current list, it is used *as well as* the others. When the tags commands scan the list of tags tables, they don't always start at the beginning of the list; they start with the first tags table (if any) that describes the current file, proceed from there to the end of the list, and then scan from the beginning of the list until they have covered all the tables in the list.

You can specify a precise list of tags tables by setting the variable **tags-table-list** to a list of strings, like this:

```
(setq tags-table-list
      '("~/emacs" "/usr/local/lib/emacs/src"))
```

This tells the tags commands to look at the 'TAGS' files in your '~/emacs' directory and in the '/usr/local/lib/emacs/src' directory. The order depends on which file you are in and which tags table mentions that file, as explained above.

Do not set both **tags-file-name** and **tags-table-list**.

21.12.4 Finding a Tag

The most important thing that a tags table enables you to do is to find the definition of a specific tag.

M-. *tag* RET

> Find first definition of *tag* (`find-tag`).

C-u M-.   Find next alternate definition of last tag specified.

C-u - M-.   Go back to previous tag found.

C-M-. *pattern* RET

> Find a tag whose name matches *pattern* (`find-tag-regexp`).

C-u C-M-.   Find the next tag whose name matches the last pattern used.

C-x 4 . *tag* RET

> Find first definition of *tag*, but display it in another window (`find-tag-other-window`).

C-x 5 . *tag* RET

> Find first definition of *tag*, and create a new frame to select the buffer (`find-tag-other-frame`).

M-. (`find-tag`) is the command to find the definition of a specified tag. It searches through the tags table for that tag, as a string, and then uses the tags table info to determine the file that the definition is in and the approximate character position in the file of the definition. Then `find-tag` visits that file, moves point to the approximate character position, and searches ever-increasing distances away to find the tag definition.

If an empty argument is given (just type RET), the sexp in the buffer before or around point is used as the *tag* argument. See Section 21.2 [Lists], page 200, for info on sexps.

You don't need to give M-. the full name of the tag; a part will do. This is because M-. finds tags in the table which contain *tag* as a substring. However, it prefers an exact match to a substring match. To find other tags that match the same substring, give `find-tag` a numeric argument, as in C-u M-.; this does not read a tag name, but continues searching the tags table's text for another tag containing the same substring last used. If you have a real META key, M-0 M-. is an easier alternative to C-u M-..

Like most commands that can switch buffers, `find-tag` has a variant that displays the new buffer in another window, and one that makes a new frame for it. The former is C-x 4 ., which invokes the command `find-tag-other-window`. The latter is C-x 5 ., which invokes `find-tag-other-frame`.

To move back to places you've found tags recently, use C-u - M-.; more generally, M-. with a negative numeric argument. This command can take you to another buffer. `C-x 4 .` with a negative argument finds the previous tag location in another window.

The command `C-M-.` (`find-tag-regexp`) visits the tags that match a specified regular expression. It is just like `M-.` except that it does regexp matching instead of substring matching.

21.12.5 Searching and Replacing with Tags Tables

The commands in this section visit and search all the files listed in the selected tags table, one by one. For these commands, the tags table serves only to specify a sequence of files to search.

`M-x tags-search RET` *regexp* `RET`

> Search for *regexp* through the files in the selected tags table.

`M-x tags-query-replace RET` *regexp* `RET` *replacement* `RET`

> Perform a `query-replace-regexp` on each file in the selected tags table.

`M-,`   Restart one of the commands above, from the current location of point (`tags-loop-continue`).

`M-x tags-search` reads a regexp using the minibuffer, then searches for matches in all the files in the selected tags table, one file at a time. It displays the name of the file being searched so you can follow its progress. As soon as it finds an occurrence, `tags-search` returns.

Having found one match, you probably want to find all the rest. To find one more match, type `M-,` (`tags-loop-continue`) to resume the `tags-search`. This searches the rest of the current buffer, followed by the remaining files of the tags table.

`M-x tags-query-replace` performs a single `query-replace-regexp` through all the files in the tags table. It reads a regexp to search for and a string to replace with, just like ordinary `M-x query-replace-regexp`. It searches much like `M-x tags-search`, but repeatedly, processing matches according to your input. See Section 12.7 [Replace], page 93, for more information on query replace.

It is possible to get through all the files in the tags table with a single invocation of `M-x tags-query-replace`. But often it is useful to exit temporarily, which you can do with any input event that has no special query replace meaning. You can resume the query replace subsequently by typing `M-,`; this command resumes the last tags search or replace command that you did.

The commands in this section carry out much broader searches than the `find-tag` family. The `find-tag` commands search only for definitions of tags that match your substring or regexp. The commands `tags-search` and `tags-query-replace` find every occurrence of the regexp, as ordinary search commands and replace commands do in the current buffer.

These commands create buffers only temporarily for the files that they have to search (those which are not already visited in Emacs buffers). Buffers in which no match is found are quickly killed; the others continue to exist.

It may have struck you that `tags-search` is a lot like `grep`. You can also run `grep` itself as an inferior of Emacs and have Emacs show you the matching lines one by one. This works much like running a compilation; finding the source locations of the `grep` matches works like finding the compilation errors. See Section 22.1 [Compilation], page 239.

21.12.6 Stepping Through a Tags Table

If you wish to process all the files in the selected tags table, but not in the specific ways that `M-x tags-search` and `M-x tags-query-replace` do, you can use `M-x next-file` to visit the files one by one.

`C-u M-x next-file`
> Visit the first file in the tags table, and prepare to advance sequentially by files.

`M-x next-file`
> Visit the next file in the selected tags table.

21.12.7 Tags Table Inquiries

`M-x list-tags RET` *file* `RET`
> Display a list of the tags defined in the program file 'file'.

`M-x tags-apropos RET` *regexp* `RET`
> Display a list of all tags matching *regexp*.

`M-x list-tags` reads the name of one of the files described by the selected tags table, and displays a list of all the tags defined in that file. The "file name" argument is really just a string to compare against the file names recorded in the tags table; it is read as a string rather than as a file name. Therefore, completion and defaulting are not available, and you must enter the file name the same way it appears in the tag table. Do not include a directory as part of the file name unless the file name recorded in the tags table includes a directory.

`M-x tags-apropos` is like `apropos` for tags (see Section 7.3 [Apropos], page 49). It reads a regexp, then finds all the tags in the selected tags table whose entries match that regexp, and displays the tag names found.

You can also perform completion in the buffer on the name space of tag names in the current tags tables. See Section 21.9 [Symbol Completion], page 213.

21.13 Merging Files with Emerge

It's not unusual for programmers to get their signals crossed and modify the same program in two different directions. To recover from this confusion, you need to merge the two versions. Emerge makes this easier. See also Section 14.9 [Comparing Files], page 130.

21.13.1 Overview of Emerge

To start Emerge, run one of these four commands:

M-x emerge-files
> Merge two specified files.

M-x emerge-files-with-ancestor
> Merge two specified files, with reference to a common ancestor.

M-x emerge-buffers
> Merge two buffers.

M-x emerge-buffers-with-ancestor
> Merge two buffers with reference to a common ancestor in a third buffer.

The Emerge commands compare two files or buffers, and display the comparison in three buffers: one for each input text (the *A buffer* and the *B buffer*), and one (the *merge buffer*) where merging takes place. The merge buffer shows the full merged text, not just the differences. Wherever the two input texts differ, you can choose which one of them to include in the merge buffer.

The Emerge commands that take input from existing buffers use only the accessible portions of those buffers, if they are narrowed (see Section 29.7 [Narrowing], page 335).

If a common ancestor version is available, from which the two texts to be merged were both derived, Emerge can use it to guess which alternative is right. Wherever one current version agrees with the ancestor, Emerge presumes that the other current version is a deliberate change which should be kept in the merged version. Use the 'with-ancestor' commands if you want to specify a common ancestor text. These commands read three file or buffer names—variant A, variant B, and the common ancestor.

After the comparison is done and the buffers are prepared, the interactive merging starts. You control the merging by typing special *merge commands* in the merge buffer. The merge buffer shows you a full merged text, not just differences. For each run of differences between the input texts, you can choose which one of them to keep, or edit them both together.

The merge buffer uses a special major mode, Emerge mode, with commands for making these choices. But you can also edit the buffer with ordinary Emacs commands.

At any given time, the attention of Emerge is focused on one particular difference, called the *selected* difference. This difference is marked off in the three buffers like this:

```
vvvvvvvvvvvvvvvvvvvvv
text that differs
^^^^^^^^^^^^^^^^^^^^^^^
```

Emerge numbers all the differences sequentially and the mode line always shows the number of the selected difference.

Normally, the merge buffer starts out with the A version of the text. But when the A version of a difference agrees with the common ancestor, then the B version is initially preferred for that difference.

Emerge leaves the merged text in the merge buffer when you exit. At that point, you can save it in a file with C-x C-w. If you give a numeric argument to `emerge-files` or `emerge-files-with-ancestor`, it reads the name of the output file using the minibuffer. (This is the last file name those commands read.) Then exiting from Emerge saves the merged text in the output file.

Normally, Emerge commands save the output buffer in its file when you exit. If you abort Emerge with C-], the Emerge command does not save the output buffer, but you can save it yourself if you wish.

21.13.2 Submodes of Emerge

You can choose between two modes for giving merge commands: Fast mode and Edit mode. In Fast mode, basic merge commands are single characters, but ordinary Emacs commands are disabled. This is convenient if you use only merge commands. In Edit mode, all merge commands start with the prefix key C-c C-c, and the normal Emacs commands are also available. This allows editing the merge buffer, but slows down Emerge operations.

Use e to switch to Edit mode, and C-c C-c f to switch to Fast mode. The mode line indicates Edit and Fast modes with 'E' and 'F'.

Emerge has two additional submodes that affect how particular merge commands work: Auto Advance mode and Skip Prefers mode.

If Auto Advance mode is in effect, the a and b commands advance to the next difference. This lets you go through the merge faster as long as you simply choose one of the alternatives from the input. The mode line indicates Auto Advance mode with 'A'.

If Skip Prefers mode is in effect, the n and p commands skip over differences in states prefer-A and prefer-B (see Section 21.13.3 [State of Difference], page 225). Thus you see only differences for which neither version is presumed "correct". The mode line indicates Skip Prefers mode with 'S'.

Use the command s a (emerge-auto-advance-mode) to set or clear Auto Advance mode. Use s s (emerge-skip-prefers-mode) to set or clear Skip Prefers mode. These commands turn on the mode with a positive argument, turns it off with a negative or zero argument, and toggle the mode with no argument.

21.13.3 State of a Difference

In the merge buffer, a difference is marked with lines of 'v' and '^' characters. Each difference has one of these seven states:

A   The difference is showing the A version. The a command always produces this state; the mode line indicates it with 'A'.

B   The difference is showing the B version. The b command always produces this state; the mode line indicates it with 'B'.

default-A
default-B   The difference is showing the A or the B state by default, because you haven't made a choice. All differences start in the default-A state (and thus the merge buffer is a copy of the A buffer), except those for which one alternative is "preferred" (see below).

When you select a difference, its state changes from default-A or default-B to plain A or B. Thus, the selected difference never has state default-A or default-B, and these states are never displayed in the mode line.

The command d a chooses default-A as the default state, and d b chooses default-B. This chosen default applies to all differences which you haven't ever selected and for which no alternative is preferred. If you are moving through the merge sequentially, the differences you haven't selected are those following the selected one. Thus, while moving sequentially, you can effectively make the A version the default for some sections of the merge buffer and the B version the default for others by using d a and d b between sections.

prefer-A
prefer-B   The difference is showing the A or B state because it is *preferred*. This means that you haven't made an explicit choice, but one alternative seems likely to be right because the other alternative agrees with the common ancestor. Thus, where the A buffer

agrees with the common ancestor, the B version is preferred, because chances are it is the one that was actually changed.

These two states are displayed in the mode line as 'A*' and 'B*'.

combined   The difference is showing a combination of the A and B states, as a result of the x c or x C commands.

Once a difference is in this state, the a and b commands don't do anything to it unless you give them a numeric argument.

The mode line displays this state as 'comb'.

21.13.4 Merge Commands

Here are the Merge commands for Fast mode; in Edit mode, precede them with C-c C-c:

p   Select the previous difference.

n   Select the next difference.

a   Choose the A version of this difference.

b   Choose the B version of this difference.

C-u n j   Select difference number n.

.   Select the difference containing point. You can use this command in the merge buffer or in the A or B buffer.

q   Quit—finish the merge.

C-]   Abort—exit merging and do not save the output.

f   Go into Fast mode. (In Edit mode, this is actually C-c C-c f.)

e   Go into Edit mode.

l   Recenter (like C-l) all three windows.

–   Specify part of a prefix numeric argument.

digit   Also specify part of a prefix numeric argument.

d a   Choose the A version as the default from here down in the merge buffer.

d b   Choose the B version as the default from here down in the merge buffer.

c a   Copy the A version of this difference into the kill ring.

c b   Copy the B version of this difference into the kill ring.

i a   Insert the A version of this difference at point.

i b   Insert the B version of this difference at point.

m   Put point and mark around the difference.

^   Scroll all three windows down (like M-v).

v   Scroll all three windows up (like C-v).

<   Scroll all three windows left (like C-x <).

>   Scroll all three windows right (like C-x >).

| Reset horizontal scroll on all three windows.

x 1   Shrink the merge window to one line. (Use C-u 1 to restore it to full size.)

x c   Combine the two versions of this difference (see Section 21.13.6 [Combining in Emerge], page 228).

x f   Show the names of the files/buffers Emerge is operating on, in a Help window. (Use C-u 1 to restore windows.)

x j   Join this difference with the following one. (C-u x j joins this difference with the previous one.)

x s   Split this difference into two differences. Before you use this command, position point in each of the three buffers at the place where you want to split the difference.

x t   Trim identical lines off top and bottom of the difference. Such lines occur when the A and B versions are identical but differ from the ancestor version.

21.13.5 Exiting Emerge

The q command (emerge-quit) finishes the merge, storing the results into the output file if you specified one. It restores the A and B buffers to their proper contents, or kills them if they were created by Emerge and you haven't changed them. It also disables the Emerge commands in the merge buffer, since executing them later could damage the contents of the various buffers.

C-] aborts the merge. This means exiting without writing the output file. If you didn't specify an output file, then there is no real difference between aborting and finishing the merge.

If the Emerge command was called from another Lisp program, then its return value is t for successful completion, or nil if you abort.

21.13.6 Combining the Two Versions

Sometimes you want to keep *both* alternatives for a particular difference.
To do this, use x c, which edits the merge buffer like this:

```
#ifdef NEW
version from A buffer
#else /* NEW */
version from B buffer
#endif /* NEW */
```

While this example shows C preprocessor conditionals delimiting the two
alternative versions, you can specify the strings to use by setting the variable
emerge-combine-versions-template to a string of your choice. In the
string, '%a' says where to put version A, and '%b' says where to put version
B. The default setting, which produces the results shown above, looks like
this:

```
"#ifdef NEW\n%a#else /* NEW */\n%b#endif /* NEW */\n"
```

21.13.7 Fine Points of Emerge

During the merge, you mustn't try to edit the A and B buffers yourself.
Emerge modifies them temporarily, but ultimately puts them back the way
they were.

You can have any number of merges going at once—just don't use any
one buffer as input to more than one merge at once, since the temporary
changes made in these buffers would get in each other's way.

Starting Emerge can take a long time because it needs to compare the
files fully. Emacs can't do anything else until diff finishes. Perhaps in the
future someone will change Emerge to do the comparison in the background
when the input files are large—then you could keep on doing other things
with Emacs until Emerge gets ready to accept commands.

After setting up the merge, Emerge runs the hook emerge-startup-hook
(see Section 30.2.3 [Hooks], page 347).

21.14 C Mode

In addition to the facilities of typical programming language major modes
(see Section 21.1 [Program Modes], page 199), C mode has various special
facilities.

M-a
M-e   In C mode, M-a and M-e move by complete C statements (c-
                 beginning-of-statement and c-end-of-statement). These

commands do ordinary, textual sentence motion when in or next to a comment.

M-q   M-q in C mode runs c-fill-paragraph, which is designed for filling C comments. (We assume you don't want to fill the actual C code in a C program.)

C-c C-u   Move back to the containing preprocessor conditional, setting the mark at the starting point (c-up-conditional).

           A numeric argument acts as a repeat count. With a negative argument, this command moves forward to the end of the containing preprocessor conditional. When going backwards, '#elif' acts like '#else' followed by '#if'. When going forwards, '#elif' is ignored.

C-c C-n   Move forward across the next preprocessor conditional, setting the mark at the starting point (c-forward-conditional).

C-c C-p   Move backward across the previous preprocessor conditional, setting the at the starting point (c-backward-conditional).

M-x c-macro-expand
           When you are debugging C code that uses macros, sometimes it is hard to figure out precisely how the macros expand. The command M-x c-macro-expand runs the C preprocessor and shows you what expansion results from the region. The portion of the buffer before the region is also included in preprocessing, for the sake of macros defined there, but the output from this part isn't shown.

M-x c-backslash-region
           Insert or align '\' characters at the ends of the lines of the region, except for the last such line. This is useful after writing or editing a C macro definition.

           If a line already ends in '\', this command adjusts the amount of whitespace before it. Otherwise, it inserts a new '\'.

M-x cpp-highlight-buffer
           Highlight parts of the text according to its preprocessor conditionals. This command displays another buffer named '*CPP Edit*', which serves as a graphic menu for selecting how to display particular kinds of conditionals and their contents. After changing various settings, click on '[A]pply these settings' (or go to that buffer and type a) to rehighlight the C mode buffer accordingly.

    C++ mode is like C mode, except that it understands C++ comment syntax and certain other differences between C and C++. It also has a command M-x fill-c++-comment, which fills a paragraph made of C++ comment lines.

The command `comment-region` is useful in C++ mode for commenting out several consecutive lines, or removing the commenting out of such lines. (You don't need this command with C comment syntax because you don't need to put comment delimiters on each line.) See Section 21.7 [Comments], page 210.

21.15 Fortran Mode

Fortran mode provides special motion commands for Fortran statements and subprograms, and indentation commands that understand Fortran conventions of nesting, line numbers and continuation statements. Fortran mode has its own Auto Fill mode that breaks long lines into proper Fortran continuation lines.

Special commands for comments are provided because Fortran comments are unlike those of other languages. Built-in abbrevs optionally save typing when you insert Fortran keywords.

Use `M-x fortran-mode` to switch to this major mode. This command runs the hook `fortran-mode-hook` (see Section 30.2.3 [Hooks], page 347).

21.15.1 Motion Commands

Fortran mode provides special commands to move by subprograms (functions and subroutines) and by statements. There is also a command to put the region around one subprogram, convenient for killing it or moving it.

C-M-a   Move to beginning of subprogram (`beginning-of-fortran-subprogram`).

C-M-e   Move to end of subprogram (`end-of-fortran-subprogram`).

C-M-h   Put point at beginning of subprogram and mark at end (`mark-fortran-subprogram`).

C-c C-n   Move to beginning of current or next statement (`fortran-next-statement`).

C-c C-p   Move to beginning of current or previous statement (`fortran-previous-statement`).

21.15.2 Fortran Indentation

Special commands and features are needed for indenting Fortran code in order to make sure various syntactic entities (line numbers, comment line indicators and continuation line flags) appear in the columns that are required for standard Fortran.

21.15.2.1 Fortran Indentation Commands

TAB   Indent the current line (`fortran-indent-line`).

LFD   Indent the current and start a new indented line (`fortran-indent-new-line`).

M-LFD   Break the current line and set up a continuation line.

C-M-q   Indent all the lines of the subprogram point is in (`fortran-indent-subprogram`).

Fortran mode redefines TAB to reindent the current line for Fortran (`fortran-indent-line`). This command indents Line numbers and continuation markers to their required columns, and independently indents the body of the statement based on its nesting in the program.

The key LFD runs the command `fortran-indent-new-line`, which reindents the current line then makes and indents a new line. This command is useful to reindent the closing statement of 'do' loops and other blocks before starting a new line.

The key C-M-q runs `fortran-indent-subprogram`, a command to reindent all the lines of the Fortran subprogram (function or subroutine) containing point.

The key M-LFD runs `fortran-split-line`, which splits a line in the appropriate fashion for Fortran. In a non-comment line, the second half becomes a continuation line and is indented accordingly. In a comment line, both halves become separate comment lines.

21.15.2.2 Continuation Lines

Most modern Fortran compilers allow two ways of writing continuation lines. If the first non-space character on a line is in column 5, then that line is a continuation of the previous line. We call this *fixed format*. (In GNU Emacs we always count columns from 0.) The variable `fortran-continuation-string` specifies what character to put on column 5. A line that starts with a tab character followed by any digit except '0' is also a continuation line. We call this style of continuation *tab format*.

Fortran mode can make either style of continuation line, but you must specify which one you prefer. The value of the variable `indent-tabs-mode` controls the choice: `nil` for fixed format, and non-`nil` for tab format. You can tell which style is presently in effect by the presence or absence of the string 'Tab' in the mode line.

If the text on a line starts with the conventional Fortran continuation marker '$', or if it begins with any non-whitespace character in column 5,

Fortran mode treats it as a continuation line. When you indent a continuation line with TAB, it converts the line to the current continuation style. When you split a Fortran statement with M-LFD, the continuation marker on the newline is created according to the continuation style.

The setting of continuation style affects several other aspects of editing in Fortran mode. In fixed format mode, the minimum column number for the body of a statement is 6. Lines inside of Fortran blocks that are indented to larger column numbers always use only the space character for whitespace. In tab format mode, the minimum column number for the statement body is 8, and the whitespace before column 8 must always consist of one tab character.

When you enter Fortran mode for an existing file, it tries to deduce the proper continuation style automatically from the file contents. The first line that begins with either a tab character or six spaces determines the choice. The variable `fortran-analyze-depth` specifies how many lines to consider (at the beginning of the file); if none of those lines indicates a style, then the variable `fortran-tab-mode-default` specifies the style. If it is `nil`, that specifies fixed format, and non-`nil` specifies tab format.

21.15.2.3 Line Numbers

If a number is the first non-whitespace in the line, Fortran indentation assumes it is a line number and moves it to columns 0 through 4. (Columns always count from 0 in GNU Emacs.)

Line numbers of four digits or less are normally indented one space. The variable `fortran-line-number-indent` controls this; it specifies the maximum indentation a line number can have. Line numbers are indented to right-justify them to end in column 4 unless that would require more than this maximum indentation. The default value of the variable is 1.

Simply inserting a line number is enough to indent it according to these rules. As each digit is inserted, the indentation is recomputed. To turn off this feature, set the variable `fortran-electric-line-number` to `nil`. Then inserting line numbers is like inserting anything else.

21.15.2.4 Syntactic Conventions

Fortran mode assumes that you follow certain conventions that simplify the task of understanding a Fortran program well enough to indent it properly:

- Two nested 'do' loops never share a '`continue`' statement.
- Fortran keywords such as 'if', '`else`', '`then`', 'do' and others are written without embedded whitespace or line breaks.

Fortran compilers generally ignore whitespace outside of string constants, but Fortran mode does not recognize these keywords if they are not contiguous. Constructs such as 'else if' or 'end do' are acceptable, but the second word should be on the same line as the first and not on a continuation line.

If you fail to follow these conventions, the indentation commands may indent some lines unaesthetically. However, a correct Fortran program retains its meaning when reindented even if the conventions are not followed.

21.15.2.5 Variables for Fortran Indentation

Several additional variables control how Fortran indentation works:

`fortran-do-indent`
> Extra indentation within each level of 'do' statement (default 3).

`fortran-if-indent`
> Extra indentation within each level of 'if' statement (default 3). This value is also used for extra indentation within each level of the Fortran 90 'where' statement.

`fortran-structure-indent`
> Extra indentation within each level of 'structure', 'union', or 'map' statements (default 3).

`fortran-continuation-indent`
> Extra indentation for bodies of continuation lines (default 5).

`fortran-check-all-num-for-matching-do`
> If this is nil, indentation assumes that each 'do' statement ends on a 'continue' statement. Therefore, when computing indentation for a statement other than 'continue', it can save time by not checking for a 'do' statement ending there. If this is non-nil, indenting any numbered statement must check for a 'do' that ends there. The default is nil.

`fortran-blink-matching-if`
> If this is t, indenting an 'endif' statement moves the cursor momentarily to the matching 'if' statement to show where it is. The default is nil.

`fortran-minimum-statement-indent-fixed`
> Minimum indentation for fortran statements when using fixed format continuation line style. Statement bodies are never indented less than this much. The default is 6.

`fortran-minimum-statement-indent-tab`

> Minimum indentation for fortran statements for tab format continuation line style. Statement bodies are never indented less than this much. The default is 8.

21.15.3 Fortran Comments

The usual Emacs comment commands assume that a comment can follow a line of code. In Fortran, the standard comment syntax requires an entire line to be just a comment. Therefore, Fortran mode replaces the standard Emacs comment commands and defines some new variables.

Fortran mode can also handle a nonstandard comment syntax where comments start with '!' and can follow other text. Because only some Fortran compilers accept this syntax, Fortran mode will not insert such comments unless you have said in advance to do so. To do this, set the variable `comment-start` to '"!"' (see Section 30.2 [Variables], page 345).

`M-;`   Align comment or insert new comment (`fortran-comment-indent`).

`C-x ;`   Applies to nonstandard '!' comments only.

`C-c ;`   Turn all lines of the region into comments, or (with argument) turn them back into real code (`fortran-comment-region`).

`M-;` in Fortran mode is redefined as the command `fortran-comment-indent`. Like the usual `M-;` command, this recognizes any kind of existing comment and aligns its text appropriately; if there is no existing comment, a comment is inserted and aligned. But inserting and aligning comments are not the same in Fortran mode as in other modes.

When a new comment must be inserted, if the current line is blank, a full-line comment is inserted. On a non-blank line, a nonstandard '!' comment is inserted if you have said you want to use them. Otherwise a full-line comment is inserted on a new line before the current line.

Nonstandard '!' comments are aligned like comments in other languages, but full-line comments are different. In a standard full-line comment, the comment delimiter itself must always appear in column zero. What can be aligned is the text within the comment. You can choose from three styles of alignment by setting the variable `fortran-comment-indent-style` to one of these values:

`fixed`   Align the text at a fixed column, which is the sum of `fortran-comment-line-extra-indent` and the minimum statement indentation. This is the default.

> The minimum statement indentation is `fortran-minimum-statement-indent-fixed` for fixed format continuation line

style and `fortran-minimum-statement-indent-tab` for tab format style.

relative   Align the text as if it were a line of code, but with an additional `fortran-comment-line-extra-indent` columns of indentation.

nil   Don't move text in full-line columns automatically at all.

In addition, you can specify the character to be used to indent within full-line comments by setting the variable `fortran-comment-indent-char` to the single-character string you want to use.

Fortran mode introduces two variables `comment-line-start` and `comment-line-start-skip` which play for full-line comments the same roles played by `comment-start` and `comment-start-skip` for ordinary text-following comments. Normally these are set properly by Fortran mode so you do not need to change them.

The normal Emacs comment command `C-x ;` has not been redefined. If you use '!' comments, this command can be used with them. Otherwise it is useless in Fortran mode.

The command `C-c ;` (`fortran-comment-region`) turns all the lines of the region into comments by inserting the string 'C$$$' at the front of each one. With a numeric argument, it turns the region back into live code by deleting 'C$$$' from the front of each line in it. The string used for these comments can be controlled by setting the variable `fortran-comment-region`. Note that here we have an example of a command and a variable with the same name; these two uses of the name never conflict because in Lisp and in Emacs it is always clear from the context which one is meant.

21.15.4 Fortran Auto Fill Mode

Fortran Auto Fill mode is a minor mode which automatically splits Fortran statements as you insert them when they become too wide. Splitting a statement involves making continuation lines using `fortran-continuation-string` (See Section 21.15.2.2 [ForIndent Cont], page 231). This splitting happens when you type SPC, RET, or TAB, and also in the Fortran indentation commands.

`M-x fortran-auto-fill-mode` turns Fortran Auto Fill mode on if it was off, or off if it was on. This command works the same as `M-x auto-fill-mode` does for normal Auto Fill mode (see Section 20.5 [Filling], page 174). A positive numeric argument turns Fortran Auto Fill mode on, and a negative argument turns it off. You can see when Fortran Auto Fill mode is in effect by the presence of the word 'Fill' in the mode line, inside the parentheses. Fortran Auto Fill mode is a minor mode, turned on or off for each buffer individually. See Section 30.1 [Minor Modes], page 343.

Fortran Auto Fill mode breaks lines at spaces or delimiters when the lines get longer than the desired width (the value of `fill-column`). The delimiters that Fortran Auto Fill mode may break at are ',', ''', '+', '-', '/', '*', '=', and ')'. The line break comes after the delimiter if the variable `fortran-break-before-delimiters` is `nil`. Otherwise (and by default), the break comes before the delimiter.

By default, Fortran Auto Fill mode is not enabled. If you want this feature turned on permanently, add a hook function to `fortran-mode-hook` to execute (`fortran-auto-fill-mode 1`). See Section 30.2.3 [Hooks], page 347.

21.15.5 Checking Columns in Fortran

C-c C-r   Display a "column ruler" momentarily above the current line (`fortran-column-ruler`).

C-c C-w   Split the current window horizontally temporarily so that it is 72 columns wide. This may help you avoid making lines longer than the 72 character limit that some fortran compilers impose (`fortran-window-create-momentarily`).

The command C-c C-r (`fortran-column-ruler`) shows a column ruler momentarily above the current line. The comment ruler is two lines of text that show you the locations of columns with special significance in Fortran programs. Square brackets show the limits of the columns for line numbers, and curly brackets show the limits of the columns for the statement body. Column numbers appear above them.

Note that the column numbers count from zero, as always in GNU Emacs. As a result, the numbers may be one less than those you are familiar with; but the positions they indicate in the line are standard for Fortran.

The text used to display the column ruler depends on the value of the variable `indent-tabs-mode`. If `indent-tabs-mode` is `nil`, then the value of the variable `fortran-column-ruler-fixed` is used as the column ruler. Otherwise, the variable `fortran-column-ruler-tab` is displayed. By changing these variables, you can change the column ruler display.

For even more help, use C-c C-w (`fortran-window-create`), a command which splits the current window horizontally, making a window 72 columns wide. By editing in this window you can immediately see when you make a line too wide to be correct Fortran.

21.15.6 Fortran Keyword Abbrevs

Fortran mode provides many built-in abbrevs for common keywords and declarations. These are the same sort of abbrev that you can define yourself.

To use them, you must turn on Abbrev mode. See Chapter 23 [Abbrevs], page 251.

The built-in abbrevs are unusual in one way: they all start with a semicolon. You cannot normally use semicolon in an abbrev, but Fortran mode makes this possible by changing the syntax of semicolon to "word constituent."

For example, one built-in Fortran abbrev is ';c' for 'continue'. If you insert ';c' and then insert a punctuation character such as a space or a newline, the ';c' expands automatically to 'continue', provided Abbrev mode is enabled.

Type ';?' or ';C-h' to display a list of all the built-in Fortran abbrevs and what they stand for.

21.16 Asm Mode

Asm mode is a major mode for editing files of assembler code. It defines these commands:

TAB   `tab-to-tab-stop`.

LFD   Insert a newline and then indent using `tab-to-tab-stop`.

:   Insert a colon and then remove the indentation from before the label preceding colon. Then do `tab-to-tab-stop`.

;   Insert or align a comment.

The variable `asm-comment-char` specifies which character starts comments in assembler syntax.

22 Compiling and Testing Programs

The previous chapter discusses the Emacs commands that are useful for making changes in programs. This chapter deals with commands that assist in the larger process of developing and maintaining programs.

22.1 Running Compilations under Emacs

Emacs can run compilers for noninteractive languages such as C and Fortran as inferior processes, feeding the error log into an Emacs buffer. It can also parse the error messages and show you the source lines where compilation errors occurred.

M-x compile
> Run a compiler asynchronously under Emacs, with error messages to '*compilation*' buffer.

M-x grep   Run grep asynchronously under Emacs, with matching lines listed in the buffer named '*grep*'.

M-x kill-compilation
M-x kill-grep
> Kill the running compilation or grep subprocess.

C-x '   Visit the locus of the next compiler error message or grep match.

RET   Visit the locus of the error message that point is on. This command is used in the compilation buffer.

Mouse-2   Visit the locus of the error message that you click on.

To run make or another compilation command, do M-x compile. This command reads a shell command line using the minibuffer, and then executes the command in an inferior shell, putting output in the buffer named '*compilation*'. The current buffer's default directory is used as the working directory for the execution of the command; normally, therefore, the compilation happens in this directory.

When the shell command line is read, the minibuffer appears containing a default command line, which is the command you used the last time you did M-x compile. If you type just RET, the same command line is used again. For the first M-x compile, the default is 'make -k'. The default compilation command comes from the variable compile-command; if the appropriate compilation command for a file is something other than 'make -k', it can be useful for the file to specify a local value for compile-command (see Section 30.2.5 [File Variables], page 350).

Starting a compilation displays the buffer '*compilation*' in another window but does not select it. The buffer's mode line tells you whether compilation is finished, with the word 'run' or 'exit' inside the parentheses. You do not have to keep this buffer visible; compilation continues in any case. While a compilation is going on, the string 'Compiling' appears in the mode lines of all windows. When this string disappears, the compilation is finished.

To kill the compilation process, do M-x kill-compilation. When the compiler process terminates, the mode line of the '*compilation*' buffer changes to say 'signal' instead of 'run'. Starting a new compilation also kills any running compilation, as only one can exist at any time. However, M-x compile asks for confirmation before actually killing a compilation that is running.

The '*compilation*' buffer uses a special major mode, Compilation mode. This mode provides the keys SPC and DEL to scroll by screenfuls, and M-n and M-p to move to the next or previous error message. You can also use M-{ and M-} to move up or down to an error message for a different source file.

You can visit the source for any particular error message by moving point in '*compilation*' to that error message and typing RET (compile-goto-error). Or click Mouse-2 on the error message; you need not switch to the '*compilation*' buffer first.

To parse the compiler error messages sequentially, type C-x ' (next-error). The character following the C-x is the backquote or "grave accent," not the single-quote. This command is available in all buffers, not just in '*compilation*'; it displays the next error message at the top of one window and source location of the error in another window.

The first time C-x ' is used after the start of a compilation, it moves to the first error's location. Subsequent uses of C-x ' advance down to subsequent errors. If you visit a specific error message with RET or Mouse-2, subsequent C-x ' commands advance from there. When C-x ' gets to the end of the buffer and finds no more error messages to visit, it fails and signals an Emacs error.

C-u C-x ' starts scanning from the beginning of the compilation buffer. This way, you can process the same set of errors again.

Just as you can run a compiler, you can also run grep and then visit the lines on which matches were found. To do this, type M-x grep with an argument line that contains the same arguments you would give grep when running it normally: a grep-style regexp (usually in single-quotes to quote the shell's special characters) followed by file names which may use wildcards. The output from grep goes in the '*grep*' buffer, and you can find the matching lines in the source with C-x ' and RET just like compiler errors.

Note: a shell is used to run the compile command, but the shell is told that it should be noninteractive. This means in particular that the shell starts up with no prompt. If you find your usual shell prompt making an unsightly appearance in the '*compilation*' buffer, it means you have made a mistake in your shell's init file by setting the prompt unconditionally. (The init file name may be '.profile', '.cshrc', '.shrc', or various other things, depending on the shell you use.) The shell init file should set the prompt only if there already is a prompt. In csh, here is how to do it:

```
if ($?prompt) set prompt = ...
```

And here's how to do it in bash:

```
if [ "${PS1+set}" = set ]
then prompt=...
fi
```

There may well be other things that your shell's init file ought to do only for an interactive shell. You can use the same method to conditionalize them.

The features of Compilation mode are also available in a minor mode called Compilation Minor mode. This lets you parse error messages in any buffer, not just a normal compilation output buffer. Type M-x compilation-minor-mode to enable the minor mode. This defines the keys RET and Mouse-2, as in the Compilation major mode. In an Rlogin buffer (see Section 29.2.6 [Remote Host], page 330), Compilation minor mode automatically accesses remote source files by FTP (see Section 14.1 [File Names], page 103).

The MS-DOS "operating system" does not support asynchronous subprocesses; to work around this lack, M-x compile runs the compilation command synchronously on MS-DOS. As a consequence, you must wait until the command finishes before you can do anything else in Emacs. See Appendix C [MS-DOS], page 409.

22.2 Running Debuggers Under Emacs

The GUD (Grand Unified Debugger) library provides an interface to various symbolic debuggers from within Emacs. We recommend the debugger GDB, which is free software, but you can also run DBX, SDB or XDB if you have them. GUD can also serve as an interface to the Perl's debugging mode.

22.2.1 Starting GUD

There are five commands for starting a debugger, each corresponding to a particular debugger program.

M-x gdb RET *file* RET

> Run GDB as a subprocess of Emacs. This command creates a buffer for input and output to GDB, and switches to it. If a GDB buffer already exists, it just switches to that buffer.

M-x dbx RET *file* RET

> Similar, but run DBX instead of GDB.

M-x xdb RET *file* RET

> Similar, but run XDB instead of GDB. Use the variable `gud-xdb-directories` to specify directories to search for source files.

M-x sdb RET *file* RET

> Similar, but run SDB instead of GDB.

> Some versions of SDB do not mention source file names in their messages. When you use them, you need to have a valid tags table (see Section 21.12 [Tags], page 216) in order for GUD to find functions in the source code. If you have not visited a tags table or the tags table doesn't list one of the functions, you get a message saying 'The sdb support requires a valid tags table to work'. If this happens, generate a valid tags table in the working directory and try again.

M-x perldb RET *file* RET

> Run the Perl interpreter in debug mode to debug *file*, a Perl program.

You can only run one debugger process at a time.

Each of these commands takes one argument: a command line to invoke the debugger. In the simplest case, specify just the name of the executable file you want to debug. You may also use options that the debugger supports. However, shell wild cards and variables are not allowed. GUD assumes that the first argument not preceded by a '-' is the executable file name.

22.2.2 Debugger Operation

When you run a debugger with GUD, the debugger uses an Emacs buffer for its ordinary input and output. This is called the GUD buffer. The debugger displays the source files of the program by visiting them in Emacs buffers. An arrow ('=>') in one of these buffers indicates the current execution line. Moving point in this buffer does not move the arrow.

You can start editing these source files at any time in the buffers that were made to display them. The arrow is not part of the file's text; it appears only on the screen. If you do modify a source file, keep in mind that inserting or deleting lines will throw off the arrow's positioning; GUD has no way of figuring out which line corresponded before your changes to the line number in a debugger message. Also, you'll typically have to recompile and restart the program for your changes to be reflected in the debugger's tables.

If you wish, you can control your debugger process entirely through the debugger buffer, which uses a variant of Shell mode. All the usual commands for your debugger are available, and you can use the Shell mode history commands to repeat them. See Section 29.2.3 [Shell Mode], page 324.

22.2.3 Commands of GUD

The GUD interaction buffer uses a variant of Shell mode, so the commands of Shell mode are available (see Section 29.2.3 [Shell Mode], page 324). GUD mode also provides commands for setting and clearing breakpoints, for selecting stack frames, and for stepping through the program. These commands are available both in the GUD buffer and globally, but with different key bindings.

The breakpoint commands are usually used in source file buffers, because that is the way to specify where to set or clear the breakpoint. Here's the global command to set a breakpoint:

C-x SPC   Set a breakpoint on the source line that point is on.

Here are the other special commands provided by GUD. The keys starting with C-c are available only in the GUD interaction buffer. The bindings that start with C-x C-a are available in the GUD buffer and also in source files.

C-c C-l
C-x C-a C-l
> Display in another window the last line referred to in the GUD buffer (that is, the line indicated in the last location message). This runs the command gud-refresh.

C-c C-s
C-x C-a C-s
> Execute a single line of code (gud-step). If the line contains a function call, execution stops after entering the called function.

C-c C-n
C-x C-a C-n
> Execute a single line of code, stepping across entire function calls at full speed (gud-next).

C-c C-i
C-x C-a C-i
> Execute a single machine instruction (gud-stepi).

C-c C-r
C-x C-a C-r
> Continue execution without specifying any stopping point. The
> program will run until it hits a breakpoint, terminates, or gets
> a signal that the debugger is checking for (gud-cont).

C-c C-d
C-x C-a C-d
> Delete the breakpoint(s) on the current source line, if any (gud-
> remove). If you use this command in the GUD interaction buffer,
> it applies to the line where the program last stopped.

C-c C-t
C-x C-a C-t
> Set a temporary breakpoint on the current source line, if any. If
> you use this command in the GUD interaction buffer, it applies
> to the line where the program last stopped.

The above commands are common to all supported debuggers. If you
are using GDB or (some versions of) DBX, these additional commands are
available:

C-c <
C-x C-a <   Select the next enclosing stack frame (gud-up). This is equiva-
            lent to the 'up' command.

C-c >
C-x C-a >   Select the next inner stack frame (gud-down). This is equivalent
            to the 'down' command.

If you are using GDB, these additional key bindings are available:

TAB   With GDB, complete a symbol name (gud-gdb-complete-
            command). This key is available only in the GUD interaction
            buffer, and requires GDB versions 4.13 and later.

C-c C-f
C-x C-a C-f
> Run the program until the selected stack frame returns (or until
> it stops for some other reason).

These commands interpret a numeric argument as a repeat count, when
that makes sense.

22.2.4 GUD Customization

On startup, GUD runs one of the following hooks: gdb-mode-hook, if
you are using GDB; dbx-mode-hook, if you are using DBX; sdb-mode-hook,

if you are using SDB; `xdb-mode-hook`, if you are using XDB; `perldb-mode-hook`, for Perl debugging mode. You can use these hooks to define custom key bindings for the debugger interaction buffer. See Section 30.2.3 [Hooks], page 347.

Here is a convenient way to define a command that sends a particular command string to the debugger, and set up a key binding for it in the debugger interaction buffer:

> (`gud-def` *function cmdstring binding docstring*)

This defines a command named *function* which sends *cmdstring* to the debugger process, and gives it the documentation string *docstring*. You can use the command thus defined in any buffer. If *binding* is non-`nil`, `gud-def` also binds the command to `C-c` *binding* in the GUD buffer's mode and to `C-x C-a` *binding* generally.

The command string *cmdstring* may contain certain '%'-sequences that stand for data to be filled in at the time *function* is called:

'`%f`'   The name of the current source file. If the current buffer is the GUD buffer, then the "current source file" is the file that the program stopped in.

'`%l`'   The number of the current source line. If the current buffer is the GUD buffer, then the "current source line" is the line that the program stopped in.

'`%e`'   The text of the C lvalue or function-call expression at or adjacent to point.

'`%a`'   The text of the hexadecimal address at or adjacent to point.

'`%p`'   The numeric argument of the called function, as a decimal number. If the command is used without a numeric argument, '`%p`' stands for the empty string.

If you don't use '`%p`' in the command string, the command you define ignores any numeric argument.

22.3 Executing Lisp Expressions

Emacs has several different major modes for Lisp and Scheme. They are the same in terms of editing commands, but differ in the commands for executing Lisp expressions. Each mode has its own purpose.

Emacs-Lisp mode

The mode for editing source files of programs to run in Emacs Lisp. This mode defines `C-M-x` to evaluate the current defun. See Section 22.4 [Lisp Libraries], page 246.

Lisp Interaction mode

> The mode for an interactive session with Emacs Lisp. It defines
> LFD to evaluate the sexp before point and insert its value in the
> buffer. See Section 22.6 [Lisp Interaction], page 249.

Lisp mode The mode for editing source files of programs that run in Lisps
> other than Emacs Lisp. This mode defines C-M-x to send the
> current defun to an inferior Lisp process. See Section 22.7 [Ex-
> ternal Lisp], page 249.

Inferior Lisp mode

> The mode for an interactive session with an inferior Lisp process.
> This mode combines the special features of Lisp mode and Shell
> mode (see Section 29.2.3 [Shell Mode], page 324).

Scheme mode

> Like Lisp mode but for Scheme programs.

Inferior Scheme mode

> The mode for an interactive session with an inferior Scheme
> process.

Most editing commands for working with Lisp programs are in fact available globally. See Chapter 21 [Programs], page 199.

22.4 Libraries of Lisp Code for Emacs

Lisp code for Emacs editing commands is stored in files whose names
conventionally end in '.el'. This ending tells Emacs to edit them in Emacs-
Lisp mode (see Section 22.3 [Executing Lisp], page 245).

To execute a file of Emacs Lisp code, use M-x load-file. This command
reads a file name using the minibuffer and then executes the contents of that
file as Lisp code. It is not necessary to visit the file first; in any case, this
command reads the file as found on disk, not text in an Emacs buffer.

Once a file of Lisp code is installed in the Emacs Lisp library directories,
users can load it using M-x load-library. Programs can load it by calling
load-library, or with load, a more primitive function that is similar but
accepts some additional arguments.

M-x load-library differs from M-x load-file in that it searches a sequence of directories and tries three file names in each directory. Suppose
your argument is *lib*; the three names are '*lib*.elc', '*lib*.el', and lastly just
'*lib*'. If '*lib*.elc' exists, it is by convention the result of compiling '*lib*.el';
it is better to load the compiled file, since it will load and run faster.

If load-library finds that '*lib*.el' is newer than '*lib*.elc' file, it prints
a warning, because it's likely that somebody made changes to the '.el' file
and forgot to recompile it.

Because the argument to `load-library` is usually not in itself a valid file name, file name completion is not available. Indeed, when using this command, you usually do not know exactly what file name will be used.

The sequence of directories searched by `M-x load-library` is specified by the variable `load-path`, a list of strings that are directory names. The default value of the list contains the directory where the Lisp code for Emacs itself is stored. If you have libraries of your own, put them in a single directory and add that directory to `load-path`. `nil` in this list stands for the current default directory, but it is probably not a good idea to put `nil` in the list. If you find yourself wishing that `nil` were in the list, most likely what you really want to do is use `M-x load-file` this once.

Often you do not have to give any command to load a library, because the commands defined in the library are set up to *autoload* that library. Trying to run any of those commands calls `load` to load the library; this replaces the autoload definitions with the real ones from the library.

Emacs Lisp code can be compiled into byte-code which loads faster, takes up less space when loaded, and executes faster. See section "Byte Compilation" in *the Emacs Lisp Reference Manual*. By convention, the compiled code for a library goes in a separate file whose name consists of the library source file with 'c' appended. Thus, the compiled code for 'foo.el' goes in 'foo.elc'. That's why `load-library` searches for '.elc' files first.

22.5 Evaluating Emacs-Lisp Expressions

Lisp programs intended to be run in Emacs should be edited in Emacs-Lisp mode; this happens automatically for file names ending in '.el'. By contrast, Lisp mode itself is used for editing Lisp programs intended for other Lisp systems. To switch to Emacs-Lisp mode explicitly, use the command `M-x emacs-lisp-mode`.

For testing of Lisp programs to run in Emacs, it is often useful to evaluate part of the program as it is found in the Emacs buffer. For example, after changing the text of a Lisp function definition, evaluating the definition installs the change for future calls to the function. Evaluation of Lisp expressions is also useful in any kind of editing, for invoking noninteractive functions (functions that are not commands).

`M-:` Read a single Lisp expression in the minibuffer, evaluate it, and print the value in the echo area (`eval-expression`).

`C-x C-e` Evaluate the Lisp expression before point, and print the value in the echo area (`eval-last-sexp`).

`C-M-x` Evaluate the defun containing or after point, and print the value in the echo area (`eval-defun`).

`M-x eval-region`
>   Evaluate all the Lisp expressions in the region.

`M-x eval-current-buffer`
>   Evaluate all the Lisp expressions in the buffer.

`M-:` (`eval-expression`) is the most basic command for evaluating a Lisp expression interactively. It reads the expression using the minibuffer, so you can execute any expression on a buffer regardless of what the buffer contains. When the expression is evaluated, the current buffer is once again the buffer that was current when `M-:` was typed.

`M-:` can easily confuse users who do not understand it. Therefore, `eval-expression` is normally a disabled command. Attempting to use this command asks for confirmation and gives you the option of enabling it; once you enable the command, confirmation will no longer be required for it. See Section 30.4.10 [Disabling], page 365.

In Emacs-Lisp mode, the key `C-M-x` is bound to the command `eval-defun`, which parses the defun containing or following point as a Lisp expression and evaluates it. The value is printed in the echo area. This command is convenient for installing in the Lisp environment changes that you have just made in the text of a function definition.

`C-M-x` treats `defvar` expressions specially. Normally, evaluating a `defvar` expression does nothing if the variable it defines already has a value. But `C-M-x` unconditionally resets the variable to the initial value specified in the `defvar` expression. This special feature is convenient for debugging Lisp programs.

The command `C-x C-e` (`eval-last-sexp`) evaluates the Lisp expression preceding point in the buffer, and displays the value in the echo area. It is available in all major modes, not just Emacs-Lisp mode. It does not treat `defvar` specially.

If `C-M-x` or `C-x C-e` is given a numeric argument, it inserts the value into the current buffer at point, rather than displaying it in the echo area. The argument's value does not matter.

The most general command for evaluating Lisp expressions from a buffer is `eval-region`. `M-x eval-region` parses the text of the region as one or more Lisp expressions, evaluating them one by one. `M-x eval-current-buffer` is similar but evaluates the entire buffer. This is a reasonable way to install the contents of a file of Lisp code that you are just ready to test. Later, as you find bugs and change individual functions, use `C-M-x` on each function that you change. This keeps the Lisp world in step with the source file.

22.6 Lisp Interaction Buffers

The buffer '*scratch*' which is selected when Emacs starts up is provided for evaluating Lisp expressions interactively inside Emacs.

The simplest way to use the '*scratch*' buffer is to insert Lisp expressions and type LFD after each expression. This command reads the Lisp expression before point, evaluates it, and inserts the value in printed representation before point. The result is a complete typescript of the expressions you have evaluated and their values.

The '*scratch*' buffer's major mode is Lisp Interaction mode, which is the same as Emacs-Lisp mode except for the binding of LFD.

The rationale for this feature is that Emacs must have a buffer when it starts up, but that buffer is not useful for editing files since a new buffer is made for every file that you visit. The Lisp interpreter typescript is the most useful thing I can think of for the initial buffer to do. Type M-x lisp-interaction-mode to put the current buffer in Lisp Interaction mode.

22.7 Running an External Lisp

Emacs has facilities for running programs in other Lisp systems. You can run a Lisp process as an inferior of Emacs, and pass expressions to it to be evaluated. You can also pass changed function definitions directly from the Emacs buffers in which you edit the Lisp programs to the inferior Lisp process.

To run an inferior Lisp process, type M-x run-lisp. This runs the program named lisp, the same program you would run by typing lisp as a shell command, with both input and output going through an Emacs buffer named '*lisp*'. That is to say, any "terminal output" from Lisp will go into the buffer, advancing point, and any "terminal input" for Lisp comes from text in the buffer. (You can change the name of the Lisp executable file by setting the variable inferior-lisp-program.)

To give input to Lisp, go to the end of the buffer and type the input, terminated by RET. The '*lisp*' buffer is in Inferior Lisp mode, which combines the special characteristics of Lisp mode with most of the features of Shell mode (see Section 29.2.3 [Shell Mode], page 324). The definition of RET to send a line to a subprocess is one of the features of Shell mode.

For the source files of programs to run in external Lisps, use Lisp mode. This mode can be selected with M-x lisp-mode, and is used automatically for files whose names end in '.l', '.lsp', or '.lisp', as most Lisp systems usually expect.

When you edit a function in a Lisp program you are running, the easiest way to send the changed definition to the inferior Lisp process is the key

`C-M-x`. In Lisp mode, this runs the function `lisp-eval-defun`, which finds the defun around or following point and sends it as input to the Lisp process. (Emacs can send input to any inferior process regardless of what buffer is current.)

Contrast the meanings of `C-M-x` in Lisp mode (for editing programs to be run in another Lisp system) and Emacs-Lisp mode (for editing Lisp programs to be run in Emacs): in both modes it has the effect of installing the function definition that point is in, but the way of doing so is different according to where the relevant Lisp environment is found. See Section 22.3 [Executing Lisp], page 245.

23 Abbrevs

A defined *abbrev* is a word which *expands*, if you insert it, into some different text. Abbrevs are defined by the user to expand in specific ways. For example, you might define 'foo' as an abbrev expanding to 'find outer otter'. Then you would be able to insert 'find outer otter ' into the buffer by typing f o o SPC.

A second kind of abbreviation facility is called *dynamic abbrev expansion*. You use dynamic abbrev expansion with an explicit command to expand the letters in the buffer before point by looking for other words in the buffer that start with those letters. See Section 23.6 [Dynamic Abbrevs], page 255.

23.1 Abbrev Concepts

An *abbrev* is a word which has been defined to *expand* into a specified *expansion*. When you insert a word-separator character following the abbrev, that expands the abbrev—replacing the abbrev with its expansion. For example, if 'foo' is defined as an abbrev expanding to 'find outer otter', then you can insert 'find outer otter.' into the buffer by typing f o o ..

Abbrevs expand only when Abbrev mode (a minor mode) is enabled. Disabling Abbrev mode does not cause abbrev definitions to be forgotten, but they do not expand until Abbrev mode is enabled again. The command M-x abbrev-mode toggles Abbrev mode; with a numeric argument, it turns Abbrev mode on if the argument is positive, off otherwise. See Section 30.1 [Minor Modes], page 343. abbrev-mode is also a variable; Abbrev mode is on when the variable is non-nil. The variable abbrev-mode automatically becomes local to the current buffer when it is set.

Abbrev definitions can be *mode-specific*—active only in one major mode. Abbrevs can also have *global* definitions that are active in all major modes. The same abbrev can have a global definition and various mode-specific definitions for different major modes. A mode specific definition for the current major mode overrides a global definition.

Abbrevs can be defined interactively during the editing session. Lists of abbrev definitions can also be saved in files and reloaded in later sessions. Some users keep extensive lists of abbrevs that they load in every session.

23.2 Defining Abbrevs

C-x a g   Define an abbrev, using one or more words before point as its expansion (add-global-abbrev).

C-x a l   Similar, but define an abbrev specific to the current major mode (add-mode-abbrev).

C-x a i g   Define a word in the buffer as an abbrev (`inverse-add-global-abbrev`).

C-x a i l   Define a word in the buffer as a mode-specific abbrev (`inverse-add-mode-abbrev`).

M-x kill-all-abbrevs

> This command discards all abbrev definitions currently in effect, leaving a blank slate.

The usual way to define an abbrev is to enter the text you want the abbrev to expand to, position point after it, and type `C-x a g` (`add-global-abbrev`). This reads the abbrev itself using the minibuffer, and then defines it as an abbrev for one or more words before point. Use a numeric argument to say how many words before point should be taken as the expansion. For example, to define the abbrev 'foo' as mentioned above, insert the text 'find outer otter' and then type `C-u 3 C-x a g f o o RET`.

An argument of zero to `C-x a g` means to use the contents of the region as the expansion of the abbrev being defined.

The command `C-x a l` (`add-mode-abbrev`) is similar, but defines a mode-specific abbrev. Mode specific abbrevs are active only in a particular major mode. `C-x a l` defines an abbrev for the major mode in effect at the time `C-x a l` is typed. The arguments work the same as for `C-x a g`.

If the text already in the buffer is the abbrev, rather than its expansion, use command `C-x a i g` (`inverse-add-global-abbrev`) instead of `C-x a g`, or use `C-x a i l` (`inverse-add-mode-abbrev`) instead of `C-x a l`. These commands are called "inverse" because they invert the meaning of the two text strings they use (one from the buffer and one read with the minibuffer).

To change the definition of an abbrev, just define a new definition. When the abbrev has a prior definition, the abbrev definition commands ask for confirmation for replacing it.

To remove an abbrev definition, give a negative argument to the abbrev definition command: `C-u - C-x a g` or `C-u - C-x a l`. The former removes a global definition, while the latter removes a mode-specific definition.

`M-x kill-all-abbrevs` removes all the abbrev definitions there are, both global and local.

23.3 Controlling Abbrev Expansion

An abbrev expands whenever it is present in the buffer just before point and you type a self-inserting whitespace or punctuation character (SPC, comma, etc.). More precisely, any character that is not a word constituent expands an abbrev, and any word constituent character can be part of an abbrev. The most common way to use an abbrev is to insert it and then insert a punctuation character to expand it.

Abbrev expansion preserves case; thus, 'foo' expands into 'find outer otter'; 'Foo' into 'Find outer otter', and 'FOO' into 'FIND OUTER OTTER' or 'Find Outer Otter' according to the variable abbrev-all-caps (a non-nil value chooses the first of the two expansions).

These commands are used to control abbrev expansion:

M-'   Separate a prefix from a following abbrev to be expanded
            (abbrev-prefix-mark).

C-x a e   Expand the abbrev before point (expand-abbrev). This is ef-
            fective even when Abbrev mode is not enabled.

M-x expand-region-abbrevs
            Expand some or all abbrevs found in the region.

You may wish to expand an abbrev with a prefix attached; for example, if 'cnst' expands into 'construction', you might want to use it to enter 'reconstruction'. It does not work to type recnst, because that is not necessarily a defined abbrev. What you can do is use the command M-' (abbrev-prefix-mark) in between the prefix 're' and the abbrev 'cnst'. First, insert 're'. Then type M-'; this inserts a hyphen in the buffer to indicate that it has done its work. Then insert the abbrev 'cnst'; the buffer now contains 're-cnst'. Now insert a non-word character to expand the abbrev 'cnst' into 'construction'. This expansion step also deletes the hyphen that indicated M-' had been used. The result is the desired 'reconstruction'.

If you actually want the text of the abbrev in the buffer, rather than its expansion, you can accomplish this by inserting the following punctuation with C-q. Thus, foo C-q , leaves 'foo,' in the buffer.

If you expand an abbrev by mistake, you can undo the expansion and bring back the abbrev itself by typing C-_ to undo (see Section 4.4 [Undo], page 30). This also undoes the insertion of the non-word character that expanded the abbrev. If the result you want is the terminating non-word character plus the unexpanded abbrev, you must reinsert the terminating character, quoting it with C-q.

M-x expand-region-abbrevs searches through the region for defined abbrevs, and for each one found offers to replace it with its expansion. This command is useful if you have typed in text using abbrevs but forgot to turn on Abbrev mode first. It may also be useful together with a special set of abbrev definitions for making several global replacements at once. This command is effective even if Abbrev mode is not enabled.

Expanding an abbrev runs the hook pre-abbrev-expand-hook (see Section 30.2.3 [Hooks], page 347).

23.4 Examining and Editing Abbrevs

M-x list-abbrevs
>Display a list of all abbrev definitions.

M-x edit-abbrevs
>Edit a list of abbrevs; you can add, alter or remove definitions.

The output from M-x list-abbrevs looks like this:

```
(lisp-mode-abbrev-table)
"dk"          0     "define-key"
(global-abbrev-table)
"dfn"          0     "definition"
```

(Some blank lines of no semantic significance, and some other abbrev tables, have been omitted.)

A line containing a name in parentheses is the header for abbrevs in a particular abbrev table; global-abbrev-table contains all the global abbrevs, and the other abbrev tables that are named after major modes contain the mode-specific abbrevs.

Within each abbrev table, each nonblank line defines one abbrev. The word at the beginning of the line is the abbrev. The number that follows is the number of times the abbrev has been expanded. Emacs keeps track of this to help you see which abbrevs you actually use, so that you can eliminate those that you don't use often. The string at the end of the line is the expansion.

M-x edit-abbrevs allows you to add, change or kill abbrev definitions by editing a list of them in an Emacs buffer. The list has the same format described above. The buffer of abbrevs is called '*Abbrevs*', and is in Edit-Abbrevs mode. Type C-c C-c in this buffer to install the abbrev definitions as specified in the buffer—and delete any abbrev definitions not listed.

The command edit-abbrevs is actually the same as list-abbrevs except that it selects the buffer '*Abbrevs*' whereas list-abbrevs merely displays it in another window.

23.5 Saving Abbrevs

These commands allow you to keep abbrev definitions between editing sessions.

M-x write-abbrev-file RET *file* RET
>Write a file *file* describing all defined abbrevs.

M-x read-abbrev-file RET *file* RET
>Read the file *file* and define abbrevs as specified therein.

`M-x quietly-read-abbrev-file RET` *file* `RET`
> Similar but do not display a message about what is going on.

`M-x define-abbrevs`
> Define abbrevs from definitions in current buffer.

`M-x insert-abbrevs`
> Insert all abbrevs and their expansions into current buffer.

`M-x write-abbrev-file` reads a file name using the minibuffer and then writes a description of all current abbrev definitions into that file. This is used to save abbrev definitions for use in a later session. The text stored in the file is a series of Lisp expressions that, when executed, define the same abbrevs that you currently have.

`M-x read-abbrev-file` reads a file name using the minibuffer and then reads the file, defining abbrevs according to the contents of the file. `M-x quietly-read-abbrev-file` is the same except that it does not display a message in the echo area saying that it is doing its work; it is actually useful primarily in the '`.emacs`' file. If an empty argument is given to either of these functions, they use the file name specified in the variable `abbrev-file-name`, which is by default `"~/.abbrev_defs"`.

Emacs will offer to save abbrevs automatically if you have changed any of them, whenever it offers to save all files (for `C-x s` or `C-x C-c`). This feature can be inhibited by setting the variable `save-abbrevs` to `nil`.

The commands `M-x insert-abbrevs` and `M-x define-abbrevs` are similar to the previous commands but work on text in an Emacs buffer. `M-x insert-abbrevs` inserts text into the current buffer before point, describing all current abbrev definitions; `M-x define-abbrevs` parses the entire current buffer and defines abbrevs accordingly.

23.6 Dynamic Abbrev Expansion

The abbrev facility described above operates automatically as you insert text, but all abbrevs must be defined explicitly. By contrast, *dynamic abbrevs* allow the meanings of abbrevs to be determined automatically from the contents of the buffer, but dynamic abbrev expansion happens only when you request it explicitly.

`M-/`
> Expand the word in the buffer before point as a *dynamic abbrev*, by searching in the buffer for words starting with that abbreviation (`dabbrev-expand`).

`C-M-/`
> Complete the word before point as a dynamic abbrev (`dabbrev-completion`).

For example, if the buffer contains '`does this follow `' and you type `f o` `M-/`, the effect is to insert '`follow`' because that is the last word in the buffer that starts with 'fo'. A numeric argument to M-/ says to take the second, third, etc. distinct expansion found looking backward from point. Repeating M-/ searches for an alternative expansion by looking farther back. After considering the entire buffer before point, it searches the text after point. After searching all of the current buffer, M-/ searches other buffers.

A negative argument to M-/, as in C-u - M-/, says to search first for expansions after point, and second for expansions before point. If you repeat the M-/ to look for another expansion, do not specify an argument. This tries all the expansions after point and then the expansions before point.

After you have expanded a dynamic abbrev, you can copy additional words that follow the expansion in its original context. Simply type SPC M-/ for each word you want to copy. The spacing and punctuation between words is copied along with the words.

In shell scripts and makefiles, a variable name is sometimes prefixed with '$' and sometimes not. Major modes for this kind of text can customize dynamic abbreviation to handle optional prefixes by setting the variable `dabbrev-abbrev-skip-leading-regexp`. Its value should be a regular expression that matches the optional prefix that dynamic abbreviation should ignore.

The command C-M-/ (`dabbrev-completion`) performs completion of a dynamic abbreviation. Instead of trying the possible expansions one by one, it finds all of them, then inserts the text that they have in common. If they have nothing in common, C-M-/ displays a list of completions, from which you can select a choice in the usual manner. See Section 5.3 [Completion], page 39.

Dynamic abbrev expansion is completely independent of Abbrev mode; the expansion of a word with M-/ is completely independent of whether it has a definition as an ordinary abbrev.

24 Editing Pictures

To edit a picture made out of text characters (for example, a picture of the division of a register into fields, as a comment in a program), use the command M-x edit-picture to enter Picture mode.

In Picture mode, editing is based on the *quarter-plane* model of text, according to which the text characters lie studded on an area that stretches infinitely far to the right and downward. The concept of the end of a line does not exist in this model; the most you can say is where the last nonblank character on the line is found.

Of course, Emacs really always considers text as a sequence of characters, and lines really do have ends. But Picture mode replaces the most frequently-used commands with variants that simulate the quarter-plane model of text. They do this by inserting spaces or by converting tabs to spaces.

Most of the basic editing commands of Emacs are redefined by Picture mode to do essentially the same thing but in a quarter-plane way. In addition, Picture mode defines various keys starting with the C-c prefix to run special picture editing commands.

One of these keys, C-c C-c, is pretty important. Often a picture is part of a larger file that is usually edited in some other major mode. M-x edit-picture records the name of the previous major mode so you can use the C-c C-c command (picture-mode-exit) later to go back to that mode. C-c C-c also deletes spaces from the ends of lines, unless given a numeric argument.

The special commands of Picture mode all work in other modes (provided the 'picture' library is loaded), but are not bound to keys except in Picture mode. The descriptions below talk of moving "one column" and so on, but all the picture mode commands handle numeric arguments as their normal equivalents do.

Turning on Picture mode runs the hook picture-mode-hook (see Section 30.2.3 [Hooks], page 347).

24.1 Basic Editing in Picture Mode

Most keys do the same thing in Picture mode that they usually do, but do it in a quarter-plane style. For example, C-f is rebound to run picture-forward-column, a command which moves point one column to the right, inserting a space if necessary so that the actual end of the line makes no difference. C-b is rebound to run picture-backward-column, which always moves point left one column, converting a tab to multiple spaces if necessary. C-n and C-p are rebound to run picture-move-down and picture-move-up, which can either insert spaces or convert tabs as necessary to make sure that point stays in exactly the same column. `C-e` runs `picture-end-of-line`, which moves to after the last nonblank character on the line. There is no need to change `C-a`, as the choice of screen model does not affect beginnings of lines.

Insertion of text is adapted to the quarter-plane screen model through the use of Overwrite mode (see Section 30.1 [Minor Modes], page 343). Self-inserting characters replace existing text, column by column, rather than pushing existing text to the right. `RET` runs `picture-newline`, which just moves to the beginning of the following line so that new text will replace that line.

Picture mode provides erasure instead of deletion and killing of text. `DEL` (`picture-backward-clear-column`) replaces the preceding character with a space rather than removing it; this moves point backwards. `C-d` (`picture-clear-column`) replaces the next character or characters with spaces, but does not move point. (If you want to clear characters to spaces and move forward over them, use `SPC`.) `C-k` (`picture-clear-line`) really kills the contents of lines, but does not delete the newlines from the buffer.

To do actual insertion, you must use special commands. `C-o` (`picture-open-line`) creates a blank line after the current line; it never splits a line. `C-M-o`, `split-line`, makes sense in Picture mode, so it is not changed. `LFD` (`picture-duplicate-line`) inserts below the current line another line with the same contents.

To do actual deletion in Picture mode, use `C-w`, `C-c C-d` (which is defined as `delete-char`, as `C-d` is in other modes), or one of the picture rectangle commands (see Section 24.4 [Rectangles in Picture], page 259).

24.2 Controlling Motion after Insert

Since "self-inserting" characters in Picture mode overwrite and move point, there is no essential restriction on how point should be moved. Normally point moves right, but you can specify any of the eight orthogonal or diagonal directions for motion after a "self-inserting" character. This is useful for drawing lines in the buffer.

C-c <   Move left after insertion (`picture-movement-left`).

C-c >   Move right after insertion (`picture-movement-right`).

C-c ^   Move up after insertion (`picture-movement-up`).

C-c .   Move down after insertion (`picture-movement-down`).

C-c '   Move up and left ("northwest") after insertion (`picture-movement-nw`).

C-c '   Move up and right ("northeast") after insertion (`picture-movement-ne`).

C-c /   Move down and left ("southwest") after insertion
            (`picture-movement-sw`).

C-c \   Move down and right ("southeast") after insertion
            (`picture-movement-se`).

Two motion commands move based on the current Picture insertion direction. The command `C-c C-f` (`picture-motion`) moves in the same direction as motion after "insertion" currently does, while `C-c C-b` (`picture-motion-reverse`) moves in the opposite direction.

24.3 Picture Mode Tabs

Two kinds of tab-like action are provided in Picture mode. Use `M-TAB` (`picture-tab-search`) for context-based tabbing. With no argument, it moves to a point underneath the next "interesting" character that follows whitespace in the previous nonblank line. "Next" here means "appearing at a horizontal position greater than the one point starts out at." With an argument, as in `C-u M-TAB`, this command moves to the next such interesting character in the current line. `M-TAB` does not change the text; it only moves point. "Interesting" characters are defined by the variable `picture-tab-chars`, which should define a set of characters. The syntax for this variable is like the syntax used inside of '[...]' in a regular expression—but without the '[' and the ']'. Its default value is "!-~".

`TAB` itself runs `picture-tab`, which operates based on the current tab stop settings; it is the Picture mode equivalent of `tab-to-tab-stop`. Normally it just moves point, but with a numeric argument it clears the text that it moves over.

The context-based and tab-stop-based forms of tabbing are brought together by the command `C-c TAB`, `picture-set-tab-stops`. This command sets the tab stops to the positions which `M-TAB` would consider significant in the current line. The use of this command, together with `TAB`, can get the effect of context-based tabbing. But `M-TAB` is more convenient in the cases where it is sufficient.

24.4 Picture Mode Rectangle Commands

Picture mode defines commands for working on rectangular pieces of the text in ways that fit with the quarter-plane model. The standard rectangle commands may also be useful (see Section 9.4 [Rectangles], page 67).

C-c C-k   Clear out the region-rectangle with spaces (`picture-clear-rectangle`). With argument, delete the text.

C-c C-w r Similar but save rectangle contents in register r first (`picture-clear-rectangle-to-register`).

C-c C-y   Copy last killed rectangle into the buffer by overwriting, with
           upper left corner at point (`picture-yank-rectangle`). With
           argument, insert instead.

C-c C-x r Similar, but use the rectangle in register r (`picture-yank-rectangle-from-register`).

   The picture rectangle commands C-c C-k (`picture-clear-rectangle`)
and C-c C-w (`picture-clear-rectangle-to-register`) differ from the
standard rectangle commands in that they normally clear the rectangle instead of deleting it; this is analogous with the way C-d is changed in Picture
mode.

   However, deletion of rectangles can be useful in Picture mode, so these
commands delete the rectangle if given a numeric argument. C-c C-k either
with or without a numeric argument saves the rectangle for C-c C-y.

   The Picture mode commands for yanking rectangles differ from the
standard ones in overwriting instead of inserting. This is the same way
that Picture mode insertion of other text differs from other modes. C-c
C-y (`picture-yank-rectangle`) inserts (by overwriting) the rectangle that
was most recently killed, while C-c C-x (`picture-yank-rectangle-from-register`) does likewise for the rectangle found in a specified register.

25 Sending Mail

To send a message in Emacs, you start by typing a command (C-x m) to select and initialize the '*mail*' buffer. Then you edit the text and headers of the message in this buffer, and type another command (C-c C-s or C-c C-c) to send the message.

C-x m   Begin composing a message to send (mail).

C-x 4 m   Likewise, but display the message in another window (mail-other-window).

C-x 5 m   Likewise, but make a new frame (mail-other-frame).

C-c C-s   In Mail mode, send the message (mail-send).

C-c C-c   Send the message and bury the mail buffer (mail-send-and-exit).

The command C-x m (mail) selects a buffer named '*mail*' and initializes it with the skeleton of an outgoing message. C-x 4 m (mail-other-window) selects the '*mail*' buffer in a different window, leaving the previous current buffer visible. C-x 5 m (mail-other-frame) creates a new frame to select the '*mail*' buffer.

Because the mail composition buffer is an ordinary Emacs buffer, you can switch to other buffers while in the middle of composing mail, and switch back later (or never). If you use the C-x m command again when you have been composing another message but have not sent it, you are asked to confirm before the old message is erased. If you answer n, the '*mail*' buffer is left selected with its old contents, so you can finish the old message and send it. C-u C-x m is another way to do this. Sending the message marks the '*mail*' buffer "unmodified", which avoids the need for confirmation when C-x m is next used.

If you are composing a message in the '*mail*' buffer and want to send another message before finishing the first, rename the '*mail*' buffer using M-x rename-uniquely (see Section 15.3 [Misc Buffer], page 135). Then you can use C-x m or its variants described above to make a new '*mail*' buffer. Once you've done that, you can work with each mail buffer independently.

25.1 The Format of the Mail Buffer

In addition to the *text* or *body*, a message has *header fields* which say who sent it, when, to whom, why, and so on. Some header fields such as the date and sender are created automatically after the message is sent. Others, such as the recipient names, must be specified by you in order to send the message properly.

Mail mode provides a few commands to help you edit some header fields, and some are preinitialized in the buffer automatically at times. You can insert and edit header fields using ordinary editing commands.

The line in the buffer that says

```
--text follows this line--
```

is a special delimiter that separates the headers you have specified from the text. Whatever follows this line is the text of the message; the headers precede it. The delimiter line itself does not appear in the message actually sent. The text used for the delimiter line is controlled by the variable `mail-header-separator`.

Here is an example of what the headers and text in the mail buffer might look like.

```
To: gnu@prep.ai.mit.edu
CC: lungfish@spam.org, byob@spam.org
Subject: The Emacs Manual
--Text follows this line--
Please ignore this message.
```

25.2 Mail Header Fields

A header field in the mail buffer starts with a field name at the beginning of a line, terminated by a colon. Upper and lower case are equivalent in field names (and in mailing addresses also). After the colon and optional whitespace comes the contents of the field.

You can use any name you like for a header field, but normally people use only standard field names with accepted meanings. Here is a table of fields commonly used in outgoing messages.

'To'   This field contains the mailing addresses to which the message is addressed.

'Subject'   The contents of the 'Subject' field should be a piece of text that says what the message is about. The reason 'Subject' fields are useful is that most mail-reading programs can provide a summary of messages, listing the subject of each message but not its text.

'CC'   This field contains additional mailing addresses to send the message to, but whose readers should not regard the message as addressed to them.

'BCC'   This field contains additional mailing addresses to send the message to, which should not appear in the header of the message actually sent. Copies sent this way are called *blind carbon copies*.

To send a blind carbon copy of every outgoing message to yourself, set the variable `mail-self-blind` to t.

'FCC'   This field contains the name of one file and directs Emacs to append a copy of the message to that file when you send the message. If the file is in Rmail format, Emacs writes the message to Rmail format; otherwise, Emacs writes the message in system mail file format.

To put a fixed file name as in 'FCC' field each time you start editing an outgoing message, set the variable `mail-archive-file-name` to that file name. Unless you remove the 'FCC' field before sending, the message will be written into that file when it is sent.

'From'   Use the 'From' field to say who you are, when the account you are using to send the mail is not your own. The contents of the 'From' field should be a valid mailing address, since replies will normally go there.

'Reply-to'

Use this field to direct replies to a different address. Most mail-reading programs (including Rmail) automatically send replies to the 'Reply-to' address in preference to the 'From' address. By adding a 'Reply-to' field to your header, you can work around any problems your 'From' address may cause for replies.

To put a fixed 'Reply-to' address into every outgoing message, set the variable `mail-default-reply-to` to that address (as a string). Then `mail` initializes the message with a 'Reply-to' field as specified. You can delete or alter that header field before you send the message, if you wish. When Emacs starts up, if the environment variable REPLYTO is set, `mail-default-reply-to` is initialized from that environment variable.

'In-reply-to'

This field contains a piece of text describing a message you are replying to. Some mail systems can use this information to correlate related pieces of mail. Normally this field is filled in by Rmail when you reply to a message in Rmail, and you never need to think about it (see Chapter 26 [Rmail], page 269).

The 'To', 'CC', 'BCC' and 'FCC' fields can appear any number of times, to specify many places to send the message. The 'To', 'CC', and 'BCC' fields can have continuation lines. All the lines starting with whitespace, following the line on which the field starts, are considered part of the field. For example,

```
To: foo@here.net, this@there.net,
    me@gnu.cambridge.mass.usa.earth.spiral3281
```

When you send the message, if you didn't write a 'From' field yourself, Emacs puts in one for you. The variable `mail-from-style` controls the format:

nil   Just the email address, as in 'king@grassland.com'.

parens   Both email address and full name, as in 'king@grassland.com (Elvis Parsley)'.

angles   Both email address and full name, as in 'Elvis Parsley <king@grassland.com>'.

25.3 Mail Aliases

You can define *mail aliases* in a file named '~/.mailrc'. These are short mnemonic names which stand for mail addresses or groups of mail addresses. Like many other mail programs, Emacs expands aliases when they occur in the 'To', 'From', 'CC', 'BCC', and 'Reply-to' fields, plus their 'Resent-' variants.

To define an alias in '~/.mailrc', write a line in the following format:

    alias *shortaddress* *fulladdresses*

Here *fulladdresses* stands for one or more mail addresses for *shortaddress* to expand into. Separate multiple addresses with spaces; if an address contains a space, quote the whole address with a pair of double-quotes.

For instance, to make `maingnu` stand for `gnu@prep.ai.mit.edu` plus a local address of your own, put in this line:

    alias maingnu gnu@prep.ai.mit.edu local-gnu

Emacs also recognizes include commands in '.mailrc' files. They look like this:

    source *filename*

The file '~/.mailrc' is used primarily by other mail-reading programs; it can contain various other commands. Emacs ignores everything in it except for alias definitions and include commands.

Another way to define a mail alias, within Emacs alone, is with the `define-mail-alias` command. It prompts for the alias and then the full address. You can use it to define aliases in your '.emacs' file, like this:

    (define-mail-alias "maingnu" "gnu@prep.ai.mit.edu")

`define-mail-alias` records aliases by adding them to a variable named `mail-aliases`. If you are comfortable with manipulating Lisp lists, you can set `mail-aliases` directly. The initial value of `mail-aliases` is t, which means that Emacs should read '.mailrc' to get the proper value.

You can specify a different file name to use instead of '~/.mailrc' by setting the variable `mail-personal-alias-file`.

Normally, Emacs expands aliases when you send the message. If you like, you can have mail aliases expand as abbrevs, as soon as you type them in (see Chapter 23 [Abbrevs], page 251). To enable this feature, execute the following:

```
(add-hook 'mail-setup-hook 'mail-abbrevs-setup)
```

This can go in your '.emacs' file. See Section 30.2.3 [Hooks], page 347. If you use this feature, you must use define-mail-abbrev instead of define-mail-alias; the latter does not work with this package. Note that the mail abbreviation package uses the variable mail-abbrevs instead of mail-aliases, and that all alias names are converted to lower case.

The mail abbreviation package also provides the C-c C-a (mail-interactive-insert-alias) command, which reads an alias name (with completion) and inserts its definition at point. This is useful when editing the message text itself or a header field such as 'Subject' in which Emacs does not normally expand aliases.

Note that abbrevs expand only if you insert a word-separator character afterward. However, you can rebind C-n and M-> to cause expansion as well. Here's how to do that:

```
(define-key mail-mode-map "\C-n" 'mail-abbrev-next-line)
(define-key mail-mode-map "\M->" 'mail-abbrev-end-of-buffer)
```

25.4 Mail Mode

The major mode used in the mail buffer is Mail mode, which is much like Text mode except that various special commands are provided on the C-c prefix. These commands all have to do specifically with editing or sending the message.

C-c C-s   Send the message, and leave the mail buffer selected (mail-send).

C-c C-c   Send the message, and select some other buffer (mail-send-and-exit).

C-c C-f C-t
           Move to the 'To' header field, creating one if there is none (mail-to).

C-c C-f C-s
           Move to the 'Subject' header field, creating one if there is none (mail-subject).

C-c C-f C-c
           Move to the 'CC' header field, creating one if there is none (mail-cc).

C-c C-f C-b
>   Move to the 'BCC' header field, creating one if there is none
>   (mail-bcc).

C-c C-f C-f
>   Move to the 'FCC' header field, creating one if there is none
>   (mail-fcc).

C-c C-t   Move to the beginning of the message body text (mail-text).

C-c C-w   Insert the file '~/.signature' at the end of the message text
>   (mail-signature).

C-c C-y   Yank the selected message from Rmail (mail-yank-original).
>   This command does nothing unless your command to start send-
>   ing a message was issued with Rmail.

C-c C-q   Fill all paragraphs of yanked old messages, each individually
>   (mail-fill-yanked-message).

M-x ispell-message
>   Do spelling correction on the message text, but not on citations
>   from other messages.

There are two ways to send the message. C-c C-s (mail-send) sends
the message and marks the mail buffer unmodified, but leaves that buffer
selected so that you can modify the message (perhaps with new recipients)
and send it again. C-c C-c (mail-send-and-exit) sends and then deletes
the window or switches to another buffer. It puts the mail buffer at the
lowest priority for reselection by default, since you are finished with using
it. This is the usual way to send the message.

Mail mode provides special commands for editing the headers and text
of the message before you send it. There are five commands defined to
move point to particular header fields, all based on the prefix C-c C-f ('C-f'
is for "field"). They are C-c C-f C-t (mail-to) to move to the 'To' field,
C-c C-f C-s (mail-subject) for the 'Subject' field, C-c C-f C-c (mail-cc)
for the 'CC' field, C-c C-f C-b (mail-bcc) for the 'BCC' field, and C-c C-f
C-f (mail-fcc) for the 'FCC' field. If the field in question does not exist,
these commands create one. We provide special motion commands for these
particular fields because they are the fields users most often want to edit.

C-c C-t (mail-text) moves point to just after the header separator line—
that is, to the beginning of the message body text.

C-c C-w (mail-signature) adds a standard piece text at the end of the
message to say more about who you are. The text comes from the file
'.signature' in your home directory. To insert your signature automatically,
set the variable mail-signature non-nil; then starting a mail message
automatically inserts the contents of your '.signature' file. If you want

to omit your signature from a particular message, delete it from the buffer before you send the message.

When mail sending is invoked from the Rmail mail reader using an Rmail command, C-c C-y can be used inside the mail buffer to insert the text of the message you are replying to. Normally it indents each line of that message four spaces and eliminates most header fields. A numeric argument specifies the number of spaces to indent. An argument of just C-u says not to indent at all and not to eliminate anything. C-c C-y always uses the current message from the Rmail buffer, so you can insert several old messages by selecting one in Rmail, switching to '*mail*' and yanking it, then switching back to Rmail to select another.

You can specify the text for C-c C-y to insert at the beginning of each line: set mail-yank-prefix to the desired string. (A value of nil means to use indentation; this is the default.) However, C-u C-c C-y never adds anything at the beginning of the inserted lines, regardless of the value of mail-yank-prefix.

After using C-c C-y, you can use the command C-c C-q (mail-fill-yanked-message) to fill the paragraphs of the yanked old message or messages. One use of C-c C-q fills all such paragraphs, each one individually. See Section 20.5 [Filling], page 174.

You can do spelling correction on the message text you have written with the command M-x ispell-message. If you have yanked an incoming message into the outgoing draft, this command skips what was yanked, but it checks the text that you yourself inserted. (It looks for indentation or mail-yank-prefix to distinguish the cited lines from your input.) See Section 13.4 [Spelling], page 99.

Mail mode defines the character '%' as a word separator; this is helpful for using the word commands to edit mail addresses.

Mail mode is normally used in buffers set up automatically by the mail command and related commands. However, you can also switch to Mail mode in a file-visiting buffer. That is a useful thing to do if you have saved draft message text in a file. In a file-visiting buffer, C-c C-c does not clear the modified flag, because only saving the file should do that. As a result, you don't get a warning about trying to send the same message twice.

Turning on Mail mode (which C-x m does automatically) runs the normal hooks text-mode-hook and mail-mode-hook. Initializing a new outgoing message runs the normal hook mail-setup-hook; if you want to add special fields to your mail header or make other changes to the appearance of the mail buffer, use that hook. See Section 30.2.3 [Hooks], page 347.

The main difference between these hooks is just when they are invoked. Whenever you type M-x mail, mail-mode-hook runs as soon as the '*mail*' buffer is created. Then the mail-setup function puts in the default contents of the buffer. After these default contents are inserted, `mail-setup-hook` runs.

25.5 Distracting the NSA

`M-x spook` adds a line of randomly chosen keywords to an outgoing mail message. The keywords are chosen from a list of words that suggest you are discussing something subversive.

The idea behind this feature is that the suspicion that the NSA snoops on all electronic mail messages that contain keywords suggesting they might be interested. (The NSA says they don't, but that's what they *would* say.) The idea is that if lots of people add suspicious words to their messages, the NSA will get so busy with spurious input that they will have to give up reading it all.

Here's how to insert spook keywords automatically whenever you start entering an outgoing message:

```
(add-hook 'mail-setup-hook 'spook)
```

Whether or not this confuses the NSA, it at least amuses people.

26 Reading Mail with Rmail

Rmail is an Emacs subsystem for reading and disposing of mail that you receive. Rmail stores mail messages in files called Rmail files. Reading the message in an Rmail file is done in a special major mode, Rmail mode, which redefines most letters to run commands for managing mail.

26.1 Basic Concepts of Rmail

Using Rmail in the simplest fashion, you have one Rmail file '~/RMAIL' in which all of your mail is saved. It is called your *primary Rmail file*. The command M-x rmail reads your primary Rmail file, merges new mail in from your inboxes, displays the first message you haven't read yet, and lets you begin reading.

Rmail uses narrowing to hide all but one message in the Rmail file. The message that is shown is called the *current message*. Rmail mode's special commands can do such things as delete the current message, copy it into another file, send a reply, or move to another message. You can also create multiple Rmail files and use Rmail to move messages between them.

Within the Rmail file, messages are normally arranged sequentially in order of receipt; you can specify other ways to sort them. Messages are assigned consecutive integers as their *message numbers*. The number of the current message is displayed in Rmail's mode line, followed by the total number of messages in the file. You can move to a message by specifying its message number with the j key (see Section 26.3 [Rmail Motion], page 270).

Following the usual conventions of Emacs, changes in an Rmail file become permanent only when the file is saved. You can save it with s (rmail-save), which also expunges deleted messages from the file first (see Section 26.4 [Rmail Deletion], page 271). To save the file without expunging, use C-x C-s. Rmail also saves the Rmail file after merging new mail from an inbox file (see Section 26.5 [Rmail Inbox], page 272).

You can exit Rmail with q (rmail-quit); this expunges and saves the Rmail file and then switches to another buffer. But there is no need to 'exit' formally. If you switch from Rmail to editing in other buffers, and never happen to switch back, you have exited. (The Rmail command b, rmail-bury, does this for you.) Just make sure to save the Rmail file eventually (like any other file you have changed). C-x s is a good enough way to do this (see Section 14.3 [Saving], page 107).

26.2 Scrolling Within a Message

When Rmail displays a message that does not fit on the screen, you must scroll through it to read the rest. You could do this with `C-v`, `M-v` and `M-<`, but in Rmail scrolling is so frequent that it deserves to be easier to type.

SPC   Scroll forward (`scroll-up`).

DEL   Scroll backward (`scroll-down`).

.   Scroll to start of message (`rmail-beginning-of-message`).

Since the most common thing to do while reading a message is to scroll through it by screenfuls, Rmail makes `SPC` and `DEL` synonyms of `C-v` (`scroll-up`) and `M-v` (`scroll-down`)

The command `.` (`rmail-beginning-of-message`) scrolls back to the beginning of the selected message. This is not quite the same as `M-<`: for one thing, it does not set the mark; for another, it resets the buffer boundaries to the current message if you have changed them.

26.3 Moving Among Messages

The most basic thing to do with a message is to read it. The way to do this in Rmail is to make the message current. The usual practice is to move sequentially through the file, since this is the order of receipt of messages. When you enter Rmail, you are positioned at the first message that you have not yet made current (that is, the first one that has the 'unseen' attribute; see Section 26.8 [Rmail Labels], page 276). Move forward to see the other new messages; move backward to reexamine old messages.

n   Move to the next nondeleted message, skipping any intervening deleted messages (`rmail-next-undeleted-message`).

p   Move to the previous nondeleted message (`rmail-previous-undeleted-message`).

M-n   Move to the next message, including deleted messages (`rmail-next-message`).

M-p   Move to the previous message, including deleted messages (`rmail-previous-message`).

j   Move to the first message. With argument n, move to message number n (`rmail-show-message`).

>   Move to the last message (`rmail-last-message`).

<   Move to the first message (`rmail-first-message`).

M-s *regexp* RET
>   Move to the next message containing a match for *regexp* (rmail-
>   search).

- M-s *regexp* RET
>   Move to the previous message containing a match for *regexp*.

n and p are the usual way of moving among messages in Rmail. They move through the messages sequentially, but skip over deleted messages, which is usually what you want to do. Their command definitions are named rmail-next-undeleted-message and rmail-previous-undeleted-message. If you do not want to skip deleted messages—for example, if you want to move to a message to undelete it—use the variants M-n and M-p (rmail-next-message and rmail-previous-message). A numeric argument to any of these commands serves as a repeat count.

In Rmail, you can specify a numeric argument by typing just the digits. You don't need to type C-u first.

The M-s (rmail-search) command is Rmail's version of search. The usual incremental search command C-s works in Rmail, but it searches only within the current message. The purpose of M-s is to search for another message. It reads a regular expression (see Section 12.5 [Regexps], page 88) nonincrementally, then searches starting at the beginning of the following message for a match. It then selects that message. If *regexp* is empty, M-s reuses the regexp used the previous time.

To search backward in the file for another message, give M-s a negative argument. In Rmail you can do this with - M-s.

It is also possible to search for a message based on labels. See Section 26.8 [Rmail Labels], page 276.

To move to a message specified by absolute message number, use j (rmail-show-message) with the message number as argument. With no argument, j selects the first message. < (rmail-first-message) also selects the first message. > (rmail-last-message) selects the last message.

26.4 Deleting Messages

When you no longer need to keep a message, you can *delete* it. This flags it as ignorable, and some Rmail commands pretend it is no longer present; but it still has its place in the Rmail file, and still has its message number.

Expunging the Rmail file actually removes the deleted messages. The remaining messages are renumbered consecutively. Expunging is the only action that changes the message number of any message, except for undigestifying (see Section 26.14 [Rmail Digest], page 284).

d   Delete the current message, and move to the next nondeleted
             message (`rmail-delete-forward`).

C-d   Delete the current message, and move to the previous nondeleted
             message (`rmail-delete-backward`).

u   Undelete the current message, or move back to a deleted message
             and undelete it (`rmail-undelete-previous-message`).

x   Expunge the Rmail file (`rmail-expunge`).

There are two Rmail commands for deleting messages. Both delete the current message and select another message. d (`rmail-delete-forward`) moves to the following message, skipping messages already deleted, while C-d (`rmail-delete-backward`) moves to the previous nondeleted message. If there is no nondeleted message to move to in the specified direction, the message that was just deleted remains current.

To make all the deleted messages finally vanish from the Rmail file, type x (`rmail-expunge`). Until you do this, you can still *undelete* the deleted messages. The undeletion command, u (`rmail-undelete-previous-message`), is designed to cancel the effect of a d command in most cases. It undeletes the current message if the current message is deleted. Otherwise it moves backward to previous messages until a deleted message is found, and undeletes that message.

You can usually undo a d with a u because the u moves back to and undeletes the message that the d deleted. But this does not work when the d skips a few already-deleted messages that follow the message being deleted; then the u command undeletes the last of the messages that were skipped. There is no clean way to avoid this problem. However, by repeating the u command, you can eventually get back to the message that you intend to undelete. You can also select a particular deleted message with the M-p command, then type u to undelete it.

A deleted message has the '`deleted`' attribute, and as a result '`deleted`' appears in the mode line when the current message is deleted. In fact, deleting or undeleting a message is nothing more than adding or removing this attribute. See Section 26.8 [Rmail Labels], page 276.

26.5 Rmail Files and Inboxes

The operating system places incoming mail for you in a file that we call your *inbox*. When you start up Rmail, it runs a C program called `movemail` to copy the new messages from your inbox into your primary Rmail file, which also contains other messages saved from previous Rmail sessions. It is in this file that you actually read the mail with Rmail. This operation is called *getting new mail*. You can get new mail at any time in Rmail by typing g.

The variable `rmail-primary-inbox-list` contains a list of the files which are inboxes for your primary Rmail file. If you don't set this variable explicitly, it is initialized from the `MAIL` environment variable, or, as a last resort, set to `nil`, which means to use the default inbox. The default inbox is '`/var/mail/`*username*', '`/usr/spool/mail/`*username*', or '`/usr/mail/`*username*', depending on your operating system.

Some sites use a method called POP for accessing users' inbox data instead of storing the data in inbox files. `movemail` can work with POP if you compile it with the macro `MAIL_USE_POP` defined, and then install it setuid to `root`. It is safe to install `movemail` in this way.

Assuming you have compiled and installed `movemail` appropriately, you can specify a POP inbox with a "file name" of the form '`po:`*username*'. `movemail` handles such a name by opening a connection to the POP server. The `MAILHOST` environment variable specifies the machine to look for the server on.

There are three reason for having separate Rmail files and inboxes.

1. The inbox file format varies between operating systems and according to the other mail software in use. Only one part of Rmail needs to know about the alternatives, and it need only understand how to convert all of them to Rmail's own format.

2. The inbox file format usually doesn't provide a place for all the information that Rmail records.

3. It is very cumbersome to access an inbox file without danger of losing mail, because it is necessary to interlock with mail delivery. Moreover, different operating systems use different interlocking techniques. The strategy of moving mail out of the inbox once and for all into a separate Rmail file avoids the need for interlocking in all the rest of Rmail, since only Rmail operates on the Rmail file.

When getting new mail, Rmail first copies the new mail from the inbox file to the Rmail file; then it saves the Rmail file; then it truncates the inbox file. This way, a system crash may cause duplication of mail between the inbox and the Rmail file, but cannot lose mail.

When `movemail` copies mail from an inbox in the system's mailer directory, it actually puts it in an intermediate file '`~/.newmail-`*inboxname*'. Once it finishes, Rmail reads that file, merges the new mail, saves the Rmail file, and only then deletes the intermediate file. If there is a crash at the wrong time, this file continues to exist and Rmail will use it again the next time it gets new mail from that inbox.

26.6 Multiple Rmail Files

Rmail operates by default on your *primary Rmail file*, which is named
'~/RMAIL' and receives your incoming mail from your system inbox file. But
you can also have other Rmail files and edit them with Rmail. These files can
receive mail through their own inboxes, or you can move messages into them
with explicit Rmail commands (see Section 26.7 [Rmail Output], page 275).

i *file* RET   Read *file* into Emacs and run Rmail on it (`rmail-input`).

M-x set-rmail-inbox-list RET *files* RET
                Specify inbox file names for current Rmail file to get mail from.

g   Merge new mail from current Rmail file's inboxes (`rmail-get-`
                `new-mail`).

C-u g *file* RET
                Merge new mail from inbox file *file*.

To run Rmail on a file other than your primary Rmail file, you may use
the i (`rmail-input`) command in Rmail. This visits the file in Rmail mode.
You can use M-x rmail-input even when not in Rmail.

The file you read with i should normally be a valid Rmail file. If it is
not, Rmail tries to decompose it into a stream of messages in various known
formats. If it succeeds, it converts the whole file to an Rmail file. If you
specify a file name that doesn't exist, i initializes a new buffer for creating
a new Rmail file.

You can also select an Rmail file from a menu. Choose first the menu
bar Classify item, then from the Classify menu choose the Input Rmail File
item; then choose the Rmail file you want. The variables `rmail-secondary-`
`file-directory` and `rmail-secondary-file-regexp` specify which files to
offer in the menu: the first variable says which directory to find them in; the
second says which files in that directory to offer (all those that match the
regular expression). These variables also apply to choosing a file for output
(see Section 26.7 [Rmail Output], page 275).

Each Rmail file can contain a list of inbox file names; you can specify
this list with M-x set-rmail-inbox-list RET *files* RET. The argument can
contain any number of file names, separated by commas. It can also be
empty, which specifies that this file should have no inboxes. Once a list
of inboxes is specified, the Rmail file remembers it permanently until you
specify a different list.

As a special exception, if your primary Rmail file does not specify any
inbox files, it uses your standard system inbox.

The g command (`rmail-get-new-mail`) merges mail into the current
Rmail file from its specified inboxes. If the Rmail file has no inboxes, g does

nothing. The command M-x rmail also merges new mail into your primary Rmail file.

To merge mail from a file that is not the usual inbox, give the g key a numeric argument, as in C-u g. Then it reads a file name and merges mail from that file. The inbox file is not deleted or changed in any way when g with an argument is used. This is, therefore, a general way of merging one file of messages into another.

26.7 Copying Messages Out to Files

These commands copy messages from an Rmail file into another file.

o *file* RET   Append a copy of the current message to the file *file*, using Rmail file format by default (rmail-output-to-rmail-file).

C-o *file* RET

Append a copy of the current message to the file *file*, using system inbox file format by default (rmail-output).

The commands o and C-o copy the current message into a specified file. This file may be an Rmail file or it may be in system inbox format; the output commands ascertain the file's format and write the copied message in that format.

The o and C-o commands differ in two ways: each has its own separate default file name, and each specifies a choice of format to use when the file does not already exist. The o command uses Rmail format when it creates a new file, while C-o uses system inbox format for a new file. The default file name for o is the file name used last with o, and the default file name for C-o is the file name used last with C-o.

If the output file is an Rmail file currently visited in an Emacs buffer, the output commands copy the message into that buffer. It is up to you to save the buffer eventually in its file.

You can also output a message to an Rmail file chosen with a menu. Choose first the menu bar Classify item, then from the Classify menu choose the Output Rmail Menu item; then choose the Rmail file you want. This outputs the current message to that file, like the o command. The variables rmail-secondary-file-directory and rmail-secondary-file-regexp specify which files to offer in the menu: the first variable says which directory to find them in; the second says which files in that directory to offer (all those that match the regular expression).

Copying a message gives the original copy of the message the 'filed' attribute, so that 'filed' appears in the mode line when such a message is current. If you like to keep just a single copy of every mail message, set the variable rmail-delete-after-output to t; then the o and C-o commands delete the original message after copying it. (You can undelete the original afterward if you wish.)

Copying messages into files in system inbox format uses the header fields that are displayed in Rmail at the time. Thus, if you use the t command to view the entire header and then copy the message, the entire header is copied. See Section 26.12 [Rmail Display], page 283.

The variable `rmail-output-file-alist` lets you specify intelligent defaults for the output file, based on the contents of the current message. The value should be a list whose elements have this form:

> (*regexp* . *name-exp*)

If there's a match for *regexp* in the current message, then the default file name for output is *name-exp*. If multiple elements match the message, the first matching element decides the default file name. The subexpression *name-exp* may be a string constant giving the file name to use, or more generally it may be any Lisp expression that returns a file name as a string. `rmail-output-file-alist` applies to both o and C-o.

26.8 Labels

Each message can have various *labels* assigned to it as a means of classification. Each label has a name; different names are different labels. Any given label is either present or absent on a particular message. A few label names have standard meanings and are given to messages automatically by Rmail when appropriate; these special labels are called *attributes*. All other labels are assigned only by users.

a *label* RET
> Assign the label *label* to the current message (`rmail-add-label`).

k *label* RET
> Remove the label *label* from the current message (`rmail-kill-label`).

C-M-n *labels* RET
> Move to the next message that has one of the labels *labels* (`rmail-next-labeled-message`).

C-M-p *labels* RET
> Move to the previous message that has one of the labels *labels* (`rmail-previous-labeled-message`).

C-M-l *labels* RET
> Make a summary of all messages containing any of the labels *labels* (`rmail-summary-by-labels`).

The a (`rmail-add-label`) and k (`rmail-kill-label`) commands allow you to assign or remove any label on the current message. If the *label* argument is empty, it means to assign or remove the same label most recently assigned or removed.

Once you have given messages labels to classify them as you wish, there are two ways to use the labels: in moving and in summaries.

The command `C-M-n` *labels* RET (`rmail-next-labeled-message`) moves to the next message that has one of the labels *labels*. The argument *labels* specifies one or more label names, separated by commas. `C-M-p` (`rmail-previous-labeled-message`) is similar, but moves backwards to previous messages. A numeric argument to either command serves as a repeat count.

The command `C-M-l` *labels* RET (`rmail-summary-by-labels`) displays a summary containing only the messages that have at least one of a specified set of messages. The argument *labels* is one or more label names, separated by commas. See Section 26.10 [Rmail Summary], page 280, for information on summaries.

If the *labels* argument to `C-M-n`, `C-M-p` or `C-M-l` is empty, it means to use the last set of labels specified for any of these commands.

Some labels such as '`deleted`' and '`filed`' have built-in meanings and are assigned to or removed from messages automatically at appropriate times; these labels are called *attributes*. Here is a list of Rmail attributes:

'`unseen`'   Means the message has never been current. Assigned to messages when they come from an inbox file, and removed when a message is made current. When you start Rmail, it initially shows the first message that has this attribute.

'`deleted`'   Means the message is deleted. Assigned by deletion commands and removed by undeletion commands (see Section 26.4 [Rmail Deletion], page 271).

'`filed`'   Means the message has been copied to some other file. Assigned by the file output commands (see Section 26.6 [Rmail Files], page 274).

'`answered`'

Means you have mailed an answer to the message. Assigned by the r command (`rmail-reply`). See Section 26.9 [Rmail Reply], page 278.

'`forwarded`'

Means you have forwarded the message. Assigned by the f command (`rmail-forward`). See Section 26.9 [Rmail Reply], page 278.

'`edited`'   Means you have edited the text of the message within Rmail. See Section 26.13 [Rmail Editing], page 283.

'resent'   Means you have resent the message. Assigned by the command
             M-x rmail-resend. See Section 26.9 [Rmail Reply], page 278.

All other labels are assigned or removed only by the user, and have no
standard meaning.

26.9 Sending Replies

Rmail has several commands that use Mail mode to send outgoing mail.
See Chapter 25 [Sending Mail], page 261, for information on using Mail
mode. What are documented here are the special commands of Rmail for
entering Mail mode. Note that the usual keys for sending mail—C-x m, C-x
4 m, and C-x 5 m—are available in Rmail mode and work just as they usually
do.

m   Send a message (rmail-mail).

c   Continue editing already started outgoing message (rmail-
             continue).

r   Send a reply to the current Rmail message (rmail-reply).

f   Forward current message to other users (rmail-forward).

C-u f   Resend the current message to other users (rmail-resend).

M-m   Try sending a bounced message a second time (rmail-retry-
             failure).

The most common reason to send a message while in Rmail is to reply to the message you are reading. To do this, type r (rmail-reply).
This displays the '*mail*' buffer in another window, much like C-x 4 m, but
preinitializes the 'Subject', 'To', 'CC' and 'In-reply-to' header fields based
on the message you are replying to. The 'To' field starts out as the address
of the person who sent the message you received, and the 'CC' field starts
out with all the other recipients of that message.

You can exclude certain recipients from being placed automatically in the
'CC', using the variable rmail-dont-reply-to-names. Its value should be
a regular expression (as a string); any recipient that the regular expression
matches, is excluded from the 'CC' field. The default value matches your own
name, and any name starting with 'info-'. (Those names are excluded because there is a convention of using them for large mailing lists to broadcast
announcements.)

To omit the 'CC' field completely for a particular reply, enter the reply
command with a numeric argument: C-u r or 1 r.

Once the '*mail*' buffer has been initialized, editing and sending the
mail goes as usual (see Chapter 25 [Sending Mail], page 261). You can edit

the presupplied header fields if they are not right for you. You can also use the commands of Mail mode, including C-c C-y to yank in the message that you are replying to, and C-c C-q to fill what was thus yanked. You can also switch to the Rmail buffer, select a different message, switch back, and yank the new current message.

Sometimes a message does not reach its destination. Mailers usually send the failed message back to you, enclosed in a *failure message*. The Rmail command M-m (rmail-retry-failure) prepares to send the same message a second time: it sets up a '*mail*' buffer with the same text and header fields as before. If you type C-c C-c right away, you send the message again exactly the same as the first time. Alternatively, you can edit the text or headers and then send it. The variable rmail-retry-ignored-headers, in the same format as rmail-ignored-headers (see Section 26.12 [Rmail Display], page 283), controls which headers are stripped from the failed message when retrying it; it defaults to nil.

Another frequent reason to send mail in Rmail is to *forward* the current message to other users. f (rmail-forward) makes this easy by preinitializing the '*mail*' buffer with the current message as the text, and a subject designating a forwarded message. All you have to do is fill in the recipients and send. When you forward a message, recipients get a message which is "from" you, and which has the original message in its contents.

Resending is an alternative similar to forwarding; the difference is that resending sends a message that is "from" the original sender, just as it reached you—with a few added header fields 'Resent-from' and 'Resent-to' to indicate that it came via you. To resend a message in Rmail, use C-u f. (f runs rmail-forward, which is programmed to invoke rmail-resend if you provide a numeric argument.)

The m (rmail-mail) command is used to start editing an outgoing message that is not a reply. It leaves the header fields empty. Its only difference from C-x 4 m is that it makes the Rmail buffer accessible for C-c C-y, just as r does. Thus, m can be used to reply to or forward a message; it can do anything r or f can do.

The c (rmail-continue) command resumes editing the '*mail*' buffer, to finish editing an outgoing message you were already composing, or to alter a message you have sent.

If you set the variable rmail-mail-new-frame to a non-nil value, then all the Rmail commands to start sending a message create a new frame to edit it in. This frame is deleted when you send the message, or when you use the 'Don't Send' item in the 'Mail' menu.

26.10 Summaries

A *summary* is a buffer containing one line per message to give you an
overview of the mail in an Rmail file. Each line shows the message number,
the sender, the labels, and the subject. Almost all Rmail commands are
valid in the summary buffer also; these apply to the message described by
the current line of the summary. Moving point in the summary buffer selects
messages as you move to their summary lines.

A summary buffer applies to a single Rmail file only; if you are editing
multiple Rmail files, each one can have its own summary buffer. The summary buffer name is made by appending '`-summary`' to the Rmail buffer's
name. Normally only one summary buffer is displayed at a time.

26.10.1 Making Summaries

Here are the commands to create a summary for the current Rmail file.
Once the Rmail file has a summary buffer, changes in the Rmail file (such as
deleting or expunging messages, and getting new mail) automatically update
the summary.

h
C-M-h   Summarize all messages (`rmail-summary`).

l *labels* RET
C-M-l *labels* RET
               Summarize message that have one or more of the specified labels
               (`rmail-summary-by-labels`).

C-M-r *rcpts* RET
               Summarize messages that have one or more of the specified re-
               cipients (`rmail-summary-by-recipients`).

C-M-t *topic* RET
               Summarize messages that have a match for the specified regexp
               topic in their subjects (`rmail-summary-by-topic`).

The h or C-M-h (`rmail-summary`) command fills the summary buffer for
the current Rmail file with a summary of all the messages in the file. It then
displays and selects the summary buffer in another window.

C-M-l *labels* RET (`rmail-summary-by-labels`) makes a partial summary
mentioning only the messages that have one or more of the labels *labels*.
labels should contain label names separated by commas.

C-M-r *rcpts* RET (`rmail-summary-by-recipients`) makes a partial summary mentioning only the messages that have one or more of the recipients
rcpts. *rcpts* should contain mailing addresses separated by commas.

C-M-t *topic* RET (`rmail-summary-by-topic`) makes a partial summary mentioning only the messages whose subjects have a match for the regular expression *topic*.

Note that there is only one summary buffer for any Rmail file; making one kind of summary discards any previously made summary.

The variable `rmail-summary-window-size` says how many lines to use for the summary window.

26.10.2 Editing in Summaries

You can use the Rmail summary buffer to do almost anything you can do in the Rmail buffer itself. In fact, once you have a summary buffer, there's no need to switch back to the Rmail buffer.

You can select and display various messages in the Rmail buffer, from the summary buffer, just by moving point in the summary buffer to different lines. It doesn't matter what Emacs command you use to move point; whichever line point is on at the end of the command, that message is selected in the Rmail buffer.

Almost all Rmail commands work in the summary buffer as well as in the Rmail buffer. Thus, d in the summary buffer deletes the current message, u undeletes, and x expunges. o and C-o output the current message to a file; r starts a reply to it. You can scroll the current message while remaining in the summary buffer using SPC and DEL.

The Rmail commands to move between messages also work in the summary buffer, but with a twist: they move through the set of messages included in the summary. They also ensure the Rmail buffer appears on the screen (unlike cursor motion commands, which update the contents of the Rmail buffer but don't display it in a window unless it already appears). Here is a list of these commands:

n   Move to next line, skipping lines saying 'deleted', and select its message.

p   Move to previous line, skipping lines saying 'deleted', and select its message.

M-n   Move to next line and select its message.

M-p   Move to previous line and select its message.

>   Move to the last line, and select its message.

<   Move to the first line, and select its message.

M-s *pattern* RET
            Search through messages for *pattern* starting with the current message; select the message found, and move point in the summary buffer to that message's line.

Deletion, undeletion, and getting new mail, and even selection of a different message all update the summary buffer when you do them in the Rmail buffer. If the variable `rmail-redisplay-summary` is non-`nil`, these actions also bring the summary buffer back onto the screen.

When you are finished using the summary, type `w` (`rmail-summary-wipe`) to delete the summary buffer's window. You can also exit Rmail while in the summary: `q` (`rmail-summary-quit`) deletes the summary window, then exits from Rmail by saving the Rmail file and switching to another buffer.

26.11 Sorting the Rmail File

`M-x rmail-sort-by-date`
> Sort messages of current Rmail file by date.

`M-x rmail-sort-by-subject`
> Sort messages of current Rmail file by subject.

`M-x rmail-sort-by-author`
> Sort messages of current Rmail file by author's name.

`M-x rmail-sort-by-recipient`
> Sort messages of current Rmail file by recipient's names.

`M-x rmail-sort-by-correspondent`
> Sort messages of current Rmail file by the name of the other correspondent.

`M-x rmail-sort-by-lines`
> Sort messages of current Rmail file by size (number of lines).

`M-x rmail-sort-by-keywords` RET *labels* RET
> Sort messages of current Rmail file by labels. The argument *labels* should be a comma-separated list of labels. The order of these labels specifies the order of messages; messages with the first label come first, messages with the second label come second, and so on. Messages which have none of these labels come last.

The Rmail sort commands perform a *stable sort*: if there is no reason to prefer either one of two messages, their order remains unchanged. You can use this to sort by more than one criterion. For example, if you use `rmail-sort-by-date` and then `rmail-sort-by-author`, messages from the same author appear in order by date.

With a numeric argument, all these commands reverse the order of comparison. This means they sort messages from newest to oldest, from biggest to smallest, or in reverse alphabetical order.

26.12 Display of Messages

Rmail reformats the header of each message before displaying it for the first time. Reformatting hides uninteresting header fields to reduce clutter. You can use the `t` command to show the entire header or to repeat the header reformatting operation.

`t`   Toggle display of complete header (`rmail-toggle-headers`).

Reformatting the header involves deleting most header fields, on the grounds that they are not interesting. The variable `rmail-ignored-headers` holds a regular expression that specifies which header fields to hide in this way—if it matches the beginning of a header field, that whole field is hidden.

Rmail saves the complete original header before reformatting; to see it, use the `t` command (`rmail-toggle-headers`). This discards the reformatted headers of the current message and displays it with the original header. Repeating `t` reformats the message again. Selecting the message again also reformats.

One consequence of this is that if you edit the reformatted header (using `e`; see Section 26.13 [Rmail Editing], page 283), subsequent use of `t` will discard your edits. On the other hand, if you use `e` after `t`, to edit the original (unreformatted) header, those changes are permanent.

When used with a window system that supports multiple fonts, Rmail highlights certain header fields that are especially interesting—by default, the 'From' and 'Subject' fields. The variable `rmail-highlighted-headers` holds a regular expression that specifies the header fields to highlight; if it matches the beginning of a header field, that whole field is highlighted.

If you specify unusual colors for your text foreground and background, the colors used for highlighting may not go well with them. If so, specify different colors for the `highlight` face. That is worth doing because the `highlight` face is used for other kinds of highlighting as well. See Section 17.12 [Faces], page 156, for how to do this.

To turn off highlighting entirely in Rmail, set `rmail-highlighted-headers` to `nil`.

26.13 Editing Within a Message

Most of the usual Emacs commands are available in Rmail mode, though a few, such as `C-M-n` and `C-M-h`, are redefined by Rmail for other purposes. However, the Rmail buffer is normally read only, and most of the letters are redefined as Rmail commands. If you want to edit the text of a message, you must use the Rmail command `e`.

`e`   Edit the current message as ordinary text.

The e command (`rmail-edit-current-message`) switches from Rmail mode into Rmail Edit mode, another major mode which is nearly the same as Text mode. The mode line indicates this change.

In Rmail Edit mode, letters insert themselves as usual and the Rmail commands are not available. When you are finished editing the message and are ready to go back to Rmail, type `C-c C-c`, which switches back to Rmail mode. Alternatively, you can return to Rmail mode but cancel all the editing that you have done, by typing `C-c C-]`.

Entering Rmail Edit mode runs the hook `text-mode-hook`; then it runs the hook `rmail-edit-mode-hook` (see Section 30.2.3 [Hooks], page 347). It adds the attribute 'edited' to the message.

26.14 Digest Messages

A *digest message* is a message which exists to contain and carry several other messages. Digests are used on some moderated mailing lists; all the messages that arrive for the list during a period of time such as one day are put inside a single digest which is then sent to the subscribers. Transmitting the single digest uses much less computer time than transmitting the individual messages even though the total size is the same, because the per-message overhead in network mail transmission is considerable.

When you receive a digest message, the most convenient way to read it is to *undigestify* it: to turn it back into many individual messages. Then you can read and delete the individual messages as it suits you.

To do this, select the digest message and type the command `M-x undigestify-rmail-message`. This extracts the submessages as separate Rmail messages, and inserts them following the digest. The digest message itself is flagged as deleted.

26.15 Converting an Rmail File to Inbox Format

The command `M-x unrmail` converts a file in Rmail format to inbox format (also known as the system mailbox format), so that you can use it with other mail-editing tools. You must specify two arguments, the name of the Rmail file and the name to use for the converted file. `M-x unrmail` does not alter the Rmail file itself.

26.16 Reading Rot13 Messages

Mailing list messages that might offend some readers are sometimes encoded in a simple code called *rot13*—so named because it rotates the alphabet by 13 letters. This code is not for secrecy, as it provides none; rather, it enables those who might be offended to avoid ever seeing the real text of the message.

To view a buffer using the rot13 code, use the command `M-x rot13-other-window`. This displays the current buffer in another window which applies the code when displaying the text.

27 Dired, the Directory Editor

Dired makes an Emacs buffer containing a listing of a directory, and optionally some of its subdirectories as well. You can use the normal Emacs commands to move around in this buffer, and special Dired commands to operate on the files listed.

27.1 Entering Dired

To invoke Dired, do `C-x d` or `M-x dired`. The command reads a directory name or wildcard file name pattern as a minibuffer argument to specify which files to list. Where `dired` differs from `list-directory` is in putting the buffer into Dired mode so that the special commands of Dired are available.

The variable `dired-listing-switches` specifies the options to give to `ls` for listing directory; this string *must* contain '-l'. If you use a numeric prefix argument with the `dired` command, you can specify the `ls` switches with the minibuffer after you finish entering the directory specification.

To display the Dired buffer in another window rather than in the selected window, use `C-x 4 d` (`dired-other-window`) instead of `C-x d`. `C-x 5 d` (`dired-other-frame`) uses a separate frame to display the Dired buffer.

27.2 Commands in the Dired Buffer

The Dired buffer is "read-only", and inserting text in it is not useful, so ordinary printing characters such as `d` and `x` are used for special Dired commands. Some Dired commands *mark* or *flag* the *current file* (that is, the file on the current line); other commands operate on the marked files or on the flagged files.

All the usual Emacs cursor motion commands are available in Dired buffers. Some special purpose cursor motion commands are also provided. The keys `C-n` and `C-p` are redefined to put the cursor at the beginning of the file name on the line, rather than at the beginning of the line.

For extra convenience, `SPC` and `n` in Dired are equivalent to `C-n`. `p` is equivalent to `C-p`. (Moving by lines is so common in Dired that it deserves to be easy to type.) `DEL` (move up and unflag) is often useful simply for moving up.

27.3 Deleting Files with Dired

The primary use of Dired is to *flag* files for deletion and then delete the files previously flagged.

d   Flag this file for deletion.

u   Remove deletion flag on this line.

DEL   Move point to previous line and remove the deletion flag on that
               line.

x   Delete the files that are flagged for deletion.

You can flag a file for deletion by moving to the line describing the file
and typing d. The deletion flag is visible as a 'D' at the beginning of the line.
This command moves point to the next line, so that repeated d commands
flag successive files. A numeric argument serves as a repeat count.

The files are flagged for deletion rather than deleted immediately to reduce the danger of deleting a file accidentally. Until you direct Dired to
expunge the flagged files, you can remove deletion flags using the commands
u and DEL. u works just like d, but removes flags rather than making flags.
DEL moves upward, removing flags; it is like u with numeric argument automatically negated.

To delete the flagged files, type x (dired-expunge). This command first
displays a list of all the file names flagged for deletion, and requests confirmation with yes. If you confirm, Dired deletes the flagged files, then deletes
their lines from the text of the Dired buffer. The shortened Dired buffer
remains selected.

If you answer no or quit with C-g when asked to confirm, you return
immediately to Dired, with the deletion flags still present in the buffer, and
no files actually deleted.

27.4 Flagging Many Files

\#   Flag all auto-save files (files whose names start and end with '#')
               for deletion (see Section 14.5 [Auto Save], page 113).

~   Flag all backup files (files whose names end with '~') for deletion
               (see Section 14.3.1 [Backup], page 109).

. (Period)   Flag excess numeric backup files for deletion. The oldest and
               newest few backup files of any one file are exempt; the middle
               ones are flagged.

% d regexp RET
               Flag for deletion all files whose names match the regular expres-
               sion regexp (dired-flag-files-regexp).

The #, ~ and . commands flag many files for deletion, based on their file
names. These commands are useful precisely because they do not actually
delete any files; you can remove the deletion flags from any flagged files that
you really wish to keep.

flags for deletion all files whose names look like auto-save files (see Section 14.5 [Auto Save], page 113)—that is, files whose names begin and end with '#'. ~ flags for deletion all files whose names say they are backup files (see Section 14.3.1 [Backup], page 109)—that is, whose names end in '~'.

. (Period) flags just some of the backup files for deletion: all but the oldest few and newest few backups of any one file. Normally `dired-kept-versions` (**not** `kept-new-versions`; that applies only when saving) specifies the number of newest versions of each file to keep, and `kept-old-versions` specifies the number of oldest versions to keep.

Period with a positive numeric argument, as in C-u 3 ., specifies the number of newest versions to keep, overriding `dired-kept-versions`. A negative numeric argument overrides `kept-old-versions`, using minus the value of the argument to specify the number of oldest versions of each file to keep.

The % d command flags all files whose names match a specified regular expression (`dired-flag-files-regexp`). Only the non-directory part of the file name is used in matching. You can use '^' and '$' to anchor matches. You can exclude subdirectories by hiding them (see Section 27.13 [Hiding Subdirectories], page 296).

27.5 Visiting Files in Dired

There are several Dired commands for visiting or examining the files listed in the Dired buffer. All of them apply to the current line's file; if that file is really a directory, these commands invoke Dired on that subdirectory (making a separate Dired buffer).

f   Visit the file described on the current line, like typing C-x C-f
            and supplying that file name (`dired-find-file`). See Sec-
            tion 14.2 [Visiting], page 104.

RET   Equivalent to f.

o   Like f, but uses another window to display the file's buffer
            (`dired-find-file-other-window`). The Dired buffer remains
            visible in the first window. This is like using C-x 4 C-f to visit
            the file. See Chapter 16 [Windows], page 141.

C-o   Visit the file described on the current line, and display the buffer
            in another window, but do not select that window (`dired-
            display-file`).

Mouse-2   Visit the file named by the line you click on (`dired-mouse-
            find-file-other-window`). This uses another window to dis-
            play the file, like the o command.

v   View the file described on the current line, using `M-x view-file`
             (`dired-view-file`).

             Viewing a file is like visiting it, but is slanted toward moving
             around in the file conveniently and does not allow changing the
             file. See Section 14.10 [Misc File Ops], page 131.

27.6 Dired Marks vs. Flags

Instead of flagging a file with 'D', you can *mark* the file with some other
character (usually '*'). Most Dired commands to operate on files, aside from
"expunge" (x), look for files marked with '*'.

Here are some commands for marking with '*' (and also for unmarking).
(See Section 27.3 [Dired Deletion], page 287, for commands to flag and unflag
files.)

m   Mark the current file with '*' (`dired-mark`). With a numeric
             argument *n*, mark the next *n* files starting with the current file.
             (If *n* is negative, mark the previous −*n* files.)

*   Mark all executable files with '*' (`dired-mark-executables`).
             With a numeric argument, unmark all those files.

@   Mark all symbolic links with '*' (`dired-mark-symlinks`). With
             a numeric argument, unmark all those files.

/   Mark with '*' all files which are actually directories, except for
             '.' and '..' (`dired-mark-directories`). With a numeric argu-
             ment, unmark all those files.

M-DEL *markchar*
             Remove all marks that use the character *markchar* (`dired-`
             `unmark-all-files`). If you specify RET as *markchar*, this com-
             mand removes all marks, no matter what the marker character
             is.

             With a numeric argument, this command queries about each
             marked file, asking whether to remove its mark. You can answer
             y meaning yes, n meaning no, ! to remove the marks from the
             remaining files without asking about them.

c *old new*   Replace all marks that use the character *old* with marks that
             use the character *new* (`dired-change-marks`). This command
             is the primary way to create or use marks other than '*' or
             'D'. The arguments are single characters—do not use RET to
             terminate them.

             You can use almost any character as a mark character by means
             of this command, to distinguish various classes of files. If *old* is

a space (' '), then the command operates on all unmarked files; if *new* is a space, then the command unmarks the files it acts on.

To illustrate the power of this command, here is how to put '*' marks on all the files that are unmarked, while unmarking all those that have '*' marks:

          c * t   c SPC *   c t SPC

% m *regexp* **RET**

Mark (with '*') all files whose names match the regular expression *regexp* (`dired-mark-files-regexp`). **% m** is like **% d**, except that it marks files with '*' instead of flagging with 'D'. See Section 27.4 [Flagging Many Files], page 288.

Only the non-directory part of the file name is used in matching. Use '^' and '$' to anchor matches. Exclude subdirectories by hiding them (see Section 27.13 [Hiding Subdirectories], page 296).

27.7 Operating on Files

This section describes the basic Dired commands to operate on one file or several files. All of these commands are capital letters; all of them use the minibuffer, either to read an argument or to ask for confirmation, before they act. All use the following convention to decide which files to manipulate:

- If you give the command a numeric prefix argument *n*, it operates on the next *n* files, starting with the current file. (If *n* is negative, the command operates on the −*n* files preceding the current line.)
- Otherwise, if some files are marked with '*', the command operates on all those files.
- Otherwise, the command operates on the current file only.

Here are the file-manipulating commands that operate on files in this way. (Some other Dired commands, such as ! and the '%' commands, also use these conventions to decide which files to work on.)

C *new* **RET** Copy the specified files (`dired-do-copy`). The argument *new* is the directory to copy into, or (if copying a single file) the new name.

If `dired-copy-preserve-time` is non-nil, then copying with this command sets the modification time of the new file to be the same as that of the old file.

R *new* **RET** Rename the specified files (`dired-do-rename`). The argument *new* is the directory to rename into, or (if renaming a single file) the new name.

Dired automatically changes the visited file name of buffers associated with renamed files so that they refer to the new names.

H *new* RET   Make hard links to the specified files (`dired-do-hardlink`). The argument *new* is the directory to make the links in, or (if making just one link) the name to give the link.

S *new* RET   Make symbolic links to the specified files (`dired-do-symlink`). The argument *new* is the directory to make the links in, or (if making just one link) the name to give the link.

M *modespec* RET
Change the mode (also called "permission bits") of the specified files (`dired-do-chmod`). This uses the `chmod` program, so *modespec* can be any argument that `chmod` can handle.

G *newgroup* RET
Change the group of the specified files to *newgroup* (`dired-do-chgrp`).

O *newowner* RET
Change the owner of the specified files to *newowner* (`dired-do-chown`). (On most systems, only the superuser can do this.)

The variable `dired-chown-program` specifies the name of the program to use to do the work (different systems put `chown` in different places).

P *command* RET
Print the specified files (`dired-do-print`). You must specify the command to print them with, but the minibuffer starts out with a suitable guess made using the variables `lpr-command` and `lpr-switches` (the same variables that `lpr-file` uses; see Section 29.4 [Hardcopy], page 331).

Z   Compress or uncompress the specified files (`dired-do-compress`). If the file appears to be a compressed file, it is uncompressed; otherwise, it is compressed.

L   Load the specified Emacs Lisp files (`dired-do-load`). See Section 22.4 [Lisp Libraries], page 246.

B   Byte compile the specified Emacs Lisp files (`dired-do-byte-compile`). See section "Byte Compilation" in *The Emacs Lisp Reference Manual*.

A *regexp* RET
Search all the specified files for the regular expression *regexp* (`dired-do-search`).

This command is a variant of `tags-search`. The search stops at the first match it finds; use M-, to resume the search and find the next match. See Section 21.12.5 [Tags Search], page 221.

Q *from* RET *to* RET

> Perform `query-replace-regexp` on each of the specified files,
> replacing matches for *from* (a regular expression) with the string
> *to* (`dired-do-query-replace`).
>
> This command is a variant of `tags-query-replace`. If you exit
> the query replace loop, you can use M-, to resume the scan
> and replace more matches. See Section 21.12.5 [Tags Search],
> page 221.

One special file-operation command is + (`dired-create-directory`).
This command reads a directory name and creates the directory if it does
not already exist.

27.8 Shell Commands in Dired

The dired command ! (`dired-do-shell-command`) reads a shell command string in the minibuffer and runs that shell command on all the specified files. There are two ways of applying a shell command to multiple
files:

- If you use '*' in the shell command, then it runs just once, with the list
  of file names substituted for the '*'. The order of file names is the order
  of appearance in the Dired buffer.

  Thus, ! `tar cf foo.tar` * RET runs `tar` on the entire list of file names,
  putting them into one tar file '`foo.tar`'.

- If the command string doesn't contain '*', then it runs once *for each
  file*, with the file name added at the end.

  For example, ! `uudecode` RET runs `uudecode` on each file.

What if you want to run the shell command once for each file but with
the file name inserted in the middle? Or if you want to use the file names
in a more complicated fashion? Use a shell loop. For example, this shell
command would run `uuencode` on each of the specified files, writing the
output into a corresponding '`.uu`' file:

```
for file in *; uuencode $file $file >$file.uu; done
```

The working directory for the shell command is the top level directory of
the Dired buffer.

The ! command does not attempt to update the Dired buffer to show new
or modified files, because it doesn't really understand shell commands, and
does not know what files the shell command changed. Use the g command
to update the Dired buffer (see Section 27.14 [Dired Updating], page 296).

27.9 Transforming File Names in Dired

Here are commands that alter file names in a systematic way:

% u   Rename each of the selected files to an upper case name (`dired-upcase`). If the old file names are 'Foo' and 'bar', the new names are 'FOO' and 'BAR'.

% l   Rename each of the selected files to a lower case name (`dired-downcase`). If the old file names are 'Foo' and 'bar', the new names are 'foo' and 'bar'.

% R *from* RET *to* RET
% C *from* RET *to* RET
% H *from* RET *to* RET
% S *from* RET *to* RET
             These four commands rename, copy, make hard links and make soft links, in each case computing the new name by regular expression substitution from the name of the old file.

The four regular expression substitution commands effectively perform a search-and-replace on the selected file names in the Dired buffer. They read two arguments: a regular expression *from*, and a substitution pattern *to*.

The commands match each "old" file name against the regular expression *from*, and then replace the matching part with *to*. You can use '\&' and '*digit*' in *to* to refer to all or part of what the pattern matched in the old file name, as in `query-replace-regexp` (see Section 12.7.4 [Query Replace], page 94). If the regular expression matches more than once in a file name, only the first match is replaced.

For example, % R ^.*$ RET x-\& RET renames each selected file by prepending 'x-' to its name. The inverse of this, removing 'x-' from the front of each file name, is also possible: one method is % R ^x-\(.*\)$ RET \1 RET; another is % R ^x- RET RET. (Use '^' and '$' to anchor matches that should span the whole filename.)

Normally, the replacement process does not consider the files' directory names; it operates on the file name within the directory. If you specify a numeric argument of zero, then replacement affects the entire absolute file name including directory name.

Often you will want to apply the command to all files matching the same *regexp* that you use in the command. To do this, mark those files with % m *regexp* RET, then use the same regular expression in the command to operate on the files. To make this easier, the % commands to operate on files use the last regular expression specified in any % command as a default.

27.10 File Comparison with Dired

Here are two Dired commands that compare specified files using `diff`.

=   Compare the current file (the file at point) with another file (the
                     file at the mark) using the `diff` program (`dired-diff`). The file
                     at the mark is the first argument of `diff`, and the file at point
                     is the second argument.

M-=   Compare the current file with its latest backup file (`dired-`
                     `backup-diff`). If the current file is itself a backup, compare
                     it with the file it is a backup of; this way, you can compare a file
                     with any backup version of your choice.

                     The backup file is the first file given to `diff`.

27.11 Subdirectories in Dired

A Dired buffer displays just one directory in the normal case; but you
can optionally include its subdirectories as well.

The simplest way to include multiple directories in one Dired buffer is to
specify the options '`-lR`' for running `ls`. (If you give a numeric argument
when you run Dired, then you can specify these options in the minibuffer.)
That produces a recursive directory listing showing all subdirectories at all
levels.

But usually all the subdirectories are too many; usually you will prefer to
include specific subdirectories only. You can do this with the `i` command:

i   Insert the contents of a subdirectory later in the buffer.

Use the `i` (`dired-maybe-insert-subdir`) command on a line that describes a file which is a directory. It inserts the contents of that directory
into the same Dired buffer, and moves there. Inserted subdirectory contents
follow the top-level directory of the Dired buffer, just as they do in '`ls -lR`'
output.

If the subdirectory's contents are already present in the buffer, the `i`
command just moves to it.

In either case, `i` sets the Emacs mark before moving, so `C-u C-SPC` takes
you back to the old position in the buffer (the line describing that subdirectory).

Use the `l` command (`dired-do-redisplay`) to update the subdirectory's
contents. Use `k` to delete the subdirectory. See Section 27.14 [Dired Updat-
ing], page 296.

27.12 Moving Over Subdirectories

When a Dired buffer lists subdirectories, you can use the page motion commands C-x [and C-x] to move by entire directories.

The following commands move across, up and down in the tree of directories within one Dired buffer. They move to *directory header lines*, which are the lines that give a directory's name, at the beginning of the directory's contents.

C-M-n   Go to next subdirectory header line, regardless of level (dired-next-subdir).

C-M-p   Go to previous subdirectory header line, regardless of level (dired-prev-subdir).

C-M-u   Go up to the parent directory's header line (dired-tree-up).

C-M-d   Go down in the directory tree, to the first subdirectory's header line (dired-tree-down).

27.13 Hiding Subdirectories

Hiding a subdirectory means to make it invisible, except for its header line, via selective display (see Section 11.3 [Selective Display], page 77).

$ Hide or reveal the subdirectory that point is in, and move point to the next subdirectory (dired-hide-subdir). A numeric argument serves as a repeat count.

M-$ Hide all subdirectories in this Dired buffer, leaving only their header lines (dired-hide-all). Or, if any subdirectory is currently hidden, make all subdirectories visible again. You can use this command to get an overview in very deep directory trees or to move quickly to subdirectories far away.

Ordinary Dired commands never consider files inside a hidden subdirectory. For example, the commands to operate on marked files ignore files in hidden directories even if they are marked. Thus you can use hiding to temporarily exclude subdirectories from operations without having to remove the markers.

The subdirectory hiding commands toggle; that is, they hide what was visible, and show what was hidden.

27.14 Updating the Dired Buffer

This section describes commands to update the Dired buffer to reflect outside (non-Dired) changes in the directories and files, and to delete part of the Dired buffer.

g   Update the entire contents of the Dired buffer (`revert-buffer`).

l   Update the specified files (`dired-do-redisplay`).

k   Delete the specified *file lines*—not the files, just the lines (`dired-do-kill-lines`).

s   Toggle between sorting by file name and sorting by date/time (`dired-sort-toggle-or-edit`).

C-u s *switches* RET

Refresh the Dired buffer using *switches* as `dired-listing-switches`.

Type g (`revert-buffer`) to update the contents of the Dired buffer, based on changes in the files and directories listed. This preserves all marks except for those on files that have vanished. Hidden subdirectories are updated but remain hidden.

To update only some of the files, type l (`dired-do-redisplay`). This command applies to the next *n* files, or to the marked files if any, or to the current file. Updating them means reading their current status from the file system and changing the buffer to reflect it properly.

If you use l on a subdirectory header line, it updates the contents of the corresponding subdirectory.

To delete the specified *file lines*—not the files, just the lines—type k (`dired-do-kill-lines`). This command applies to the next *n* files, or to the marked files if any, or to the current file.

If you kill the line for a file that is a directory, the directory's contents are also deleted from the buffer. Typing C-u k on the header line for a subdirectory is another way to delete a subdirectory from the Dired buffer.

The g command brings back any individual lines that you have killed in this way, but not subdirectories—you must use i to reinsert each subdirectory.

The files in a Dired buffers are normally in listed alphabetical order by file names. Alternatively Dired can sort them by date/time. The Dired command s (`dired-sort-toggle-or-edit`) switches between these two sorting modes. The mode line in a Dired buffer indicates which way it is currently sorted—by name, or by date.

C-u s *switches* RET lets you specify a new value for `dired-listing-switches`.

27.15 Dired and `find`

You can select a set of files for display in a Dired buffer more flexibly by using the `find` utility to choose the files.

To search for files with names matching a wildcard pattern use `M-x find-name-dired`. It reads arguments *directory* and *pattern*, and chooses all the files in *directory* or its subdirectories whose individual names match *pattern*.

The files thus chosen are displayed in a Dired buffer in which the ordinary Dired commands are available.

If you want to test the contents of files, rather than their names, use `M-x find-grep-dired`. This command reads two minibuffer arguments, *directory* and *regexp*; it chooses all the files in *directory* or its subdirectories that contain a match for *regexp*. It works by running the programs `find` and `grep`.

The most general command in this series is `M-x find-dired`, which lets you specify any condition that `find` can test. It takes two minibuffer arguments, *directory* and *find-args*; it runs `find` in *directory*, passing *find-args* to tell `find` what condition to test. To use this command, you need to know how to use `find`.

The format of listing produced by these commands is controlled by the variable `find-ls-option`, whose default value specifies using options '-ldi' for `ls`. If your listings are corrupted, you may need to change the value of this variable.

28 The Calendar and the Diary

Emacs provides the functions of a desk calendar, with a diary of planned or past events. To enter the calendar, type `M-x calendar`; this displays a three-month calendar centered on the current month, with point on the current date. With a numeric argument, as in `C-u M-x calendar`, it prompts you for the month and year to be the center of the three-month calendar. The calendar uses its own buffer, whose major mode is Calendar mode.

`Mouse-2` in the calendar brings up a menu of operations on a particular date; `C-Mouse-3` brings up a menu of commonly used calendar features that are independent of any particular date. To exit the calendar, type q. See section "Calendar" in *The Emacs Lisp Reference Manual*, for customization information about the calendar and diary.

28.1 Movement in the Calendar

Calendar mode lets you move through the calendar in logical units of time such as days, weeks, months, and years. If you move outside the three months originally displayed, the calendar display "scrolls" automatically through time to make the selected date visible. Moving to a date lets you view its holidays or diary entries, convert it to other calendars; moving longer time periods is also useful simply to scroll the calendar.

28.1.1 Motion by Standard Lengths of Time

The commands for movement in the calendar buffer parallel the commands for movement in text. You can move forward and backward by days, weeks, months, and years.

`C-f`	Move point one day forward (`calendar-forward-day`).
`C-b`	Move point one day backward (`calendar-backward-day`).
`C-n`	Move point one week forward (`calendar-forward-week`).
`C-p`	Move point one week backward (`calendar-backward-week`).
`M-}`	Move point one month forward (`calendar-forward-month`).
`M-{`	Move point one month backward (`calendar-backward-month`).
`C-x ]`	Move point one year forward (`calendar-forward-year`).
`C-x [`	Move point one year backward (`calendar-forward-year`).

The day and week commands are natural analogues of the usual Emacs commands for moving by characters and by lines. Just as `C-n` usually moves to the same column in the following line, in Calendar mode it moves to the same day in the following week. And C-p moves to the same day in the previous week.

The arrow keys are equivalent to C-f, C-b, C-n and C-p, just as they normally are in other modes.

The commands for motion by months and years work like those for weeks, but move a larger distance. The month commands M-} and M-{ move forward or backward by an entire month's time. The year commands C-x] and C-x [move forward or backward a whole year.

The easiest way to remember these commands is to consider months and years analogous to paragraphs and pages of text, respectively. But the commands themselves are not quite analogous. The ordinary Emacs paragraph commands move to the beginning or end of a paragraph, whereas these month and year commands move by an entire month or an entire year, which usually involves skipping across the end of a month or year.

All these commands accept a numeric argument as a repeat count. For convenience, the digit keys and the minus sign specify numeric arguments in Calendar mode even without the Meta modifier. For example, 100 C-f moves point 100 days forward from its present location.

28.1.2 Beginning or End of Week, Month or Year

A week (or month, or year) is not just a quantity of days; we think of weeks (months, years) as starting on particular dates. So Calendar mode provides commands to move to the beginning or end of a week, month or year:

C-a   Move point to start of week (calendar-beginning-of-week).

C-e   Move point to end of week (calendar-end-of-week).

M-a   Move point to start of month (calendar-beginning-of-month).

M-e   Move point to end of month (calendar-end-of-month).

M-<   Move point to start of year (calendar-beginning-of-year).

M->   Move point to end of year (calendar-end-of-year).

These commands also take numeric arguments as repeat counts, with the repeat count indicating how many weeks, months, or years to move backward or forward.

By default, weeks begin on Sunday. To make them begin on Monday instead, set the variable calendar-week-start-day to 1.

28.1.3 Specified Dates

Calendar mode provides commands for moving to a particular date specified in various ways.

g d   Move point to specified date (`calendar-goto-date`).

o   Center calendar around specified month (`calendar-other-month`).

.   Move point to today's date (`calendar-goto-today`).

g d (`calendar-goto-date`) prompts for a year, a month, and a day of the month, and then moves to that date. Because the calendar includes all dates from the beginning of the current era, you must type the year in its entirety; that is, type '1990', not '90'.

o (`calendar-other-month`) prompts for a month and year, then centers the three-month calendar around that month.

You can return to today's date with . (`calendar-goto-today`).

28.2 Scrolling in the Calendar

The calendar display scrolls automatically through time when you move out of the visible portion. You can also scroll it manually. Imagine that the calendar window contains a long strip of paper with the months on it. Scrolling it means moving the strip so that new months become visible in the window.

C-x <   Scroll calendar one month forward (`scroll-calendar-left`).

C-x >   Scroll calendar one month backward (`scroll-calendar-right`).

C-v
NEXT   Scroll calendar three months forward (`scroll-calendar-left-three-months`).

M-v
PRIOR   Scroll calendar three months backward (`scroll-calendar-right-three-months`).

The most basic calendar scroll commands scroll by one month at a time. This means that there are two months of overlap between the display before the command and the display after. C-x < scrolls the calendar contents one month to the left; that is, it moves the display forward in time. C-x > scrolls the contents to the right, which moves backwards in time.

The commands C-v and M-v scroll the calendar by an entire "screenful"—three months—in analogy with the usual meaning of these commands. C-v makes later dates visible and M-v makes earlier dates visible. These commands take a numeric argument as a repeat count; in particular, since C-u multiplies the next command by four, typing C-u C-v scrolls the calendar forward by a year and typing C-u M-v scrolls the calendar backward by a year.

The function keys NEXT and PRIOR are equivalent to C-v and M-v, just as they are in other modes.

28.3 Counting Days

M-=   Display the number of days in the current region (calendar-
            count-days-region).

To determine the number of days in the region, type M-= (calendar-count-days-region). The numbers of days printed is *inclusive*; that is, it includes the days specified by mark and point.

28.4 Miscellaneous Calendar Commands

p d   Display day-in-year (calendar-print-day-of-year).

C-c C-l   Regenerate the calendar window (redraw-calendar).

SPC   Scroll the next window (scroll-other-window).

q   Exit from calendar (exit-calendar).

To print the number of days elapsed since the start of the year, or the number of days remaining in the year, type the p d command (calendar-print-day-of-year). This displays both of those numbers in the echo area. The number of days elapsed includes the selected date. The number of days remaining does not include that date.

If the calendar window text gets corrupted, type C-c C-l (redraw-calendar) to redraw it. (This can only happen if you use non-Calendar-mode editing commands.)

In Calendar mode, you can use SPC (scroll-other-window) to scroll the other window. This is handy when you display a list of holidays or diary entries in another window.

To exit from the calendar, type q (exit-calendar). This buries all buffers related to the calendar, selecting other buffers. (If a frame contains a dedicated calendar window, exiting from the calendar iconifies that frame.)

28.5 Holidays

The Emacs calendar knows about all major and many minor holidays, and can display them.

h   Display holidays for the selected date (`calendar-cursor-holidays`).

Mouse-2 Holidays
          Display any diary entries for the date you click on.

x   Mark holidays in the calendar window (`mark-calendar-holidays`).

u   Unmark calendar window (`calendar-unmark`).

a   List all holidays for the displayed three months in another window (`list-calendar-holidays`).

M-x holidays
          List all holidays for three months around today's date in another window.

To see if any holidays fall on a given date, position point on that date in the calendar window and use the h command. Alternatively, click on that date with Mouse-2 and then choose Holidays from the menu that appears. Either way, this displays the holidays for that date, in the echo area if they fit there, otherwise in a separate window.

To view the distribution of holidays for all the dates shown in the calendar, use the x command. This displays the dates that are holidays in a different face (or places a '*' after these dates, if display with multiple faces is not available). The command applies both to the currently visible months and to other months that subsequently become visible by scrolling. To turn marking off and erase the current marks, type u, which also erases any diary marks (see Section 28.9 [Diary], page 309).

To get even more detailed information, use the a command, which displays a separate buffer containing a list of all holidays in the current three-month range. You can use SPC in the calendar window to scroll that list.

The command M-x holidays displays the list of holidays for the current month and the preceding and succeeding months; this works even if you don't have a calendar window. If you want the list of holidays centered around a different month, use C-u M-x holidays, which prompts for the month and year.

The holidays known to Emacs include American holidays and the major Christian, Jewish, and Islamic holidays; also the solstices and equinoxes.

The dates used by Emacs for holidays are based on *current practice*, not historical fact. Historically, for instance, the start of daylight savings time and even its existence have varied from year to year, but present American law mandates that daylight savings time begins on the first Sunday in April. In an American locale, Emacs always uses this definition, even though it is wrong for some prior years.

28.6 Times of Sunrise and Sunset

Special calendar commands can tell you, to within a minute or two, the times of sunrise and sunset for any date.

S   Display times of sunrise and sunset for the selected date (`calendar-sunrise-sunset`).

`Mouse-2 Sunrise/Sunset`
Display times of sunrise and sunset for the date you click on.

`M-x sunrise-sunset`
Display times of sunrise and sunset for today's date.

`C-u M-x sunrise-sunset`
Display times of sunrise and sunset for a specified date.

Within the calendar, to display the *local times* of sunrise and sunset in the echo area, move point to the date you want, and type S. Alternatively, click `Mouse-2` on the date, then choose `Sunrise/Sunset` from the menu that appears. The command `M-x sunrise-sunset` is available outside the calendar to display this information for today's date or a specified date. To specify a date other than today, use `C-u M-x sunrise-sunset`, which prompts for the year, month, and day.

You can display the times of sunrise and sunset for any location and any date with `C-u C-u M-x sunrise-sunset`. This asks you for a longitude, latitude, number of minutes difference from Coordinated Universal Time, and date, and then tells you the times of sunrise and sunset for that location on that date.

Because the times of sunrise and sunset depend on the location on earth, you need to tell Emacs your latitude, longitude, and location name before using these commands. Here is an example of what to set:

```
(setq calendar-latitude 40.1)
(setq calendar-longitude -88.2)
(setq calendar-location-name "Urbana, IL")
```

Use one decimal place in the values of `calendar-latitude` and `calendar-longitude`.

Your time zone also affects the local time of sunrise and sunset. Emacs usually gets time zone information from the operating system, but if these values are not what you want (or if the operating system does not supply them), you must set them yourself. Here is an example:

```
(setq calendar-time-zone -360)
(setq calendar-standard-time-zone-name "CST")
(setq calendar-daylight-time-zone-name "CDT")
```

The value of `calendar-time-zone` is the number of minutes difference between your local standard time and Coordinated Universal Time (Greenwich time). The values of `calendar-standard-time-zone-name` and `calendar-daylight-time-zone-name` are the abbreviations used in your time zone. Emacs displays the times of sunrise and sunset *corrected for daylight savings time*. See Section 28.11 [Daylight Savings], page 317, for how daylight savings time is determined.

As a user, you might find it convenient to set the calendar location variables for your usual physical location in your '`.emacs`' file. And when you install Emacs on a machine, you can create a '`default.el`' file which sets them properly for the typical location of most users of that machine. See Section 30.7 [Init File], page 366.

28.7 Phases of the Moon

These calendar commands display the dates and times of the phases of the moon (new moon, first quarter, full moon, last quarter). This feature is useful for debugging problems that "depend on the phase of the moon."

M   Display the dates and times for all the quarters of the moon for the three-month period shown (`calendar-phases-of-moon`).

M-x phases-of-moon
                   Display dates and times of the quarters of the moon for three months around today's date.

Within the calendar, use the M command to display a separate buffer of the phases of the moon for the current three-month range. The dates and times listed are accurate to within a few minutes.

Outside the calendar, use the command `M-x phases-of-moon` to display the list of the phases of the moon for the current month and the preceding and succeeding months. For information about a different month, use `C-u M-x phases-of-moon`, which prompts for the month and year.

The dates and times given for the phases of the moon are given in local time (corrected for daylight savings, when appropriate); but if the variable `calendar-time-zone` is void, Coordinated Universal Time (the Greenwich time zone) is used. See Section 28.11 [Daylight Savings], page 317.

28.8 Conversion To and From Other Calendars

The Emacs calendar displayed is *always* the Gregorian calendar, sometimes called the "new style" calendar, which is used in most of the world today. However, this calendar did not exist before the sixteenth century and was not widely used before the eighteenth century; it did not fully displace the Julian calendar and gain universal acceptance until the early twentieth century. The Emacs calendar can display any month since January, year 1 of the current era, but the calendar displayed is the Gregorian, even for a date at which the Gregorian calendar did not exist.

While Emacs cannot display other calendars, it can convert dates to and from several other calendars.

28.8.1 Supported Calendar Systems

The ISO commercial calendar is used largely in Europe.

The Julian calendar, named after Julius Caesar, was the one used in Europe throughout medieval times, and in many countries up until the nineteenth century.

Astronomers use a simple counting of days elapsed since noon, Monday, January 1, 4713 B.C. on the Julian calendar. The number of days elapsed is called the *Julian day number* or the *Astronomical day number*.

The Hebrew calendar is used by tradition in the Jewish religion. The Emacs calendar program uses the Hebrew calendar to determine the dates of Jewish holidays. Hebrew calendar dates begin and end at sunset.

The Islamic calendar is used in many predominantly Islamic countries. Emacs uses it to determine the dates of Islamic holidays. There is no universal agreement in the Islamic world about the calendar; Emacs uses a widely accepted version, but the precise dates of Islamic holidays often depend on proclamation by religious authorities, not on calculations. As a consequence, the actual dates of observance can vary slightly from the dates computed by Emacs. Islamic calendar dates begin and end at sunset.

The French Revolutionary calendar was created by the Jacobins after the 1789 revolution, to represent a more secular and nature-based view of the annual cycle, and to install a 10-day week in a rationalization measure similar to the metric system. The French government officially abandoned this calendar at the end of 1805.

The Maya of Central America used three separate, overlapping calendar systems, the *long count*, the *tzolkin*, and the *haab*. Emacs knows about all three of these calendars. Experts dispute the exact correlation between the Mayan calendar and our calendar; Emacs uses the Goodman-Martinez-Thompson correlation in its calculations.

28.8.2 Converting To Other Calendars

The following commands describe the selected date (the date at point) in various other calendar systems:

Mouse-2 Other Calendars

> Display the date that you click on, expressed in various other calendars.

p c
> Display ISO commercial calendar equivalent for selected day (`calendar-print-iso-date`).

p j
> Display Julian date for selected day (`calendar-print-julian-date`).

p a
> Display astronomical (Julian) day number for selected day (`calendar-print-astro-day-number`).

p h
> Display Hebrew date for selected day (`calendar-print-hebrew-date`).

p i
> Display Islamic date for selected day (`calendar-print-islamic-date`).

p f
> Display French Revolutionary date for selected day (`calendar-print-french-date`).

p m
> Display Mayan date for selected day (`calendar-print-mayan-date`).

If you are using X windows, the easiest way to translate a date into other calendars is to click on it with Mouse-2, then choose Other Calendars from the menu that appears. This displays the equivalent forms of the date in all the calendars Emacs understands, in the form of a menu. (Choosing an alternative from this menu doesn't actually do anything—the menu is used only for display.)

Put point on the desired date of the Gregorian calendar, then type the appropriate keys. The p is a mnemonic for "print" since Emacs "prints" the equivalent date in the echo area.

28.8.3 Converting From Other Calendars

You can use the other supported calendars to specify a date to move to. This section describes the commands for doing this using calendars other than Mayan; for the Mayan calendar, see the following section.

g c
> Move to a date specified in the ISO commercial calendar (`calendar-goto-iso-date`).

g j
> Move to a date specified in the Julian calendar (`calendar-goto-julian-date`).

g a   Move to a date specified in astronomical (Julian) day number
               (`calendar-goto-astro-day-number`).

g h   Move to a date specified in the Hebrew calendar (`calendar-goto-hebrew-date`).

g i   Move to a date specified in the Islamic calendar (`calendar-goto-islamic-date`).

g f   Move to a date specified in the French Revolutionary calendar
               (`calendar-goto-french-date`).

These commands ask you for a date on the other calendar, move point
to the Gregorian calendar date equivalent to that date, and display the
other calendar's date in the echo area. Emacs uses strict completion (see
Section 5.3 [Completion], page 39) whenever it asks you to type a month
name, so you don't have to worry about the spelling of Hebrew, Islamic, or
French names.

One common question concerning the Hebrew calendar is the computa-
tion of the anniversary of a date of death, called a "yahrzeit." The Emacs
calendar includes a facility for such calculations. If you are in the calendar,
the command `M-x list-yahrzeit-dates` asks you for a range of years and
then displays a list of the yahrzeit dates for those years for the date given
by point. If you are not in the calendar, this command first asks you for the
date of death and the range of years, and then displays the list of yahrzeit
dates.

28.8.4 Converting from the Mayan Calendar

Here are the commands to select dates based on the Mayan calendar:

g m l   Move to a date specified by the long count calendar (`calendar-goto-mayan-long-count-date`).

g m n t   Move to the next occurrence of a place in the tzolkin calendar
               (`calendar-next-tzolkin-date`).

g m p t   Move to the previous occurrence of a place in the tzolkin calen-
               dar (`calendar-previous-tzolkin-date`).

g m n h   Move to the next occurrence of a place in the haab calendar
               (`calendar-next-haab-date`).

g m p h   Move to the previous occurrence of a place in the haab calendar
               (`calendar-previous-haab-date`).

g m n c   Move to the next occurrence of a place in the calendar round
               (`calendar-next-calendar-round-date`).

g m p c   Move to the previous occurrence of a place in the calendar round (`calendar-previous-calendar-round-date`).

To understand these commands, you need to understand the Mayan calendars. The *long count* is a counting of days with these units:

1 kin = 1 day   1 uinal = 20 kin   1 tun = 18 uinal
1 katun = 20 tun   1 baktun = 20 katun

Thus, the long count date 12.16.11.16.6 means 12 baktun, 16 katun, 11 tun, 16 uinal, and 6 kin. The Emacs calendar can handle Mayan long count dates as early as 7.17.18.13.1, but no earlier. When you use the g m l command, type the Mayan long count date with the baktun, katun, tun, uinal, and kin separated by periods.

The Mayan tzolkin calendar is a cycle of 260 days formed by a pair of independent cycles of 13 and 20 days. Since this cycle repeats endlessly, Emacs provides commands to move backward and forward to the previous or next point in the cycle. Type g m p t to go to the previous tzolkin date; Emacs asks you for a tzolkin date and moves point to the previous occurrence of that date. Similarly, type g m n t to go to the next occurrence of a tzolkin date.

The Mayan haab calendar is a cycle of 365 days arranged as 18 months of 20 days each, followed a 5-day monthless period. Like the tzolkin cycle, this cycle repeats endlessly, and there are commands to move backward and forward to the previous or next point in the cycle. Type g m p h to go to the previous haab date; Emacs asks you for a haab date and moves point to the previous occurrence of that date. Similarly, type g m n h to go to the next occurrence of a haab date.

The Maya also used the combination of the tzolkin date and the haab date. This combination is a cycle of about 52 years called a *calendar round*. If you type g m p c, Emacs asks you for both a haab and a tzolkin date and then moves point to the previous occurrence of that combination. Use g m p c to move point to the next occurrence of a combination. These commands signal an error if the haab/tzolkin date combination you have typed is impossible.

Emacs uses strict completion (see Section 5.3.3 [Strict Completion], page 41) whenever it asks you to type a Mayan name, so you don't have to worry about spelling.

28.9 The Diary

The Emacs diary keeps track of appointments or other events on a daily basis, in conjunction with the calendar. To use the diary feature, you must first create a *diary file* containing a list of events and their dates. Then

Emacs can automatically pick out and display the events for today, for the immediate future, or for any specified date.

By default, Emacs uses '~/diary' as the diary file. This is the same file that the `calendar` utility uses. A sample '~/diary' file is:

```
12/22/1988  Twentieth wedding anniversary!!
&1/1.       Happy New Year!
10/22       Ruth's birthday.
* 21, *:    Payday
Tuesday--weekly meeting with grad students at 10am
            Supowit, Shen, Bitner, and Kapoor to attend.
1/13/89     Friday the thirteenth!!
&thu 4pm    squash game with Lloyd.
mar 16      Dad's birthday
April 15, 1989 Income tax due.
&* 15       time cards due.
```

This example uses extra spaces to align the event descriptions of most of the entries. Such formatting is purely a matter of taste.

Although you probably will start by creating a diary manually, Emacs provides a number of commands to let you view, add, and change diary entries.

28.9.1 Commands Displaying Diary Entries

Once you have created a '~/diary' file, you can use the calendar to view it. You can also view today's events outside of Calendar mode.

d
          Display all diary entries for the selected date (`view-diary-entries`).

Mouse-2 Diary
          Display all diary entries for the date you click on.

s
          Display the entire diary file (`show-all-diary-entries`).

m
          Mark all visible dates that have diary entries (`mark-diary-entries`).

u
          Unmark the calendar window (`calendar-unmark`).

M-x print-diary-entries
          Print hard copy of the diary display as it appears.

M-x diary   Display all diary entries for today's date.

Displaying the diary entries with d shows in a separate window the diary entries for the selected date in the calendar. The mode line of the new window shows the date of the diary entries and any holidays that fall on that date. If you specify a numeric argument with d, it shows all the diary entries for that many successive days. Thus, 2 d displays all the entries for the selected date and for the following day.

Another way to display the diary entries for a date is to click Mouse-2 on the date, and then choose Diary from the menu that appears.

To get a broader view of which days are mentioned in the diary, use the m command. This displays the dates that have diary entries fall in a different face (or places a '+' after these dates, if display with multiple faces is not available). The command applies both to the currently visible months and to other months that subsequently become visible by scrolling. To turn marking off and erase the current marks, type u, which also turns off holiday marks (see Section 28.5 [Holidays], page 303).

To see the full diary file, rather than just some of the entries, use the s command.

Display of selected diary entries uses the selective display feature to hide entries that don't apply. This is the same feature that Outline mode uses to show part of an outline (see Section 20.8 [Outline Mode], page 179).

The diary buffer as you see it is an illusion, so simply printing the buffer does not print what you see on your screen. There is a special command to print hard copy of the diary buffer *as it appears*; this command is M-x print-diary-entries. It sends the data directly to the printer. You can customize it like lpr-region (see Section 29.4 [Hardcopy], page 331).

The command M-x diary displays the diary entries for the current date, independently of the calendar display, and optionally for the next few days as well; the variable number-of-diary-entries specifies how many days to include. See section "Calendar/Diary Options" in *The Emacs Lisp Reference Manual*.

If you put (diary) in your '.emacs' file, this automatically displays a window with the day's diary entries, when you enter Emacs. The mode line of the displayed window shows the date and any holidays that fall on that date.

28.9.2 The Diary File

Your *diary file* is a file that records events associated with particular dates. The name of the diary file is specified by the variable diary-file; '~/diary' is the default. The calendar utility program supports a subset of the format allowed by the Emacs diary facilities, so you can use that utility to view the diary file, with reasonable results aside from the entries it cannot understand.

Each entry in the diary file describes one event and consists of one or more lines. An entry always begins with a date specification at the left margin.

The rest of the entry is simply text to describe the event. If the entry has more than one line, then the lines after the first must begin with whitespace to indicate they continue a previous entry. Lines that do not begin with valid dates and do not continue a preceding entry are ignored.

You can inhibit the marking of certain diary entries in the calendar window; to do this, insert an ampersand ('&') at the beginning of the entry, before the date. This has no effect on display of the entry in the diary window; it affects only marks on dates in the calendar window. Nonmarking entries are especially useful for generic entries that would otherwise mark many different dates.

If the first line of a diary entry consists only of the date or day name with no following blanks or punctuation, then the diary window display doesn't include that line; only the continuation lines appear. For example, this entry:

```
02/11/1989
        Bill B. visits Princeton today
        2pm Cognitive Studies Committee meeting
        2:30-5:30 Liz at Lawrenceville
        4:00pm Dentist appt
        7:30pm Dinner at George's
        8:00-10:00pm concert
```

appears in the diary window without the date line at the beginning. This style of entry looks neater when you display just a single day's entries, but can cause confusion if you ask for more than one day's entries.

You can edit the diary entries as they appear in the window, but it is important to remember that the buffer displayed contains the *entire* diary file, with portions of it concealed from view. This means, for instance, that the C-f (forward-char) command can put point at what appears to be the end of the line, but what is in reality the middle of some concealed line.

Be careful when editing the diary entries! Inserting additional lines or adding/deleting characters in the middle of a visible line cannot cause problems, but editing at the end of a line may not do what you expect. Deleting a line may delete other invisible entries that follow it. Before editing the diary, it is best to display the entire file with s (show-all-diary-entries).

28.9.3 Date Formats

Here are some sample diary entries, illustrating different ways of formatting a date. The examples all show dates in American order (month, day, year), but Calendar mode supports European order (day, month, year) as an option.

```
4/20/93  Switch-over to new tabulation system
apr. 25  Start tabulating annual results
```

```
4/30   Results for April are due
*/25   Monthly cycle finishes
Friday  Don't leave without backing up files
```

The first entry appears only once, on April 20, 1993. The second and third appear every year on the specified dates, and the fourth uses a wildcard (asterisk) for the month, so it appears on the 25th of every month. The final entry appears every week on Friday.

You can use just numbers to express a date, as in '*month/day*' or '*month/day/year*'. This must be followed by a nondigit. In the date itself, *month* and *day* are numbers of one or two digits. The optional *year* is also a number, and may be abbreviated to the last two digits; that is, you can use '11/12/1989' or '11/12/89'.

Dates can also have the form '*monthname day*' or '*monthname day, year*', where the month's name can be spelled in full or abbreviated to three characters (with or without a period). Case is not significant.

A date may be *generic*; that is, partially unspecified. Then the entry applies to all dates that match the specification. If the date does not contain a year, it is generic and applies to any year. Alternatively, *month*, *day*, or *year* can be a '*'; this matches any month, day, or year, respectively. Thus, a diary entry '3/*/*' matches any day in March of any year; so does 'march *'.

If you prefer the European style of writing dates—in which the day comes before the month—type M-x european-calendar while in the calendar, or set the variable european-calendar-style to t *before* using any calendar or diary command. This mode interprets all dates in the diary in the European manner, and also uses European style for displaying diary dates. (Note that there is no comma after the *monthname* in the European style.) To go back to the (default) American style of writing dates, type M-x american-calendar.

You can use the name of a day of the week as a generic date which applies to any date falling on that day of the week. You can abbreviate the day of the week to three letters (with or without a period) or spell it in full; case is not significant.

28.9.4 Commands to Add to the Diary

While in the calendar, there are several commands to create diary entries:

i d   Add a diary entry for the selected date (insert-diary-entry).

i w   Add a diary entry for the selected day of the week (insert-weekly-diary-entry).

i m   Add a diary entry for the selected day of the month (insert-monthly-diary-entry).

i y   Add a diary entry for the selected day of the year (`insert-yearly-diary-entry`).

You can make a diary entry for a specific date by selecting that date in the calendar window and typing the `i d` command. This command displays the end of your diary file in another window and inserts the date; you can then type the rest of the diary entry.

If you want to make a diary entry that applies to a specific day of the week, select that day of the week (any occurrence will do) and type `i w`. This inserts the day-of-week as a generic date; you can then type the rest of the diary entry. You can make a monthly diary entry in the same fashion. Select the day of the month, use the `i m` command, and type rest of the entry. Similarly, you can insert a yearly diary entry with the `i y` command.

All of the above commands make marking diary entries by default. To make a nonmarking diary entry, give a numeric argument to the command. For example, `C-u i w` makes a nonmarking weekly diary entry.

When you modify the diary file, be sure to save the file before exiting Emacs.

28.9.5 Special Diary Entries

In addition to entries based on calendar dates, the diary file can contain *special entries* for regular events such as anniversaries. These entries are based on Lisp expressions (sexps) that Emacs evaluates as it scans the diary file. Instead of a date, a special entry contains '%%' followed by a Lisp expression which must begin and end with parentheses. The Lisp expression determines which dates the entry applies to.

Calendar mode provides commands to insert certain commonly used special entries:

i a   Add an anniversary diary entry for the selected date (`insert-anniversary-diary-entry`).

i b   Add a block diary entry for the current region (`insert-block-diary-entry`).

i c   Add a cyclic diary entry starting at the date (`insert-cyclic-diary-entry`).

If you want to make a diary entry that applies to the anniversary of a specific date, move point to that date and use the `i a` command. This displays the end of your diary file in another window and inserts the anniversary description; you can then type the rest of the diary entry. The entry looks like this:

```
%%(diary-anniversary 10 31 1948) Arthur's birthday
```

This entry applies to October 31 in any year after 1948; '10 31 1948' specifies the date. (If you are using the European calendar style, the month and day are interchanged.) The reason this expression requires a beginning year is that advanced diary functions can use it to calculate the number of elapsed years.

A *block* diary entry applies to a specified range of consecutive dates. Here is a block diary entry that applies to all dates from June 24, 1990 through July 10, 1990:

```
%%(diary-block 6 24 1990 7 10 1990) Vacation
```

The '6 24 1990' indicates the starting date and the '7 10 1990' indicates the stopping date. (Again, if you are using the European calendar style, the month and day are interchanged.)

To insert a block entry, place point and the mark on the two dates that begin and end the range, and type i b. This command displays the end of your diary file in another window and inserts the block description; you can then type the diary entry.

Cyclic diary entries repeat after a fixed interval of days. To create one, select the starting date and use the i c command. The command prompts for the length of interval, then inserts the entry, which looks like this:

```
%%(diary-cyclic 50 3 1 1990) Renew medication
```

This entry applies to March 1, 1990 and every 50th day following; '3 1 1990' specifies the starting date. (If you are using the European calendar style, the month and day are interchanged.)

All three of these commands make marking diary entries. To insert a nonmarking entry, give a numeric argument to the command. For example, C-u i a makes a nonmarking anniversary diary entry.

Marking sexp diary entries in the calendar is *extremely* time-consuming, since every date visible in the calendar window must be individually checked. So it's a good idea to make sexp diary entries nonmarking (with '&') when possible.

Another sophisticated kind of sexp entry, a *floating* diary entry, specifies a regularly-occurring event by offsets specified in days, weeks, and months. It is comparable to a crontab entry interpreted by the cron utility. Here is a nonmarking, floating diary entry that applies to the last Thursday in November:

```
&%%(diary-float 11 4 -1) American Thanksgiving
```

The 11 specifies November (the eleventh month), the 4 specifies Thursday (the fourth day of the week, where Sunday is numbered zero), and the −1 specifies "last" (1 would mean "first", 2 would mean "second", −2 would mean "second-to-last", and so on). The month can be a single month or a list of months. Thus you could change the 11 above to ''(1 2 3)' and have the entry apply to the last Thursday of January, February, and March. If the month is t, the entry applies to all months of the year.

Most generally, special diary entries can perform arbitrary computations to determine when they apply. See section "Sexp Diary Entries" in *The Emacs Lisp Reference Manual*.

28.10 Appointments

If you have a diary entry for an appointment, and that diary entry begins with a recognizable time of day, Emacs can warn you, several minutes beforehand, that that appointment is pending. Emacs alerts you to the appointment by displaying a message in the mode line.

To enable appointment notification, you must enable the time display feature of Emacs, M-x display-time (see Section 1.3 [Mode Line], page 17). You must also add the function appt-make-list to the diary-hook, like this:

```
(add-hook 'diary-hook 'appt-make-list)
```

With these preparations done, when you display the diary (either with the d command in the calendar window or with the M-x diary command), it sets up an appointment list of all the diary entries found with recognizable times of day, and reminds you just before each of them.

For example, suppose the diary file contains these lines:

```
Monday
  9:30am Coffee break
 12:00pm Lunch
```

Then on Mondays, after you have displayed the diary, you will be reminded at 9:20am about your coffee break and at 11:50am about lunch.

You can write times in conventional American am/pm style, or 24-hour European/military style. You need not be consistent; your diary file can have a mixture of the two styles.

Emacs updates the appointments list automatically just after midnight. This also displays the next day's diary entries in the diary buffer, unless you set appt-display-diary to nil.

You can also use the appointment notification facility like an alarm clock. The command M-x appt-add adds entries to the appointment list without affecting your diary file. You delete entries from the appointment list with M-x appt-delete.

You can turn off the appointment notification feature at any time by setting appt-issue-message to nil.

28.11 Daylight Savings Time

Emacs understands the difference between standard time and daylight savings time—the times given for sunrise, sunset, solstices, equinoxes, and the phases of the moon take that into account. The rules for daylight savings time vary from place to place and have also varied historically from year to year. To do the job properly, Emacs needs to know which rules to use.

Some operating systems keep track of the rules that apply to the place where you are; on these systems, Emacs gets the information it needs from the system automatically. If some or all of this information is missing, Emacs fills in the gaps with the rules currently used in Cambridge, Massachusetts. If the resulting rules are not what you want, you can tell Emacs the rules to use by setting certain variables.

These values should be Lisp expressions that refer to the variable `year`, and evaluate to the Gregorian date on which daylight savings time starts or (respectively) ends, in the form of a list (*month day year*). The values should be `nil` if your area does not use daylight savings time.

Emacs uses these expressions to determine the starting date of daylight savings time for the holiday list and for correcting times of day in the solar and lunar calculations.

The values for Cambridge, Massachusetts are as follows:

```
(calendar-nth-named-day 1 0 4 year)
(calendar-nth-named-day -1 0 10 year)
```

That is, the first 0th day (Sunday) of the fourth month (April) in the year specified by `year`, and the last Sunday of the tenth month (October) of that year. If daylight savings time were changed to start on October 1, you would set `calendar-daylight-savings-starts` to this:

```
(list 10 1 year)
```

If there is no daylight savings time at your location, or if you want all times in standard time, set `calendar-daylight-savings-starts` and `calendar-daylight-savings-ends` to `nil`.

The variable `calendar-daylight-time-offset` specifies the difference between daylight savings time and standard time, measured in minutes. The value for Cambridge, Massachusetts is 60.

The two variables `calendar-daylight-savings-starts-time` and `calendar-daylight-savings-ends-time` specify the number of minutes after midnight local time when the transition to and from daylight savings time should occur. For Cambridge, both variables' values are 120.

29 Miscellaneous Commands

This chapter contains several brief topics that do not fit anywhere else: reading netnews, running shell commands and shell subprocesses, using a single shared Emacs for utilities that expect to run an editor as a subprocess, printing hardcopy, sorting text, narrowing display to part of the buffer, editing double-column files and binary files, saving an Emacs session for later resumption, emulating other editors, various diversions and amusements.

29.1 GNUS

GNUS is an Emacs subsystem for reading and responding to netnews. You can use GNUS to browse through news groups, look at summaries of articles in specific group, and read articles of interest. You can respond to authors or write replies to all the readers of a news group.

This section introduces GNUS and describes several basic features. For more information, run `M-x info` and select the GNUS manual.

To start GNUS, type `M-x gnus RET`.

29.1.1 GNUS's Three Buffers

GNUS creates and uses three Emacs buffers, each with its own particular purpose and its own major mode.

The *Newsgroup buffer* contains a list of newsgroups. This is the first buffer that GNUS displays when it starts up. Normally the list contains only the newsgroups to which you subscribe (which are listed in your '`.newsrc`' file) and which contain unread articles. Use this buffer to select a specific newsgroup.

The *Summary buffer* lists the articles in a single newsgroup, including their subjects, their numbers, and who posted them. GNUS creates a Summary buffer for a newsgroup when you select the group in the Newsgroup buffer. Use this buffer to select an article.

The *Article buffer* displays the text of an article. You rarely need to select this buffer because you can scroll through it while remaining in the Summary buffer.

29.1.2 When GNUS Starts Up

At startup, GNUS reads your '`.newsrc`' news initialization file and attempts to communicate with the local news server, which is a repository of news articles. The news server need not be the same computer you are logged in on.

If you start GNUS and connect to the server, but do not see any news-groups listed in the Newsgroup buffer, type L to get a listing of all the newsgroups. Then type u to unsubscribe from the newsgroups you don't want to read. (You can move point to a particular group using n and p or the usual Emacs commands.)

The first time you start GNUS, it subscribes automatically to every news-group that exists. Subsequently, GNUS subscribes automatically to all newly created newsgroups. You can unsubscribe groups with u. You can inhibit automatic subscription by adding the following line to your '~/.newsrc' file:

```
options -n !all !all.all
```

When you quit GNUS with q, it automatically records in your '.newsrc' initialization file the subscribed or unsubscribed status of all newsgroups, except for groups you have "killed". (You do not need to edit this file yourself, but you may.) When new newsgroups come into existence, GNUS subscribes to them automatically; if you don't want to read them, use u to unsubscribe from them.

29.1.3 Summary of GNUS Commands

Reading news is a two step process:

1. Choose a newsgroup in the Newsgroup buffer.

2. Select articles from the Summary buffer. Each article selected is dis-played in the Article buffer in a large window, below the Summary buffer in its small window.

Each GNUS buffer has its own special commands, but commands that do the similar things have similar key bindings. Here are commands for the Newsgroup and Summary buffers:

z   In the Newsgroup buffer, suspend GNUS. You can return to GNUS later by selecting the Newsgroup buffer and typing g to get newly arrived articles.

q   In the Newsgroup buffer, update your '.newsrc' initialization file and quit GNUS.

             In the Summary buffer, exit the current newsgroup and return to the Newsgroup buffer. Thus, typing q twice quits GNUS.

L   In the Newsgroup buffer, list all the newsgroups available on your news server (except those you have killed). This may be a long list!

l   In the Newsgroup buffer, list only the newsgroups to which you subscribe and which contain unread articles.

u   In the Newsgroup buffer, unsubscribe from (or subscribe to) the newsgroup listed in the line that point is on. When you quit GNUS by typing q, GNUS lists in your '.newsrc' file which groups you have subscribed to. The next time you start GNUS, you won't see this group initially, because GNUS normally displays only subscribed-to groups.

C-k   In the Newsgroup buffer, "kill" the current line's newsgroup— don't even list it in '.newsrc' from now on. This affects future GNUS sessions as well as the present session.

                When you quit GNUS by typing q, GNUS writes information in the file '.newsrc' describing all newsgroups except those you have "killed."

SPC   In the Newsgroup buffer, select the group on the line under the cursor and display the first unread article in that group.

                In the Summary buffer,

                - Select the article on the line under the cursor if none is selected.
                - Scroll the text of the selected article (if there is one).
                - Select the next unread article if at the end of the current article.

                Thus, you can move through all the articles by repeatedly typing SPC.

DEL   In the Newsgroup Buffer, move point to the previous newsgroup containing unread articles.

                In the Summary buffer, scroll the text of the article backwards.

n   Move point to the next unread newsgroup, or select the next unread article.

p   Move point to the previous unread newsgroup, or select the previous unread article.

C-n
C-p   Move point to the next or previous item, even if it is marked as read. This does not select the article or newsgroup on that line.

s   In the Summary buffer, do an incremental search of the current text in the Article buffer, just as if you switched to the Article buffer and typed C-s.

M-s *regexp* RET
                In the Summary buffer, search forward for articles containing a match for *regexp*.

```
C-c C-s C-n
C-c C-s C-s
C-c C-s C-d
C-c C-s C-a
```
In the Summary buffer, sort the list of articles by number, subject, date, or author.

```
C-M-n
C-M-p
```
In the Summary buffer, read the next or previous article with the same subject as the current article.

29.2 Running Shell Commands from Emacs

Emacs has commands for passing single command lines to inferior shell processes; it can also run a shell interactively with input and output to an Emacs buffer named '*shell*'.

M-! *cmd* RET
Run the shell command line *cmd* and display the output (shell-command).

M-| *cmd* RET
Run the shell command line *cmd* with region contents as input; optionally replace the region with the output (shell-command-on-region).

M-x shell Run a subshell with input and output through an Emacs buffer. You can then give commands interactively.

29.2.1 Single Shell Commands

M-! (shell-command) reads a line of text using the minibuffer executes it as a shell command in a subshell made just for this command. Standard input for the command comes from the null device. If the shell command produces any output, the output goes into an Emacs buffer named '*Shell Command Output*', which is displayed in another window but not selected. A numeric argument, as in M-1 M-!, directs this command to insert any output into the current buffer. In that case, point is left before the output and the mark is set after the output.

If the shell command line ends in '&', it runs asynchronously.

M-| (shell-command-on-region) is like M-! but passes the contents of the region as the standard input to the shell command, instead of no input. If a numeric argument is used, meaning insert the output in the current buffer, then the old region is deleted first and the output replaces it as the contents of the region.

Both M-! and M-| use `shell-file-name` to specify the shell to use. This variable is initialized based on your SHELL environment variable when Emacs is started. If the file name does not specify a directory, the directories in the list `exec-path` are searched; this list is initialized based on the environment variable PATH when Emacs is started. Your '.emacs' file can override either or both of these default initializations.

Both M-! and M-| wait for the shell command to complete. To stop waiting, type C-g to quit; that terminates the shell command with the signal SIGINT—the same signal that C-c normally generates in the shell. Emacs waits until the command actually terminates. If the shell command doesn't stop (because it ignores the SIGINT signal), type C-g again; this sends the command a SIGKILL signal which is impossible to ignore.

29.2.2 Interactive Inferior Shell

To run a subshell interactively, putting its typescript in an Emacs buffer, use M-x shell. This creates (or reuses) a buffer named '*shell*' and runs a subshell with input coming from and output going to that buffer. That is to say, any "terminal output" from the subshell goes into the buffer, advancing point, and any "terminal input" for the subshell comes from text in the buffer. To give input to the subshell, go to the end of the buffer and type the input, terminated by RET.

Emacs does not wait for the subshell to do anything. You can switch windows or buffers and edit them while the shell is waiting, or while it is running a command. Output from the subshell waits until Emacs has time to process it; this happens whenever Emacs is waiting for keyboard input or for time to elapse.

To make multiple subshells, rename the buffer '*shell*' to something different using M-x rename-uniquely. Then type M-x shell again to create a new buffer '*shell*' with its own subshell. If you rename this buffer as well, you can create a third one, and so on. All the subshells run independently and in parallel.

The file name used to load the subshell is the value of the variable `explicit-shell-file-name`, if that is non-nil. Otherwise, the environment variable ESHELL is used, or the environment variable SHELL if there is no ESHELL. If the file name specified is relative, the directories in the list `exec-path` are searched; this list is initialized based on the environment variable PATH when Emacs is started. Your '.emacs' file can override either or both of these default initializations.

As soon as the subshell is started, it is sent as input the contents of the file '~/.emacs_*shellname*', if that file exists, where *shellname* is the name of the file that the shell was loaded from. For example, if you use bash, the file sent to it is '~/.emacs_bash'.

cd, pushd and popd commands given to the inferior shell are watched by Emacs so it can keep the '*shell*' buffer's default directory the same as the shell's working directory. These commands are recognized syntactically by examining lines of input that are sent. If you use aliases for these commands, you can tell Emacs to recognize them also. For example, if the value of the variable shell-pushd-regexp matches the beginning of a shell command line, that line is regarded as a pushd command. Change this variable when you add aliases for 'pushd'. Likewise, shell-popd-regexp and shell-cd-regexp are used to recognize commands with the meaning of 'popd' and 'cd'. These commands are recognized only at the beginning of a shell command line.

If Emacs gets an error while trying to handle what it believes is a 'cd', 'pushd' or 'popd' command, it runs the hook shell-set-directory-error-hook (see Section 30.2.3 [Hooks], page 347).

If Emacs does not properly track changes in the current directory of the subshell, use the command M-x dirs to ask the shell what its current directory is. This command works for shells that support the most common command syntax; it may not work for unusual shells.

29.2.3 Shell Mode

Shell buffer use Shell mode, which defines several special keys attached to the C-c prefix. They are chosen to resemble the usual editing and job control characters present in shells that are not under Emacs, except that you must type C-c first. Here is a complete list of the special key bindings of Shell mode:

RET   At end of buffer send line as input; otherwise, copy current line
           to end of buffer and send it (comint-send-input). When a line
           is copied, any text at the beginning of the line that matches the
           variable shell-prompt-pattern is left out; this variable's value
           should be a regexp string that matches the prompts that your
           shell uses.

TAB   Complete the command name or file name before point in the
           shell buffer (comint-dynamic-complete). TAB also completes
           history references (see Section 29.2.4.3 [History References],
           page 328) and environment variable names.

           The variable shell-completion-fignore specifies a list of file
           name extensions to ignore in Shell mode completion. The default
           setting ignores file names ending in '~', '#' or '%'. Other related
           Comint modes use the variable comint-completion-fignore
           instead.

M-?   Display temporarily a list of the possible completions of the file
           name before point in the shell buffer (`comint-dynamic-list-
           filename-completions`).

C-d   Either delete a character or send EOF (`comint-delchar-or-
           maybe-eof`). Typed at the end of the shell buffer, C-d sends
           EOF to the subshell. Typed at any other position in the buffer,
           C-d deletes a character as usual.

C-c C-a   Move to the beginning of the line, but after the prompt if any
           (`comint-bol`).

C-c C-u   Kill all text pending at end of buffer to be sent as input (`comint-
           kill-input`).

C-c C-w   Kill a word before point (`backward-kill-word`).

C-c C-c   Interrupt the shell or its current subjob if any (`comint-
           interrupt-subjob`).

C-c C-z   Stop the shell or its current subjob if any (`comint-stop-
           subjob`).

C-c C-\   Send quit signal to the shell or its current subjob if any (`comint-
           quit-subjob`).

C-c C-o   Kill the last batch of output from a shell command (`comint-
           kill-output`). This is useful if a shell command spews out lots
           of output that just gets in the way.

C-c C-r
C-M-l   Scroll to display the beginning of the last batch of output at the
           top of the window; also move the cursor there (`comint-show-
           output`).

C-c C-e   Scroll to put the end of the buffer at the bottom of the window
           (`comint-show-maximum-output`).

C-c C-f   Move forward across one shell command, but not beyond the
           current line (`shell-forward-command`). The variable `shell-
           command-regexp` specifies how to recognize the end of a com-
           mand.

C-c C-b   Move backward across one shell command, but not beyond the
           current line (`shell-backward-command`).

C-c C-l   Display the buffer's history of shell commands in another win-
           dow (`comint-dynamic-list-input-ring`).

M-x dirs   Ask the shell what its current directory is, so that Emacs can
           agree with the shell.

M-x send-invisible RET *text* **RET**

> Send *text* as input to the shell, after reading it without echoing. This is useful when a shell command runs a program that asks for a password.
>
> Alternatively, you can arrange for Emacs to notice password prompts and turn off echoing for them, as follows:
>
> ```
> (add-hook 'comint-output-filter-functions
>           'comint-watch-for-password-prompt)
> ```

M-x comint-continue-subjob

> Continue the shell process. This is useful if you accidentally suspend the shell process.[1]

M-x comint-strip-ctrl-m

> Discard all control-m characters from the shell output. The most convenient way to use this command is to make it run automatically when you get output from the subshell. To do that, evaluate this Lisp expression:
>
> ```
> (add-hook 'comint-output-filter-functions
>           'comint-strip-ctrl-m)
> ```

M-x comint-truncate-buffer

> This command truncates the shell buffer to a certain maximum number of lines, specified by the variable `comint-buffer-maximum-size`. Here's how to do this automatically each time you get output from the subshell:
>
> ```
> (add-hook 'comint-output-filter-functions
>           'comint-truncate-buffer)
> ```

Shell mode also customizes the paragraph commands so that only shell prompts start new paragraphs. Thus, a paragraph consists of an input command plus the output that follows it in the buffer.

Shell mode is a derivative of Comint mode, a general purpose mode for communicating with interactive subprocesses. Most of the features of Shell mode actually come from Comint mode, as you can see from the command names listed above. The specialization of Shell mode in particular include the choice of regular expression for detecting prompts, the directory tracking feature, and a few user commands.

Other Emacs features that use variants of Comint mode include GUD (see Section 22.2 [Debuggers], page 241) and `M-x run-lisp` (see Section 22.7 [External Lisp], page 249).

---

[1] You should not suspend the shell process. Suspending a subjob of the shell is a completely different matter—that is normal practice, but you must use the shell to continue the subjob; this command won't do it.

You can use `M-x comint-run` to execute any program of your choice in a subprocess using unmodified Comint mode—without the specializations of Shell mode.

29.2.4 Shell Command History

Shell buffers support three ways of repeating earlier commands. You can use the same keys used in the minibuffer; these work much as they do in the minibuffer, inserting text from prior commands while point remains always at the end of the buffer. You can move through the buffer to previous inputs in their original place, then resubmit them or copy them to the end. Or you can use a '!'-style history reference.

29.2.4.1 Shell History Ring

M-p   Fetch the next earlier old shell command.

M-n   Fetch the next later old shell command.

M-r *regexp* RET
M-s *regexp* RET
            Search backwards or forwards for old shell commands that match *regexp*.

Shell buffers provide a history of previously entered shell commands. To reuse shell commands from the history, use the editing commands M-p, M-n, M-r and M-s. These work just like the minibuffer history commands except that they operate on the text at the end of the shell buffer, where you would normally insert text to send to the shell.

M-p fetches an earlier shell command to the end of the shell buffer. Successive use of M-p fetches successively earlier shell commands, each replacing any text that was already present as potential shell input. M-n does likewise except that it finds successively more recent shell commands from the buffer.

The history search commands M-r and M-s read a regular expression and search through the history for a matching command. Aside from the choice of which command to fetch, they work just like M-p and M-r. If you enter an empty regexp, these commands reuse the same regexp used last time.

When you find the previous input you want, you can resubmit it by typing RET, or you can edit it first and then resubmit it if you wish.

These commands get the text of previous shell commands from a special history list, not from the shell buffer itself. Thus, editing the shell buffer, or even killing large parts of it, does not affect the history that these commands access.

Some shells store their command histories in files so that you can refer to previous commands from previous shell sessions. Emacs reads the command history file for your chosen shell, to initialize its own command history. The file name is '`~/.bash_history`' for bash, '`~/.sh_history`' for ksh, and '`~/.history`' for other shells.

29.2.4.2 Shell History Copying

C-c C-p   Move point to the previous prompt (`comint-previous-prompt`).

C-c C-n   Move point to the following prompt (`comint-next-prompt`).

.C-c RET   Copy the input command which point is in, inserting the copy at the end of the buffer (`comint-copy-old-input`). This is useful if you move point back to a previous command. After you copy the command, you can submit the copy as input with RET. If you wish, you can edit the copy before resubmitting it.

Moving to a previous input and then copying it with C-c RET produces the same results—the same buffer contents—that you would get by using M-p enough times to fetch that previous input from the history list. However, C-c RET copies the text from the buffer, which can be different from what is in the history list if you edit the input text in the buffer after it has been sent.

29.2.4.3 Shell History References

Various shells including csh and bash support *history references* that begin with '`!`' and '`^`'. Shell mode can understands these constructs and perform the history substitution for you. If you insert a history reference and type TAB, this searches the input history for a matching command, performs substitution if necessary, and places the result in the buffer in place of the history reference. For example, you can fetch the most recent command beginning with 'mv' with ! m v TAB. You can edit the command if you wish, and then resubmit the command to the shell by typing RET.

History references take effect only following a shell prompt. The variable `shell-prompt-pattern` specifies how to recognize a shell prompt. Comint modes in general use the variable `comint-prompt-regexp` to specify how to find a prompt; Shell mode uses `shell-prompt-pattern` to set up the local value of `comint-prompt-regexp`.

Shell mode can optionally expand history references in the buffer when you send them to the shell. To request this, set the variable `comint-input-autoexpand` to `input`.

You can make SPC perform history expansion by binding SPC to the command `comint-magic-space`.

29.2.5 Shell Mode Options

If the variable `comint-scroll-to-bottom-on-input` is non-`nil`, insertion and yank commands scroll the selected window to the bottom before inserting.

If `comint-scroll-show-maximum-output` is non-`nil` (which is the default), then scrolling due to arrival of output tries to place the last line of text at the bottom line of the window, so as to show as much useful text as possible. (This mimics the scrolling behavior of many terminals.)

By setting `comint-scroll-to-bottom-on-output`, you can opt for having point jump to the end of the buffer whenever output arrives—no matter where in the buffer point was before. If the value is `this`, point jumps in the selected window. If the value is `all`, point jumps in each window that shows the comint buffer. If the value is `other`, point jumps in all nonselected windows that show the current buffer. The default value is `nil`, which means point does not jump to the end.

The variable `comint-input-ignoredups` controls whether successive identical inputs are stored in the input history. A non-`nil` value means to omit an input that is the same as the previous input. The default is `nil`, which means to store each input even if it is equal to the previous input.

Three variables customize file name completion. The variable `comint-completion-addsuffix` controls whether completion inserts a space or a slash to indicate a fully completed file or directory name (non-`nil` means do insert a space or slash). `comint-completion-recexact`, if non-`nil`, directs TAB to choose the shortest possible completion if the usual Emacs completion algorithm cannot add even a single character. `comint-completion-autolist`, if non-`nil`, says to list all the possible completions whenever completion is not exact.

The command `comint-dynamic-complete-variable` does variable name completion using the environment variables as set within Emacs. The variables controlling file name completion apply to variable name completion too. This command is normally available through the menu bar.

Command completion normally considers only executable files. If you set `shell-command-execonly` to `nil`, it considers nonexecutable files as well.

You can configure the behavior of 'pushd'. Variables control whether 'pushd' behaves like 'cd' if no argument is given (`shell-pushd-tohome`), pop rather than rotate with a numeric argument (`shell-pushd-dextract`), and only add directories to the directory stack if they are not already on it (`shell-pushd-dunique`). The values you choose should match the underlying shell, of course.

29.2.6 Remote Host Shell

Emacs provides two commands for logging in to another computer and communicating with it through an Emacs buffer.

M-x telnet RET *hostname* RET
>   Set up a Telnet connection to the computer named *hostname*.

M-x rlogin RET *hostname* RET
>   Set up an Rlogin connection to the computer named *hostname*.

Use M-x telnet to set up a Telnet connection to another computer. (Telnet is the standard Internet protocol for remote login.) It reads the host name of the other computer as an argument with the minibuffer. Once the connection is established, talking to the other computer works like talking to a subshell: you can edit input with the usual Emacs commands, and send it a line at a time by typing RET. The output is inserted in the Telnet buffer interspersed with the input.

Use M-x rlogin to set up an Rlogin connection. Rlogin is another remote login communication protocol, essentially much like the Telnet protocol but incompatible with it, and supported only by certain systems. Rlogin's advantages are that you can arrange not to have to give your user name and password when communicating between two machines you frequently use, and that you can make an 8-bit-clean connection. (To do that in Emacs, set rlogin-explicit-args to ("-8") before you run Rlogin.)

M-x rlogin sets up the default file directory of the Emacs buffer to access the remote host via FTP (see Section 14.1 [File Names], page 103), and it tracks the shell commands that change the current directory just like Shell mode.

29.3 Using Emacs as a Server

Various programs such as mail can invoke your choice of editor to edit a particular piece of text, such as a message that you are sending. By convention, most of these programs use the environment variable EDITOR to specify which editor to run. If you set EDITOR to 'emacs', they invoke Emacs—but in an inconvenient fashion, by starting a new, separate Emacs process. This is inconvenient because it takes time and because the new Emacs process doesn't share the buffers in the existing Emacs process.

You can arrange to use your existing Emacs process as the editor for programs like mail by using the Emacs client and Emacs server programs. Here is how.

First, the preparation. Within Emacs, call the function server-start. (Your '.emacs' file can do this automatically if you add the expression (server-start) to it.) Then, outside Emacs, set the EDITOR environment variable to 'emacsclient'. (Note that some programs use a different environment variable; for example, to make TEX use 'emacsclient', you should set the TEXEDIT environment variable to 'emacsclient +%d %s'.)

Then, whenever any program invokes your specified EDITOR program, the effect is to send a message to your principal Emacs telling it to visit a file. (That's what the program emacsclient does.) Emacs displays the buffer immediately and you can immediately begin editing it.

When you've finished editing that buffer, type C-x # (server-edit). This saves the file and sends a message back to the emacsclient program telling it to exit. The programs that use EDITOR wait for the "editor" (actually, emacsclient) to exit. C-x # also checks for other pending external requests to edit various files, and selects the next such file.

You can switch to a server buffer manually if you wish; you don't have to arrive at it with C-x #. But C-x # is the only way to say that you are "finished" with one.

If you set the variable server-window to a window or a frame, C-x # displays the server buffer in that window or in that frame.

While mail or another application is waiting for emacsclient to finish, emacsclient does not read terminal input. So the terminal that mail was using is effectively blocked for the duration. In order to edit with your principal Emacs, you need to be able to use it without using that terminal. There are two ways to do this:

- Using a window system, run mail and the principal Emacs in two separate windows. While mail is waiting for emacsclient, the window where it was running is blocked, but you can use Emacs by switching windows.

- Use Shell mode in Emacs to run the other program such as mail; then, emacsclient blocks only the subshell under Emacs, and you can still use Emacs to edit the file.

Some programs write temporary files for you to edit. After you edit the temporary file, the program reads it back and deletes it. If the Emacs server is later asked to edit the same file name, it should assume this has nothing to do with the previous occasion for that file name. The server accomplishes this by killing the temporary file's buffer when you finish with the file. Use the variable server-temp-file-regexp to specify which files are temporary in this sense; its value should be a regular expression that matches file names that are temporary.

29.4 Hardcopy Output

The Emacs commands for making hardcopy let you print either an entire buffer or just part of one, either with or without page headers. See also the hardcopy commands of Dired (see Section 14.10 [Misc File Ops], page 131) and the diary (see Section 28.9.1 [Diary Commands], page 310).

M-x print-buffer

> Print hardcopy of current buffer with page headings containing the file name and page number.

M-x lpr-buffer

> Print hardcopy of current buffer without page headings. makes no page headings.

M-x print-region

> Like `print-buffer` but print only the current region.

M-x lpr-region

> Like `lpr-buffer` but print only the current region.

The hardcopy commands (aside from the Postscript commands) pass extra switches to the `lpr` program based on the value of the variable `lpr-switches`. Its value should be a list of strings, each string an option starting with '-'. For example, to use a printer named 'nearme', set `lpr-switches` like this:

```
(setq lpr-switches '("-Pnearme"))
```

The variable `lpr-header-switches` similarly specifies the extra switches to use to make page headers.

29.5 Postscript Hardcopy

These commands convert buffer contents to Postscript, either printing it or leaving it in another Emacs buffer.

M-x ps-print-buffer

> Print hardcopy of the current buffer in Postscript form.

M-x ps-print-region

> Print hardcopy of the current region in Postscript form.

M-x ps-print-buffer-with-faces

> Print hardcopy of the current buffer in Postscript form, showing the faces used in the text by means of Postscript features.

M-x ps-print-region-with-faces

> Print hardcopy of the current region in Postscript form, showing the faces used in the text.

M-x ps-spool-buffer

> Generate Postscript for the current buffer text.

M-x ps-spool-region

> Generate Postscript for the current region.

`M-x ps-spool-buffer-with-faces`
> Generate Postscript for the current buffer, showing the faces used.

`M-x ps-spool-region-with-faces`
> Generate Postscript for the current region, showing the faces used.

The Postscript commands, `ps-print-buffer` and `ps-print-region`, print buffer contents in Postscript form. One command prints the entire buffer; the other, just the region. The corresponding '`-with-faces`' commands, `ps-print-buffer-with-faces` and `ps-print-region-with-faces`, use Postscript features to show the faces (fonts and colors) in the text properties of the text being printed.

All four of the commands above use the variables `ps-lpr-command` and `ps-lpr-switches` to specify how to print the output. `ps-lpr-command` specifies the command name to run, and `ps-lpr-switches` specifies command line options to use. If you don't set these variables yourself, they take their initial values from `lpr-command` and `lpr-switches`.

The variable `ps-print-header` controls whether these commands add header lines to each page—set it to `nil` to turn headers off. You can turn off color processing by setting `ps-print-color-p` to `nil`. Many other customization variables for these commands are defined and described in the Lisp file '`ps-print.el`'.

The commands whose names have '`spool`' instead of '`print`' generate the Postscript output in an Emacs buffer instead of sending it to the printer.

29.6 Sorting Text

Emacs provides several commands for sorting text in the buffer. All operate on the contents of the region (the text between point and the mark). They divide the text of the region into many *sort records*, identify a *sort key* for each record, and then reorder the records into the order determined by the sort keys. The records are ordered so that their keys are in alphabetical order, or, for numeric sorting, in numeric order. In alphabetic sorting, all upper case letters 'A' through 'Z' come before lower case 'a', in accord with the ASCII character sequence.

The various sort commands differ in how they divide the text into sort records and in which part of each record is used as the sort key. Most of the commands make each line a separate sort record, but some commands use paragraphs or pages as sort records. Most of the sort commands use each entire sort record as its own sort key, but some use only a portion of the record as the sort key.

`M-x sort-lines`
> Divide the region into lines, and sort by comparing the entire text of a line. A numeric argument means sort into descending order.

`M-x sort-paragraphs`
> Divide the region into paragraphs, and sort by comparing the entire text of a paragraph (except for leading blank lines). A numeric argument means sort into descending order.

`M-x sort-pages`
> Divide the region into pages, and sort by comparing the entire text of a page (except for leading blank lines). A numeric argument means sort into descending order.

`M-x sort-fields`
> Divide the region into lines, and sort by comparing the contents of one field in each line. Fields are defined as separated by whitespace, so the first run of consecutive non-whitespace characters in a line constitutes field 1, the second such run constitutes field 2, etc.
>
> Specify which field to sort by with a numeric argument: 1 to sort by field 1, etc. A negative argument means count fields from the right instead of from the left; thus, minus 1 means sort by the last field. If several lines have identical contents in the field being sorted, they keep same relative order that they had in the original buffer.
>
> A negative argument means count fields from the right (from the end of the line).

`M-x sort-numeric-fields`
> Like `M-x sort-fields` except the specified field is converted to an integer for each line, and the numbers are compared. '10' comes before '2' when considered as text, but after it when considered as a number.

`M-x sort-columns`
> Like `M-x sort-fields` except that the text within each line used for comparison comes from a fixed range of columns. See below for an explanation.

`M-x reverse-region`
> Reverse the order of the lines in the region. This is useful for sorting into descending order by fields or columns, since those sort commands do not have a feature for doing that.

For example, if the buffer contains this:

```
On systems where clash detection (locking of files being edited) is
implemented, Emacs also checks the first time you modify a buffer
whether the file has changed on disk since it was last visited or
saved.  If it has, you are asked to confirm that you want to change
the buffer.
```

applying `M-x sort-lines` to the entire buffer produces this:

```
On systems where clash detection (locking of files being edited) is
implemented, Emacs also checks the first time you modify a buffer
saved.  If it has, you are asked to confirm that you want to change
the buffer.
whether the file has changed on disk since it was last visited or
```

where the upper case 'O' sorts before all lower case letters. If you use `C-u 2 M-x sort-fields` instead, you get this:

```
implemented, Emacs also checks the first time you modify a buffer
saved.  If it has, you are asked to confirm that you want to change
the buffer.
On systems where clash detection (locking of files being edited) is
whether the file has changed on disk since it was last visited or
```

where the sort keys were 'Emacs', 'If', 'buffer', 'systems' and 'the'.

`M-x sort-columns` requires more explanation. You specify the columns by putting point at one of the columns and the mark at the other column. Because this means you cannot put point or the mark at the beginning of the first line to sort, this command uses an unusual definition of 'region': all of the line point is in is considered part of the region, and so is all of the line the mark is in, as well as all the lines in between.

For example, to sort a table by information found in columns 10 to 15, you could put the mark on column 10 in the first line of the table, and point on column 15 in the last line of the table, and then run `sort-columns`. Equivalently, you could run it with the mark on column 15 in the first line and point on column 10 in the last line.

This can be thought of as sorting the rectangle specified by point and the mark, except that the text on each line to the left or right of the rectangle moves along with the text inside the rectangle. See Section 9.4 [Rectangles], page 67.

Many of the sort commands ignore case differences when comparing, if `sort-fold-case` is non-nil.

29.7 Narrowing

Narrowing means focusing in on some portion of the buffer, making the rest temporarily inaccessible. The portion which you can still get to is called the *accessible portion*. Canceling the narrowing, which makes the entire buffer once again accessible, is called *widening*. The amount of narrowing in effect in a buffer at any time is called the buffer's *restriction*.

Narrowing can make it easier to concentrate on a single subroutine or paragraph by eliminating clutter. It can also be used to restrict the range of operation of a replace command or repeating keyboard macro.

C-x n n   Narrow down to between point and mark (`narrow-to-region`).

C-x n w   Widen to make the entire buffer accessible again (`widen`).

C-x n p   Narrow down to the current page (`narrow-to-page`).

When you have narrowed down to a part of the buffer, that part appears to be all there is. You can't see the rest, you can't move into it (motion commands won't go outside the accessible part), you can't change it in any way. However, it is not gone, and if you save the file all the inaccessible text will be saved. The word '`Narrow`' appears in the mode line whenever narrowing is in effect.

The primary narrowing command is C-x n n (`narrow-to-region`). It sets the current buffer's restrictions so that the text in the current region remains accessible but all text before the region or after the region is inaccessible. Point and mark do not change.

Alternatively, use C-x n p (`narrow-to-page`) to narrow down to the current page. See Section 20.4 [Pages], page 173, for the definition of a page.

The way to cancel narrowing is to widen with C-x n w (`widen`). This makes all text in the buffer accessible again.

You can get information on what part of the buffer you are narrowed down to using the C-x = command. See Section 4.9 [Position Info], page 33.

Because narrowing can easily confuse users who do not understand it, `narrow-to-region` is normally a disabled command. Attempting to use this command asks for confirmation and gives you the option of enabling it; if you enable the command, confirmation will no longer be required for it. See Section 30.4.10 [Disabling], page 365.

29.8 Two-Column Editing

Two-column mode lets you conveniently edit two side-by-side columns of text. It uses two side-by-side windows, each showing its own buffer.

There are three ways to enter two-column mode:

C-x 6 2   Enter two-column mode with the current buffer on the left, and on the right, a buffer whose name is based on the current buffer's name (`tc-two-columns`). If the right-hand buffer doesn't already exist, it starts out empty; the current buffer's contents are not changed.

This command is appropriate when the current buffer contains just one column and you want to add another column.

C-x 6 s   Split the current buffer, which contains two-column text, into two buffers, and display them side by side (tc-split). The current buffer becomes the left-hand buffer, but the text in the right-hand column is moved into the right-hand buffer. The current column specifies the split point. Splitting starts with the current line and continues to the end of the buffer.

This command is appropriate when you have a buffer that already contains two-column text, and you wish to separate the columns temporarily.

C-x 6 b *buffer* RET
Enter two-column mode using the current buffer as the left-hand buffer, and using buffer *buffer* as the right-hand buffer (tc-associate-buffer).

C-x 6 s looks for a column separator which is a string that appears on each line between the two columns. You can specify the width of the separator with a numeric argument to C-x 6 s; that many characters, before point, constitute the separator string. By default, the width is 1, so the column separator is the character before point.

When a line has the separator at the proper place, C-x 6 s puts the text after the separator into the right-hand buffer, and deletes the separator. Lines that don't have the column separator at the proper place remain unsplit; they stay in the left-hand buffer, and the right-hand buffer gets an empty line to correspond. (This is the way to write a line that spans both columns while in two-column mode: write it in the left-hand buffer, and put an empty line in the right-hand buffer.)

It's not a good idea to use ordinary scrolling commands during two-column editing, because that separates the two parts of each split line. Instead, use these special scroll commands:

C-x 6 SPC   Scroll both buffers up, in lock step (tc-scroll-up).

C-x 6 DEL   Scroll both buffers down, in lock step (tc-scroll-down).

C-x 6 C-l   Recenter both buffers, in lock step (tc-recenter).

When you have edited both buffers as you wish, merge them with C-x 6 1 (tc-merge). This copies the text from the right-hand buffer as a second column in the other buffer. To go back to two-column editing, use C-x 6 s.

Use C-x 6 d to disassociate the two buffers, leaving each as it stands (tc-dissociate). If the other buffer, the one not current when you type C-x 6 d, is empty, C-x 6 d kills it.

29.9 Editing Binary Files

There is a special major mode for editing binary files: Hexl mode. To use it, use `M-x hexl-find-file` instead of `C-x C-f` to visit the file. This command converts the file's contents to hexadecimal and lets you edit the translation. When you save the file, it is converted automatically back to binary.

You can also use `M-x hexl-mode` to translate an existing buffer into hex. This is useful if you visit a file normally and then discover it is a binary file.

Ordinary text characters overwrite in Hexl mode. This is to reduce the risk of accidentally spoiling the alignment of data in the file. There are special commands for insertion. Here is a list of the commands of Hexl mode:

`C-M-d`	Insert a byte with a code typed in decimal.
`C-M-o`	Insert a byte with a code typed in octal.
`C-M-x`	Insert a byte with a code typed in hex.
`C-x [`	Move to the beginning of a 1k-byte "page".
`C-x ]`	Move to the end of a 1k-byte "page".
`M-g`	Move to an address specified in hex.
`M-j`	Move to an address specified in decimal.
`C-c C-c`	Leave Hexl mode, going back to the major mode this buffer had before you invoked `hexl-mode`.

29.10 Saving Emacs Sessions

You can use the Desktop library to save the state of Emacs from one session to another. Saving the state means that Emacs starts up with the same set of buffers, major modes, buffer positions, and so on that the previous Emacs session had.

To use Desktop, you should first add these lines to your '`.emacs`' file, preferably at or near the end:

```
(load "desktop")
(desktop-load-default)
(desktop-read)
```

Then, to enable state saving in a particular Emacs session, use the command `M-x desktop-save`. Once you have done this, the state of this Emacs session will be saved when you exit Emacs.

In order for Emacs to recover the state from a previous session, you must start it with the same current directory as you used when you started the previous session.

The variable `desktop-files-not-to-save` controls which files are excluded from state saving. Its value is a regular expression that matches the files to exclude. By default, remote (ftp-accessed) files are excluded; this is because visiting them again in the subsequent session would be slow. If you want to include these files in state saving, set `desktop-files-not-to-save` to `"^$"`.

29.11 Recursive Editing Levels

A *recursive edit* is a situation in which you are using Emacs commands to perform arbitrary editing while in the middle of another Emacs command. For example, when you type `C-r` inside of a `query-replace`, you enter a recursive edit in which you can change the current buffer. On exiting from the recursive edit, you go back to the `query-replace`.

Exiting the recursive edit means returning to the unfinished command, which continues execution. The command to exit is `C-M-c` (`exit-recursive-edit`).

You can also *abort* the recursive edit. This is like exiting, but also quits the unfinished command immediately. Use the command `C-]` (`abort-recursive-edit`) to do this. See Section 31.1 [Quitting], page 373.

The mode line shows you when you are in a recursive edit by displaying square brackets around the parentheses that always surround the major and minor mode names. Every window's mode line shows this, in the same way, since being in a recursive edit is true of Emacs as a whole rather than any particular window or buffer.

It is possible to be in recursive edits within recursive edits. For example, after typing `C-r` in a `query-replace`, you may type a command that enters the debugger. This begins a recursive editing level for the debugger, within the recursive editing level for `C-r`. Mode lines display a pair of square brackets for each recursive editing level currently in progress.

Exiting the inner recursive edit (such as, with the debugger `c` command) resumes the command running in the next level up. When that command finishes, you can then use `C-M-c` to exit another recursive editing level, and so on. Exiting applies to the innermost level only. Aborting also gets out of only one level of recursive edit; it returns immediately to the command level of the previous recursive edit. If you wish, you can then abort the next recursive editing level.

Alternatively, the command `M-x top-level` aborts all levels of recursive edits, returning immediately to the top level command reader.

The text being edited inside the recursive edit need not be the same text that you were editing at top level. It depends on what the recursive edit is for. If the command that invokes the recursive edit selects a different buffer first, that is the buffer you will edit recursively. In any case, you can switch buffers within the recursive edit in the normal manner (as long as the buffer-switching keys have not been rebound). You could probably do all the rest of your editing inside the recursive edit, visiting files and all. But this could have surprising effects (such as stack overflow) from time to time. So remember to exit or abort the recursive edit when you no longer need it.

In general, we try to minimize the use of recursive editing levels in GNU Emacs. This is because they constrain you to "go back" in a particular order—from the innermost level toward the top level. When possible, we present different activities in separate buffers so that you can switch between them as you please. Some commands switch to a new major mode which provides a command to switch back. These approaches give you more flexibility to go back to unfinished tasks in the order you choose.

29.12 Emulation

GNU Emacs can be programmed to emulate (more or less) most other editors. Standard facilities can emulate these:

EDT (DEC VMS editor)

> Turn on EDT emulation with `M-x edt-emulation-on`. `M-x edt-emulation-off` restores normal Emacs command bindings.

> Most of the EDT emulation commands are keypad keys, and most standard Emacs key bindings are still available. The EDT emulation rebindings are done in the global keymap, so there is no problem switching buffers or major modes while in EDT emulation.

vi (Berkeley editor)

> Viper is the newest emulator for vi. It implements several levels of emulation; level 1 is closest to vi itself, while level 5 departs somewhat from strict emulation to take advantage of the capabilities of Emacs. To invoke Viper, type `M-x viper-mode`; it will guide you the rest of the way and ask for the emulation level.

vi (another emulator)

> `M-x vi-mode` enters a major mode that replaces the previously established major mode. All of the vi commands that, in real vi, enter "input" mode are programmed instead to return to the previous major mode. Thus, ordinary Emacs serves as vi's "input" mode.

> Because vi emulation works through major modes, it does not work to switch buffers during emulation. Return to normal Emacs first.

If you plan to use vi emulation much, you probably want to bind a key to the `vi-mode` command.

vi (alternate emulator)

> `M-x vip-mode` invokes another vi emulator, said to resemble real vi more thoroughly than `M-x vi-mode`. "Input" mode in this emulator is changed from ordinary Emacs so you can use `ESC` to go back to emulated vi command mode. To get from emulated vi command mode back to ordinary Emacs, type `C-z`.

> This emulation does not work through major modes, and it is possible to switch buffers in various ways within the emulator. It is not so necessary to assign a key to the command `vip-mode` as it is with `vi-mode` because terminating insert mode does not use it.

> For full information, see the long comment at the beginning of the source file, which is '`lisp/vip.el`' in the Emacs distribution.

29.13 Dissociated Press

`M-x dissociated-press` is a command for scrambling a file of text either word by word or character by character. Starting from a buffer of straight English, it produces extremely amusing output. The input comes from the current Emacs buffer. Dissociated Press writes its output in a buffer named '`*Dissociation*`', and redisplays that buffer after every couple of lines (approximately) so you can read the output as it comes out.

Dissociated Press asks every so often whether to continue generating output. Answer n to stop it. You can also stop at any time by typing `C-g`. The dissociation output remains in the '`*Dissociation*`' buffer for you to copy elsewhere if you wish.

Dissociated Press operates by jumping at random from one point in the buffer to another. In order to produce plausible output rather than gibberish, it insists on a certain amount of overlap between the end of one run of consecutive words or characters and the start of the next. That is, if it has just printed out 'president' and then decides to jump to a different point in the file, it might spot the 'ent' in 'pentagon' and continue from there, producing 'presidentagon'.[2] Long sample texts produce the best results.

A positive argument to `M-x dissociated-press` tells it to operate character by character, and specifies the number of overlap characters. A negative argument tells it to operate word by word and specifies the number of overlap words. In this mode, whole words are treated as the elements

---

[2] This dissociword actually appeared during the Vietnam War, when it was very appropriate.

to be permuted, rather than characters. No argument is equivalent to an argument of two. For your againformation, the output goes only into the buffer '*Dissociation*'. The buffer you start with is not changed.

Dissociated Press produces nearly the same results as a Markov chain based on a frequency table constructed from the sample text. It is, however, an independent, ignoriginal invention. Dissociated Press techniquitously copies several consecutive characters from the sample between random choices, whereas a Markov chain would choose randomly for each word or character. This makes for more plausible sounding results, and runs faster.

It is a mustatement that too much use of Dissociated Press can be a developediment to your real work. Sometimes to the point of outragedy. And keep dissociwords out of your documentation, if you want it to be well userenced and properbose. Have fun. Your buggestions are welcome.

29.14 Other Amusements

If you are a little bit bored, you can try M-x hanoi. If you are considerably bored, give it a numeric argument. If you are very very bored, try an argument of 9. Sit back and watch.

If you want a little more personal involvement, try M-x gomoku, which plays the game Go Moku with you.

M-x blackbox and M-x mpuz are two kinds of puzzles. blackbox challenges you to determine the location of objects inside a box by tomography. mpuz displays a multiplication puzzle with letters standing for digits in a code that you must guess—to guess a value, type a letter and then the digit you think it stands for.

M-x dunnet runs an adventure-style exploration game, which is a bigger sort of puzzle.

When you are frustrated, try the famous Eliza program. Just do M-x doctor. End each input by typing RET twice.

When you are feeling strange, type M-x yow.

30 Customization

This chapter talks about various topics relevant to adapting the behavior of Emacs in minor ways. See *The Emacs Lisp Reference Manual* for how to make more far-reaching changes.

All kinds of customization affect only the particular Emacs session that you do them in. They are completely lost when you kill the Emacs session, and have no effect on other Emacs sessions you may run at the same time or later. The only way an Emacs session can affect anything outside of it is by writing a file; in particular, the only way to make a customization 'permanent' is to put something in your '.emacs' file or other appropriate file to do the customization in each session. See Section 30.7 [Init File], page 366.

30.1 Minor Modes

Minor modes are optional features which you can turn on or off. For example, Auto Fill mode is a minor mode in which SPC breaks lines between words as you type. All the minor modes are independent of each other and of the selected major mode. Most minor modes say in the mode line when they are on; for example, 'Fill' in the mode line means that Auto Fill mode is on.

Append -mode to the name of a minor mode to get the name of a command function that turns the mode on or off. Thus, the command to enable or disable Auto Fill mode is called M-x auto-fill-mode. These commands are usually invoked with M-x, but you can bind keys to them if you wish. With no argument, the function turns the mode on if it was off and off if it was on. This is known as *toggling*. A positive argument always turns the mode on, and an explicit zero argument or a negative argument always turns it off.

Enabling or disabling some minor modes applies only to the current buffer; each buffer is independent of the other buffers. Therefore, you can enable the mode in particular buffers and disable it in others. The per-buffer minor modes include Auto Fill mode, Auto Save mode, Font-Lock mode, ISO Accents mode, Outline minor mode, Overwrite mode, and Binary Overwrite mode.

Auto Fill mode allows you to enter filled text without breaking lines explicitly. Emacs inserts newlines as necessary to prevent lines from becoming too long. See Section 20.5 [Filling], page 174.

Auto Save mode causes the contents of a buffer to be saved periodically to reduce the amount of work you can lose in case of a system crash. See Section 14.5 [Auto Save], page 113.

Enriched mode enables editing and saving of formatted text. See Section 20.11 [Formatted Text], page 190.

Font-Lock mode automatically highlights certain textual units found in programs, such as comments, strings, and function names being defined. This requires a window system that can display multiple fonts. See Section 17.12 [Faces], page 156.

ISO Accents mode makes the characters '`'', ''', '"', '^', '/' and '~' combine with the following letter, to produce an accented letter in the ISO Latin-1 character set. See Section 11.4 [European Display], page 77.

Outline minor mode provides the same facilities as the major mode called Outline mode; but since it is a minor mode instead, you can combine it with any major mode. See Section 20.8 [Outline Mode], page 179.

Overwrite mode causes ordinary printing characters to replace existing text instead of shoving it to the right. For example, if point is in front of the 'B' in 'FOOBAR', then in Overwrite mode typing a G changes it to 'FOOGAR', instead of producing it 'FOOGBAR' as usual. Binary Overwrite mode is a variant of Overwrite mode for editing binary files; it treats newlines and tabs like other characters, so that they overwrite other characters and can be overwritten by them.

The following minor modes normally apply to all buffers at once. Since each is enabled or disabled by the value of a variable, you *can* set them differently for particular buffers, by explicitly making the corresponding variables local in those buffers. See Section 30.2.4 [Locals], page 348.

Abbrev mode allows you to define abbreviations that automatically expand as you type them. For example, 'amd' might expand to 'abbrev mode'. See Chapter 23 [Abbrevs], page 251, for full information.

Icomplete mode displays an indication of available completions when you are in the minibuffer and completion is active. See Section 5.3.4 [Completion Options], page 41.

Line Number mode enables continuous display in the mode line of the line number of point. See Section 1.3 [Mode Line], page 17.

Resize-Minibuffer mode makes the minibuffer expand as necessary to hold the text that you put in it. See Section 5.2 [Minibuffer Edit], page 38.

Scroll Bar mode gives each window a scroll bar (see Section 17.10 [Scroll Bars], page 155). Menu Bar mode gives each frame a menu bar (see Section 17.11 [Menu Bars], page 155). Both of these modes are enabled by default when you use the X Window System.

In Transient Mark mode, every change in the buffer contents "deactivates" the mark, so that commands that operate on the region will get an error. This means you must either set the mark, or explicitly "reactivate" it, before each command that uses the region. The advantage of Transient

Mark mode is that Emacs can display the region highlighted (currently only when using X). See Section 8.1 [Setting Mark], page 55.

For most minor modes, the command name is also the name of a variable which directly controls the mode. The mode is enabled whenever this variable's value is non-`nil`, and the minor mode command works by setting the variable. For example, the command `outline-minor-mode` works by setting the value of `outline-minor-mode` as a variable; it is this variable that directly turns Outline minor mode on and off. To check whether a given minor mode works this way, use `C-h v` to ask for documentation on the variable name.

These minor mode variables provide a good way for Lisp programs to turn minor modes on and off; they are also useful in a file's local variables list. But please think twice before setting minor modes with a local variables list, because most minor modes are matter of user preference—other users editing the same file might not want the same minor modes you prefer.

30.2 Variables

A *variable* is a Lisp symbol which has a value. The symbol's name is also called the name of the variable. A variable name can contain any characters that can appear in a file, but conventionally variable names consist of words separated by hyphens. A variable can have a documentation string which describes what kind of value it should have and how the value will be used.

Lisp allows any variable to have any kind of value, but most variables that Emacs uses require a value of a certain type. Often the value should always be a string, or should always be a number. Sometimes we say that a certain feature is turned on if a variable is "non-`nil`," meaning that if the variable's value is `nil`, the feature is off, but the feature is on for *any* other value. The conventional value to use to turn on the feature—since you have to pick one particular value when you set the variable—is `t`.

Emacs uses many Lisp variables for internal record keeping, as any Lisp program must, but the most interesting variables for you are the ones that exist for the sake of customization. Emacs does not (usually) change the values of these variables; instead, you set the values, and thereby alter and control the behavior of certain Emacs commands. These variables are called *options*. Most options are documented in this manual, and appear in the Variable Index (see [Variable Index], page 459).

One example of a variable which is an option is `fill-column`, which specifies the position of the right margin (as a number of characters from the left margin) to be used by the fill commands (see Section 20.5 [Filling], page 174).

30.2.1 Examining and Setting Variables

C-h v *var* RET
>   Display the value and documentation of variable *var* (describe-
>   variable).

M-x set-variable RET *var* RET *value* RET
>   Change the value of variable *var* to *value*.

To examine the value of a single variable, use C-h v (describe-variable), which reads a variable name using the minibuffer, with completion. It displays both the value and the documentation of the variable. For example,

        C-h v fill-column RET

displays something like this:

        fill-column's value is 75

        Documentation:
        *Column beyond which automatic line-wrapping should happen.
        Automatically becomes buffer-local when set in any fashion.

The star at the beginning of the documentation indicates that this variable is an option. C-h v is not restricted to options; it allows any variable name.

The most convenient way to set a specific option is with M-x set-variable. This reads the variable name with the minibuffer (with completion), and then reads a Lisp expression for the new value using the minibuffer a second time. For example,

        M-x set-variable RET fill-column RET 75 RET

sets fill-column to 75.

You can set any variable with a Lisp expression using the function setq. Here's how to use it to set fill-column:

        (setq fill-column 75)

Setting variables, like all means of customizing Emacs except where otherwise stated, affects only the current Emacs session.

30.2.2 Editing Variable Values

These two functions make it easy to display all the Emacs option variables, and to change some of them if you wish.

M-x list-options
>   Display a buffer listing names, values and documentation of all
>   options.

M-x edit-options
>   Change option values by editing a list of options.

M-x list-options displays a list of all Emacs option variables, in an Emacs buffer named '*List Options*'. Each option is shown with its documentation and its current value. Here is what a portion of it might look like:

```
;; exec-path:
("." "/usr/local/bin" "/usr/ucb" "/bin" "/usr/bin" "/u2/emacs/etc")
*List of directories to search programs to run in subprocesses.
Each element is a string (directory name)
or nil (try the default directory).
;;
;; fill-column:
75
*Column beyond which automatic line-wrapping should happen.
Automatically becomes buffer-local when set in any fashion.
;;
```

M-x edit-options goes one step further and immediately selects the '*List Options*' buffer; this buffer uses the major mode Options mode, which provides commands that allow you to point at an option and change its value:

s   Set the variable point is in or near to a new value read using the minibuffer.

x   Toggle the variable point is in or near: if the value was nil, it becomes t; otherwise it becomes nil.

1   Set the variable point is in or near to t.

0   Set the variable point is in or near to nil.

n
p   Move to the next or previous variable.

Any changes take effect immediately, and last until you exit from Emacs.

30.2.3 Hooks

A *hook* is a variable where you can store a function or functions to be called on a particular occasion by an existing program. Emacs provides a number of hooks for the sake of customization.

Most of the hooks in Emacs are *normal hooks*. These variables contain lists of functions to be called with no arguments. The reason most hooks are normal hooks is so that you can use them in a uniform way. Every variable in Emacs whose name ends in '-hook' is a normal hook.

Most major modes run hooks as the last step of initialization. This makes it easy for a user to customize the behavior of the mode, by overriding the local variable assignments already made by the mode. But hooks may also be used in other contexts. For example, the hook suspend-hook runs just before Emacs suspends itself (see Section 3.1 [Exiting], page 24).

The recommended way to add a hook function to a normal hook is by calling `add-hook`. You can use any valid Lisp function as the hook function. For example, here's how to set up a hook to turn on Auto Fill mode when entering Text mode and other modes based on Text mode:

```
(add-hook 'text-mode-hook 'turn-on-auto-fill)
```

The next example shows how to use a hook to customize the indentation of C code. (People often have strong personal preferences for one format compared to another.) Here the hook function is an anonymous lambda expression.

```
(add-hook 'c-mode-hook
  (function (lambda ()
              (setq c-indent-level 4
                    c-argdecl-indent 0
                    c-label-offset -4
                    c-continued-statement-indent 0
                    c-brace-offset 0
                    comment-column 40))))
```

```
(setq c++-mode-hook c-mode-hook)
```

It is best to design your hook functions so that the order in which they are executed does not matter. Any dependence on the order is "asking for trouble." However, the order is predictable: the most recently added hook functions are executed first.

30.2.4 Local Variables

`M-x make-local-variable RET` *var* `RET`
> Make variable *var* have a local value in the current buffer.

`M-x kill-local-variable RET` *var* `RET`
> Make variable *var* use its global value in the current buffer.

`M-x make-variable-buffer-local RET` *var* `RET`
> Mark variable *var* so that setting it will make it local to the buffer that is current at that time.

Almost any variable can be made *local* to a specific Emacs buffer. This means that its value in that buffer is independent of its value in other buffers. A few variables are always local in every buffer. Every other Emacs variable has a *global* value which is in effect in all buffers that have not made the variable local.

`M-x make-local-variable` reads the name of a variable and makes it local to the current buffer. Further changes in this buffer will not affect others, and further changes in the global value will not affect this buffer.

M-x make-variable-buffer-local reads the name of a variable and changes the future behavior of the variable so that it will become local automatically when it is set. More precisely, once a variable has been marked in this way, the usual ways of setting the variable automatically do make-local-variable first. We call such variables *per-buffer* variables.

Major modes (see Chapter 18 [Major Modes], page 161) always make variables local to the buffer before setting the variables. This is why changing major modes in one buffer has no effect on other buffers. Minor modes also work by setting variables—normally, each minor mode has one controlling variable which is non-nil when the mode is enabled (see Section 30.1 [Minor Modes], page 343). For most minor modes, the controlling variable is per buffer.

Emacs contains a number of variables that are always per-buffer. These include abbrev-mode, auto-fill-function, case-fold-search, comment-column, ctl-arrow, fill-column, fill-prefix, indent-tabs-mode, left-margin, mode-line-format, overwrite-mode, selective-display-ellipses, selective-display, tab-width, and truncate-lines. Some other variables are always local in every buffer, but they are used for internal purposes.

A few variables cannot be local to a buffer because they are always local to each display instead (See Section 17.7 [Multiple Displays], page 152). If you try to make one of these variables buffer-local, you'll get an error message.

M-x kill-local-variable reads the name of a variable and makes it cease to be local to the current buffer. The global value of the variable henceforth is in effect in this buffer. Setting the major mode kills all the local variables of the buffer except for a few variables specially marked as *permanent locals*.

To set the global value of a variable, regardless of whether the variable has a local value in the current buffer, you can use the Lisp construct setq-default. This construct is used just like setq, but it sets variables' global values instead of their local values (if any). When the current buffer does have a local value, the new global value may not be visible until you switch to another buffer. Here is an example:

```
(setq-default fill-column 75)
```

setq-default is the only way to set the global value of a variable that has been marked with make-variable-buffer-local.

Lisp programs can use default-value to look at a variable's default value. This function takes a symbol as argument and returns its default value. The argument is evaluated; usually you must quote it explicitly. For example, here's how to obtain the default value of fill-column:

```
(default-value 'fill-column)
```

30.2.5 Local Variables in Files

A file can specify local variable values for use when you edit the file with Emacs. Visiting the file checks for local variables specifications; it automatically makes these variables local to the buffer, and sets them to the values specified in the file.

There are two ways to specify local variable values: in the first line, or with a local variables list. Here's how to specify them in the first line:

```
-*- mode: modename; var: value; ... -*-
```

You can specify any number of variables/value pairs in this way, each pair with a colon and semicolon as shown above. `mode: modename;` specifies the major mode; this should come first in the line. The *values* are not evaluated; they are used literally. Here is an example that specifies Lisp mode and sets two variables with numeric values:

```
;; -*-mode: Lisp; fill-column: 75; comment-column: 50; -*-
```

A *local variables list* goes near the end of the file, in the last page. (It is often best to put it on a page by itself.) The local variables list starts with a line containing the string '`Local Variables:`', and ends with a line containing the string '`End:`'. In between come the variable names and values, one set per line, as '*variable*: *value*'. The *values* are not evaluated; they are used literally. If a file has both a local variables list and a '-*-' line, Emacs processes *everything* in the '-*-' line first, and *everything* in the local variables list afterward.

Here is an example of a local variables list:

```
;;; Local Variables: ***
;;; mode:lisp ***
;;; comment-column:0 ***
;;; comment-start: ";;; "  ***
;;; comment-end:"***" ***
;;; End: ***
```

As you see, each line starts with the prefix ';;; ' and each line ends with the suffix ' ***'. Emacs recognizes these as the prefix and suffix based on the first line of the list, by finding them surrounding the magic string '`Local Variables:`'; then it automatically discards them from the other lines of the list.

The usual reason for using a prefix and/or suffix is to embed the local variables list in a comment, so it won't confuse other programs that the file is intended as input for. The example above is for a language where comment lines start with ';;; ' and end with '***'; the local values for `comment-start` and `comment-end` customize the rest of Emacs for this unusual syntax. Don't use a prefix (or a suffix) if you don't need one.

Two "variable names" have special meanings in a local variables list: a value for the variable `mode` really sets the major mode, and a value for the variable `eval` is simply evaluated as an expression and the value is ignored. `mode` and `eval` are not real variables; setting variables named `mode` and `eval` in any other context has no special meaning. If `mode` is used to set a major mode, it should be the first "variable" in the list.

You can use the `mode` "variable" to set minor modes as well as major modes; in fact, you can use it more than once, first to set the major mode and then to set minor modes which are specific to particular buffers. But most minor modes should not be specified in the file in any fashion, because they represent user preferences. For example, you should not try to specify Auto Fill mode with file local variables, because whether to use Auto Fill mode for editing a particular kind of text is a matter of personal taste, not an aspect of the format of the text.

The start of the local variables list must be no more than 3000 characters from the end of the file, and must be in the last page if the file is divided into pages. Otherwise, Emacs will not notice it is there. The purpose of this rule is so that a stray 'Local Variables:' not in the last page does not confuse Emacs, and so that visiting a long file that is all one page and has no local variables list need not take the time to search the whole file.

You may be tempted to try to turn on Auto Fill mode with a local variable list. That is a mistake. The choice of Auto Fill mode or not is a matter of individual taste, not a matter of the contents of particular files. If you want to use Auto Fill, set up major mode hooks with your '.emacs' file to turn it on (when appropriate) for you alone (see Section 30.7 [Init File], page 366). Don't try to use a local variable list that would impose your taste on everyone.

The variable `enable-local-variables` controls whether to process local variables lists, and thus gives you a chance to override them. Its default value is `t`, which means do process local variables lists. If you set the value to `nil`, Emacs simply ignores local variables lists. Any other value says to query you about each local variables list, showing you the local variables list to consider.

The `eval` "variable", and certain actual variables, create a special risk; when you visit someone else's file, local variable specifications for these could affect your Emacs in arbitrary ways. Therefore, the option `enable-local-eval` controls whether Emacs processes `eval` variables, as well variables with names that end in '-hook', '-hooks', '-function' or '-functions', and certain other variables. The three possibilities for the option's value are `t`, `nil`, and anything else, just as for `enable-local-variables`. The default is `maybe`, which is neither `t` nor `nil`, so normally Emacs does ask for confirmation about file settings for these variables.

Use the command `normal-mode` to reset the local variables and major mode of a buffer according to the file name and contents, including the local variables list if any. See Section 18.1 [Choosing Modes], page 161.

30.3 Keyboard Macros

A *keyboard macro* is a command defined by the user to stand for another sequence of keys. For example, if you discover that you are about to type `C-n C-d` forty times, you can speed your work by defining a keyboard macro to do `C-n C-d` and calling it with a repeat count of forty.

C-x (Start defining a keyboard macro (`start-kbd-macro`).

C-x)   End the definition of a keyboard macro (`end-kbd-macro`).

C-x e   Execute the most recent keyboard macro (`call-last-kbd-macro`).

C-u C-x (Re-execute last keyboard macro, then add more keys to its definition.

C-x q   When this point is reached during macro execution, ask for confirmation (`kbd-macro-query`).

M-x name-last-kbd-macro
               Give a command name (for the duration of the session) to the most recently defined keyboard macro.

M-x insert-kbd-macro
               Insert in the buffer a keyboard macro's definition, as Lisp code.

C-x C-k   Edit a previously defined keyboard macro (`edit-kbd-macro`).

Keyboard macros differ from ordinary Emacs commands in that they are written in the Emacs command language rather than in Lisp. This makes it easier for the novice to write them, and makes them more convenient as temporary hacks. However, the Emacs command language is not powerful enough as a programming language to be useful for writing anything intelligent or general. For such things, Lisp must be used.

You define a keyboard macro while executing the commands which are the definition. Put differently, as you define a keyboard macro, the definition is being executed for the first time. This way, you can see what the effects of your commands are, so that you don't have to figure them out in your head. When you are finished, the keyboard macro is defined and also has been, in effect, executed once. You can then do the whole thing over again by invoking the macro.

30.3.1 Basic Use

To start defining a keyboard macro, type the `C-x (` command (`start-kbd-macro`). From then on, your keys continue to be executed, but also become part of the definition of the macro. 'Def' appears in the mode line to remind you of what is going on. When you are finished, the `C-x )` command (`end-kbd-macro`) terminates the definition (without becoming part of it!). For example,

    C-x (M-f foo C-x)

defines a macro to move forward a word and then insert 'foo'.

The macro thus defined can be invoked again with the `C-x e` command (`call-last-kbd-macro`), which may be given a repeat count as a numeric argument to execute the macro many times. `C-x )` can also be given a repeat count as an argument, in which case it repeats the macro that many times right after defining it, but defining the macro counts as the first repetition (since it is executed as you define it). Therefore, giving `C-x )` an argument of 4 executes the macro immediately 3 additional times. An argument of zero to `C-x e` or `C-x )` means repeat the macro indefinitely (until it gets an error or you type `C-g`).

If you wish to repeat an operation at regularly spaced places in the text, define a macro and include as part of the macro the commands to move to the next place you want to use it. For example, if you want to change each line, you should position point at the start of a line, and define a macro to change that line and leave point at the start of the next line. Then repeating the macro will operate on successive lines.

After you have terminated the definition of a keyboard macro, you can add to the end of its definition by typing `C-u C-x (`. This is equivalent to plain `C-x (` followed by retyping the whole definition so far. As a consequence it re-executes the macro as previously defined.

You can use function keys in a keyboard macro, just like keyboard keys. You can even use mouse events, but be careful about that: when the macro replays the mouse event, it uses the original mouse position of that event, the position that the mouse had while you were defining the macro. The effect of this may be hard to predict. (Using the current mouse position would be even less predictable.)

One thing that doesn't always work well in a keyboard macro is the command `C-M-c` (`exit-recursive-edit`). When this command exits a recursive edit that started within the macro, it works as you'd expect. But if it exits a recursive edit that started before you invoked the keyboard macro, it also necessarily exits the keyboard macro as part of the process.

You can edit a keyboard macro already defined by typing `C-x C-k` (`edit-kbd-macro`). Follow that with the keyboard input that you would use to invoke the macro—C-x e or M-x *name* or some other key sequence. This formats the macro definition in a buffer and enters a specialized major mode for editing it. Type C-h m once in that buffer to display details of how to edit the macro. When you are finished editing, type C-c C-c.

30.3.2 Naming and Saving Keyboard Macros

If you wish to save a keyboard macro for longer than until you define the next one, you must give it a name using M-x name-last-kbd-macro. This reads a name as an argument using the minibuffer and defines that name to execute the macro. The macro name is a Lisp symbol, and defining it in this way makes it a valid command name for calling with M-x or for binding a key to with global-set-key (see Section 30.4.1 [Keymaps], page 355). If you specify a name that has a prior definition other than another keyboard macro, an error message is printed and nothing is changed.

Once a macro has a command name, you can save its definition in a file. Then it can be used in another editing session. First, visit the file you want to save the definition in. Then use this command:

> M-x insert-kbd-macro RET *macroname* RET

This inserts some Lisp code that, when executed later, will define the same macro with the same definition it has now. (You need not understand Lisp code to do this, because insert-kbd-macro writes the Lisp code for you.) Then save the file. You can load the file later with load-file (see Section 22.4 [Lisp Libraries], page 246). If the file you save in is your init file '~/.emacs' (see Section 30.7 [Init File], page 366) then the macro will be defined each time you run Emacs.

If you give insert-kbd-macro a numeric argument, it makes additional Lisp code to record the keys (if any) that you have bound to the keyboard macro, so that the macro will be reassigned the same keys when you load the file.

30.3.3 Executing Macros with Variations

Using C-x q (kbd-macro-query), you can get an effect similar to that of query-replace, where the macro asks you each time around whether to make a change. While defining the macro, type C-x q at the point where you want the query to occur. During macro definition, the C-x q does nothing, but when you run the macro later, C-x q asks you interactively whether to continue.

The valid responses when C-x q asks are SPC (or y), DEL (or n), ESC (or q), C-l and C-r. The answers are the same as in query-replace, though not all of the query-replace options are meaningful.

These responses include SPC to continue, and DEL to skip the remainder of this repetition of the macro and start right away with the next repetition. ESC means to skip the remainder of this repetition and cancel further repetitions. C-l redraws the screen and asks you again for a character to say what to do.

C-r enters a recursive editing level, in which you can perform editing which is not part of the macro. When you exit the recursive edit using C-M-c, you are asked again how to continue with the keyboard macro. If you type a SPC at this time, the rest of the macro definition is executed. It is up to you to leave point and the text in a state such that the rest of the macro will do what you want.

C-u C-x q, which is C-x q with a numeric argument, performs a completely different function. It enters a recursive edit reading input from the keyboard, both when you type it during the definition of the macro, and when it is executed from the macro. During definition, the editing you do inside the recursive edit does not become part of the macro. During macro execution, the recursive edit gives you a chance to do some particularized editing on each repetition. See Section 29.11 [Recursive Edit], page 339.

30.4 Customizing Key Bindings

This section describes *key bindings* which map keys to commands, and the *keymaps* which record key bindings. It also explains how to customize key bindings.

Recall that a command is a Lisp function whose definition provides for interactive use. Like every Lisp function, a command has a function name which usually consists of lower case letters and hyphens.

30.4.1 Keymaps

The bindings between key sequences and command functions are recorded in data structures called *keymaps*. Emacs has many of these, each used on particular occasions.

Recall that a *key sequence* (*key*, for short) is a sequence of *input events* that have a meaning as a unit. Input events include characters, function keys and mouse buttons—all the inputs that you can send to the computer with your terminal. A key sequence gets its meaning from its *binding*, which says what command it runs. The function of keymaps is to record these bindings.

The *global* keymap is the most important keymap because it is always in effect. The global keymap defines keys for Fundamental mode; most of these definitions are common to most or all major modes. Each major or minor mode can have its own keymap which overrides the global definitions of some keys.

For example, a self-inserting character such as `g` is self-inserting because the global keymap binds it to the command `self-insert-command`. The standard Emacs editing characters such as `C-a` also get their standard meanings from the global keymap. Commands to rebind keys, such as `M-x global-set-key`, actually work by storing the new binding in the proper place in the global map. See Section 30.4.5 [Rebinding], page 359.

Meta characters work differently; Emacs translates each Meta character into a pair of characters starting with `ESC`. When you type the character `M-a` in a key sequence, Emacs replaces it with `ESC a`. A meta key comes in as a single input event, but becomes two events for purposes of key bindings. The reason for this is historical, and we might change it someday.

Most modern keyboards have function keys as well as character keys. Function keys send input events just as character keys do, and keymaps can have bindings for them.

On many terminals, typing a function key actually sends the computer a sequence of characters; the precise details of the sequence depends on which function key and on the model of terminal you are using. (Often the sequence starts with `ESC [`.) If Emacs understands your terminal type properly, it recognizes the character sequences forming function keys wherever they occur in a key sequence (not just at the beginning). Thus, for most purposes, you can pretend the function keys reach Emacs directly and ignore their encoding as character sequences.

Mouse buttons also produce input events. These events come with other data—the window and position where you pressed or released the button, and a time stamp. But only the choice of button matters for key bindings; the other data matters only if a command looks at it. (Commands designed for mouse invocation usually do look at the other data.)

A keymap records definitions for single events. Interpreting a key sequence of multiple events involves a chain of keymaps. The first keymap gives a definition for the first event; this definition is another keymap, which is used to look up the second event in the sequence, and so on.

Key sequences can mix function keys and characters. For example, `C-x SELECT` makes sense. If you make `SELECT` a prefix key, then `SELECT C-n` makes sense. You can even mix mouse events with keyboard events, but we recommend against it, because such sequences are inconvenient to type in.

30.4.2 Prefix Keymaps

A prefix key such as `C-x` or `ESC` has its own keymap, which holds the definition for the event that immediately follows that prefix.

The definition of a prefix key is usually the keymap to use for looking up the following event. The definition can also be a Lisp symbol whose function definition is the following keymap; the effect is the same, but it provides a command name for the prefix key that can be used as a description of what the prefix key is for. Thus, the binding of C-x is the symbol Ctl-X-Prefix, whose function definition is the keymap for C-x commands. The definitions of C-c, C-x, C-h and ESC as prefix keys appear in the global map, so these prefix keys are always available.

Some prefix keymaps are stored in variables with names:

- ctl-x-map is the variable name for the map used for characters that follow C-x.

- help-map is for characters that follow C-h.

- esc-map is for characters that follow ESC. Thus, all Meta characters are actually defined by this map.

- ctl-x-4-map is for characters that follow C-x 4.

- mode-specific-map is for characters that follow C-c.

30.4.3 Local Keymaps

So far we have explained the ins and outs of the global map. Major modes customize Emacs by providing their own key bindings in *local keymaps*. For example, C mode overrides TAB to make it indent the current line for C code. Portions of text in the buffer can specify their own keymaps to substitute for the keymap of the buffer's major mode.

Minor modes can also have local keymaps. Whenever a minor mode is in effect, the definitions in its keymap override both the major mode's local keymap and the global keymap.

The local keymaps for Lisp mode, C mode, and several other major modes always exist even when not in use. These are kept in variables named lisp-mode-map, c-mode-map, and so on. For major modes less often used, the local keymap is normally constructed only when the mode is used for the first time in a session. This is to save space. If you wish to change one of these keymaps, you must use the major mode's *mode hook*—see below.

All minor mode keymaps are created in advance. There is no way to defer their creation until the first time the minor mode is enabled.

A local keymap can locally redefine a key as a prefix key by defining it as a prefix keymap. If the key is also defined globally as a prefix, then its local and global definitions (both keymaps) effectively combine: both of them are used to look up the event that follows the prefix key. Thus, if the mode's local keymap defines C-c as another keymap, and that keymap defines C-z as a command, this provides a local meaning for C-c C-z. This does not affect other sequences that start with C-c; if those sequences don't have their own local bindings, their global bindings remain in effect.

Another way to think of this is that Emacs handles a multi-event key sequence by looking in several keymaps, one by one, for a binding of the whole key sequence. First it checks the minor mode keymaps for minor modes that are enabled, then it checks the major mode's keymap, and then it checks the global keymap. This is not precisely how key lookup works, but it's good enough for understanding ordinary circumstances.

To change the local bindings of a major mode, you must change the mode's local keymap. Normally you must wait until the first time the mode is used, because most major modes don't create their keymaps until then. If you want to specify something in your '~/.emacs' file to change a major mode's bindings, you must use the mode's mode hook to delay the change until the mode is first used.

For example, the command texinfo-mode to select Texinfo mode runs the hook texinfo-mode-hook. Here's how you can use the hook to add local bindings (not very useful, we admit) for C-c n and C-c p in Texinfo mode:

```
(add-hook 'texinfo-mode-hook
          '(lambda ()
             (define-key texinfo-mode-map
                         "\C-cp"
                         'backward-paragraph)
             (define-key texinfo-mode-map
                         "\C-cn"
                         'forward-paragraph)
             ))
```

See Section 30.2.3 [Hooks], page 347.

30.4.4 Minibuffer Keymaps

The minibuffer has its own set of local keymaps; they contain various completion and exit commands.

- minibuffer-local-map is used for ordinary input (no completion).

- minibuffer-local-ns-map is similar, except that SPC exits just like RET. This is used mainly for Mocklisp compatibility.

- minibuffer-local-completion-map is for permissive completion.

- minibuffer-local-must-match-map is for strict completion and for cautious completion.

30.4.5 Changing Key Bindings Interactively

The way to redefine an Emacs key is to change its entry in a keymap. You can change the global keymap, in which case the change is effective in all major modes (except those that have their own overriding local definitions for the same key). Or you can change the current buffer's local map, which affects all buffers using the same major mode.

M-x global-set-key RET *key cmd* RET
> Define *key* globally to run *cmd*.

M-x local-set-key RET *key cmd* RET
> Define *key* locally (in the major mode now in effect) to run *cmd*.

M-x global-unset-key RET *key*
> Make *key* undefined in the global map.

M-x local-unset-key RET *key*
> Make *key* undefined locally (in the major mode now in effect).

For example, suppose you like to execute commands in a subshell within an Emacs buffer, instead of suspending Emacs and executing commands in your login shell. Normally, C-z is bound to the function suspend-emacs (when not using the X Window System), but you can change C-z to invoke an interactive subshell within Emacs, by binding it to shell as follows:

> M-x global-set-key RET C-z shell RET

global-set-key reads the command name after the key. After you press the key, a message like this appears so that you can confirm that you are binding the key you want:

> Set key C-z to command:

You can redefine function keys and mouse events in the same way; just type the function key or click the mouse when it's time to specify the key to rebind.

You can rebind a key that contains more than one event in the same way. Emacs keeps reading the key to rebind until it is a complete key (that is, not a prefix key). Thus, if you type C-f for *key*, that's the end; the minibuffer is entered immediately to read *cmd*. But if you type C-x, another character is read; if that is 4, another character is read, and so on. For example,

> M-x global-set-key RET C-x 4 $ spell-other-window RET

redefines C-x 4 $ to run the (fictitious) command spell-other-window.

The two-character keys consisting of C-c followed by a letter are reserved for user customizations. Lisp programs are not supposed to define these keys, so the bindings you make for them will be available in all major modes and will never get in the way of anything.

You can remove the global definition of a key with `global-unset-key`. This makes the key *undefined*; if you type it, Emacs will just beep. Similarly, `local-unset-key` makes a key undefined in the current major mode keymap, which makes the global definition (or lack of one) come back into effect in that major mode.

If you have redefined (or undefined) a key and you subsequently wish to retract the change, undefining the key will not do the job—you need to redefine the key with its standard definition. To find the name of the standard definition of a key, go to a Fundamental mode buffer and use `C-h c`. The documentation of keys in this manual also lists their command names.

If you want to prevent yourself from invoking a command by mistake, it is better to disable the command than to undefine the key. A disabled command is less work to invoke when you really want to. See Section 30.4.10 [Disabling], page 365.

30.4.6 Rebinding Keys in Your Init File

If you have a set of key bindings that you like to use all the time, you can specify them in your '`.emacs`' file by using their Lisp syntax.

The simplest method for doing this works for ASCII characters and Meta-modified ASCII characters only. This method uses a string to represent the key sequence you want to rebind. For example, here's how to bind `C-z` to `shell`:

```
(global-set-key "\C-z" 'shell)
```

This example uses a string constant containing one character, `C-z`. The single-quote before the command name, `shell`, marks it as a constant symbol rather than a variable. If you omit the quote, Emacs would try to evaluate `shell` immediately as a variable. This probably causes an error; it certainly isn't what you want.

Here is another example that binds a key sequence two characters long:

```
(global-set-key "\C-xl" 'make-symbolic-link)
```

When the key sequence includes function keys or mouse button events, or non-ASCII characters such as `C-=` or `H-a`, you must use the more general method of rebinding, which uses a vector to specify the key sequence.

The way to write a vector in Emacs Lisp is with square brackets around the vector elements. Use spaces to separate the elements. If an element is a symbol, simply write the symbol's name—no other delimiters or punctuation are needed. If a vector element is a character, write it as a Lisp character constant: '`?`' followed by the character as it would appear in a string.

Here are examples of using vectors to rebind `C-=` (a control character outside of ASCII), `H-a` (a Hyper character; ASCII doesn't have Hyper at all); `F7` (a function key), and `C-Mouse-1` (a keyboard-modified mouse button):

```
(global-set-key [?\C-=] 'make-symbolic-link)
(global-set-key [?\H-a] 'make-symbolic-link)
(global-set-key [f7] 'make-symbolic-link)
(global-set-key [C-mouse-1] 'make-symbolic-link)
```

You can use a vector for the simple cases too. Here's how to rewrite the first two examples, above, to use vectors:

```
(global-set-key [?\C-z] 'shell)
```

```
(global-set-key [?\C-x ?l] 'make-symbolic-link)
```

30.4.7 Rebinding Function Keys

Key sequences can contain function keys as well as ordinary characters. Just as Lisp characters (actually integers) represent keyboard characters, Lisp symbols represent function keys. If the function key has a word as its label, then that word is also the name of the corresponding Lisp symbol. Here are the conventional Lisp names for common function keys:

left, up, right, down
> Cursor arrow keys.

begin, end, home, next, prior
> Other cursor repositioning keys.

select, print, execute, backtab
insert, undo, redo, clearline
insertline, deleteline, insertchar, deletechar,
> Miscellaneous function keys.

f1, f2, ... f35
> Numbered function keys (across the top of the keyboard).

kp-add, kp-subtract, kp-multiply, kp-divide
kp-backtab, kp-space, kp-tab, kp-enter
kp-separator, kp-decimal, kp-equal
> Keypad keys (to the right of the regular keyboard), with names or punctuation.

kp-0, kp-1, ... kp-9
> Keypad keys with digits.

kp-f1, kp-f2, kp-f3, kp-f4
> Keypad PF keys.

These names are conventional, but some systems (especially when using X windows) may use different names. To make certain what symbol is used for a given function key on your terminal, type C-h c followed by that key.

A key sequence which contains function key symbols (or anything but ASCII characters) must be a vector rather than a string. The vector syntax uses spaces between the elements, and square brackets around the whole vector. Thus, to bind function key 'f1' to the command rmail, write the following:

```
(global-set-key [f1] 'rmail)
```

To bind the right-arrow key to the command forward-char, you can use this expression:

```
(global-set-key [right] 'forward-char)
```

This uses the Lisp syntax for a vector containing the symbol right. (This binding is present in Emacs by default.)

See Section 30.4.6 [Init Rebinding], page 360, for more information about using vectors for rebinding.

You can mix function keys and characters in a key sequence. This example binds C-x NEXT to the command forward-page.

```
(global-set-key [?\C-x next] 'forward-page)
```

where ?\C-x is the Lisp character constant for the character C-x. The vector element next is a symbol and therefore does not take a question mark.

You can use the modifier keys CTRL, META, HYPER, SUPER, ALT and SHIFT with function keys. To represent these modifiers, add the strings 'C-', 'M-', 'H-', 's-', 'A-' and 'S-' at the front of the symbol name. Thus, here is how to make Hyper-Meta-RIGHT move forward a word:

```
(global-set-key [H-M-right] 'forward-word)
```

30.4.8 Named ASCII Control Characters

TAB, RET, BS, LFD, ESC and DEL started out as names for certain ASCII control characters, used so often that they have special keys of their own. Later, users found it convenient to distinguish in Emacs between these keys and the "same" control characters typed with the CTRL key.

Emacs 19 distinguishes these two kinds of input, when used with the X Window System. It treats the "special" keys as function keys named tab, return, backspace, linefeed, escape, and delete. These function keys translate automatically into the corresponding ASCII characters *if* they have no bindings of their own. As a result, neither users nor Lisp programs need to pay attention to the distinction unless they care to.

If you do not want to distinguish between (for example) TAB and C-i, make just one binding, for the ASCII character TAB (octal code 011). If you do want to distinguish, make one binding for this ASCII character, and another for the "function key" tab.

With an ordinary ASCII terminal, there is no way to distinguish between `TAB` and `C-i` (and likewise for other such pairs), because the terminal sends the same character in both cases.

30.4.9 Rebinding Mouse Buttons

Emacs uses Lisp symbols to designate mouse buttons, too. The ordinary mouse events in Emacs are *click* events; these happen when you press a button and release it without moving the mouse. You can also get *drag* events, when you move the mouse while holding the button down. Drag events happen when you finally let go of the button.

The symbols for basic click events are `mouse-1` for the leftmost button, `mouse-2` for the next, and so on. Here is how you can redefine the second mouse button to split the current window:

```
(global-set-key [mouse-2] 'split-window-vertically)
```

The symbols for drag events are similar, but have the prefix 'drag-' before the word 'mouse'. For example, dragging the first button generates a `drag-mouse-1` event.

You can also define bindings for events that occur when a mouse button is pressed down. These events start with 'down-' instead of 'drag-'. Such events are generated only if they have key bindings. When you get a button-down event, a corresponding click or drag event will always follow.

If you wish, you can distinguish single, double, and triple clicks. A double click means clicking a mouse button twice in approximately the same place. The first click generates an ordinary click event. The second click, if it comes soon enough, generates a double-click event instead. The event type for a double click event starts with 'double-': for example, `double-mouse-3`.

This means that you can give a special meaning to the second click at the same place, but it must act on the assumption that the ordinary single click definition has run when the first click was received.

This constrains what you can do with double clicks, but user interface designers say that this constraint ought to be followed in any case. A double click should do something similar to the single click, only "more so". The command for the double-click event should perform the extra work for the double click.

If a double-click event has no binding, it changes to the corresponding single-click event. Thus, if you don't define a particular double click specially, it executes the single-click command twice.

Emacs also supports triple-click events whose names start with 'triple-'. Emacs does not distinguish quadruple clicks as event types; clicks beyond the third generate additional triple-click events. However, the full number of clicks is recorded in the event list, so you can distinguish if you really want to. We don't recommend distinct meanings for more than three clicks, but sometimes it is useful for subsequent clicks to cycle through the same set of three meanings, so that four clicks are equivalent to one click, five are equivalent to two, and six are equivalent to three.

Emacs also records multiple presses in drag and button-down events. For example, when you press a button twice, then move the mouse while holding the button, Emacs gets a 'double-drag-' event. And at the moment when you press it down for the second time, Emacs gets a 'double-down-' event (which is ignored, like all button-down events, if it has no binding).

The variable double-click-time specifies how long may elapse between clicks that are recognized as a pair. Its value is measured in milliseconds. If the value is nil, double clicks are not detected at all. If the value is t, then there is no time limit.

The symbols for mouse events also indicate the status of the modifier keys, with the usual prefixes 'C-', 'M-', 'H-', 's-', 'A-' and 'S-'. These always precede 'double-' or 'triple-', which always precede 'drag-' or 'down-'.

A frame includes areas that don't show text from the buffer, such as the mode line and the scroll bar. You can tell whether a mouse button comes from a special area of the screen by means of dummy "prefix keys." For example, if you click the mouse in the mode line, you get the prefix key mode-line before the ordinary mouse-button symbol. Thus, here is how to define the command for clicking the first button in a mode line to run scroll-up:

```
(global-set-key [mode-line mouse-1] 'scroll-up)
```

Here is the complete list of these dummy prefix keys and their meanings:

mode-line
> The mouse was in the mode line of a window.

vertical-line
> The mouse was in the vertical line separating side-by-side windows. (If you use scroll bars, they appear in place of these vertical lines.)

vertical-scroll-bar
> The mouse was in a vertical scroll bar. (This is the only kind of scroll bar Emacs currently supports.)

You can put more than one mouse button in a key sequence, but it isn't usual to do so.

30.4.10 Disabling Commands

Disabling a command marks the command as requiring confirmation before it can be executed. The purpose of disabling a command is to prevent beginning users from executing it by accident and being confused.

An attempt to invoke a disabled command interactively in Emacs displays a window containing the command's name, its documentation, and some instructions on what to do immediately; then Emacs asks for input saying whether to execute the command as requested, enable it and execute it, or cancel. If you decide to enable the command, you are asked whether to do this permanently or just for the current session. Enabling permanently works by automatically editing your '.emacs' file.

The direct mechanism for disabling a command is to put a non-nil disabled property on the Lisp symbol for the command. Here is the Lisp program to do this:

```
(put 'delete-region 'disabled t)
```

If the value of the disabled property is a string, that string is included in the message printed when the command is used:

```
(put 'delete-region 'disabled
    "It's better to use `kill-region' instead.\n")
```

You can make a command disabled either by editing the '.emacs' file directly or with the command M-x disable-command, which edits the '.emacs' file for you. Likewise, M-x enable-command edits '.emacs' to enable a command permanently. See Section 30.7 [Init File], page 366.

Whether a command is disabled is independent of what key is used to invoke it; disabling also applies if the command is invoked using M-x. Disabling a command has no effect on calling it as a function from Lisp programs.

30.5 Keyboard Translations

Some keyboards do not make it convenient to send all the special characters that Emacs uses. The most common problem case is the DEL character. Some keyboards provide no convenient way to type this very important character—usually because they were designed to expect the character C-h to be used for deletion. On these keyboard, if you press the key normally used for deletion, Emacs handles the C-h as a prefix character and offers you a list of help options, which is not what you want.

You can work around this problem within Emacs by setting up keyboard translations to turn C-h into DEL and DEL into C-h, as follows:

```
;; Translate C-h to DEL.
(keyboard-translate ?\C-h ?\C-?)
```

```
;; Translate DEL to C-h.
(keyboard-translate ?\C-? ?\C-h)
```

Keyboard translations are not the same as key bindings in keymaps (see Section 30.4.1 [Keymaps], page 355). Emacs contains numerous keymaps that apply in different situations, but there is only one set of keyboard translations, and it applies to every character that Emacs reads from the terminal. Keyboard translations take place at the lowest level of input processing; the keys that are looked up in keymaps contain the characters that result from keyboard translation.

Under X, the keyboard key named DELETE is a function key and is distinct from the ASCII character named DEL. See Section 30.4.8 [Named ASCII Chars], page 362. Keyboard translations affect only ASCII character input, not function keys; thus, the above example used under X does not affect the DELETE key. However, the translation above isn't necessary under X, because Emacs can also distinguish between the BACKSPACE key and C-h; and it normally treats BACKSPACE as DEL.

For full information about how to use keyboard translations, see section "Translating Input" in *The Emacs Lisp Reference Manual*.

30.6 The Syntax Table

All the Emacs commands which parse words or balance parentheses are controlled by the *syntax table*. The syntax table says which characters are opening delimiters, which are parts of words, which are string quotes, and so on. Each major mode has its own syntax table (though sometimes related major modes use the same one) which it installs in each buffer that uses that major mode. The syntax table installed in the current buffer is the one that all commands use, so we call it "the" syntax table. A syntax table is a Lisp object, a vector of length 256 whose elements are numbers.

To display a description of the contents of the current syntax table, type C-h s (describe-syntax). The description of each character includes both the string you would have to give to modify-syntax-entry to set up that character's current syntax, and some English to explain that string if necessary.

For full information on the syntax table, see section "Syntax Tables" in *The Emacs Lisp Reference Manual*.

30.7 The Init File, '~/.emacs'

When Emacs is started, it normally loads a Lisp program from the file '.emacs' in your home directory. We call this file your *init file* because it specifies how to initialize Emacs for you. You can use the command line switches '-q' and '-u' to tell Emacs whether to load an init file, and which one (see Chapter 3 [Entering Emacs], page 23).

There can also be a *default init file*, which is the library named 'default.el', found via the standard search path for libraries. The Emacs distribution contains no such library; your site may create one for local customizations. If this library exists, it is loaded whenever you start Emacs (except when you specify '-q'). But your init file, if any, is loaded first; if it sets inhibit-default-init non-nil, then 'default' is not loaded.

Your site may also have a *site startup file*; this is named 'site-start.el', if it exists. Emacs loads this library before it loads your init file. To inhibit loading of this library, use the option '-no-site-file'.

If you have a large amount of code in your '.emacs' file, you should move it into another file such as '~/*something*.el', byte-compile it, and make your '.emacs' file load it with (load "~/*something*"). See section "Byte Compilation" in *the Emacs Lisp Reference Manual*, for more information about compiling Emacs Lisp programs.

30.7.1 Init File Syntax

The '.emacs' file contains one or more Lisp function call expressions. Each of these consists of a function name followed by arguments, all surrounded by parentheses. For example, (setq fill-column 60) calls the function setq to set the variable fill-column (see Section 20.5 [Filling], page 174) to 60.

The second argument to setq is an expression for the new value of the variable. This can be a constant, a variable, or a function call expression. In '.emacs', constants are used most of the time. They can be:

Numbers: Numbers are written in decimal, with an optional initial minus sign.

Strings: Lisp string syntax is the same as C string syntax with a few extra features. Use a double-quote character to begin and end a string constant.

In a string, you can include newlines and special characters literally. But often it is cleaner to use backslash sequences for them: '\n' for newline, '\b' for backspace, '\r' for carriage return, '\t' for tab, '\f' for formfeed (control-L), '\e' for escape, '\\' for a backslash, '\"' for a double-quote, or '\ooo' for the character whose octal code is *ooo*. Backslash and double-quote are the only characters for which backslash sequences are mandatory.

'\C-' can be used as a prefix for a control character, as in '\C-s' for ASCII control-S, and '\M-' can be used as a prefix for a Meta character, as in '\M-a' for Meta-A or '\M-\C-a' for Control-Meta-A.

Characters:

Lisp character constant syntax consists of a '?' followed by either a character or an escape sequence starting with '\'. Examples: ?x, ?\n, ?\", ?\). Note that strings and characters are not interchangeable in Lisp; some contexts require one and some contexts require the other.

True: t stands for 'true'.

False: nil stands for 'false'.

Other Lisp objects:

Write a single-quote (') followed by the Lisp object you want.

30.7.2 Init File Examples

Here are some examples of doing certain commonly desired things with Lisp expressions:

- Make TAB in C mode just insert a tab if point is in the middle of a line.

    (setq c-tab-always-indent nil)

  Here we have a variable whose value is normally t for 'true' and the alternative is nil for 'false'.

- Make searches case sensitive by default (in all buffers that do not override this).

    (setq-default case-fold-search nil)

  This sets the default value, which is effective in all buffers that do not have local values for the variable. Setting case-fold-search with setq affects only the current buffer's local value, which is not what you probably want to do in an init file.

- Specify your own email address, if Emacs can't figure it out correctly.

    (setq user-mail-address "coon@yoyodyne.com")

  Various Emacs packages that need your own email address use the value of user-mail-address.

- Make Text mode the default mode for new buffers.

    (setq default-major-mode 'text-mode)

  Note that text-mode is used because it is the command for entering Text mode. The single-quote before it makes the symbol a constant; otherwise, text-mode would be treated as a variable name.

- Turn on Auto Fill mode automatically in Text mode and related modes.

```
(add-hook 'text-mode-hook
  '(lambda () (auto-fill-mode 1)))
```

This shows how to add a hook function to a normal hook variable (see Section 30.2.3 [Hooks], page 347). The function we supply is a list starting with `lambda`, with a single-quote in front of it to make it a list constant rather than an expression.

It's beyond the scope of this manual to explain Lisp functions, but for this example it is enough to know that the effect is to execute `(auto-fill-mode 1)` when Text mode is entered. You can replace that with any other expression that you like, or with several expressions in a row.

Emacs comes with a function named `turn-on-auto-fill` whose definition is `(lambda () (auto-fill-mode 1))`. Thus, a simpler way to write the above example is as follows:

```
(add-hook 'text-mode-hook 'turn-on-auto-fill)
```

- Load the installed Lisp library named 'foo' (actually a file 'foo.elc' or 'foo.el' in a standard Emacs directory).

```
(load "foo")
```

When the argument to `load` is a relative file name, not starting with '/' or '~', `load` searches the directories in `load-path` (see Section 22.4 [Lisp Libraries], page 246).

- Load the compiled Lisp file 'foo.elc' from your home directory.

```
(load "~/foo.elc")
```

Here an absolute file name is used, so no searching is done.

- Rebind the key C-x l to run the function `make-symbolic-link`.

```
(global-set-key "\C-xl" 'make-symbolic-link)
```

or

```
(define-key global-map "\C-xl" 'make-symbolic-link)
```

Note once again the single-quote used to refer to the symbol `make-symbolic-link` instead of its value as a variable.

- Do the same thing for C mode only.

```
(define-key c-mode-map "\C-xl" 'make-symbolic-link)
```

- Redefine all keys which now run `next-line` in Fundamental mode so that they run `forward-line` instead.

```
(substitute-key-definition 'next-line 'forward-line
                            global-map)
```

- Make C-x C-v undefined.

```
(global-unset-key "\C-x\C-v")
```

One reason to undefine a key is so that you can make it a prefix. Simply defining C-x C-v *anything* will make C-x C-v a prefix, but C-x C-v must first be freed of its usual non-prefix definition.

- Make '$' have the syntax of punctuation in Text mode. Note the use of a character constant for '$'.

  ```
  (modify-syntax-entry ?\$ "." text-mode-syntax-table)
  ```

- Enable the use of the command **eval-expression** without confirmation.

  ```
  (put 'eval-expression 'disabled nil)
  ```

30.7.3 Terminal-specific Initialization

Each terminal type can have a Lisp library to be loaded into Emacs when it is run on that type of terminal. For a terminal type named *termtype*, the library is called '**term/***termtype*' and it is found by searching the directories **load-path** as usual and trying the suffixes '.elc' and '.el'. Normally it appears in the subdirectory '**term**' of the directory where most Emacs libraries are kept.

The usual purpose of the terminal-specific library is to map the escape sequences used by the terminal's function keys onto more meaningful names, using **function-key-map**. See the file '**term/lk201.el**' for an example of how this is done. Many function keys are mapped automatically according to the information in the Termcap data base; the terminal-specific library needs to map only the function keys that Termcap does not specify.

When the terminal type contains a hyphen, only the part of the name before the first hyphen is significant in choosing the library name. Thus, terminal types '**aaa-48**' and '**aaa-30-rv**' both use the library '**term/aaa**'. The code in the library can use (**getenv "TERM"**) to find the full terminal type name.

The library's name is constructed by concatenating the value of the variable **term-file-prefix** and the terminal type. Your '.emacs' file can prevent the loading of the terminal-specific library by setting **term-file-prefix** to **nil**.

Emacs runs the hook **term-setup-hook** at the end of initialization, after both your '.emacs' file and any terminal-specific library have been read in. Add hook functions to this hook if you wish to override part of any of the terminal-specific libraries and to define initializations for terminals that do not have a library. See Section 30.2.3 [Hooks], page 347.

30.7.4 How Emacs Finds Your Init File

Normally Emacs uses the environment variable **HOME** to find '.emacs'; that's what '~' means in a file name. But if you have done **su**, Emacs tries to find your own '.emacs', not that of the user you are currently pretending to be. The idea is that you should get your own editor customizations even if you are running as the super user.

More precisely, Emacs first determines which user's init file to use. It gets the user name from the environment variables `LOGNAME` and `USER`; if neither of those exists, it uses effective user-ID. If that user name matches the real user-ID, then Emacs uses `HOME`; otherwise, it looks up the home directory corresponding to that user name in the system's data base of users.

31 Dealing with Common Problems

If you type an Emacs command you did not intend, the results are often mysterious. This chapter tells what you can do to cancel your mistake or recover from a mysterious situation. Emacs bugs and system crashes are also considered.

31.1 Quitting and Aborting

C-g   Quit. Cancel running or partially typed command.

C-]   Abort innermost recursive editing level and cancel the command which invoked it (**abort-recursive-edit**).

ESC ESC ESC
           Either quit or abort, whichever makes sense (**keyboard-escape-quit**).

M-x top-level
           Abort all recursive editing levels that are currently executing.

C-x u   Cancel a previously made change in the buffer contents (**undo**).

There are two ways of canceling commands which are not finished executing: *quitting* with C-g, and *aborting* with C-] or M-x top-level. Quitting cancels a partially typed command or one which is already running. Aborting exits a recursive editing level and cancels the command that invoked the recursive edit. (See Section 29.11 [Recursive Edit], page 339.)

Quitting with C-g is used for getting rid of a partially typed command, or a numeric argument that you don't want. It also stops a running command in the middle in a relatively safe way, so you can use it if you accidentally give a command which takes a long time. In particular, it is safe to quit out of killing; either your text will *all* still be in the buffer, or it will *all* be in the kill ring (or maybe both). Quitting an incremental search does special things documented under searching; in general, it may take two successive C-g characters to get out of a search (see Section 12.1 [Incremental Search], page 83).

C-g works by setting the variable **quit-flag** to **t** the instant C-g is typed; Emacs Lisp checks this variable frequently and quits if it is non-**nil**. C-g is only actually executed as a command if you type it while Emacs is waiting for input.

If you quit with C-g a second time before the first C-g is recognized, you activate the "emergency escape" feature and return to the shell. See Section 31.2.7 [Emergency Escape], page 376.

There may be times when you cannot quit. When Emacs is waiting for the operating system to do something, quitting is impossible unless special pains are taken for the particular system call within Emacs where the waiting occurs. We have done this for the system calls that users are likely to want to quit from, but it's possible you will find another. In one very common case—waiting for file input or output using NFS—Emacs itself knows how to quit, but most NFS implementations simply do not allow user programs to stop waiting for NFS when the NFS server is hung.

Aborting with C-] (abort-recursive-edit) is used to get out of a recursive editing level and cancel the command which invoked it. Quitting with C-g does not do this, and could not do this, because it is used to cancel a partially typed command *within* the recursive editing level. Both operations are useful. For example, if you are in a recursive edit and type C-u 8 to enter a numeric argument, you can cancel that argument with C-g and remain in the recursive edit.

The command ESC ESC ESC (keyboard-escape-quit) can either quit or abort. This key was defined because ESC is used to "get out" in many PC programs. It can cancel a prefix argument, clear a selected region, or get out of a Query Replace, like C-g. It can get out of the minibuffer or a recursive edit, like C-]. It can also get out of splitting the frame into multiple windows, like C-x 1. One thing it cannot do, however, is stop a command that is running. That's because it executes as an ordinary command, and Emacs doesn't notice it until it is ready for a command.

The command M-x top-level is equivalent to "enough" C-] commands to get you out of all the levels of recursive edits that you are in. C-] gets you out one level at a time, but M-x top-level goes out all levels at once. Both C-] and M-x top-level are like all other commands, and unlike C-g, in that they take effect only when Emacs is ready for a command. C-] is an ordinary key and has its meaning only because of its binding in the keymap. See Section 29.11 [Recursive Edit], page 339.

C-x u (undo) is not strictly speaking a way of canceling a command, but you can think of it as canceling a command that already finished executing. See Section 4.4 [Undo], page 30.

31.2 Dealing with Emacs Trouble

This section describes various conditions in which Emacs fails to work normally, and how to recognize them and correct them.

31.2.1 If DEL Fails to Delete

If you find that DEL enters Help like Control-h instead of deleting a character, your terminal is sending the wrong code for DEL. You can work around this problem by changing the keyboard translation table (see Section 30.5 [Keyboard Translations], page 365).

31.2.2 Recursive Editing Levels

Recursive editing levels are important and useful features of Emacs, but they can seem like malfunctions to the user who does not understand them.

If the mode line has square brackets '[...]' around the parentheses that contain the names of the major and minor modes, you have entered a recursive editing level. If you did not do this on purpose, or if you don't understand what that means, you should just get out of the recursive editing level. To do so, type M-x top-level. This is called getting back to top level. See Section 29.11 [Recursive Edit], page 339.

31.2.3 Garbage on the Screen

If the data on the screen looks wrong, the first thing to do is see whether the text is really wrong. Type C-l, to redisplay the entire screen. If the screen appears correct after this, the problem was entirely in the previous screen update. (Otherwise, see Section 31.2.4 [Text Garbled], page 375.)

Display updating problems often result from an incorrect termcap entry for the terminal you are using. The file 'etc/TERMS' in the Emacs distribution gives the fixes for known problems of this sort. 'INSTALL' contains general advice for these problems in one of its sections. Very likely there is simply insufficient padding for certain display operations. To investigate the possibility that you have this sort of problem, try Emacs on another terminal made by a different manufacturer. If problems happen frequently on one kind of terminal but not another kind, it is likely to be a bad termcap entry, though it could also be due to a bug in Emacs that appears for terminals that have or that lack specific features.

31.2.4 Garbage in the Text

If C-l shows that the text is wrong, try undoing the changes to it using C-x u until it gets back to a state you consider correct. Also try C-h l to find out what command you typed to produce the observed results.

If a large portion of text appears to be missing at the beginning or end of the buffer, check for the word 'Narrow' in the mode line. If it appears, the text you don't see is probably still present, but temporarily off-limits. To make it accessible again, type C-x n w. See Section 29.7 [Narrowing], page 335.

31.2.5 Spontaneous Entry to Incremental Search

If Emacs spontaneously displays 'I-search:' at the bottom of the screen, it means that the terminal is sending C-s and C-q according to the poorly designed xon/xoff "flow control" protocol.

If this happens to you, your best recourse is to put the terminal in a mode where it will not use flow control, or give it so much padding that it will never send a C-s. (One way to increase the amount of padding is to set the variable baud-rate to a larger value. Its value is the terminal output speed, measured in the conventional units of baud.)

If you don't succeed in turning off flow control, the next best thing is to tell Emacs to cope with it. To do this, call the function enable-flow-control.

Typically there are particular terminal types with which you must use flow control. You can conveniently ask for flow control on those terminal types only, using enable-flow-control-on. For example, if you find you must use flow control on VT-100 and H19 terminals, put the following in your '.emacs' file:

```
(enable-flow-control-on "vt100" "h19")
```

When flow control is enabled, you must type C-\ to get the effect of a C-s, and type C-^ to get the effect of a C-q. (These aliases work by means of keyboard translations; see Section 30.5 [Keyboard Translations], page 365.)

31.2.6 Running out of Memory

If you get the error message 'Virtual memory exceeded', save your modified buffers with C-x s. This method of saving them has the smallest need for additional memory. Emacs keeps a reserve of memory which it makes available when this error happens; that should be enough to enable C-x s to complete its work.

Once you have saved your modified buffers, you can exit this Emacs job and start another, or you can use M-x kill-some-buffers to free space in the current Emacs job. If you kill buffers containing a substantial amount of text, you can safely go on editing. Emacs refills its memory reserve automatically when it sees sufficient free space available, in case you run out of memory another time.

Do not use M-x buffer-menu to save or kill buffers when you run out of memory, because the buffer menu needs a fair amount memory itself, and the reserve supply may not be enough.

31.2.7 Emergency Escape

Because at times there have been bugs causing Emacs to loop without checking quit-flag, a special feature causes Emacs to be suspended immediately if you type a second C-g while the flag is already set, so you can always get out of GNU Emacs. Normally Emacs recognizes and clears quit-flag (and quits!) quickly enough to prevent this from happening.

When you resume Emacs after a suspension caused by multiple C-g, it asks two questions before going back to what it had been doing:

```
Auto-save? (y or n)
Abort (and dump core)? (y or n)
```

Answer each one with y or n followed by RET.

Saying y to 'Auto-save?' causes immediate auto-saving of all modified buffers in which auto-saving is enabled.

Saying y to 'Abort (and dump core)?' causes an illegal instruction to be executed, dumping core. This is to enable a wizard to figure out why Emacs was failing to quit in the first place. Execution does not continue after a core dump. If you answer n, execution does continue. With luck, GNU Emacs will ultimately check quit-flag and quit normally. If not, and you type another C-g, it is suspended again.

If Emacs is not really hung, just slow, you may invoke the double C-g feature without really meaning to. Then just resume and answer n to both questions, and you will arrive at your former state. Presumably the quit you requested will happen soon.

The double-C-g feature is turned off when Emacs is running under the X Window System, since you can use the window manager to kill Emacs or to create another window and run another program.

31.2.8 Help for Total Frustration

If using Emacs (or something else) becomes terribly frustrating and none of the techniques described above solve the problem, Emacs can still help you.

First, if the Emacs you are using is not responding to commands, type C-g C-g to get out of it and then start a new one.

Second, type M-x doctor RET.

The doctor will help you feel better. Each time you say something to the doctor, you must end it by typing RET RET. This lets the doctor know you are finished.

31.3 Reporting Bugs

Sometimes you will encounter a bug in Emacs. Although we cannot promise we can or will fix the bug, and we might not even agree that it is a bug, we want to hear about problems you encounter. Often we agree they are bugs and want to fix them.

To make it possible for us to fix a bug, you must report it. In order to do so effectively, you must know when and how to do it.

31.3.1 When Is There a Bug

If Emacs executes an illegal instruction, or dies with an operating system error message that indicates a problem in the program (as opposed to something like "disk full"), then it is certainly a bug.

If Emacs updates the display in a way that does not correspond to what is in the buffer, then it is certainly a bug. If a command seems to do the wrong thing but the problem corrects itself if you type C-l, it is a case of incorrect display updating.

Taking forever to complete a command can be a bug, but you must make certain that it was really Emacs's fault. Some commands simply take a long time. Type C-g and then C-h l to see whether the input Emacs received was what you intended to type; if the input was such that you *know* it should have been processed quickly, report a bug. If you don't know whether the command should take a long time, find out by looking in the manual or by asking for assistance.

If a command you are familiar with causes an Emacs error message in a case where its usual definition ought to be reasonable, it is probably a bug.

If a command does the wrong thing, that is a bug. But be sure you know for certain what it ought to have done. If you aren't familiar with the command, or don't know for certain how the command is supposed to work, then it might actually be working right. Rather than jumping to conclusions, show the problem to someone who knows for certain.

Finally, a command's intended definition may not be best for editing with. This is a very important sort of problem, but it is also a matter of judgment. Also, it is easy to come to such a conclusion out of ignorance of some of the existing features. It is probably best not to complain about such a problem until you have checked the documentation in the usual ways, feel confident that you understand it, and know for certain that what you want is not available. If you are not sure what the command is supposed to do after a careful reading of the manual, check the index and glossary for any terms that may be unclear.

If after careful rereading of the manual you still do not understand what the command should do, that indicates a bug in the manual, which you should report. The manual's job is to make everything clear to people who are not Emacs experts—including you. It is just as important to report documentation bugs as program bugs.

If the on-line documentation string of a function or variable disagrees with the manual, one of them must be wrong; that is a bug.

31.3.2 Understanding Bug Reporting

When you decide that there is a bug, it is important to report it and to report it in a way which is useful. What is most useful is an exact description of what commands you type, starting with the shell command to run Emacs, until the problem happens.

The most important principle in reporting a bug is to report *facts*, not hypotheses or categorizations. It is always easier to report the facts, but people seem to prefer to strain to posit explanations and report them instead. If the explanations are based on guesses about how Emacs is implemented, they will be useless; we will have to try to figure out what the facts must have been to lead to such speculations. Sometimes this is impossible. But in any case, it is unnecessary work for us.

For example, suppose that you type `C-x C-f /glorp/baz.ugh RET`, visiting a file which (you know) happens to be rather large, and Emacs prints out 'I feel pretty today'. The best way to report the bug is with a sentence like the preceding one, because it gives all the facts and nothing but the facts.

Do not assume that the problem is due to the size of the file and say, "When I visit a large file, Emacs prints out 'I feel pretty today'." This is what we mean by "guessing explanations". The problem is just as likely to be due to the fact that there is a 'z' in the file name. If this is so, then when we got your report, we would try out the problem with some "large file", probably with no 'z' in its name, and not find anything wrong. There is no way in the world that we could guess that we should try visiting a file with a 'z' in its name.

Alternatively, the problem might be due to the fact that the file starts with exactly 25 spaces. For this reason, you should make sure that you inform us of the exact contents of any file that is needed to reproduce the bug. What if the problem only occurs when you have typed the `C-x C-a` command previously? This is why we ask you to give the exact sequence of characters you typed since starting the Emacs session.

You should not even say "visit a file" instead of `C-x C-f` unless you *know* that it makes no difference which visiting command is used. Similarly, rather than saying "if I have three characters on the line," say "after I type RET A B C RET C-p," if that is the way you entered the text.

31.3.3 Checklist for Bug Reports

The best way to send a bug report is to mail it electronically to the Emacs maintainers at 'bug-gnu-emacs@prep.ai.mit.edu'. (If you want to suggest a change as an improvement, use the same address.)

If you'd like to read the bug reports, you can find them on the newsgroup 'gnu.emacs.bug'; keep in mind, however, that as a spectator you should not criticize anything about what you see there. The purpose of bug reports is to give information to the Emacs maintainers. Spectators are welcome only as long as they do not interfere with this. In particular, some bug reports contain large amounts of data; spectators should not complain about this.

Please do not post bug reports using netnews; mail is more reliable than netnews about reporting your correct address, which we may need in order to ask you for more information.

If you can't send electronic mail, then mail the bug report on paper or machine-readable media to this address:

GNU Emacs Bugs
Free Software Foundation
59 Temple Place, Suite 330
Boston, MA 02111-1307 USA

We do not promise to fix the bug; but if the bug is serious, or ugly, or easy to fix, chances are we will want to.

To enable maintainers to investigate a bug, your report should include all these things:

- The version number of Emacs. Without this, we won't know whether there is any point in looking for the bug in the current version of GNU Emacs.

  You can get the version number by typing `M-x emacs-version RET`. If that command does not work, you probably have something other than GNU Emacs, so you will have to report the bug somewhere else.

- The type of machine you are using, and the operating system name and version number. `M-x emacs-version RET` provides this information too. Copy its output from the '`*Messages*`' buffer, so that you get it all and get it accurately.

- The operands given to the `configure` command when Emacs was installed.

- A complete list of any modifications you have made to the Emacs source. (We may not have time to investigate the bug unless it happens in an unmodified Emacs. But if you've made modifications and you don't tell us, you are sending us on a wild goose chase.)

  Be precise about these changes. A description in English is not enough—send a context diff for them.

  Adding files of your own, or porting to another machine, is a modification of the source.

- Details of any other deviations from the standard procedure for installing GNU Emacs.

- The complete text of any files needed to reproduce the bug.

  If you can tell us a way to cause the problem without visiting any files, please do so. This makes it much easier to debug. If you do need files, make sure you arrange for us to see their exact contents. For example, it can often matter whether there are spaces at the ends of lines, or a newline after the last line in the buffer (nothing ought to care whether the last line is terminated, but try telling the bugs that).

- The precise commands we need to type to reproduce the bug.

  The easy way to record the input to Emacs precisely is to to write a dribble file. To start the file, execute the Lisp expression

  ```
  (open-dribble-file "~/dribble")
  ```

  using M-ESC or from the '*scratch*' buffer just after starting Emacs. From then on, Emacs copies all your input to the specified dribble file until the Emacs process is killed.

- For possible display bugs, the terminal type (the value of environment variable TERM), the complete termcap entry for the terminal from '/etc/termcap' (since that file is not identical on all machines), and the output that Emacs actually sent to the terminal.

  The way to collect the terminal output is to execute the Lisp expression

  ```
  (open-termscript "~/termscript")
  ```

  using M-ESC or from the '*scratch*' buffer just after starting Emacs. From then on, Emacs copies all terminal output to the specified termscript file as well, until the Emacs process is killed. If the problem happens when Emacs starts up, put this expression into your '.emacs' file so that the termscript file will be open when Emacs displays the screen for the first time.

  Be warned: it is often difficult, and sometimes impossible, to fix a terminal-dependent bug without access to a terminal of the type that stimulates the bug.

- A description of what behavior you observe that you believe is incorrect. For example, "The Emacs process gets a fatal signal," or, "The resulting text is as follows, which I think is wrong."

  Of course, if the bug is that Emacs gets a fatal signal, then one can't miss it. But if the bug is incorrect text, the maintainer might fail to notice what is wrong. Why leave it to chance?

  Even if the problem you experience is a fatal signal, you should still say so explicitly. Suppose something strange is going on, such as, your copy of the source is out of sync, or you have encountered a bug in the C library on your system. (This has happened!) Your copy might crash and the copy here might not. If you *said* to expect a crash, then when Emacs here fails to crash, we would know that the bug was not happening. If you don't say to expect a crash, then we would not know whether the bug was happening—we would not be able to draw any conclusion from our observations.

- If the manifestation of the bug is an Emacs error message, it is important to report the precise text of the error message, and a backtrace showing how the Lisp program in Emacs arrived at the error.

  To get the error message text accurately, copy it from the '*Messages*' buffer into the bug report. Copy all of it, not just part.

  To make a backtrace for the error, evaluate the Lisp expression (setq debug-on-error t) before the error happens (that is to say, you must execute that expression and then make the bug happen). This causes the error to run the Lisp debugger, which shows you a backtrace. Copy the text of the debugger's backtrace into the bug report.

  This use of the debugger is possible only if you know how to make the bug happen again. If you can't make it happen again, at least copy the whole error message.

- Check whether any programs you have loaded into the Lisp world, including your '.emacs' file, set any variables that may affect the functioning of Emacs. Also, see whether the problem happens in a freshly started Emacs without loading your '.emacs' file (start Emacs with the -q switch to prevent loading the init file.) If the problem does *not* occur then, you must report the precise contents of any programs that you must load into the Lisp world in order to cause the problem to occur.

- If the problem does depend on an init file or other Lisp programs that are not part of the standard Emacs system, then you should make sure it is not a bug in those programs by complaining to their maintainers first. After they verify that they are using Emacs in a way that is supposed to work, they should report the bug.

- If you wish to mention something in the GNU Emacs source, show the line of code with a few lines of context. Don't just give a line number.

  The line numbers in the development sources don't match those in your sources. It would take extra work for the maintainers to determine what code is in your version at a given line number, and we could not be certain.

- Additional information from a C debugger such as GDB might enable someone to find a problem on a machine which he does not have available. If you don't know how to use GDB, please read the GDB manual— it is not very long, and using GDB is easy. You can find the GDB distribution, including the GDB manual in online form, in most of the same places you can find the Emacs distribution.

  However, you need to think when you collect the additional information if you want it to show what causes the bug.

  For example, many people send just a backtrace, but that is not very useful by itself. A simple backtrace with arguments often conveys little about what is happening inside GNU Emacs, because most of the arguments listed in the backtrace are pointers to Lisp objects. The numeric values of these pointers have no significance whatever; all that matters is the contents of the objects they point to (and most of the contents are themselves pointers).

To provide useful information, you need to show the values of Lisp objects in Lisp notation. Do this for each variable which is a Lisp object, in several stack frames near the bottom of the stack. Look at the source to see which variables are Lisp objects, because the debugger thinks of them as integers.

To show a variable's value in Lisp syntax, first print its value, then use the user-defined GDB command `pr` to print the Lisp object in Lisp syntax. (If you must use another debugger, call the function `debug_print` with the object as an argument.) The `pr` command is defined by the file '.gdbinit' in the 'src' subdirectory, and it works only if you are debugging a running process (not with a core dump).

To make Lisp errors stop Emacs and return to GDB, put a breakpoint at `Fsignal`.

To find out which Lisp functions are running, using GDB, move up the stack, and each time you get to a frame for the function `Ffuncall`, type these GDB commands:

```
p *args
pr
```

To print the first argument that the function received, use these commands:

```
p args[1]
pr
```

You can print the other arguments likewise. The argument `nargs` of `Ffuncall` says how many arguments `Ffuncall` received; these include the Lisp function itself and the arguments for that function.

- If the symptom of the bug is that Emacs fails to respond, don't assume Emacs is "hung"—it may instead be in an infinite loop. To find out which, make the problem happen under GDB and stop Emacs once it is not responding. (If Emacs is using X Windows directly, you can stop Emacs by typing `C-c` at the GDB job.) Then try stepping with 'step'. If Emacs is hung, the 'step' command won't return. If it is looping, 'step' will return.

  If this shows Emacs is hung in a system call, stop it again and examine the arguments of the call. In your bug report, state exactly where in the source the system call is, and what the arguments are.

  If Emacs is in an infinite loop, please determine where the loop starts and ends. The easiest way to do this is to use the GDB command 'finish'. Each time you use it, Emacs resumes execution until it exits one stack frame. Keep typing 'finish' until it doesn't return—that means the infinite loop is in the stack frame which you just tried to finish.

Stop Emacs again, and use 'finish' repeatedly again until you get *back to* that frame. Then use 'next' to step through that frame. By stepping, you will see where the loop starts and ends. Also please examine the data being used in the loop and try to determine why the loop does not exit when it should. Include all of this information in your bug report.

Here are some things that are not necessary in a bug report:

- A description of the envelope of the bug—this is not necessary for a reproducible bug.

  Often people who encounter a bug spend a lot of time investigating which changes to the input file will make the bug go away and which changes will not affect it.

  This is often time consuming and not very useful, because the way we will find the bug is by running a single example under the debugger with breakpoints, not by pure deduction from a series of examples. You might as well save time by not searching for additional examples.

  Of course, if you can find a simpler example to report *instead* of the original one, that is a convenience. Errors in the output will be easier to spot, running under the debugger will take less time, etc.

  However, simplification is not vital; if you can't do this or don't have time to try, please report the bug with your original test case.

- A system call trace of Emacs execution.

  System call traces are very useful for certain special kinds of debugging, but in most cases they give little useful information. It is therefore strange that many people seem to think that *the* way to report information about a crash is to send a system call trace.

  In most programs, a backtrace is normally far, far more informative than a system call trace. Even in Emacs, a simple backtrace is generally more informative, though to give full information you should supplement the backtrace by displaying variable values and printing them as Lisp objects with pr (see above).

- A patch for the bug.

  A patch for the bug is useful if it is a good one. But don't omit the other information that a bug report needs, such as the test case, on the assumption that a patch is sufficient. We might see problems with your patch and decide to fix the problem another way, or we might not understand it at all. And if we can't understand what bug you are trying to fix, or why your patch should be an improvement, we mustn't install it.

- A guess about what the bug is or what it depends on.

  Such guesses are usually wrong. Even experts can't guess right about such things without first using the debugger to find the facts.

31.3.4 Sending Patches for GNU Emacs

If you would like to write bug fixes or improvements for GNU Emacs, that is very helpful. When you send your changes, please follow these guidelines to make it easy for the maintainers to use them. If you don't follow these guidelines, your information might still be useful, but using it will take extra work. Maintaining GNU Emacs is a lot of work in the best of circumstances, and we can't keep up unless you do your best to help.

- Send an explanation with your changes of what problem they fix or what improvement they bring about. For a bug fix, just include a copy of the bug report, and explain why the change fixes the bug.

  (Referring to a bug report is not as good as including it, because then we will have to look it up, and we have probably already deleted it if we've already fixed the bug.)

- Always include a proper bug report for the problem you think you have fixed. We need to convince ourselves that the change is right before installing it. Even if it is correct, we might have trouble understanding it if we don't have a way to reproduce the problem.

- Include all the comments that are appropriate to help people reading the source in the future understand why this change was needed.

- Don't mix together changes made for different reasons. Send them *individually*.

  If you make two changes for separate reasons, then we might not want to install them both. We might want to install just one. If you send them all jumbled together in a single set of diffs, we have to do extra work to disentangle them—to figure out which parts of the change serve which purpose. If we don't have time for this, we might have to ignore your changes entirely.

  If you send each change as soon as you have written it, with its own explanation, then two changes never get tangled up, and we can consider each one properly without any extra work to disentangle them.

- Send each change as soon as that change is finished. Sometimes people think they are helping us by accumulating many changes to send them all together. As explained above, this is absolutely the worst thing you could do.

  Since you should send each change separately, you might as well send it right away. That gives us the option of installing it immediately if it is important.

- Use 'diff -c' to make your diffs. Diffs without context are hard to install reliably. More than that, they are hard to study; we must always study a patch to decide whether we want to install it. Unidiff format is better than contextless diffs, but not as easy to read as '-c' format.

  If you have GNU diff, use 'diff -c -F'^[_a-zA-Z0-9$]+ *('' when making diffs of C code. This shows the name of the function that each change occurs in.

- Write the change log entries for your changes. This is both to save us the extra work of writing them, and to help explain your changes so we can understand them.

  The purpose of the change log is to show people where to find what was changed. So you need to be specific about what functions you changed; in large functions, it's often helpful to indicate where within the function the change was.

  On the other hand, once you have shown people where to find the change, you need not explain its purpose in the change log. Thus, if you add a new function, all you need to say about it is that it is new. If you feel that the purpose needs explaining, it probably does—but put the explanation in comments in the code. It will be more useful there.

  Please read the 'ChangeLog' files in the 'src' and 'lisp' directories to see what sorts of information to put in, and to learn the style that we use. If you would like your name to appear in the header line, showing who made the change, send us the header line. See Section 21.11 [Change Log], page 214.

- When you write the fix, keep in mind that we can't install a change that would break other systems. Please think about what effect your change will have if compiled on another type of system.

  Sometimes people send fixes that *might* be an improvement in general— but it is hard to be sure of this. It's hard to install such changes because we have to study them very carefully. Of course, a good explanation of the reasoning by which you concluded the change was correct can help convince us.

  The safest changes are changes to the configuration files for a particular machine. These are safe because they can't create new bugs on other machines.

  Please help us keep up with the workload by designing the patch in a form that is clearly safe to install.

31.4 How To Get Help with GNU Emacs

If you need help installing, using or changing GNU Emacs, there are two ways to find it:

- Send a message to the mailing list `help-gnu-emacs@prep.ai.mit.edu`, or post your request on newsgroup `gnu.emacs.help`. (This mailing list and newsgroup interconnect, so it does not matter which one you use.)

- Look in the service directory for someone who might help you for a fee. The service directory is found in the file named 'etc/SERVICE' in the Emacs distribution.

Appendix A Command Line Arguments

GNU Emacs supports command line arguments to request various actions when invoking Emacs. These are for compatibility with other editors and for sophisticated activities. We don't recommend using them for ordinary editing.

Arguments starting with '-' are *options*. Other arguments specify files to visit. Emacs visits the specified files while it starts up. The last file name on your command line becomes the current buffer; the other files are also present in other buffers.

You can use options to specify various other things, such as the size and position of the X window Emacs uses, its colors, and so on. A few options support advanced usage, such as running Lisp functions on files in batch mode. The sections of this chapter describe the available options, arranged according to their purpose.

There are two ways of writing options: the short forms that start with a single '-', and the long forms that start with '--'. For example, '-d' is a short form and '--display' is the corresponding long form.

The long forms with '--' are easier to remember, but longer to type. However, you don't have to spell out the whole option name; any unambiguous abbreviation is enough. When a long option takes an argument, you can use either a space or an equal sign to separate the option name and the argument. Thus, you can write either '--display sugar-bombs:0.0' or '--display=sugar-bombs:0.0'. We recommend an equal sign because it makes the relationship clearer, and the tables below always show an equal sign.

Most options specify how to initialize Emacs, or set parameters for the Emacs session. We call them *initial options*. A few options specify things to do: for example, load libraries, call functions, or exit Emacs. These are called *action options*. These and file names together are called *action arguments*. Emacs processes all the action arguments in the order they are written.

A.1 Action Arguments

Here is a table of the action arguments and options:

'*file*'   Visit *file* using `find-file`. See Section 14.2 [Visiting], page 104.

'+*linenum file*'
                  Visit *file* using `find-file`, then go to line number *linenum* in it.

'-l *file*'
'--load=*file*'

>Load a file *file* of Lisp code with the function `load`. See Section 22.4 [Lisp Libraries], page 246.

'-f *function*'
'--funcall=*function*'

>Call Lisp function *function* with no arguments.

'--insert=*file*'

>Insert the contents of *file* into the current buffer. This is like what `M-x insert-file` does. See Section 14.10 [Misc File Ops], page 131.

'--kill'   Exit from Emacs without asking for confirmation.

The init file can access the values of the action arguments as the elements of a list in the variable `command-line-args`. The init file can override the normal processing of the action arguments, or define new ones, by reading and setting this variable.

A.2 Initial Options

The initial options specify parameter for the Emacs session. This section describes the more general initial options; some other options specifically related to X Windows appear in the following sections.

Some initial options affect the loading of init files. The normal actions of Emacs are to first load 'site-start.el' if it exists, then your own init file '~/.emacs' if it exists, and finally 'default.el' if it exists; certain options prevent loading of some of these files or substitute other files for them.

'-t *device*'
'--terminal=*device*'

>Use *device* as the device for terminal input and output.

'-d *display*'
'--display=*display*'

>Use the X Window System and use the display named *display* to open the initial Emacs frame.

'-nw'
'--no-windows'

>Don't communicate directly with X, disregarding the DISPLAY environment variable even if it is set.

'-batch'

'--batch'   Run Emacs in *batch mode*, which means that the text being
             edited is not displayed and the standard terminal interrupt char-
             acters such as C-z and C-c continue to have their normal effect.
             Emacs in batch mode outputs to stderr only what would nor-
             mally be printed in the echo area under program control.

             Batch mode is used for running programs written in Emacs Lisp
             from shell scripts, makefiles, and so on. Normally the '-l' option
             or '-f' option will be used as well, to invoke a Lisp program to
             do the batch processing.

             '-batch' implies '-q' (do not load an init file). It also causes
             Emacs to kill itself after all command options have been pro-
             cessed. In addition, auto-saving is not done except in buffers for
             which it has been explicitly requested.

'-q'

'--no-init-file'
             Do not load your Emacs init file '~/.emacs', or 'default.el'
             either.

'--no-site-file'
             Do not load 'site-start.el'. The options '-q', '-u' and
             '-batch' have no effect on the loading of this file—this is the
             only option that blocks it.

'-u *user*'

'--user=*user*'
             Load *user*'s Emacs init file '~*user*/.emacs' instead of your own.

'--debug-init'
             Enable the Emacs Lisp debugger for errors in the init file.

A.3 Command Argument Example

Here is an example of using Emacs with arguments and options. It assumes you have a Lisp program file called 'hack-c.el' which, when loaded,
performs some useful operation on current buffer, expected to be a C program.

```
emacs -batch foo.c -l hack-c -f save-buffer >& log
```

This says to visit 'foo.c', load 'hack-c.el' (which makes changes in the
visited file), save 'foo.c' (note that save-buffer is the function that C-x
C-s is bound to), and then exit back to the shell (because of '-batch').
'-batch' also guarantees there will be no problem redirecting output to 'log',
because Emacs will not assume that it has a display terminal to work with.

A.4 Resuming Emacs with Arguments

You can specify action arguments for Emacs when you resume it after a suspension. To prepare for this, put the following code in your '.emacs' file (see Section 30.2.3 [Hooks], page 347):

```
(add-hook 'suspend-hook 'resume-suspend-hook)
```

As further preparation, you must execute the shell script 'emacs.csh' (if you use csh as your shell) or 'emacs.bash' (if you use bash as your shell). These scripts define an alias named `edit`, which will resume Emacs giving it new command line arguments such as files to visit.

Only action arguments work properly when you resume Emacs. Initial arguments are not recognized—it's too late to execute them anyway.

Note that resuming Emacs (with or without arguments) must be done from within the shell that is the parent of the Emacs job. This is why `edit` is an alias rather than a program or a shell script. It is not possible to implement a resumption command that could be run from other subjobs of the shell; no way to define a command that could be made the value of `EDITOR`, for example. Therefore, this feature does not take the place of the Emacs Server feature (see Section 29.3 [Emacs Server], page 330).

The aliases use the Emacs Server feature if you appear to have a server Emacs running. However, they cannot determine this with complete accuracy. They may think that a server is still running when in actuality you have killed that Emacs, because the file '/tmp/.esrv...' still exists. If this happens, find that file and delete it.

A.5 Environment Variables

This appendix describes how Emacs uses environment variables. An environment variable is a string passed from the operating system to Emacs, and the collection of environment variables is known as the environment. Environment variable names are case sensitive and it is conventional to use upper case letters only.

Because environment variables come from the operating system there is no general way to set them; it depends on the operating system and especially the shell that you are using. For example, here's how to set the environment variable `ORGANIZATION` to 'not very much' using bash:

```
export ORGANIZATION="not very much"
```

and here's how to do it in csh or tcsh:

```
setenv ORGANIZATION "not very much"
```

When Emacs is set-up to use the X windowing system, it inherits the use of a large number of environment variables from the X library. See the X documentation for more information.

A.5.1 General Variables

AUTHORCOPY

> The name of a file used to archive news articles posted with the GNUS package.

CDPATH   Used by the `cd` command.

DOMAINNAME

> The name of the internet domain that the machine running Emacs is located in. Used by the GNUS package.

EMACSDATA

> Used to initialize the variable `data-directory` used to locate the architecture-independent files that come with Emacs. Setting this variable overrides the setting in 'paths.h' when Emacs was built.

EMACSLOADPATH

> A colon-separated list of directories from which to load Emacs Lisp files. Setting this variable overrides the setting in 'paths.h' when Emacs was built.

EMACSLOCKDIR

> The directory that Emacs places lock files—files used to protect users from editing the same files simultaneously. Setting this variable overrides the setting in 'paths.h' when Emacs was built.

EMACSPATH

> The location of Emacs-specific binaries. Setting this variable overrides the setting in 'paths.h' when Emacs was built.

ESHELL   Used for shell-mode to override the SHELL environment variable.

HISTFILE   The name of the file that shell commands are saved in between logins. This variable defaults to '~/.history' if you use (t)csh as shell, to '~/.bash_history' if you use bash, to '~/.sh_history' if you use ksh, and to '~/.history' otherwise.

HOME   The location of the user's files in the directory tree; used for expansion of file names starting with a tilde ('~'). On MS-DOS, it defaults to the directory from which Emacs was started, with '/bin' removed from the end if it was present.

HOSTNAME   The name of the machine that Emacs is running on.

INCPATH   A colon-separated list of directories. Used by the `complete` package to search for files.

INFOPATH   A colon separated list of directories holding info files. Setting
            this variable overrides the setting in 'paths.el' when Emacs
            was built.

LOGNAME   The user's login name. See also USER.

MAIL   The name of the user's system mail box.

MAILRC   Name of file containing mail aliases. This defaults to
            '~/.mailrc'.

MH   Name of setup file for the mh system. This defaults to
            '~/.mh_profile'.

NAME   The real-world name of the user.

NNTPSERVER
            The name of the news server. Used by the mh and GNUS pack-
            ages.

ORGANIZATION
            The name of the organization to which you belong. Used for
            setting the 'Organization:' header in your posts from the GNUS
            package.

PATH   A colon-separated list of directories in which executables reside.
            (On MS-DOS, it is semicolon-separated instead.) This variable
            is used to set the Emacs Lisp variable exec-path which you
            should consider to use instead.

PWD   If set, this should be the default directory when Emacs was
            started.

REPLYTO   If set, this specifies an initial value for the variable mail-
            default-reply-to. See Section 25.2 [Mail Headers], page 262.

SAVEDIR   The name of a directory in which news articles are saved by
            default. Used by the GNUS package.

SHELL   The name of an interpreter used to parse and execute programs
            run from inside Emacs.

TERM   The name of the terminal that Emacs is running on. The vari-
            able must be set unless Emacs is run in batch mode. On MS-
            DOS, it defaults to 'internal', which specifies a built-in termi-
            nal emulation that handles the machine's own display.

TERMCAP   The name of the termcap library file describing how to program
            the terminal specified by the TERM variable. This defaults to
            '/etc/termcap'.

TMPDIR   Used by the Emerge package as a prefix for temporary files.

TZ   This specifies the current time zone and possibly also daylight savings information. On MS-DOS, the default is based on country code; see the file 'msdos.c' for details.

USER   The user's login name. See also LOGNAME. On MS-DOS, this defaults to 'root'.

VERSION_CONTROL
                Used to initialize the version-control variable (see Section 14.3.1.1 [Backup Names], page 109).

A.5.2 Misc Variables

These variables are used only on particular configurations:

COMSPEC   On MS-DOS, the name of the command interpreter to use. This is used to make a default value for the SHELL environment variable.

NAME   On MS-DOS, this variable defaults to the value of the USER variable.

TEMP
TMP   On MS-DOS, these specify the name of the directory for storing temporary files in.

WINDOW_GFX
                Used when initializing the Sun windows system.

A.6 Specifying the Display Name

The environment variable DISPLAY tells all X clients, including Emacs, where to display their windows. Its value is set up by default in ordinary circumstances, when you start an X server and run jobs locally. Occasionally you may need to specify the display yourself; for example, if you do a remote login and want to run a client program remotely, displaying on your local screen.

With Emacs, the main reason people change the default display is to let them log into another system, run Emacs on that system, but have the window displayed at their local terminal. You might need to use login to another system because the files you want to edit are there, or because the Emacs executable file you want to run is there.

The syntax of the DISPLAY environment variable is 'host:display.screen', where *host* is the host name of the X Window System server machine, *display* is an arbitrarily-assigned number that distinguishes your server (X terminal) from other servers on the same machine, and *screen* is a rarely-used field that allows an X server to control multiple terminal screens. The period and the *screen* field are optional. If included, *screen* is usually zero.

For example, if your host is named '`glasperle`' and your server is the first (or perhaps the only) server listed in the configuration, your `DISPLAY` is '`glasperle:0.0`'.

You can specify the display name explicitly when you run Emacs, either by changing the `DISPLAY` variable, or with the option '`-d` *display*' or '`--display=`*display*'. Here is an example:

```
emacs --display=glasperle:0 &
```

You can inhibit the direct use of X with the '`-nw`' option. This is also an initial option. It tells Emacs to display using ordinary ASCII on its controlling terminal.

Sometimes, security arrangements prevent a program on a remote system from displaying on your local system. In this case, trying to run Emacs produces messages like this:

```
Xlib:  connection to "glasperle:0.0" refused by server
```

You might be able to overcome this problem by using the `xhost` command on the local system to give permission for access from your remote machine.

A.7 Font Specification Options

By default, Emacs displays text in the font named '`9x15`', which makes each character nine pixels wide and fifteen pixels high. You can specify a different font on your command line through the option '`-fn` *name*'.

'`-fn` *name*'
> Use font *name* as the default font.

'`--font=`*name*'
> '`--font`' is an alias for '`-fn`'.

Under X, each font has a long name which consists of eleven words or numbers, separated by dashes. Some fonts also have shorter nicknames—'`9x15`' is such a nickname. You can use either kind of name. You can use wild card patterns for the font name; then Emacs lets X choose one of the fonts that match the pattern. Here is an example, which happens to specify the font whose nickname is '`6x13`':

```
emacs -fn "-misc-fixed-medium-r-semicondensed--13-*-*-*-c-60-iso8859-1" &
```

You can also specify the font in your '`.Xdefaults`' file:

```
emacs.font: -misc-fixed-medium-r-semicondensed--13-*-*-*-c-60-iso8859-1
```

A long font name has the following form:

> *-maker-family-weight-slant-widthtype-style...*
> *...-pixels-height-horiz-vert-spacing-width-charset*

family   This is the name of the font family–for example, 'courier'.

weight   This is normally 'bold', 'medium' or 'light'. Other words may appear here in some font names.

slant   This is 'r' (roman), 'i' (italic), 'o' (oblique), 'ri' (reverse italic), or 'ot' (other).

widthtype This is normally 'condensed', 'extended', 'semicondensed' or 'normal'. Other words may appear here in some font names.

style   This is an optional additional style name. Usually it is empty— most long font names have two hyphens in a row at this point.

pixels   This is the font height, in pixels.

height   This is the font height on the screen, measured in printer's points (approximately 1/72 of an inch), times ten. For a given vertical resolution, *height* and *pixels* are proportional; therefore, it is common to specify just one of them and use '*' for the other.

horiz   This is the horizontal resolution, in pixels per inch, of the screen for which the font is intended.

vert   This is the vertical resolution, in dots per inch, of the screen for which the font is intended. Normally the resolution of the fonts on your system is the right value for your screen; therefore, you normally specify '*' for this and *horiz*.

spacing   This is 'm' (monospace), 'p' (proportional) or 'c' (character cell). Emacs can use 'm' and 'c' fonts.

width   This is the average character width, in pixels, times ten.

charset   This is the character set that the font depicts. Normally you should use 'iso8859-1'.

Use only fixed width fonts—that is, fonts in which all characters have the same width; Emacs cannot yet handle display properly for variable width fonts. Any font with 'm' or 'c' in the *spacing* field of the long name is a fixed width font. Here's how to use the xlsfonts program to list all the fixed width fonts available on your system:

```
xlsfonts -fn '*x*'
xlsfonts -fn '*-*-*-*-*-*-*-*-*-*-*-m*'
xlsfonts -fn '*-*-*-*-*-*-*-*-*-*-*-c*'
```

To see what a particular font looks like, use the xfd command. For example:

```
xfd -fn 6x13
```

displays the entire font '6x13'.

While running Emacs, you can set the font of the current frame (see Section 17.9 [Frame Parameters], page 153) or for a specific kind of text (see Section 17.12 [Faces], page 156).

A.8 Window Color Options

On a color display, you can specify which color to use for various parts of the Emacs display. To find out what colors are available on your system, look at the '/usr/lib/X11/rgb.txt' file. If you do not specify colors, the default for the background is white and the default for all other colors is black. On a monochrome display, the foreground is black, the background is white, and the border is gray if the display supports that.

Here is a list of the options for specifying colors:

'-fg *color*'
'--foreground-color=*color*'
>   Specify the foreground color.

'-bg *color*'
'--background-color=*color*'
>   Specify the background color.

'-bd *color*'
'--border-color=*color*'
>   Specify the color of the border of the X window.

'-cr *color*'
'--cursor-color=*color*'
>   Specify the color of the Emacs cursor which indicates where
>   point is.

'-ms *color*'
'--mouse-color=*color*'
>   Specify the color for the mouse cursor when the mouse is in the
>   Emacs window.

'-r'
'--reverse-video'
>   Reverse video—swap the foreground and background colors.

For example, to use a coral mouse cursor and a slate blue text cursor, enter:

```
emacs -ms coral -cr 'slate blue' &
```

You can reverse the foreground and background colors through the '-r' option or with the X resource 'reverseVideo'.

A.9 Options for Window Geometry

The '-geometry' option controls the size and position of the initial Emacs frame. Here is the format for specifying the window geometry:

'**-g** *widthxheight{+-}xoffset{+-}yoffset*'
> Specify window size *width* and *height* (measured in character columns and lines), and positions *xoffset* and *yoffset* (measured in pixels).

'**--geometry=***widthxheight{+-}xoffset{+-}yoffset*'
> This is another way of writing the same thing.

{+-} means either a plus sign or a minus sign. A plus sign before *xoffset* means it is the distance from the left side of the screen; a minus sign means it counts from the right side. A plus sign before *yoffset* means it is the distance from the top of the screen, and a minus sign there indicates the distance from the bottom. The values *xoffset* and *yoffset* may themselves be positive or negative, but that doesn't change their meaning, only their direction.

Emacs uses the same units as xterm does to interpret the geometry. The *width* and *height* are measured in characters, so a large font creates a larger frame than a small font. The *xoffset* and *yoffset* are measured in pixels.

Since the mode line and the echo area occupy the last 2 lines of the frame, the height of the initial text window is 2 less than the height specified in your geometry. In non-X-toolkit versions of Emacs, the menu bar also takes one line of the specified number.

You do not have to specify all of the fields in the geometry specification.

If you omit both *xoffset* and *yoffset*, the window manager decides where to put the Emacs frame, possibly by letting you place it with the mouse. For example, '164x55' specifies a window 164 columns wide, enough for two ordinary width windows side by side, and 55 lines tall.

The default width for Emacs is 80 characters and the default height is 40 lines. You can omit either the width or the height or both. If you start the geometry with an integer, Emacs interprets it as the width. If you start with an 'x' followed by an integer, Emacs interprets it as the height. Thus, '81' specifies just the width; 'x45' specifies just the height.

If you start with '+' or '-', that introduces an offset, which means both sizes are omitted. Thus, '-3' specifies the *xoffset* only. (If you give just one offset, it is always *xoffset*.) '+3-3' specifies both the *xoffset* and the *yoffset*, placing the frame near the bottom left of the screen.

You can specify a default for any or all of the fields in '.Xdefaults' file, and then override selected fields with a '--geometry' option.

A.10 Internal and External Borders

An Emacs frame has an internal border and an external border. The internal border is an extra strip of the background color around all four edges of the frame. Emacs itself adds the internal border. The external border is added by the window manager outside the internal border; it may contain various boxes you can click on to move or iconify the window.

'-ib *width*'

'--internal-border=*width*'
>   Specify *width* as the width of the internal border.

'-bw *width*'

'--border-width=*width*'
>   Specify *width* as the width of the main border.

When you specify the size of the frame, that does not count the borders. The frame's position is measured from the outside edge of the external border.

Use the '-ib *n*' option to specify an internal border *n* pixels wide. The default is 1. Use '-bw *n*' to specify the width of the external border (though the window manager may not pay attention to what you specify). The default width of the external border is 2.

A.11 Icons

Most window managers allow the user to "iconify" a frame, removing it from sight, and leaving a small, distinctive "icon" window in its place. Clicking on the icon window makes the frame itself appear again. If you have many clients running at once, you can avoid cluttering up the screen by iconifying most of the clients.

'-i'

'--icon-type'
>   Use a picture of a gnu as the Emacs icon.

'-iconic'

'--iconic'
>   Start Emacs in iconified state.

The '-i' or '--icon-type' option tells Emacs to use an icon window containing a picture of the GNU gnu. If omitted, Emacs lets the window manager choose what sort of icon to use—usually just a small rectangle containing the frame's title.

The '-iconic' option tells Emacs to begin running as an icon, rather than opening a frame right away. In this situation, the icon window provides only indication that Emacs has started; the usual text frame doesn't appear until you deiconify it.

A.12 X Resources

Programs running under the X Window System organize their user options under a hierarchy of classes and resources. You can specify default values for these options in your X resources file, usually named '`~/.Xdefaults`'.

Each line in the file specifies a value for one option or for a collection of related options, for one program or for several programs (optionally even for all programs).

Programs define named resources with particular meanings. They also define how to group resources into named classes. For instance, in Emacs, the '`internalBorder`' resource controls the width of the internal border, and the '`borderWidth`' resource controls the width of the external border. Both of these resources are part of the '`BorderWidth`' class. Case distinctions are significant in these names.

In '`~/.Xdefaults`', you can specify a value for a single resource on one line, like this:

```
emacs.borderWidth: 2
```

Or you can use a class name to specify the same value for all resources in that class. Here's an example:

```
emacs.BorderWidth: 2
```

If you specify a value for a class, it becomes the default for all resources in that class. You can specify values for individual resources as well; these override the class value, for those particular resources. Thus, this example specifies 2 as the default width for all borders, but overrides this value with 4 for the external border:

```
emacs.Borderwidth: 2
emacs.borderwidth: 4
```

The order in which the lines appear in the file does not matter. Also, command-line options always override the X resources file.

The string '`emacs`' in the examples above is also a resource name. It actually represents the name of the executable file that you invoke to run Emacs. If Emacs is installed under a different name, it looks for resources under that name instead of '`emacs`'.

When Emacs creates a new frame, it may or may not have a specified title. The frame title, if specified, appears in window decorations and icons as the name of the frame. It is also used (instead of the Emacs executable's name) to look up all the resources for that frame. The option '`-name`' specifies a frame title for the initial frame. Subsequent frames normally have no specified frame title, but Lisp programs can specify a title when they create frames.

'-name *name*'
'--name=*name*'
>   Use *name* as the title of the initial frame.

'-xrm *resource-values*'
'--xrm=*resource-values*'
>   Specify X resource values for this Emacs job (see below).

For consistency, '-name' also specifies the name to use for other resource values that do not belong to any particular frame.

The resources that name Emacs invocations also belong to a class; its name is 'Emacs'. If you write 'Emacs' instead of 'emacs', the resource applies to all frames in all Emacs jobs, regardless of frame titles and regardless of the name of the executable file. Here is an example:

```
Emacs.BorderWidth: 2
Emacs.borderWidth: 4
```

You can specify a string of additional resource values for Emacs to use with the command line option '-xrm *resources*'. The text *resources* should have the same format that you would use inside a file of X resources. To include multiple resource specifications in *data*, put a newline between them, just as you would in a file. You can also use '#include "*filename*"' to include a file full of resource specifications. Resource values specified with '-xrm' take precedence over all other resource specifications.

The following table lists the resource names that designate options for Emacs, each with the class that it belongs to:

background (class Background)
>   Background color name.

bitmapIcon (class BitmapIcon)
>   Use a bitmap icon (a picture of a gnu) if 'on', let the window manager choose an icon if 'off'.

borderColor (class BorderColor)
>   Color name for the external border.

borderWidth (class BorderWidth)
>   Width in pixels of the external border.

cursorColor (class Foreground)
>   Color name for text cursor (point).

font (class Font)
>   Font name for text.

foreground (class Foreground)
>   Color name for text.

geometry (class Geometry)
> Window size and position. Be careful not to specify this resource as 'emacs*geometry', because that may affect individual menus as well as the Emacs frame itself. If this resource specifies a position, that affects only the initial Emacs frame; but the size (if specified) applies to all frames.

iconName (class Title)
> Name to display in the icon.

internalBorder (class BorderWidth)
> Width in pixels of the internal border.

menuBar (class MenuBar)
> Give frames menu bars if 'on'; don't have menu bars if 'off'.

paneFont (class Font)
> Font name for menu pane titles, in non-toolkit versions of Emacs.

pointerColor (class Foreground)
> Color of the mouse cursor.

reverseVideo (class ReverseVideo)
> Switch foreground and background default colors if 'on', use colors as specified if 'off'.

verticalScrollBars (class ScrollBars)
> Give frames scroll bars if 'on'; don't have scroll bars if 'off'.

selectionFont (class Font)
> Font name for pop-up menu items, in non-toolkit versions of Emacs. (For toolkit versions, see Section A.13 [Lucid Resources], page 404, also see Section A.14 [Motif Resources], page 404.)

title (class Title)
> Name to display in the title bar of the initial Emacs frame.

Here are resources for controlling the appearance of particular faces (see Section 17.12 [Faces], page 156):

face.attributeFont
> Font for face *face*.

face.attributeForeground
> Foreground color for face *face*.

face.attributeBackground
> Background color for face *face*.

face.attributeUnderline
> Underline flag for face *face*.

A.13 Lucid Menu X Resources

If the Emacs installed at your site was built to use the X toolkit with the Lucid menu widgets, then the menu bar is a separate widget and has its own resources. The resource names contain 'pane.menubar' (following, as always, the name of the Emacs invocation or 'Emacs' which stands for all Emacs invocations). Specify them like this:

        Emacs.pane.menubar.*resource*:   *value*

For example, to specify the font '8x16' for the menu bar items, write this:

        Emacs.pane.menubar.font: 8x16

Resources for toolkit popup menus have 'menu*', in like fashion. For example, to specify the font '8x16' for the popup menu items, write this:

        Emacs.menu*.font: 8x16

Experience shows that on some systems you may need to add 'shell.' before the 'pane.menubar' or 'menu*'.

Here is a list of the specific resources for menu bars and popup menus:

font   Font for menu item text.

foreground
                Color of the foreground.

background
                Color of the background.

buttonForeground
                In the menu bar, the color of the foreground for a selected item.

horizontalSpacing
                Horizontal spacing in pixels between items. Default is 3.

verticalSpacing
                Vertical spacing in pixels between items. Default is 1.

arrowSpacing
                Horizontal spacing between the arrow (which indicates a submenu) and the associated text. Default is 10.

shadowThickness
                Thickness of shadow line around the widget.

A.14 Motif Menu X Resources

If the Emacs installed at your site was built to use the X toolkit with the Motif widgets, then the menu bar is a separate widget and has its own resources. The resource names contain '**pane.menubar**' (following, as always, the name of the Emacs invocation or 'Emacs' which stands for all Emacs invocations). Specify them like this:

    Emacs.pane.menubar.*subwidget*.*resource*:   *value*

Each individual string in the menu bar is a subwidget; the subwidget's name is the same as the menu item string. For example, the word 'Files' in the menu bar is part of a subwidget named 'emacs.pane.menubar.Files'. Most likely, you want to specify the same resources for the whole menu bar. To do this, use '*' instead of a specific subwidget name. For example, to specify the font '8x16' for the menu bar items, write this:

    Emacs.pane.menubar.*.fontList: 8x16

This also specifies the resource value for submenus.

Each item in a submenu in the menu bar also has its own name for X resources; for example, the 'Files' submenu has an item named 'Save Buffer'. A resource specification for a submenu item looks like this:

    Emacs.pane.menubar.popup_*.*menu*.*item*.*resource*: *value*

For example, here's how to specify the font for the 'Save Buffer' item:

    Emacs.pane.menubar.popup_*.Files.Save Buffer.fontList: 8x16

For an item in a second-level submenu, such as 'Check Message' under 'Spell' under 'Edit', the resource fits this template:

    Emacs.pane.menubar.popup_*.popup_*.*menu*.*resource*: *value*

For example,

    Emacs.pane.menubar.popup_*.popup_*.Spell.Check Message: *value*

It's impossible to specify a resource for all the menu bar items without also specifying it for the submenus as well. So if you want the submenu items to look different from the menu bar itself, you must ask for that in two steps. First, specify the resource for all of them; then, override the value for submenus alone. Here is an example:

    Emacs.pane.menubar.*.fontList: 8x16
    Emacs.pane.menubar.popup_*.fontList: 8x16

For toolkit popup menus, use 'menu*' instead of 'pane.menubar'. For example, to specify the font '8x16' for the popup menu items, write this:

    Emacs.menu*.fontList: 8x16

Here is a list of the specific resources for menu bars and popup menus:

armColor   The color to show in an armed button.

fontList   The font to use.

```
marginBottom
marginHeight
marginLeft
marginRight
marginTop
marginWidth
```
Amount of space to leave around the item, within the border.

`borderWidth`

The width of border around the menu item, on all sides.

`shadowThickness`

The width of the border shadow.

`bottomShadowColor`

The color for the border shadow, on the bottom and the right.

`topShadowColor`

The color for the border shadow, on the bottom and the right.

Appendix B Emacs 19.28 Antinews

For those users who live backwards in time, here is information about downgrading to Emacs version 19.28. We hope you will enjoy the greater simplicity that results from the absence of certain Emacs 19.29 features.

- This version doesn't support Windows NT, or the DEC Alpha.

- There is no support for editing formatted text. The text formatter TEX does a much better job of formatting than any formatted text editor; we recommend you learn to use it.

- C-Mouse-2 now runs the menu for setting the default font.

- F1 is no longer an alias for the Help key; you must actually type C-h if you want help.

- Integers and buffer sizes are limited to 24 bits on most machines. But as memory gets more expensive, you won't want to edit such large files any more.

- There are no indirect buffers, so you can only display one view of an outline. Meanwhile, the prefix key for Outline minor mode is now C-c C-o.

- When you are in Transient Mark mode, incremental search always deactivates the mark.

- Dynamic abbrev completion has been eliminated in 19.28, and some of the other dynamic abbrev customization features are also gone.

- In Dired, Occur mode, Compilation mode, and other such modes, you must use C-c C-c to select the item point is on. RET won't do it.

- M-x buffer-menu now displays the menu buffer in another window.

- The VC (version control) package no longer supports CVS or selecting branches other than the principal branch.

- There is no recover-session command; if Emacs crashes, you simply have to remember which files you were editing before the crash, and use recover-file on the individual files.

- In Emacs Lisp mode, C-M-x now lets defvar operate as it usually does— setting the value of the variable only if it has no value yet. Use ESC ESC to evaluate a Lisp expression, instead of M-:.

- GNU-standard long option names are not supported. (Real hackers prefer the shorter single-dash names, to save typing.) All the initial options must come before all the action options, and whatever initial options you use must appear in this order: '-t', '-d', '-nw', '-batch', '-q' or '-no-init-file', '-no-site-file', '-u' or '-user', '-debug-init'.

Appendix C MS-DOS Issues

This section briefly describes the peculiarities of using Emacs under the MS-DOS "operating system" (also known as "MS-DOG").

MS-DOS normally uses a backslash, '\', to separate name units within a file name, instead of the slash used on other systems. Emacs on MS-DOS permits use of either slash or backslash.

On MS-DOS, file names are case-insensitive and limited to eight characters, plus optionally a period and three more characters. Emacs does not know about this limitation; it is up to you to specify valid file names. Excess characters before or after the period are generally ignored.

Display on MS-DOS does not support menus or multiple fonts. Support for multiple faces that specify different colors may be added later.

Emacs on MS-DOS does support a mouse (on the default terminal only). The mouse commands work as documented, aside from those that try to use menus. See Section 17.1 [Mouse Commands], page 147.

Because MS-DOS is a single-process "operating system", asynchronous subprocesses are not available. In particular, Shell mode and its derivatives do not work. Compilation under Emacs with M-x compile does work, but the compiler runs synchronously; you cannot do any more editing until the compilation finishes.

When you run a subprocess synchronously on MS-DOS, make sure the program terminates and does not try to read keyboard input. If the program does not terminate on its own, you will be unable to terminate it, because MS-DOS provides no general way to terminate a process.

The GNU Manifesto

The GNU Manifesto which appears below was written by Richard Stallman at the beginning of the GNU project, to ask for participation and support. For the first few years, it was updated in minor ways to account for developments, but now it seems best to leave it unchanged as most people have seen it.

Since that time, we have learned about certain common misunderstandings that different wording could help avoid. Footnotes added in 1993 help clarify these points.

For up-to-date information about the available GNU software, please see the latest issue of the GNU's Bulletin. The list is much too long to include here.

What's GNU? Gnu's Not Unix!

GNU, which stands for Gnu's Not Unix, is the name for the complete Unix-compatible software system which I am writing so that I can give it away free to everyone who can use it.[1] Several other volunteers are helping me. Contributions of time, money, programs and equipment are greatly needed.

So far we have an Emacs text editor with Lisp for writing editor commands, a source level debugger, a yacc-compatible parser generator, a linker, and around 35 utilities. A shell (command interpreter) is nearly completed. A new portable optimizing C compiler has compiled itself and may be released this year. An initial kernel exists but many more features are needed to emulate Unix. When the kernel and compiler are finished, it will be possible to distribute a GNU system suitable for program development. We will use TeX as our text formatter, but an nroff is being worked on. We will

---

[1] The wording here was careless. The intention was that nobody would have to pay for *permission* to use the GNU system. But the words don't make this clear, and people often interpret them as saying that copies of GNU should always be distributed at little or no charge. That was never the intent; later on, the manifesto mentions the possibility of companies providing the service of distribution for a profit. Subsequently I have learned to distinguish carefully between "free" in the sense of freedom and "free" in the sense of price. Free software is software that users have the freedom to distribute and change. Some users may obtain copies at no charge, while others pay to obtain copies—and if the funds help support improving the software, so much the better. The important thing is that everyone who has a copy has the freedom to cooperate with others in using it.

use the free, portable X window system as well. After this we will add a
portable Common Lisp, an Empire game, a spreadsheet, and hundreds of
other things, plus on-line documentation. We hope to supply, eventually,
everything useful that normally comes with a Unix system, and more.

GNU will be able to run Unix programs, but will not be identical to
Unix. We will make all improvements that are convenient, based on our experience with other operating systems. In particular, we plan to have longer
file names, file version numbers, a crashproof file system, file name completion perhaps, terminal-independent display support, and perhaps eventually
a Lisp-based window system through which several Lisp programs and ordinary Unix programs can share a screen. Both C and Lisp will be available
as system programming languages. We will try to support UUCP, MIT
Chaosnet, and Internet protocols for communication.

GNU is aimed initially at machines in the 68000/16000 class with virtual
memory, because they are the easiest machines to make it run on. The extra
effort to make it run on smaller machines will be left to someone who wants
to use it on them.

To avoid horrible confusion, please pronounce the 'G' in the word 'GNU'
when it is the name of this project.

Why I Must Write GNU

I consider that the golden rule requires that if I like a program I must
share it with other people who like it. Software sellers want to divide the
users and conquer them, making each user agree not to share with others. I
refuse to break solidarity with other users in this way. I cannot in good con-
science sign a nondisclosure agreement or a software license agreement. For
years I worked within the Artificial Intelligence Lab to resist such tendencies
and other inhospitalities, but eventually they had gone too far: I could not
remain in an institution where such things are done for me against my will.

So that I can continue to use computers without dishonor, I have decided
to put together a sufficient body of free software so that I will be able to get
along without any software that is not free. I have resigned from the AI lab
to deny MIT any legal excuse to prevent me from giving GNU away.

Why GNU Will Be Compatible with Unix

Unix is not my ideal system, but it is not too bad. The essential features
of Unix seem to be good ones, and I think I can fill in what Unix lacks without
spoiling them. And a system compatible with Unix would be convenient for
many other people to adopt.

How GNU Will Be Available

GNU is not in the public domain. Everyone will be permitted to modify and redistribute GNU, but no distributor will be allowed to restrict its further redistribution. That is to say, proprietary modifications will not be allowed. I want to make sure that all versions of GNU remain free.

Why Many Other Programmers Want to Help

I have found many other programmers who are excited about GNU and want to help.

Many programmers are unhappy about the commercialization of system software. It may enable them to make more money, but it requires them to feel in conflict with other programmers in general rather than feel as comrades. The fundamental act of friendship among programmers is the sharing of programs; marketing arrangements now typically used essentially forbid programmers to treat others as friends. The purchaser of software must choose between friendship and obeying the law. Naturally, many decide that friendship is more important. But those who believe in law often do not feel at ease with either choice. They become cynical and think that programming is just a way of making money.

By working on and using GNU rather than proprietary programs, we can be hospitable to everyone and obey the law. In addition, GNU serves as an example to inspire and a banner to rally others to join us in sharing. This can give us a feeling of harmony which is impossible if we use software that is not free. For about half the programmers I talk to, this is an important happiness that money cannot replace.

How You Can Contribute

I am asking computer manufacturers for donations of machines and money. I'm asking individuals for donations of programs and work.

One consequence you can expect if you donate machines is that GNU will run on them at an early date. The machines should be complete, ready to use systems, approved for use in a residential area, and not in need of sophisticated cooling or power.

I have found very many programmers eager to contribute part-time work for GNU. For most projects, such part-time distributed work would be very hard to coordinate; the independently-written parts would not work together. But for the particular task of replacing Unix, this problem is absent. A complete Unix system contains hundreds of utility programs, each of which is documented separately. Most interface specifications are fixed by Unix compatibility. If each contributor can write a compatible replacement for a single Unix utility, and make it work properly in place of the original on a Unix system, then these utilities will work right when put together. Even allowing for Murphy to create a few unexpected problems, assembling these components will be a feasible task. (The kernel will require closer communication and will be worked on by a small, tight group.)

If I get donations of money, I may be able to hire a few people full or part time. The salary won't be high by programmers' standards, but I'm looking for people for whom building community spirit is as important as making money. I view this as a way of enabling dedicated people to devote their full energies to working on GNU by sparing them the need to make a living in another way.

Why All Computer Users Will Benefit

Once GNU is written, everyone will be able to obtain good system software free, just like air.[2]

This means much more than just saving everyone the price of a Unix license. It means that much wasteful duplication of system programming effort will be avoided. This effort can go instead into advancing the state of the art.

Complete system sources will be available to everyone. As a result, a user who needs changes in the system will always be free to make them himself, or hire any available programmer or company to make them for him. Users will no longer be at the mercy of one programmer or company which owns the sources and is in sole position to make changes.

Schools will be able to provide a much more educational environment by encouraging all students to study and improve the system code. Harvard's computer lab used to have the policy that no program could be installed on the system if its sources were not on public display, and upheld it by actually refusing to install certain programs. I was very much inspired by this.

Finally, the overhead of considering who owns the system software and what one is or is not entitled to do with it will be lifted.

Arrangements to make people pay for using a program, including licensing of copies, always incur a tremendous cost to society through the cumbersome mechanisms necessary to figure out how much (that is, which programs) a person must pay for. And only a police state can force everyone to obey them. Consider a space station where air must be manufactured at great cost: charging each breather per liter of air may be fair, but wearing the

---

[2] This is another place I failed to distinguish carefully between the two different meanings of "free". The statement as it stands is not false—you can get copies of GNU software at no charge, from your friends or over the net. But it does suggest the wrong idea.

metered gas mask all day and all night is intolerable even if everyone can afford to pay the air bill. And the TV cameras everywhere to see if you ever take the mask off are outrageous. It's better to support the air plant with a head tax and chuck the masks.

Copying all or parts of a program is as natural to a programmer as breathing, and as productive. It ought to be as free.

Some Easily Rebutted Objections to GNU's Goals

"Nobody will use it if it is free, because that means they can't rely on any support."

"You have to charge for the program to pay for providing the support."

If people would rather pay for GNU plus service than get GNU free without service, a company to provide just service to people who have obtained GNU free ought to be profitable.[3]

We must distinguish between support in the form of real programming work and mere handholding. The former is something one cannot rely on from a software vendor. If your problem is not shared by enough people, the vendor will tell you to get lost.

If your business needs to be able to rely on support, the only way is to have all the necessary sources and tools. Then you can hire any available person to fix your problem; you are not at the mercy of any individual. With Unix, the price of sources puts this out of consideration for most businesses. With GNU this will be easy. It is still possible for there to be no available competent person, but this problem cannot be blamed on distribution arrangements. GNU does not eliminate all the world's problems, only some of them.

Meanwhile, the users who know nothing about computers need handholding: doing things for them which they could easily do themselves but don't know how.

Such services could be provided by companies that sell just hand-holding and repair service. If it is true that users would rather spend money and get a product with service, they will also be willing to buy the service having got the product free. The service companies will compete in quality and price; users will not be tied to any particular one. Meanwhile, those of us who don't need the service should be able to use the program without paying for the service.

"You cannot reach many people without advertising, and you must charge for the program to support that."

"It's no use advertising a program people can get free."

---

[3] Several such companies now exist.

There are various forms of free or very cheap publicity that can be used to inform numbers of computer users about something like GNU. But it may be true that one can reach more microcomputer users with advertising. If this is really so, a business which advertises the service of copying and mailing GNU for a fee ought to be successful enough to pay for its advertising and more. This way, only the users who benefit from the advertising pay for it.

On the other hand, if many people get GNU from their friends, and such companies don't succeed, this will show that advertising was not really necessary to spread GNU. Why is it that free market advocates don't want to let the free market decide this?[4]

"My company needs a proprietary operating system to get a competitive edge."

GNU will remove operating system software from the realm of competition. You will not be able to get an edge in this area, but neither will your competitors be able to get an edge over you. You and they will compete in other areas, while benefiting mutually in this one. If your business is selling an operating system, you will not like GNU, but that's tough on you. If your business is something else, GNU can save you from being pushed into the expensive business of selling operating systems.

I would like to see GNU development supported by gifts from many manufacturers and users, reducing the cost to each.[5]

"Don't programmers deserve a reward for their creativity?"

If anything deserves a reward, it is social contribution. Creativity can be a social contribution, but only in so far as society is free to use the results. If programmers deserve to be rewarded for creating innovative programs, by the same token they deserve to be punished if they restrict the use of these programs.

"Shouldn't a programmer be able to ask for a reward for his creativity?"

There is nothing wrong with wanting pay for work, or seeking to maximize one's income, as long as one does not use means that are destructive. But the means customary in the field of software today are based on destruction.

---

[4] The Free Software Foundation raises most of its funds from a distribution service, although it is a charity rather than a company. If *no one* chooses to obtain copies by ordering the from the FSF, it will be unable to do its work. But this does not mean that proprietary restrictions are justified to force every user to pay. If a small fraction of all the users order copies from the FSF, that is sufficient to keep the FSF afloat. So we ask users to choose to support us in this way. Have you done your part?

[5] A group of computer companies recently pooled funds to support maintenance of the GNU C Compiler.

Extracting money from users of a program by restricting their use of it is destructive because the restrictions reduce the amount and the ways that the program can be used. This reduces the amount of wealth that humanity derives from the program. When there is a deliberate choice to restrict, the harmful consequences are deliberate destruction.

The reason a good citizen does not use such destructive means to become wealthier is that, if everyone did so, we would all become poorer from the mutual destructiveness. This is Kantian ethics; or, the Golden Rule. Since I do not like the consequences that result if everyone hoards information, I am required to consider it wrong for one to do so. Specifically, the desire to be rewarded for one's creativity does not justify depriving the world in general of all or part of that creativity.

"Won't programmers starve?"

I could answer that nobody is forced to be a programmer. Most of us cannot manage to get any money for standing on the street and making faces. But we are not, as a result, condemned to spend our lives standing on the street making faces, and starving. We do something else.

But that is the wrong answer because it accepts the questioner's implicit assumption: that without ownership of software, programmers cannot possibly be paid a cent. Supposedly it is all or nothing.

The real reason programmers will not starve is that it will still be possible for them to get paid for programming; just not paid as much as now.

Restricting copying is not the only basis for business in software. It is the most common basis because it brings in the most money. If it were prohibited, or rejected by the customer, software business would move to other bases of organization which are now used less often. There are always numerous ways to organize any kind of business.

Probably programming will not be as lucrative on the new basis as it is now. But that is not an argument against the change. It is not considered an injustice that sales clerks make the salaries that they now do. If programmers made the same, that would not be an injustice either. (In practice they would still make considerably more than that.)

"Don't people have a right to control how their creativity is used?"

"Control over the use of one's ideas" really constitutes control over other people's lives; and it is usually used to make their lives more difficult.

People who have studied the issue of intellectual property rights carefully (such as lawyers) say that there is no intrinsic right to intellectual property. The kinds of supposed intellectual property rights that the government recognizes were created by specific acts of legislation for specific purposes.

For example, the patent system was established to encourage inventors to disclose the details of their inventions. Its purpose was to help society rather than to help inventors. At the time, the life span of 17 years for a patent was short compared with the rate of advance of the state of the art. Since patents are an issue only among manufacturers, for whom the cost and effort of a license agreement are small compared with setting up production, the patents often do not do much harm. They do not obstruct most individuals who use patented products.

The idea of copyright did not exist in ancient times, when authors frequently copied other authors at length in works of non-fiction. This practice was useful, and is the only way many authors' works have survived even in part. The copyright system was created expressly for the purpose of encouraging authorship. In the domain for which it was invented—books, which could be copied economically only on a printing press—it did little harm, and did not obstruct most of the individuals who read the books.

All intellectual property rights are just licenses granted by society because it was thought, rightly or wrongly, that society as a whole would benefit by granting them. But in any particular situation, we have to ask: are we really better off granting such license? What kind of act are we licensing a person to do?

The case of programs today is very different from that of books a hundred years ago. The fact that the easiest way to copy a program is from one neighbor to another, the fact that a program has both source code and object code which are distinct, and the fact that a program is used rather than read and enjoyed, combine to create a situation in which a person who enforces a copyright is harming society as a whole both materially and spiritually; in which a person should not do so regardless of whether the law enables him to.

"Competition makes things get done better."

The paradigm of competition is a race: by rewarding the winner, we encourage everyone to run faster. When capitalism really works this way, it does a good job; but its defenders are wrong in assuming it always works this way. If the runners forget why the reward is offered and become intent on winning, no matter how, they may find other strategies—such as, attacking other runners. If the runners get into a fist fight, they will all finish late.

Proprietary and secret software is the moral equivalent of runners in a fist fight. Sad to say, the only referee we've got does not seem to object to fights; he just regulates them ("For every ten yards you run, you can fire one shot"). He really ought to break them up, and penalize runners for even trying to fight.

"Won't everyone stop programming without a monetary incentive?"

Actually, many people will program with absolutely no monetary incentive. Programming has an irresistible fascination for some people, usually the people who are best at it. There is no shortage of professional musicians who keep at it even though they have no hope of making a living that way.

But really this question, though commonly asked, is not appropriate to the situation. Pay for programmers will not disappear, only become less. So the right question is, will anyone program with a reduced monetary incentive? My experience shows that they will.

For more than ten years, many of the world's best programmers worked at the Artificial Intelligence Lab for far less money than they could have had anywhere else. They got many kinds of non-monetary rewards: fame and appreciation, for example. And creativity is also fun, a reward in itself.

Then most of them left when offered a chance to do the same interesting work for a lot of money.

What the facts show is that people will program for reasons other than riches; but if given a chance to make a lot of money as well, they will come to expect and demand it. Low-paying organizations do poorly in competition with high-paying ones, but they do not have to do badly if the high-paying ones are banned.

"We need the programmers desperately. If they demand that we stop helping our neighbors, we have to obey."

You're never so desperate that you have to obey this sort of demand. Remember: millions for defense, but not a cent for tribute!

"Programmers need to make a living somehow."

In the short run, this is true. However, there are plenty of ways that programmers could make a living without selling the right to use a program. This way is customary now because it brings programmers and businessmen the most money, not because it is the only way to make a living. It is easy to find other ways if you want to find them. Here are a number of examples.

A manufacturer introducing a new computer will pay for the porting of operating systems onto the new hardware.

The sale of teaching, hand-holding and maintenance services could also employ programmers.

People with new ideas could distribute programs as freeware, asking for donations from satisfied users, or selling hand-holding services. I have met people who are already working this way successfully.

Users with related needs can form users' groups, and pay dues. A group would contract with programming companies to write programs that the group's members would like to use.

All sorts of development can be funded with a Software Tax:

Suppose everyone who buys a computer has to pay x percent of the price as a software tax. The government gives this to an agency like the NSF to spend on software development.

But if the computer buyer makes a donation to software development himself, he can take a credit against the tax. He can donate to the project of his own choosing—often, chosen because he hopes to use the results when it is done. He can take a credit for any amount of donation up to the total tax he had to pay.

The total tax rate could be decided by a vote of the payers of the tax, weighted according to the amount they will be taxed on.

The consequences:

- The computer-using community supports software development.
- This community decides what level of support is needed.
- Users who care which projects their share is spent on can choose this for themselves.

In the long run, making programs free is a step toward the post-scarcity world, where nobody will have to work very hard just to make a living. People will be free to devote themselves to activities that are fun, such as programming, after spending the necessary ten hours a week on required tasks such as legislation, family counseling, robot repair and asteroid prospecting. There will be no need to be able to make a living from programming.

We have already greatly reduced the amount of work that the whole society must do for its actual productivity, but only a little of this has translated itself into leisure for workers because much nonproductive activity is required to accompany productive activity. The main causes of this are bureaucracy and isometric struggles against competition. Free software will greatly reduce these drains in the area of software production. We must do this, in order for technical gains in productivity to translate into less work for us.

Glossary

Abbrev
An abbrev is a text string which expands into a different text string when present in the buffer. For example, you might define a few letters as an abbrev for a long phrase that you want to insert frequently. See Chapter 23 [Abbrevs], page 251.

Aborting
Aborting means getting out of a recursive edit (q.v.). The commands C-] and M-x top-level are used for this. See Section 31.1 [Quitting], page 373.

Alt
Alt is the name of a modifier bit which a keyboard input character may have. To make a character Alt, type it while holding down the ALT key. Such characters are given names that start with Alt- (usually written A- for short). (Note that many terminals have a key labeled ALT which is really a META key.) See Section 2.1 [User Input], page 19.

Auto Fill Mode
Auto Fill mode is a minor mode in which text that you insert is automatically broken into lines of fixed width. See Section 20.5 [Filling], page 174.

Auto Saving
Auto saving is the practice of saving the contents of an Emacs buffer in a specially-named file, so that the information will not be lost if the buffer is lost due to a system error or user error. See Section 14.5 [Auto Save], page 113.

Backup File
A backup file records the contents that a file had before the current editing session. Emacs makes backup files automatically to help you track down or cancel changes you later regret making. See Section 14.3.1 [Backup], page 109.

Balance Parentheses
Emacs can balance parentheses manually or automatically. Manual balancing is done by the commands to move over balanced expressions (see Section 21.2 [Lists], page 200). Automatic balancing is done by blinking or highlighting the parenthesis that matches one just inserted (see Section 21.6 [Matching Parens], page 209).

Bind
To bind a key sequence means to give it a binding (q.v.). See Section 30.4.5 [Rebinding], page 359.

Binding
A key sequence gets its meaning in Emacs by having a binding, which is a command (q.v.), a Lisp function that is run when the

user types that sequence. See Section 2.3 [Commands], page 21. Customization often involves rebinding a character to a different command function. The bindings of all key sequences are recorded in the keymaps (q.v.). See Section 30.4.1 [Keymaps], page 355.

Blank Lines

Blank lines are lines that contain only whitespace. Emacs has several commands for operating on the blank lines in the buffer.

Buffer   The buffer is the basic editing unit; one buffer corresponds to one text being edited. You can have several buffers, but at any time you are editing only one, the 'selected' buffer, though several can be visible when you are using multiple windows (q.v.). Most buffers are visiting (q.v.) some file. See Chapter 15 [Buffers], page 133.

Buffer Selection History

Emacs keeps a buffer selection history which records how recently each Emacs buffer has been selected. This is used for choosing a buffer to select. See Chapter 15 [Buffers], page 133.

Button Down Event

A button down event is the kind of input event generated right away when you press a mouse button. See Section 30.4.9 [Mouse Buttons], page 363.

C-   C- in the name of a character is an abbreviation for Control. See Section 2.1 [User Input], page 19.

C-M-   C-M- in the name of a character is an abbreviation for Control-Meta. See Section 2.1 [User Input], page 19.

Case Conversion

Case conversion means changing text from upper case to lower case or vice versa. See Section 20.6 [Case], page 178, for the commands for case conversion.

Character   Characters form the contents of an Emacs buffer; see Section 2.4 [Text Characters], page 22. Also, key sequences (q.v.) are usually made up of characters (though they may include other input events as well). See Section 2.1 [User Input], page 19.

Click Event

A click event is the kind of input event generated when you press a mouse button and release it without moving the mouse. See Section 30.4.9 [Mouse Buttons], page 363.

Command   A command is a Lisp function specially defined to be able to serve as a key binding in Emacs. When you type a key sequence (q.v.), its binding (q.v.) is looked up in the relevant keymaps (q.v.) to find the command to run. See Section 2.3 [Commands], page 21.

Command Name

A command name is the name of a Lisp symbol which is a command (see Section 2.3 [Commands], page 21). You can invoke any command by its name using M-x (see Chapter 6 [M-x], page 45).

Comment   A comment is text in a program which is intended only for humans reading the program, and which is marked specially so that it will be ignored when the program is loaded or compiled. Emacs offers special commands for creating, aligning and killing comments. See Section 21.7 [Comments], page 210.

Compilation

Compilation is the process of creating an executable program from source code. Emacs has commands for compiling files of Emacs Lisp code (see section "Byte Compilation" in *the Emacs Lisp Reference Manual*) and programs in C and other languages (see Section 22.1 [Compilation], page 239).

Complete Key

A complete key is a key sequence which fully specifies one action to be performed by Emacs. For example, X and C-f and C-x m are complete keys. Complete keys derive their meanings from being bound (q.v.) to commands (q.v.). Thus, X is conventionally bound to a command to insert 'X' in the buffer; C-x m is conventionally bound to a command to begin composing a mail message. See Section 2.2 [Keys], page 20.

Completion

Completion is what Emacs does when it automatically fills out an abbreviation for a name into the entire name. Completion is done for minibuffer (q.v.) arguments when the set of possible valid inputs is known; for example, on command names, buffer names, and file names. Completion occurs when TAB, SPC or RET is typed. See Section 5.3 [Completion], page 39.

Continuation Line

When a line of text is longer than the width of the window, it takes up more than one screen line when displayed. We say that the text line is continued, and all screen lines used for it after the first are called continuation lines. See Chapter 4 [Basic Editing], page 27.

Control Character

> ASCII characters with octal codes 0 through 037, and also code 0177, do not have graphic images assigned to them. These are the Control characters. To type a Control character, hold down the CTRL key and type the corresponding non-Control character. RET, TAB, ESC, LFD and DEL are all control characters. See Section 2.1 [User Input], page 19.
>
> When you are using the X Window System, every non-control character has a corresponding control character variant.

Copyleft

> A copyleft is a notice giving the public legal permission to redistribute a program or other work of art. Copylefts are used by left-wing programmers to give people equal rights, just as copyrights are used by right-wing programmers to gain power over other people.
>
> The particular form of copyleft used by the GNU project is called the GNU General Public License. See [Copying], page 5.

Current Buffer

> The current buffer in Emacs is the Emacs buffer on which most editing commands operate. You can select any Emacs buffer as the current one. See Chapter 15 [Buffers], page 133.

Current Line

> The line point is on (see Section 1.1 [Point], page 15).

Current Paragraph

> The paragraph that point is in. If point is between paragraphs, the current paragraph is the one that follows point. See Section 20.3 [Paragraphs], page 172.

Current Defun

> The defun (q.v.) that point is in. If point is between defuns, the current defun is the one that follows point. See Section 21.4 [Defuns], page 202.

Cursor

> The cursor is the rectangle on the screen which indicates the position called point (q.v.) at which insertion and deletion takes place. The cursor is on or under the character that follows point. Often people speak of 'the cursor' when, strictly speaking, they mean 'point'. See Chapter 4 [Basic Editing], page 27.

Customization

> Customization is making minor changes in the way Emacs works. It is often done by setting variables (see Section 30.2 [Variables], page 345) or by rebinding key sequences (see Section 30.4.1 [Keymaps], page 355).

Default Argument

> The default for an argument is the value that will be assumed if you do not specify one. When the minibuffer is used to read an argument, the default argument is used if you just type RET. See Chapter 5 [Minibuffer], page 37.

Default Directory

> When you specify a file name that does not start with '/' or '~', it is interpreted relative to the current buffer's default directory. See Section 5.1 [Minibuffer File], page 37.

Defun

> A defun is a list at the top level of parenthesis or bracket structure in a program. It is so named because most such lists in Lisp programs are calls to the Lisp function `defun`. See Section 21.4 [Defuns], page 202.

DEL

> DEL is a character that runs the command to delete one character of text. See Chapter 4 [Basic Editing], page 27.

Deletion

> Deletion means erasing text without copying it into the kill ring (q.v.). The alternative is killing (q.v.). See Section 9.1 [Killing], page 61.

Deletion of Files

> Deleting a file means erasing it from the file system. See Section 14.10 [Misc File Ops], page 131.

Deletion of Messages

> Deleting a message means flagging it to be eliminated from your mail file. Until you expunge (q.v.) the Rmail file, you can still undelete the messages you have deleted. See Section 26.4 [Rmail Deletion], page 271.

Deletion of Windows

> Deleting a window means eliminating it from the screen. Other windows expand to use up the space. The deleted window can never come back, but no actual text is thereby lost. See Chapter 16 [Windows], page 141.

Directory

> File directories are named collections in the file system, within which you can place individual files or subdirectories. See Section 14.8 [Directories], page 130.

Dired

> Dired is the Emacs facility that displays the contents of a file directory and allows you to "edit the directory", performing operations on the files in the directory. See Chapter 27 [Dired], page 287.

Disabled Command

> A disabled command is one that you may not run without special confirmation. The usual reason for disabling a command

is that it is confusing for beginning users. See Section 30.4.10 [Disabling], page 365.

Down Event

Short for 'button down event'.

Drag Event

A drag event is the kind of input event generated when you press a mouse button, move the mouse, and then release the button. See Section 30.4.9 [Mouse Buttons], page 363.

Dribble File

A file into which Emacs writes all the characters that the user types on the keyboard. Dribble files are used to make a record for debugging Emacs bugs. Emacs does not make a dribble file unless you tell it to. See Section 31.3 [Bugs], page 377.

Echo Area The echo area is the bottom line of the screen, used for echoing the arguments to commands, for asking questions, and printing brief messages (including error messages). The messages are stored in the buffer '*Messages*' so you can review them later. See Section 1.2 [Echo Area], page 16.

Echoing Echoing is acknowledging the receipt of commands by displaying them (in the echo area). Emacs never echoes single-character key sequences; longer key sequences echo only if you pause while typing them.

Error An error occurs when an Emacs command cannot execute in the current circumstances. When an error occurs, execution of the command stops (unless the command has been programmed to do otherwise) and Emacs reports the error by printing an error message (q.v.). Type-ahead is discarded. Then Emacs is ready to read another editing command.

Error Message

An error message is a single line of output displayed by Emacs when the user asks for something impossible to do (such as, killing text forward when point is at the end of the buffer). They appear in the echo area, accompanied by a beep.

ESC ESC is a character used as a prefix for typing Meta characters on keyboards lacking a META key. Unlike the META key (which, like the SHIFT key, is held down while another character is typed), the ESC key is pressed once and applies to the next character typed.

Expunging

Expunging an Rmail file or Dired buffer means really discarding the messages or files you have previously flagged for deletion.

File Name   A file name is a name that refers to a file. File names may be relative or absolute; the meaning of a relative file name depends on the current directory, but an absolute file name refers to the same file regardless of which directory is current. On GNU and Unix systems, an absolute file name starts with a slash (the root directory) or with '~/' or '~user/' (a home directory).

Some people use the term "pathname" for file names, but we do not; we use the word "path" only in the term "search path" (q.v.).

File Name Component

A file name component names a file directly within a particular directory. On GNU and Unix systems, a file name is a sequence of file name components, separated by slashes. For example, 'foo/bar' is a file name containing two components, 'foo' and 'bar'; it refers to the file named 'bar' in the directory named 'foo' in the current directory.

Fill Prefix   The fill prefix is a string that should be expected at the beginning of each line when filling is done. It is not regarded as part of the text to be filled. See Section 20.5 [Filling], page 174.

Filling   Filling text means shifting text between consecutive lines so that all the lines are approximately the same length. See Section 20.5 [Filling], page 174.

Formatted Text

Formatted text is text that displays with formatting information while you edit. Formatting information includes fonts, colors, and specified margins. See Section 20.11 [Formatted Text], page 190.

Frame   A frame is a rectangular cluster of Emacs windows. Emacs starts out with one frame, but you can create more. You can subdivide each frame into Emacs windows (q.v.). When you are using X windows, all the frames can be visible at the same time. See Chapter 17 [Frames], page 147.

Function Key

A function key is a key on the keyboard that sends input but does not correspond to any character. See Section 30.4.7 [Function Keys], page 361.

Global   Global means 'independent of the current environment; in effect throughout Emacs'. It is the opposite of local (q.v.). Particular examples of the use of 'global' appear below.

Global Abbrev
A global definition of an abbrev (q.v.) is effective in all major modes that do not have local (q.v.) definitions for the same abbrev. See Chapter 23 [Abbrevs], page 251.

Global Keymap
The global keymap (q.v.) contains key bindings that are in effect except when overridden by local key bindings in a major mode's local keymap (q.v.). See Section 30.4.1 [Keymaps], page 355.

Global Mark Ring
The global mark ring records the series of buffers you have recently set a mark in. In many cases you can use this to backtrack through buffers you have been editing in, or in which you have found tags. See Section 8.6 [Global Mark Ring], page 59.

Global Substitution
Global substitution means replacing each occurrence of one string by another string through a large amount of text. See Section 12.7 [Replace], page 93.

Global Variable
The global value of a variable (q.v.) takes effect in all buffers that do not have their own local (q.v.) values for the variable. See Section 30.2 [Variables], page 345.

Graphic Character
Graphic characters are those assigned pictorial images rather than just names. All the non-Meta (q.v.) characters except for the Control (q.v.) characters are graphic characters. These include letters, digits, punctuation, and spaces; they do not include RET or ESC. In Emacs, typing a graphic character inserts that character (in ordinary editing modes). See Chapter 4 [Basic Editing], page 27.

Highlighting
Highlighting text means displaying it with a different foreground and/or background color to make it stand out from the rest of the text in the buffer.

Hardcopy   Hardcopy means printed output. Emacs has commands for making printed listings of text in Emacs buffers. See Section 29.4 [Hardcopy], page 331.

HELP   You can type HELP at any time to ask what options you have, or to ask what any command does. The character HELP is really C-h. See Chapter 7 [Help], page 47.

Hyper   Hyper is the name of a modifier bit which a keyboard input character may have. To make a character Hyper, type it while holding down the HYPER key. Such characters are given names that start with Hyper- (usually written H- for short). See Section 2.1 [User Input], page 19.

Inbox

An inbox is a file in which mail is delivered by the operating system. Rmail transfers mail from inboxes to Rmail files (q.v.) in which the mail is then stored permanently or until explicitly deleted. See Section 26.5 [Rmail Inbox], page 272.

Indentation

Indentation means blank space at the beginning of a line. Most programming languages have conventions for using indentation to illuminate the structure of the program, and Emacs has special commands to adjust indentation. See Chapter 19 [Indentation], page 165.

Indirect Buffer

An indirect buffer is a buffer that shares the text of another buffer, called its base buffer. See Section 15.6 [Indirect Buffers], page 138.

Input Event

An input event represents, within Emacs, one action taken by the user on the terminal. Input events include typing characters, typing function keys, pressing or releasing mouse buttons, and switching between Emacs frames. See Section 2.1 [User Input], page 19.

Insertion

Insertion means copying text into the buffer, either from the keyboard or from some other place in Emacs.

Justification

Justification means adding extra spaces to lines of text to make them come exactly to a specified width. See Section 20.5 [Filling], page 174.

Keyboard Macro

Keyboard macros are a way of defining new Emacs commands from sequences of existing ones, with no need to write a Lisp program. See Section 30.3 [Keyboard Macros], page 352.

Key Sequence

A key sequence (key, for short) is a sequence of input events (q.v.) that are meaningful as a single unit. If the key sequence is enough to specify one action, it is a complete key (q.v.); if it is not enough, it is a prefix key (q.v.). See Section 2.2 [Keys], page 20.

Keymap

The keymap is the data structure that records the bindings (q.v.) of key sequences to the commands that they run. For example, the global keymap binds the character `C-n` to the command function `next-line`. See Section 30.4.1 [Keymaps], page 355.

Keyboard Translation Table

> The keyboard translation table is an array that translates the character codes that come from the terminal into the character codes that make up key sequences. See Section 30.5 [Keyboard Translations], page 365.

Kill Ring   The kill ring is where all text you have killed recently is saved. You can reinsert any of the killed text still in the ring; this is called yanking (q.v.). See Section 9.2 [Yanking], page 63.

Killing   Killing means erasing text and saving it on the kill ring so it can be yanked (q.v.) later. Some other systems call this "cutting". Most Emacs commands to erase text do killing, as opposed to deletion (q.v.). See Section 9.1 [Killing], page 61.

Killing Jobs

> Killing a job (such as, an invocation of Emacs) means making it cease to exist. Any data within it, if not saved in a file, is lost. See Section 3.1 [Exiting], page 24.

List   A list is, approximately, a text string beginning with an open parenthesis and ending with the matching close parenthesis. In C mode and other non-Lisp modes, groupings surrounded by other kinds of matched delimiters appropriate to the language, such as braces, are also considered lists. Emacs has special commands for many operations on lists. See Section 21.2 [Lists], page 200.

Local   Local means 'in effect only in a particular context'; the relevant kind of context is a particular function execution, a particular buffer, or a particular major mode. It is the opposite of 'global' (q.v.). Specific uses of 'local' in Emacs terminology appear below.

Local Abbrev

> A local abbrev definition is effective only if a particular major mode is selected. In that major mode, it overrides any global definition for the same abbrev. See Chapter 23 [Abbrevs], page 251.

Local Keymap

> A local keymap is used in a particular major mode; the key bindings (q.v.) in the current local keymap override global bindings of the same key sequences. See Section 30.4.1 [Keymaps], page 355.

Local Variable

A local value of a variable (q.v.) applies to only one buffer. See Section 30.2.4 [Locals], page 348.

M-

M- in the name of a character is an abbreviation for META, one of the modifier keys that can accompany any character. See Section 2.1 [User Input], page 19.

M-C-

M-C- in the name of a character is an abbreviation for Control-Meta; it means the same thing as C-M-. If your terminal lacks a real META key, you type a Control-Meta character by typing ESC and then typing the corresponding Control character. See Section 2.1 [User Input], page 19.

M-x

M-x is the key sequence which is used to call an Emacs command by name. This is how you run commands that are not bound to key sequences. See Chapter 6 [M-x], page 45.

Mail

Mail means messages sent from one user to another through the computer system, to be read at the recipient's convenience. Emacs has commands for composing and sending mail, and for reading and editing the mail you have received. See Chapter 25 [Sending Mail], page 261. See Chapter 26 [Rmail], page 269, for how to read mail.

Major Mode

The Emacs major modes are a mutually exclusive set of options, each of which configures Emacs for editing a certain sort of text. Ideally, each programming language has its own major mode. See Chapter 18 [Major Modes], page 161.

Mark

The mark points to a position in the text. It specifies one end of the region (q.v.), point being the other end. Many commands operate on all the text from point to the mark. Each buffer has its own mark. See Chapter 8 [Mark], page 55.

Mark Ring

The mark ring is used to hold several recent previous locations of the mark, just in case you want to move back to them. Each buffer has its own mark ring; in addition, there is a single global mark ring (q.v.). See Section 8.5 [Mark Ring], page 59.

Menu Bar

The menu bar is the line at the top of an Emacs frame. It contains words you can click on with the mouse to bring up menus. The menu bar feature is supported only with X. See Section 17.11 [Menu Bars], page 155.

Message

See 'mail'.

Meta   Meta is the name of a modifier bit which a command charac-
                ter may have. It is present in a character if the character is
                typed with the META key held down. Such characters are given
                names that start with Meta- (usually written M- for short). For
                example, M-< is typed by holding down META and at the same
                time typing < (which itself is done, on most terminals, by hold-
                ing down SHIFT and typing ,). See Section 2.1 [User Input],
                page 19.

Meta Character
                A Meta character is one whose character code includes the Meta
                bit.

Minibuffer The minibuffer is the window that appears when necessary inside
                the echo area (q.v.), used for reading arguments to commands.
                See Chapter 5 [Minibuffer], page 37.

Minibuffer History
                The minibuffer history records the text you have specified in the
                past for minibuffer arguments, so you can conveniently use the
                same text again. See Section 5.4 [Minibuffer History], page 42.

Minor Mode
                A minor mode is an optional feature of Emacs which can be
                switched on or off independently of all other features. Each
                minor mode has a command to turn it on or off. See Section 30.1
                [Minor Modes], page 343.

Minor Mode Keymap
                A keymap that belongs to a minor mode and is active when that
                mode is enabled. Minor mode keymaps take precedence over the
                buffer's local keymap, just as the local keymap takes precedence
                over the global keymap. See Section 30.4.1 [Keymaps], page 355.

Mode Line
                The mode line is the line at the bottom of each window (q.v.),
                giving status information on the buffer displayed in that window.
                See Section 1.3 [Mode Line], page 17.

Modified Buffer
                A buffer (q.v.) is modified if its text has been changed since the
                last time the buffer was saved (or since when it was created, if
                it has never been saved). See Section 14.3 [Saving], page 107.

Moving Text
                Moving text means erasing it from one place and inserting it in
                another. The usual way to move text by killing (q.v.) and then
                yanking (q.v.). See Section 9.1 [Killing], page 61.

Named Mark
> A named mark is a register (q.v.) in its role of recording a location in text so that you can move point to that location. See Chapter 10 [Registers], page 71.

Narrowing Narrowing means creating a restriction (q.v.) that limits editing in the current buffer to only a part of the text in the buffer. Text outside that part is inaccessible to the user until the boundaries are widened again, but it is still there, and saving the file saves it all. See Section 29.7 [Narrowing], page 335.

Newline Linefeed characters in the buffer terminate lines of text and are therefore also called newlines. See Section 2.4 [Text Characters], page 22.

Numeric Argument
> A numeric argument is a number, specified before a command, to change the effect of the command. Often the numeric argument serves as a repeat count. See Section 4.10 [Arguments], page 35.

Option An option is a variable (q.v.) that exists so that you can customize Emacs by setting it to a new value. See Section 30.2 [Variables], page 345.

Overwrite Mode
> Overwrite mode is a minor mode. When it is enabled, ordinary text characters replace the existing text after point rather than pushing it to the right. See Section 30.1 [Minor Modes], page 343.

Page A page is a unit of text, delimited by formfeed characters (ASCII control-L, code 014) coming at the beginning of a line. Some Emacs commands are provided for moving over and operating on pages. See Section 20.4 [Pages], page 173.

Paragraph Paragraphs are the medium-size unit of English text. There are special Emacs commands for moving over and operating on paragraphs. See Section 20.3 [Paragraphs], page 172.

Parsing We say that certain Emacs commands parse words or expressions in the text being edited. Really, all they know how to do is find the other end of a word or expression. See Section 30.6 [Syntax], page 366.

Point Point is the place in the buffer at which insertion and deletion occur. Point is considered to be between two characters, not at one character. The terminal's cursor (q.v.) indicates the location of point. See Chapter 4 [Basic], page 27.

Prefix Argument
> See 'numeric argument'.

Prefix Key

A prefix key is a key sequence (q.v.) whose sole function is to introduce a set of longer key sequences. C-x is an example of prefix key; any two-character sequence starting with C-x is therefore a legitimate key sequence. See Section 2.2 [Keys], page 20.

Primary Rmail File

Your primary Rmail file is the file named 'RMAIL' in your home directory. That's where Rmail stores your incoming mail, unless you specify a different file name. See Chapter 26 [Rmail], page 269.

Primary Selection

The primary selection is one particular X selection (q.v.); it is the selection that most X applications use for transferring text to and from other applications.

The Emacs kill commands set the primary selection and the yank command uses the primary selection when appropriate. See Section 9.1 [Killing], page 61.

Prompt   A prompt is text printed to ask the user for input. Displaying a prompt is called prompting. Emacs prompts always appear in the echo area (q.v.). One kind of prompting happens when the minibuffer is used to read an argument (see Chapter 5 [Minibuffer], page 37); the echoing which happens when you pause in the middle of typing a multi-character key sequence is also a kind of prompting (see Section 1.2 [Echo Area], page 16).

Quitting   Quitting means canceling a partially typed command or a running command, using C-g. See Section 31.1 [Quitting], page 373.

Quoting   Quoting means depriving a character of its usual special significance. In Emacs this is usually done with C-q. What constitutes special significance depends on the context and on convention. For example, an "ordinary" character as an Emacs command inserts itself; so in this context, a special character is any character that does not normally insert itself (such as DEL, for example), and quoting it makes it insert itself as if it were not special. Not all contexts allow quoting. See Chapter 4 [Basic Editing], page 27.

Read-Only Buffer

A read-only buffer is one whose text you are not allowed to change. Normally Emacs makes buffers read-only when they contain text which has a special significance to Emacs; for example, Dired buffers. Visiting a file that is write protected also makes a read-only buffer. See Chapter 15 [Buffers], page 133.

Rectangle   A rectangle consists of the text in a given range of columns on a given range of lines. Normally you specify a rectangle by putting point at one corner and putting the mark at the opposite corner. See Section 9.4 [Rectangles], page 67.

Recursive Editing Level

A recursive editing level is a state in which part of the execution of a command involves asking the user to edit some text. This text may or may not be the same as the text to which the command was applied. The mode line indicates recursive editing levels with square brackets ('[' and ']'). See Section 29.11 [Recursive Edit], page 339.

Redisplay   Redisplay is the process of correcting the image on the screen to correspond to changes that have been made in the text being edited. See Chapter 1 [Screen], page 15.

Regexp   See 'regular expression'.

Region   The region is the text between point (q.v.) and the mark (q.v.). Many commands operate on the text of the region. See Chapter 8 [Mark], page 55.

Registers   Registers are named slots in which text or buffer positions or rectangles can be saved for later use. See Chapter 10 [Registers], page 71.

Regular Expression

A regular expression is a pattern that can match various text strings; for example, '1[0-9]+' matches '1' followed by one or more digits. See Section 12.5 [Regexps], page 88.

Repeat Count

See 'numeric argument'.

Replacement

See 'global substitution'.

Restriction

A buffer's restriction is the amount of text, at the beginning or the end of the buffer, that is temporarily inaccessible. Giving a buffer a nonzero amount of restriction is called narrowing (q.v.). See Section 29.7 [Narrowing], page 335.

RET   RET is a character that in Emacs runs the command to insert a newline into the text. It is also used to terminate most arguments read in the minibuffer (q.v.). See Section 2.1 [User Input], page 19.

Rmail File   An Rmail file is a file containing text in a special format used by Rmail for storing mail. See Chapter 26 [Rmail], page 269.

Saving   Saving a buffer means copying its text into the file that was
              visited (q.v.) in that buffer. This is the way text in files actually
              gets changed by your Emacs editing. See Section 14.3 [Saving],
              page 107.

Scroll Bar   A scroll bar is a tall thin hollow box that appears at the side
              of a window. You can use mouse commands in the scroll bar to
              scroll the window. The scroll bar feature is supported only with
              X. See Section 17.10 [Scroll Bars], page 155.

Scrolling   Scrolling means shifting the text in the Emacs window so as
              to see a different part of the buffer. See Chapter 11 [Display],
              page 75.

Searching   Searching means moving point to the next occurrence of a spec-
              ified string or the next match for a specified regular expression.
              See Chapter 12 [Search], page 83.

Search Path
              A search path is a list of directory names, to be used for searching
              for files for certain purposes. For example, the variable `load-
              path` holds a search path for finding Lisp library files. See Sec-
              tion 22.4 [Lisp Libraries], page 246.

Secondary Selection
              The secondary selection is one particular X selection; some X
              applications can use it for transferring text to and from other ap-
              plications. Emacs has special mouse commands for transferring
              text using the secondary selection. See Section 17.2 [Secondary
              Selection], page 149.

Selecting   Selecting a buffer means making it the current (q.v.) buffer. See
              Chapter 15 [Buffers], page 133.

Selection   The X window system allows an application program to specify
              named selections whose values are text. A program can also
              read the selections that other programs have set up. This is the
              principal way of transferring text between window applications.
              Emacs has commands to work with the primary (q.v.) selection
              and the secondary (q.v.) selection.

Self-Documentation
              Self-documentation is the feature of Emacs which can tell you
              what any command does, or give you a list of all commands
              related to a topic you specify. You ask for self-documentation
              with the help character, C-h. See Chapter 7 [Help], page 47.

Sentences   Emacs has commands for moving by or killing by sentences. See
              Section 20.2 [Sentences], page 171.

Sexp

A sexp (short for 's-expression') is the basic syntactic unit of Lisp in its textual form: either a list, or Lisp atom. Many Emacs commands operate on sexps. The term 'sexp' is generalized to languages other than Lisp, to mean a syntactically recognizable expression. See Section 21.2 [Lists], page 200.

Simultaneous Editing

Simultaneous editing means two users modifying the same file at once. Simultaneous editing if not detected can cause one user to lose his work. Emacs detects all cases of simultaneous editing and warns one of the users to investigate. See Section 14.3.2 [Simultaneous Editing], page 111.

String

A string is a kind of Lisp data object which contains a sequence of characters. Many Emacs variables are intended to have strings as values. The Lisp syntax for a string consists of the characters in the string with a '"' before and another '"' after. A '"' that is part of the string must be written as '\"' and a '\' that is part of the string must be written as '\\'. All other characters, including newline, can be included just by writing them inside the string; however, backslash sequences as in C, such as '\n' for newline or '\241' using an octal character code, are allowed as well.

String Substitution

See 'global substitution'.

Syntax Table

The syntax table tells Emacs which characters are part of a word, which characters balance each other like parentheses, etc. See Section 30.6 [Syntax], page 366.

Super

Super is the name of a modifier bit which a keyboard input character may have. To make a character Super, type it while holding down the SUPER key. Such characters are given names that start with Super- (usually written s- for short). See Section 2.1 [User Input], page 19.

Tags Table

A tags table is a file that serves as an index to the function definitions in one or more other files. See Section 21.12 [Tags], page 216.

Termscript File

A termscript file contains a record of all characters sent by Emacs to the terminal. It is used for tracking down bugs in Emacs redisplay. Emacs does not make a termscript file unless you tell it to. See Section 31.3 [Bugs], page 377.

Text   Two meanings (see Chapter 20 [Text], page 169):

              • Data consisting of a sequence of characters, as opposed to
                binary numbers, images, graphics commands, executable
                programs, and the like. The contents of an Emacs buffer
                are always text in this sense.

              • Data consisting of written human language, as opposed to
                programs, or following the stylistic conventions of human
                language.

Top Level   Top level is the normal state of Emacs, in which you are edit-
              ing the text of the file you have visited. You are at top level
              whenever you are not in a recursive editing level (q.v.) or the
              minibuffer (q.v.), and not in the middle of a command. You can
              get back to top level by aborting (q.v.) and quitting (q.v.). See
              Section 31.1 [Quitting], page 373.

Transposition
              Transposing two units of text means putting each one into the
              place formerly occupied by the other. There are Emacs com-
              mands to transpose two adjacent characters, words, sexps (q.v.)
              or lines (see Section 13.2 [Transpose], page 97).

Truncation
              Truncating text lines in the display means leaving out any text
              on a line that does not fit within the right margin of the window
              displaying it. See also 'continuation line'. See Chapter 4 [Basic
              Editing], page 27.

Undoing   Undoing means making your previous editing go in reverse,
              bringing back the text that existed earlier in the editing ses-
              sion. See Section 4.4 [Undo], page 30.

Variable   A variable is an object in Lisp that can store an arbitrary value.
              Emacs uses some variables for internal purposes, and has others
              (known as 'options' (q.v.)) just so that you can set their values
              to control the behavior of Emacs. The variables used in Emacs
              that you are likely to be interested in are listed in the Variables
              Index in this manual. See Section 30.2 [Variables], page 345, for
              information on variables.

Version Control
              Version control systems keep track of multiple versions of a
              source file. They provide a more powerful alternative to keeping
              backup files (q.v.). See Section 14.7 [Version Control], page 116.

Visiting   Visiting a file means loading its contents into a buffer (q.v.)
              where they can be edited. See Section 14.2 [Visiting], page 104.

Whitespace

Whitespace is any run of consecutive formatting characters (space, tab, newline, and backspace).

Widening Widening is removing any restriction (q.v.) on the current buffer; it is the opposite of narrowing (q.v.). See Section 29.7 [Narrowing], page 335.

Window Emacs divides a frame (q.v.) into one or more windows, each of which can display the contents of one buffer (q.v.) at any time. See Chapter 1 [Screen], page 15, for basic information on how Emacs uses the screen. See Chapter 16 [Windows], page 141, for commands to control the use of windows.

Word Abbrev

Synonymous with 'abbrev'.

Word Search

Word search is searching for a sequence of words, considering the punctuation between them as insignificant. See Section 12.3 [Word Search], page 86.

WYSIWYG

WYSIWYG stands for "What you see is what you get." Emacs generally provides WYSIWYG editing for files of characters; in Enriched mode (see Section 20.11 [Formatted Text], page 190), it provides WYSIWYG editing for files that include text formatting information.

Yanking Yanking means reinserting text previously killed. It can be used to undo a mistaken kill, or for copying or moving text. Some other systems call this "pasting". See Section 9.2 [Yanking], page 63.

Key (Character) Index

Command and Function Index

F

G

H

I

J

K

R

S

Variable Index

T

U

V

W

X

Concept Index

Y

Z